Business Data Processing

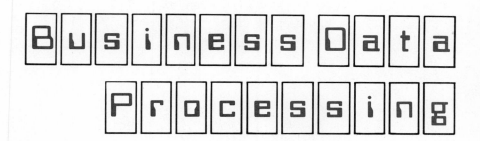

Business

ELIAS M. AWAD

School of Business and Organizational Sciences
Florida International University
Miami, Florida

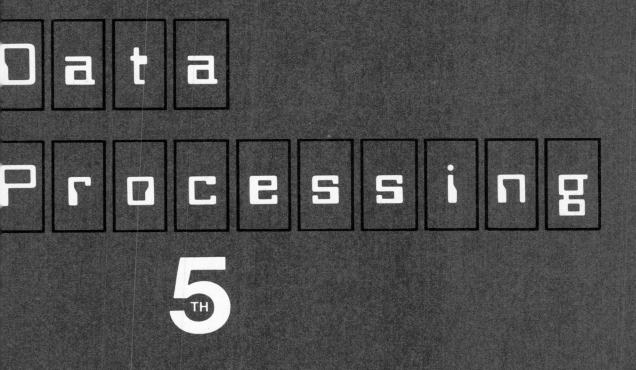

Data Processing

5TH

Prentice-Hall, Inc., Englewood Cliffs, New Jersey 07632

Awad, Elias M
 Business data processing.

 Includes index.
 1. Business—Data processing. 2. Punched
card systems. I. Tittle.
HF5548.2.A9   1980   651.8   79-29749
ISBN 0-13-093807-6

Business Data Processing
5th Edition
Elias M. Awad

Printed in the United States of America

10 9 8 7 6 5 4 3 2 1

Editorial/production supervision by Fred Dahl and Ken Cashman
Interior Design by Mark A. Binn
Cover Design by Mark A. Binn
Manufacturing buyer: Tony Caruso
Cover photograph by Joanna Ferrone of Five By Five
and Micro chip insert by Reginald Wickham

Prentice-Hall International, Inc., *London*
Prentice-Hall of Australia Pty. Limited, *Sydney*
Prentice-Hall of Canada, Ltd., *Toronto*
Prentice-Hall of India Private Limited, *New Delhi*
Prentice-Hall of Japan, Inc., *Tokyo*
Prentice-Hall of Southeast Asia Pte. Ltd., *Singapore*
Whitehall Books Limited, *Wellington, New Zealand*

To Sandy, Michael, Bruce, and Brenda

Contents

chapter 2

Computer Systems and Management Information 22

chapter 3

Developments and Trends in Computer Technology 50

chapter 4

The Classification of Computers 77

part two

Internal Makeup and Structure of a Computer System 105

chapter 5

Main Memory and Data Representation 107

chapter 6

Basic Input and Output 137

chapter 7

Magnetic Tape Input and Output 166

chapter 8

Direct-Access Data Processing 187

chapter 9

Card Replacement and Data Entry Devices 205

chapter 10

Communicating with the Computer 235

part three

Systems Applications Development   269

chapter 11

Systems Analysis for Information Processing   271

chapter 12

Systems Design and Implementation 294

chapter 13

Computer Systems Software 319

part four
Programming and Software Basics 339

chapter 14

Tools for Program Planning 341

chapter 15

Program Design and Structured Programming 369

chapter 16

Basic 399

chapter 17

Cobol 432

part five
Management Considerations of the Computer 461

chapter 18

Acquisition of Computer Resources 463

chapter 19

Managing Computer Resources 486

Preface

For over two years, the data processing literature has focused more and more on the "age of the end user," as well as on the end user's role in the planning and development of computer systems. Computer manufacturers have made a clear effort in today's systems designs. Rather than designing computers with programmers and analysts in mind, today's technology and the programming sophistication needed for generating information through the computer have been simplified for the nontechnical mind of the user. High-level, powerful software packages and a "programmed" approach to problem solving now enable the user to "talk" to the computer in very little time. This orientation, in conjunction with the developments relating to the makeup, operation, applications, design, and management of the computer necessitated the production of this revision.

This edition of *Business Data Processing*, like the four previous editions, is written more than ever for entry-level students, who are preparing for management or staff positions in areas such as production, marketing, accounting, finance, or information systems. It is also for those who are planning a career in government, health, and educational organizations that require processing of information for decision making. In many programs, students entering computer science could benefit from the unique coverage of the field in this revision.

The purpose of this text, then, is to introduce the data processing beginners and the future users to the important topics that are relevant to their career goals. More specifically, the objective of this edition is to provide:

1. the fundamentals, concepts, and developments in computer-based information processing,

2. a comprehensive orientation to the computer — what it is, what it can do, its limitations, and potential —

3. the analysis, design, and implementation of systems projects, and

4. some insights and procedures relevant to the acquisition, installation, and management of computer systems.

This edition underwent more extensive revision in organization, content, and presentation than any previous editions. The contents of seventeen of these earlier chapters have been extensively revised, reorganized, and condensed into thirteen chapters. Four of the earlier chapters have been dropped, and six new chapters have been added. An appendix covering the essence of word processing is also included. Although the net effect of the total project has been a reduction of the text size by over 150 pages, the material represents a comprehensive coverage of the technology and the latest in data processing methods and procedures.

Like previous editions, the opening pages of each chapter contain *learning objectives* and a *chapter outline*. A *chapter summary*, *"terms to learn,"* and *review questions* conclude each chapter, to test and reinforce the learning objectives and the important points. (Additionally, the words and phrases in the "terms to learn" list are set in heavy, boldface type in the text for easy reference.)

This text is organized into five parts. The key features and a brief description of the revisions are summarized below:

Part I, consisting of the first four chapters, discusses the capabilities and uses of a computer. *Chapter 1* is a new chapter. It presents an overview of the makeup, benefits, and drawbacks of computers. *Chapter 2* summarizes the data processing cycle and computer applications in various industries. *Chapter 3* deals with key developments in computer technology, the future impact of the power of the computer, and trends and projections in the computer field. The latter section includes trends in main memory and the emerging concept of distributed data processing. *Chapter 4* summarizes the different ways of classifying computer systems. The uses of microcomputers, personal computing, and the various types of distributed data processing are all new additions.

Part II emphasizes the internal makeup and structure of a computer system, detailed in *Chapters 5 – 10*. The chapters illustrate the equipment needed for a computer system, why they are used, and how the user communicates with the computer as a system.

Chapter 5 examines the types of main memory, how advanced memory systems function, and how data is represented in memory. New additions include bubble and laser memory systems, along with data structure and organization.

Chapter 6 explains the input and ouput devices for computer systems and shows how input data is prepared and entered into the computer for processing. Special-purpose output technology (relating to COM and to computer micrographics) is also included.

Chapter 7 focuses on the characteristics, uses, and makeup of magnetic tape as an alternative input/output medium.

Chapter 8 describes the characteristics, layout, and file organization of magnetic disc for direct-access data processing. The section on disc layout, file organization, and disc file capacity is all new.

Chapter 9 features card replacement, direct data entry, and pattern recognition devices. Included is a new section on source data automation, with a discussion of electronic funds transfer, automated teller machines, and intelligent point of sale transfer.

Chapter 10 is an extensive revision of the telecommunications area. The major topics include fundamental communications concepts, application categories, telecommunication hardware, and the various services offered by common carriers.

Part III consists of three new chapters on the development of systems applications. Chapter 11 focuses on analysis of the elements of an application in order to determine if conversion is feasible, why companies decide on converting applications, how an analyst gathers and organizes data for analysis, and what constitutes a systems proposal. Chapter 12 discusses the major steps in systems design, how files are organized, the basics of forms design, and the steps taken in systems testing and conversion. Chapter 13 describes the functions, the basic programs, and the advanced facilities of operating systems. The latter section includes an overview of the features of real-time, time-sharing, and virtual storage systems.

Part IV is a section on the basics of programming and software. Chapter 14 is a major revision of the tools used for program planning. Chapter 15 is a new chapter detailing the programming cycle, how a program is converted into a machine-readable language, the uses of compilers and assemblers, and the basics of structured programming. The latter section explains the makeup and uses of top-down program design, structured walkthrough, and the HIPO diagram. Chapters 16 and 17 are updated versions of earlier chapters on Basic and Cobol, respectively. They can be easily deleted in classes where students have had a prior programming course or language.

Part V emphasizes management considerations of the computer. It consists of new material in Chapter 18 on the criteria for evaluating computer acquisitions, financial considerations in computer acquisitions, and the cost of computer resources. Chapter 19 is a fresh outlook at the functions of the computer center, the personnel positions that make up a computer center, the different approaches to locating a center, and the control measures designed to safeguard data against fraud or embezzlement.

This text is designed for use as a first course in computer data processing for one quarter or one semester at the college or university level. No prior mathematical or computer background is required. The material is representative of computers in general. No specific computer system or manufacturer is featured. The material can also be covered without access to any computer, although a visit to one would be helpful.

The material is organized into five parts to provide continuity in the way an introduction to data processing course should be taught. It is based on the author's twenty years of teaching and publishing experience in the field. It should be noted, however, that the parts provide some *modular* flexibility in meeting unique sets of needs. For example, if programming is taught as a part of the course, part I can be covered, followed by the first chapter in part IV to teach the procedure in program preparation.

Many individuals have provided input in the preparation of this text. The author thanks Ron Ledwith of Prentice-Hall, Inc., for his interest in and support of the project from its inception and for his valued counsel. Special thanks go to Fred Dahl, whose talent and years of experience are reflected in the production of this volume. Most important, several persons were especially constructive with their comments on initial drafts. Professor Nilo Niccolai of the University of North Carolina–Charlotte and Victor Streeter of the University of Michigan–Dearborn were especially helpful, as well as Instructor Glenn A. Mitchell of Vanderbilt University. The author also recognizes with deep appreciation the invaluable input that hundreds of his students at Florida International University have provided regarding various sections of the manuscript.

Elias M. Awad

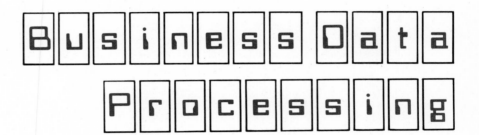

part one

Computers and Computer Processing

chapter 1

The Computer and You

Learning Objectives

The staggering implications of the computer age are full upon us. To most people, the worst thing about a computer is that nobody tells them how the "thing" works and how it can be used to solve problems. The story about computers and computer processing therefore starts by speaking to these objectives. By the end of this chapter, you should know

1. the basics behind the use of computers,

2. the general attitude toward computers,

3. the definition and the makeup of computer systems,

4. the capabilities and limitations of computers, and

5. the objectives of the text and how it is organized.

Overview
The People-Powered Computer
The Computer — in a Nutshell

Definition

The Makeup of a Computer System

Hardware

1. Data Preparation
2. Input
3. Processing
4. Output

Software
Peopleware (Manpower)

Capabilities and Limitations of Computers

Capabilities
Limitations

Computers: A Curse or a Blessing?

Objectives of the Text

> *The visible world is no longer a reality and the unseen world is no longer a dream*
>
> — *William B. Yeats*
>
> *This declaration will become truer and truer as the computerized age goes on.*

Overview

A bank somewhere in America knows which of its customers paid a streetwalker last night. The bank knows because of its computer. The bank in question has a 24-hour automated teller machine. This device allows customers with a special card to withdraw or deposit money anytime, day or night. The computer handles the transactions as quickly as they are received. Alarmed to discover a flurry of withdrawals between midnight and 2:30 AM, the bank president put an investigator on the trail. He discovered the bank was in the neighborhood of a "red light" district and that customers were stopping for cash en route![1]

The staggering implications of the Computer Age are full upon us, whether we're ready or not. Few technological developments are conspicuous enough to mark turning points in human history. Yet one such phenomenon has occurred in our time: *the Computer.* That its implications — now only barely comprehended — will be profound is already apparent. Indeed, the potential for good in the computer and the danger inherent in its misuse exceed our ability to imagine. Between reading this book and the daily newspaper, you can be sure of two things: You will understand basic computer technology, and you'll know why you can't afford not to.

To most people, the worst thing about a computer is that nobody tells them how the "thing" works and how it can be used to solve problems. This chapter answers the basic questions regarding the use of computers; the answers make up a skeletal summary of this book: Why study computers? What are computers made of? How are they used? What benefits do they offer? What are their limitations? The entering student and the new reader must have these questions answered before learning any more about computers and information processing. The answers center around four major areas:

1. The *hardware.*   The equipment that makes up a computer system.

2. The *software.*   The programs that provide the instructions for the computer to solve problems.

3. The *professionals.*   The systems analysts, programmers, and computer operators who work together in helping the end user find solutions through the computer.

4. The *end user.*   The person (manager, supervisor, administrator, or anyone) who asks for and uses the information generated by the computer.

[1]*Chicago Tribune* (August 12, 1976), Section 3, p. 1.

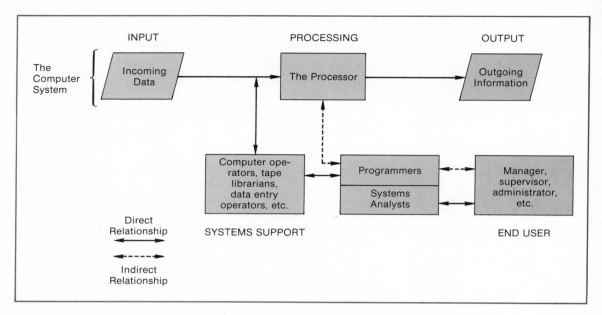

Figure 1−1. The major users in a computerized environment.

Figure 1−1 illustrates the computer system and its major users. The operators and librarians operate the equipment to provide information ultimately for the end user. Systems analysts design procedures to be used in writing the programs for running the computer. The programmer works from the systems design to write computer programs that produce the desired information. Thus, people and machines work together for the common good of the end user.

The People-Powered Computer

In our complex, industrial world, information is the building block of our society. However, at a time when the acquisition of scientific information alone exceeds 300 million pages each year, the tide of knowledge is taxing man's capacity for dealing with it. So a machine was needed to contain the tide and channel the information where needed. The electronic computer handles millions of facts with the speed of light. It solves problems in seconds or minutes that previously took a roomful of people all their lives. It does simple problems in millionths of a second (microseconds, msec) and in billionths of a second (nanoseconds, nsec). By transforming the way in which information is collected, stored, retrieved, and used, this revolutionary tool is helping humankind overcome mental and physical limitations. The computer is an *extension of the brain*—the partner, and possibly the master, of humanity.

In light of this service, the computer is becoming more and more a part of our everyday lives. A decade ago, a person rarely had direct contact with a computer. Computer applications were typically payroll, accounts receivables, computerized billing systems, and the like. Today, rare is the person who is not

Table 1–1. Popular opinion regarding 8 areas of computerization.

Area	Percentage of Total (%)	Statement
Job involvement	49	Have had a job requiring either direct or indirect contact with a computer.
	30	Currently have such a job.
Current problems	24	Difficulties in having a computerized bill corrected. Most of the respondents blamed company personnel rather than the computer for the errors.
Computers and the consumer	89	Computers will provide useful information and services in our homes.
	68	Computers have helped improve the quality of products and services.
	65	Computers will help to raise the standard of living.
	63	The use of computers should be decreased in sending "junk mail" to the home.
	48	Computers make it easier to get credit.
Computers in business	89	We can do many things today that couldn't be done without computers.
	81	"Computer mistakes" are made by people who use computers.
	60	American business would be in serious trouble without computers (33% disagreed).
Computers in government	84	Government should be concerned about regulating the use of computers.
	78	Increased use of computers to keep track of criminals.
	70	The use of computers will *not* increase the chance of war.
	63	Large computerized files will improve the efficiency of government.
Computers and privacy	62	Concern about large organizations keeping information about millions of people.
	54	Computers do not pose a major threat to people's privacy (38% disagreed).
Computers and life	91	Computers are affecting the lives of all of us.
	86	Computers will create more leisure time.
	75	Computers will improve our lives.
	55	People are becoming too dependent on computers.
	54	Computers dehumanize people by treating them as a number.**
Career opportunities	80	The jobs in the computer field are interesting (secure, 73%; having high salaries, 72%; require a lot of training, 71%; offer rapid advancement, 67%).
	76	Favor a young person entering the computer field as a career (5% opposed).

*Time-AFIPS, Inc., *A National Survey of the Public's Attitudes Toward Computers* (Montvale, N.J.: 1971). See also the summary of another study in *Computerworld* (June 14, 1976), p. 11. **A similar study conducted in 1976 by *Creative Computing* showed that 37 percent (versus 54% in 1971) of the adult population felt computers dehumanize people. If this is a trend, it may suggest improved acceptance of the computer as a way of life [*Computerworld* (June 14, 1976), p. 11].

in someway involved with computers.[2] The general public's attitudes toward the computer and its uses shows positive acceptance of this "quiet revolution." Drawn from a national survey of the adult population's attitudes toward computers, the conclusions in Table 1–1 show how the popular attitude is changing in eight basic areas involving computers.

All this indicates that society is making a quiet but positive adjustment to living with the computer. There's no turning back. The capacity that lies within the computer's circuitry for lightening the human burden is beyond imagining.

If the computer fulfills its promise, the future will differ more significantly from the present than the present from the past. For example, unless you are very old, you will live to see a society without cash or even checks—both replaced by electronic fund transfer (EFT) systems. The customer hands the clerk a plastic card, which is then pushed into the store's computer terminal. When the right keys are depressed, funds are transferred automatically from the customer's bank account to the store's account. This development, among so many others, makes it important that we familiarize ourselves with the uses and the operation of the computer.

The Computer— in a Nutshell

Before learning about computer programming, systems analysis and design, and computer applications, you need a general picture of the whole system. Like any other foreign language, you have to learn certain vocabulary to converse with the people in the field. This section provides a bird's-eye view of the makeup of a computer and the key terms used in describing it.

Definition

A **computer** is an electronic system designed to manipulate data and provide useful information. It does its job through a set of instructions called a **program.** More than a calculator, the computer is capable of solving problems in their entirety. In fact, its data-processing manner is at times almost "human." A computer follows instructions that a human would follow in solving most problems; it simulates the pattern of human thought—but it does not do the thinking. Although it seems to simulate human thought process, it is no more human than an electric saw or an automobile.

The benefits of the modern computer are basically *speed, low cost,* and *automation.* The computer's electronic nature is the reason for the *speed* with which it solves problems. The fastest computer today processes approximately 5 million instructions per second, compared to 2 million in 1960. What makes the use of the computer even more attractive is the relatively low processing *cost.* In 1960, processing power cost the equivalent of $1.87 per instruction. This cost

---

[2]In a 1976 survey by *Creative Computing,* only 25 percent of the adult population agreed with the statement that computers are beyond understanding of the common person. The implication is that more and more people have been "sold" on the uses of computers [*Computerworld* (June 14, 1976), p. 11].

dropped to $1 in 1965 and to 1 cent in 1979! The computer is also automatic or **self-directing.** Once it receives a set of instructions, it performs the job independently of human intervention. The computer's self-direction, however, is limited by the instructions made available to it by the programmer. Although the computer is not the answer to all problems and applications, its use where needed can be cost-effective and productive, if it is given adequate instructions.

The Makeup of a Computer System

Used in everyday English, the term *computer system* consists of the hardware (physical equipment) and software (programs) required for processing applications. In an operational sense, the people—or "peopleware"—are also part of the system. The people are the analysts, programmers, and the operations personnel who manage the system. Each of these three types of "ware" must function in line with the overall design of the computer as a system. Details on hardware are covered in Chapters 5–10; software is discussed in Chapters 13–17; and "peopleware" in Chapters 18–19.

Hardware

The term **hardware** refers to the physical equipment or components of a computer. (See Table 1–2.) Each component is designed to perform one or more of the following functions:

1. *Data preparation* prepare data for input to the computer.

2. *Input* read input data for computer processing.

3. *Processing* process input data based on a stored program.

4. *Output* print out the output for the end user.

Table 1–2. Function of key computer components.

Data Preparation	Input	Processing	Output
Key punch devices	Punched card reader	Central processing	Card punch
Paper tape punch devices	Paper tape reader	unit (main memory,	Paper tape punch
Paper-tape-to-magnetic	Magnetic tape unit	arithmetic, control)	Visual display
tape converters	Magnetic disc unit		(TV screen)
Key-to-tape devices	Magnetic ink		Line printer
Key-to-disc devices	character reader		Audio response
Magnetic tape encoders	Optical scanner		Console typewriter
Magnetic ink character	Console typewriter		
encoders			

1. Data preparation. Several devices are used to prepare data for input. For example, a keypunch codes data onto cards to be read later by a card reader. The keypunch operates independently of the computer system and can be placed in a separate room, if necessary.

2. Input.   Coded data is placed into an input device designed to read the data and transmit it to the computer's main memory for processing. Thus, an input device is the "eye" of the computer. It must be **on-line** or direct, equipment— that is, it is physically connected to the computer itself by cable, forming a permanent component of the computer system.

Input comes from many sources—the punched cards we have been warned not to fold, spindle, or mutilate; a human operator typing at a keyboard; reels of magnetic tape that resemble recording tape; or magnetic discs comparable to phonographic records (Figure 1–2).

3. Processing.   Inside the computer is a "logic unit" or a "central processing unit" (CPU) to do the calculating or processing. This unit is made of thousands of interconnected chips made from materials such as gold, aluminum, and silicon. Processing consists of three elements: main memory, **arithmetic-logic,** and the stored **program.** The data read by the input device is transmitted to the memory section of the CPU and held there for processing.

Figure 1–2.   Major functional elements and units of a computer system.

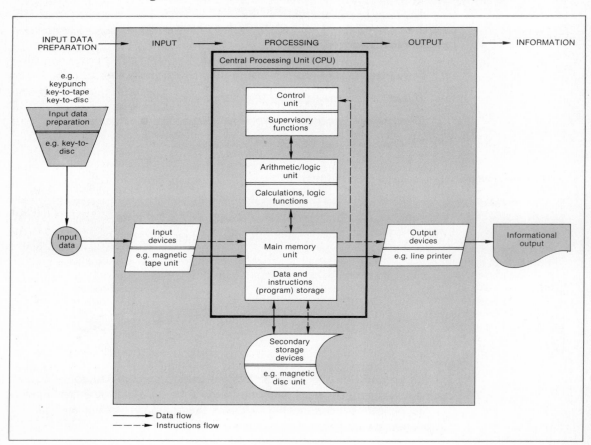

Main memory, the heart of the computer system, is analogous to the human brain (Figure 1–1). It can store the balance in your bank account or the program for compounding your interest on that account. This "brain" is composed of millions of tiny elements called "semiconductors," far too small to see. In them, data and program instructions are stored in specific locations, and each location has an address so that they can be accessed when necessary. Obviously, the capacity of main memory depends a great deal on the physical size of the computer: A pocket calculator may have six to twenty locations, while a super-sized computer may have several million. Details on the CPU are explained in Chapter 5.

In the heart of the computer are two units of great importance: the arithmetic logic unit and the control unit. The **arithmetic-logic unit (ALU)** performs arithmetic, compares values, and "logically" determines their equality. It can also distinguish between positive and negative numbers, determining whether a number is greater than, equal to, or less than zero. For example, an "add" instruction causes the transfer of two numbers to the ALU. Once added, the sum of these numbers is returned to main memory. Other arithmetic operations are handled the same way.

In addition to arithmetic, the ALU performs logical operations. It can compare two values and select (or "branch to") a program path resulting from the comparison. For example, suppose you wish to have the computer determine the balance owed by customers of your friendly corner store. Each customer's account consists of two numbers: previous balance and today's payment. You wish the computer to print the balance outstanding if the payment is less than the previous balance. Otherwise, you instruct the computer to continue with further calculations. The logic of this simple problem is flowcharted[3] in Figure 1–3.

The **control unit** interprets the program instructions and monitors their execution. It also determines the time when data are read into memory, when arithmetic is performed on the data, and when output is printed. Thus, program instructions have to be made available to the control unit before any action is taken.

4. Output.   The computer's output is the outcome of the computations and related activities carried out in the CPU. It can be a message or a diagram flashed on a TV screen. It can be a drawing or a report on paper. It can even be what sounds like a human voice, produced by assembling pre-recorded fragments or a real voice stored on tape.

Software

For the computer to read, make "decisions," update files, and print out information, it must have programs designed for these purposes. Stored programs tell the computer what steps to take, what data to work on, and what to

[3]A flowchart is a graphic means of describing the operations performed on data. Details on flowcharting are covered in Chapter 13.

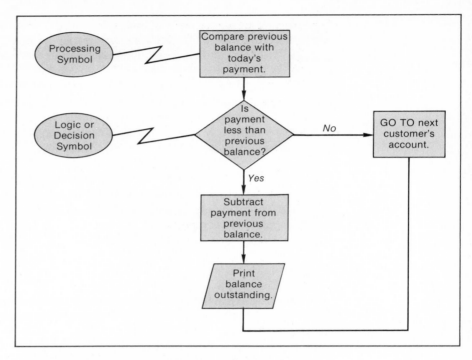

Figure 1–3. An example of a logical operation.

do with the results. In the CPU, the control unit monitors the programs and sets the timing for the functions of all the devices included in the system. **Software** commonly includes such programs as well as any operating aids (made available by the manufacturer) that extend the capabilities of the computer as a system.

Sophisticated software requires sophisticated hardware. Computers have been described as "incredibly fast, incredibly accurate, and incredibly dumb." Data-carrying electrical impulses, created by programming, move through the circuitry at the incredibly high speed of light (186,000 miles/second). Yet a computer multiplies a number only by adding it over and over; it divides only by subtracting the number over and over—incredibly dumb. Even at the speed of light, the computer loses much time when a problem requires millions of separate steps. So shorter electrical routes allow impulses to travel less and the computer to work faster. As a result, computer circuitry has been made too small to be seen with the human eye. It is designed by hand and then reduced by a photomechanical process, much as the photographs of computers were reduced by a special camera to appear in this text.

Peopleware (Manpower)

The term "peopleware" represents the personnel involved in systems analysis, programming, computer operations, system maintenance, and the like.

Their jobs include the following activities:

1. **Systems analysis.**   Separating a system into its key elements and studying each element individually and in relation to the other elements. The objective is to look into a way of improving the present system.

2. **Systems design.**   Putting together the separate elements of a system, including program development, into an operational whole. It is also a detailed concentration on the technical specifications that will implement the new system.

3. **Program development.**   With the analyst's flowcharts of the final design, the programmer uses them to write programs for implementing the new system.

4. **System implementation.**   The program testing and staff training in the operation of the new system.

5. **System maintenance.**   The detection and correction of errors in the new system. The objective is to keep the system in line with the requirements of the user.

Figure 1 – 4 summarizes the primary activities in a computer-based environment. Systems analysis and design are the jobs of the systems analyst. Program development is the specialty of the programmer. Systems development is carried out by computer operators, input data preparation staff, and output preparation clerks. Output preparation involves collating, bursting, and binding the reports before they are delivered to the user. Commonly, analysts (called "analyst-programmers") do some programming in addition to analysis. Correspondingly, programmers (called "programmer-analysts") do some systems work in addition to programming. Such an arrangement distributes the total load (and risk) among the existing staff. It also helps programmers prepare for greater involvement in systems analysis in the future.

Capabilities and Limitations of Computers

The need for (and interest in) computer systems developed over a long time. One hundred years ago, electronic computers were not really needed for the slow pace of a relatively agricultural economy. As our economy became less agricultural and ever more industrial, the need for automated data gathering and faster processing methods became apparent. Business executives began to realize that competing in rapidly growing markets requires access to essential reports as quickly as possible and in usable form. Therefore, *timeliness, speed,* and *accuracy* in information processing become more crucial than ever as economies grow and markets expand.

Computers, then, are built to boost productivity and to improve the quality of work. They achieve these goals in several ways:

1. Because the speed of the computer is measured in billionths and trillionths of a second, it is faster than any other machine designed to do similar work. With this capability, a business can update its records without delay.

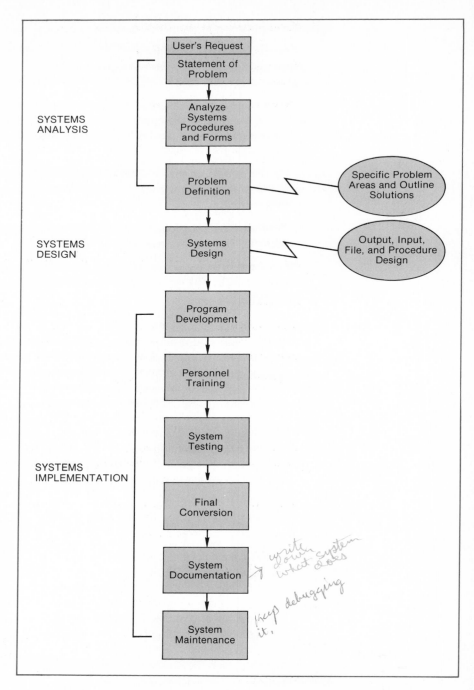

Figure 1—4. The primary activities in a computer-based environment.

2. A computer's greater versatility in tirelessly performing millions of operations frees greater amounts of time for creative and intelligent planning.

3. High-speed processing is accompanied by high-accuracy results. No other system can operate with as much accuracy as the electronic system.

4. Although the initial cost of installing a computer system is substantial, many applications are found to be cost-effective. In many cases, the speed of data processing and accuracy of the output justify the installation. Since the computer is not the answer to *all* users' problems, systems and cost-benefit analyses must be carried out before a decision to recommend a computerized environment can be justified.

Capabilities

Among the unique capabilities of computers used in business are the following:

1. **Processing** of *repetitive,* high-volume *applications.*

2. **Self-operation.** Once the data and program become available in main memory, the computer executes the instructions on its own without human intervention.

3. **"Decision-making."** A computer cannot do anything a person could not do if he or she had the time. The computer chooses between alternative paths to perform a routine. The choice, however, is limited to those prepared for it by the programmer.

4. **Self-checking.** A computer verifies the accuracy of its own work by means of a *parity check.* It counts the number of characters it has in storage to make sure there is no loss of data during processing.

5. **Performing new and additional tasks.** A computer can calculate or summarize quantitative information more efficiently than any human clerk, because it is not subject to "boredom." For example, it can be instructed to print an order every time the stock level falls below a specific minimum.

Limitations

Although computers are powerful and even marvelous tools, they have limitations. Thus, they cannot be used indiscriminately. Among the major limitations of computers are:

1. **Insufficient speed** for certain applications. Although a large-sized computer handles over 4 million operations per second, certain problems are

of such a magnitude that even this speed will not solve them. For example, take a game of chess. Even if the computer could perform at the rate of 1 billion operations per second, it would take more than 10 years of computation to foresee the consequences of a move. As another example, an accurate weather forecast makes it necessary to change the computer programs from "accurate" to "approximate," to get answers in time to be of use.

2. *Failure to derive meanings from objects.* An inexperienced dog learns the hard way about cats—by getting painful scratches in its face. But the dog soon learns by backing away or fighting back. Unlike a living system, a computer does not recognize (and therefore does not respond) to living objects. Accordingly, the meanings of the objects (data or programs) it deals with mean nothing to it. Whatever meanings the computer deals with (at least at present) are fed to it by the human programmer.

3. *Inability to generate information on its own.* Once, in a backyard, this author watched a squirrel raid a bird feeder. The feeder was tied to a string and hung from a tree branch 4 feet beyond a little bush. The squirrel first investigated the setup and ate the fallen bird seeds. A little later, he tried to reach the feeder, but it was too high. Then, he leaped on the tree branch, lowered himself along the feeder, stretching his full length upside-down toward the mouth of the feeder. He used his front paws downward. Finally, he reversed himself, crawled along the branch, and disappeared into the woods.

   The squirrel did not have instructions as a computer might have had from a programmer. The squirrel's "understanding" showed he was able to perceive relevant aspects of the situation and adopt means to fulfill his goal. A computer has the capacity to put information together from many sources, but only if programmed—never independently.

4. *Failure to correct wrong instructions.* When you tell a boy to wash the car and the windows are down, the boy usually rolls up the windows even if you didn't specifically say so. A human being is likely to do what you mean and not what you say when you don't give every detail. The computer, on the other hand, will do what you say, regardless of what you mean. And it will do the wrong thing over 4 million times a second!

Although these limitations make us appreciate the superiority of man over machine, the day may eventually come when a computer will apply "common sense" and correct wrong instructions. This capacity is sometime in the future. To date, no programmer has claimed a program with "common sense."

Computers: A Curse or a Blessing?

Powerful tools invariably have powerful effects. Hence the computer's powerful impact cannot go unnoticed. Emotional reaction led some people to view the computer as a curse; others, as a blessing. It seems to have become a symbol of all that is good and all that is "evil" in our society. As a tool with applications in every aspect of human activity, it is a blessing. Business firms, schools, government, hospitals, police, law firms, and churches all find uses for computers. (Business and other applications are discussed in Chapter 2.) With all this activity going on, people fear that facts regarding their personal lives will become encoded on discs, tapes, and cards, making them vulnerable to investigations. Yet the same power of the computer that evokes hostility in some people generates hope in others who view the computer as an extension of the human brain and reasoning power.

Both points of view at least show that with the benefits come certain risks. The risks of using computers are somewhat analogous to the risks of driving automobiles. Cars kill an estimated 60,000 people a year, but we continue to use them since their contributions outweigh the risks. Hundreds of stories have been told about the "outrageous conduct" of the computer. Following are examples:

- A computer system of a bank sent a young man a letter thanking him for repaying a loan very quickly. The man was making the first payment but had used the last ticket in the payment book. He didn't exactly steal from the bank, but he left the next move up to the computer.

- A programming error in Maryland brought overpayment under the new welfare program to over $400 million in its first 18 months of operation.

- In Washington and Florida, the State Security Departments decided against taking a chance of overpaying. So two living recipients were declared dead. Consequently, all payments were stopped immediately.[4]

- An accountant sued J. C. Penney Co. for $100,000 punitive damages due to an error of $16.78 which he claimed he was charged for a returned item (rather than given credit). After being promised by the store employees that the error would be corrected, he received threatening letters with additional service charges added to increase the amount. Eight months later, he heard from the collection agency about the matter. He went to see the store manager. The manager admitted the error. He opened a new account for the customer, but the store carried the old charge over. Within the 16-month lapse prior to the law suit, the accountant received 42 letters and bills from the company regarding the charge.[5]

- A New York bank teller embezzled $1.5 million over three years by transferring funds out of dormant accounts into his own. The only way he was caught was when the police raided a betting joint and found his name on several of the betting slips. They became suspicious that a man earning $12,000 a year could support a $30,000-a-day betting habit.

[4]Catherine Arnst, "Another Year Proves Computers Don't Err—People Do," *Computerworld* (December 31, 1975/January 5, 1976), p. 12.
[5]Catherine Arnst, "DP 'Billing Errors Victims' Sue Penney for $100,000," *Computerworld* (April 9, 1975), p. 4.

- Some officers at Equity Funding set up 56,000 phony insurance policies with a total face value of $2 billion which were sold to insurance companies for quick cash.

- A man had his account number encoded on a batch of blank deposit slips. He placed the slips in the slots of blank deposit slips provided for customers who have forgotten their slips. Unknowingly, customers used the encoded slips. The bank processed them in the usual way and the deposits were credited to the man's account. By the time the customers complained about their checks bouncing, over a quarter million dollars had been withdrawn and the man disappeared.

The advent of computers has spawned a new breed of sophisticated criminals. Unfortunately, few crimes are detected — and then only by accident. Most companies let the "crooks" go to avoid embarrassment and to prevent having their records made public. Of all the known computer "ripoff" artists, less than 5 percent serve time for their fraud. Even then, the jail sentences are relatively light. For example, a man who used a computer program from a West Coast utility to order $800,000 in electronic equipment from the company's warehouse was sentenced to 40 days in jail and had to pay $800 fine. After his release, he became a recruiting consultant, specializing in computer security and control.

With freedom comes responsibility. The freedom we have in choosing computers to do work in business and government carries the responsibility in protecting the consumer and society from the invasion of privacy and unauthorized access. Perhaps the best way to harness computer misuse is to recognize this potential for fraud.

Objectives of the Text

Today's revolution focuses not on hardware, as such, but on the user. It is a revolution to make computer systems responsive to the needs of the user. The classical single, centralized computer facility designed to serve all purposes has proved too slow to respond quickly to simple requests. Today's mini- and microcomputers distributed data processing for more individualized use by end users. This distributed data processing (DDP) system focuses on the user's needs.

Thus, one objective of this text is to familiarize the lay student with the new computer technology and its use in solving problems. The book frames out the inner workings of a computer system, enabling students to fully utilize the new technology in any profession.

The second objective is to offer the essential prerequisites for systems analysis and design — a second course in the field. A student needs to know first about computer structure, programming basics, and computer operations. This background makes it easier to learn how to analyze, design, and implement applications through a computer system. Two summary chapters on systems analysis and design are provided in a later section of the text.

The third objective of this text is to provide prerequisite background to students planning to major in information systems. It is the "union ticket" to advanced courses in the data processing program.

How This Text is Organized

An understanding of computer systems requires familiarity with five areas of knowledge:

1. *Capabilities and uses of a computer.* Chapters 2 and 3 review key computer applications, the data processing cycle, and computer classifications. Chapter 4 summarizes historical and futuristic developments in the computer field.

2. *The makeup and structure of a computer system.* Chapters 5–9 provide the student an overview of the equipment needed for a computer system, why they're used, and how the user communicates with the computer as a system.

3. *Programming the computer.* This area deals with the "how-to" aspects of programming a computer to solve a user's problem. Emphasis is on Cobol (Chapter 17) as a widely used business language and Basic (Chapter 16) as a common language used in schools and for small computers in industry.

4. *Systems analysis and design.* The "how" of computer programming is performed within the framework of an application that the user needs to update or computerize. System design is the basis for programming, because a program simply generates required information based on a system design developed in advance (Chapters 11 and 12).

5. *Structure and management of the computer center.* With the foregoing knowledge as background, the next question is, "How do we acquire, organize, and manage a computer center?" The answer has to do with feasibility study techniques, management principles unique to data processing operations, and organization basics designed to keep the overall facility in tune with the continued demands of the end user.

SUMMARY

1. This chapter presents an overview of computers, their makeup, benefits, and drawbacks. A computer is an electronic system designed to solve problems in their entirety at high speed. It performs the job through a program which provides the necessary instructions for problem solution.

2. A computer system consists of hardware (physical equipment), software (programs), and the people behind the operation of the system. The hardware handles data preparation, reading input data, processing the data, and printing out the output to the end user. The processing unit contains main memory, an arithmetic-logic unit, and a control unit. The control unit interprets the program instructions and monitors their execution.

The people involved in computer system operation are essentially the systems analysts, programmers, and computer operators. Their jobs include analysis and design of systems projects (applications), program development, system implementation, and system maintenance.

3. The primary capabilities of computers are:
    a. processing of repetitive, high-volume applications,
    b. handling applications on their own without human intervention,
    c. making critical "choices" for problem solving, and
    d. performing new and additional tasks based on programmed routines.
    Among the major limitations of computers are:
    a. insufficient speed for certain applications,
    b. failure to derive meanings from objects,
    c. failure to correct wrong instructions, and
    d. inability to put information on its own.

4. Computers have been viewed as a curse and as a blessing. As a tool with application in every aspect of our life, it is a blessing. However, the vulnerability of an individual's personal life to unauthorized access evokes hostility in many people. Looking at the computer picture in its totality, remember that the freedom we have in choosing computers to work in business and government carries the responsibility in protecting computer files from abuse.

TERMS TO LEARN

Arithmetic-logic unit
Computer
Control unit
End user
Hardware
On-line
Program
Self-directing
Software

REVIEW QUESTIONS

1. Define in your own words the terms "computer," "hardware," "system." Compare your definitions with those in a dictionary. Explain the differences.

2. Who is the "user"? Give two examples of users in a bank or in the firm where you work.

3. Describe several situations in which people can become slaves of the computer. How can these be minimized or avoided?

4. What makes the computer a system? Discuss.

5. Summarize the makeup of a computer system. Explain the primary function(s) of the CPU.

6. In what way is the control unit related to the arithmetric-logic unit? Explain.

7. List and briefly explain the capabilities and limitations of computers.

8. Give an example of how a computer violates an individual's privacy.

9. Search the classified section (Yellow Pages) of your local telephone directory and find the section dealing with computer products and services. Classify them into hardware manufacturers, data processing service bureaus, and software companies.

10. Our lives have undoubtedly been changed by the computer. Can you think of two other inventions that have done the same? Explain.

11. Give two illustrations of drastic losses that could be attributed to the failure of an information system. For example, a house burned to the ground because the fire department transposed the house number in question.

12. What is systems analysis? How does it differ from systems design? Explain.

13. Is the computer a curse or a blessing? Justify your answer by giving an example.

14. Write a 100-word summary of this chapter.

chapter 2

Computer Systems and Management Information

Learning Objectives

Everybody must process data, whether performing a decision making function as an individual, a student, a political leader, or a business owner. A basic understanding of the concepts and process of data transformation is essential for studying computer applications for the user. By the end of this chapter, you should know:

1. the relationship between data processing and management as it relates to the user,

2. the data processing cycle that makes it possible to produce information, and

3. representative computer applications in various areas of business.

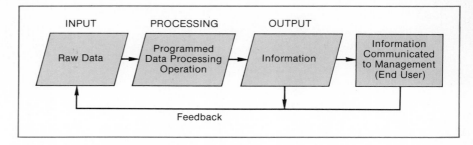

Figure 2–1. Transformation process of data.

A computer has one key function: To provide the user with information needed to make decisions or to solve problems. The transformation of raw data into usable information starts with source data (input). The computer then operates on the data according to a stored program (processing). The outcome of processing is management (or user) information (output). See Figure 2–1. You must understand the concepts and process of data transformation before studying computer applications. This chapter therefore discusses:

1. the relationships between data processing and management from a user's point of view,

2. the data processing cycle that produces information, and

3. representative computer applications in various areas of business.

Data Processing Versus Management Information

Users and practitioners often interchange the terms "data," "information," or "management information." Data and information, however, are not the same. **"Data"** refers to facts, the raw material of a computer application. When the user requests work to run through the computer, the staff provides the source data as a basis for computer processing. Upon receiving the data, the computer transforms (processes) the data into information for management. Thus, management **information** is the output of a data processing operation. Figure 2–2 illustrates examples of data and information. This three-part function is known as **data processing.**

Why Data Processing?

Everybody processes data. Anyone who makes a decision as an individual, as a head of a family, as a student, as a political leader, or as the owner of a business — large or small — has to process data. In most cases, pencil and paper are used as manual aids in problem solving. As you begin to read this chapter, you are already engaged in *collecting* and *storing* data (words, sentences) and *processing* them through the brain. The output of the transformation within the

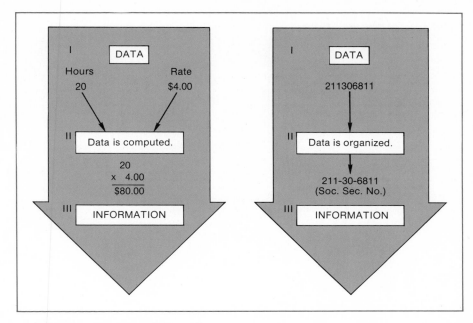

Figure 2–2. Data versus information.

brain takes the form of useful knowledge to help you as a potential user. In fact, not only are you engaged in a data processing exercise, but you *are* also a data processing system and a *part* of an academic information system.

In the distant past, under a barter system, a business person was not required to account for or document his or her work. Calculations were so few that mental calculations went as quickly as today's computer electronic processing. As communities expanded and the barter system was replaced with monetary systems, the basis of business conduct changed from intimate and informal to impersonal and formal. This change led larger business firms to organize, document, and retain records for analysis and reference.

Levels of Management Information

The competitive nature and complexity of business today means that the right kind of information must be available when needed. Managers utilize information differently, depending on their level in the organization and their assigned tasks. As shown in Figure 2–3, upper management needs information for developing policies and for drafting long-range plans. A president, for example, works with environmental information (customers, suppliers, and the like) and spends more time in planning than do lower-level managers. Given the time pressures, the president likely requires information presented in more summarized forms than those produced for lower management. Lower management,

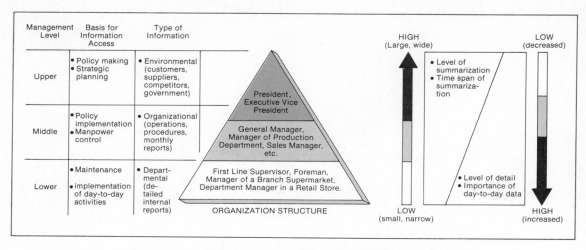

Figure 2–3. Differential requirements for management information.

on the other hand, expects detailed internal information for handling the day-to-day activities in the department. Thus, the level of detail is critical for effective implementation.

To perform its tasks, management has to rely on a system capable of producing management information when needed. Unlike a hardware-oriented data processing system, an information system is user-oriented. It often utilizes more than one data processing system to produce the required information to the end users. Thus, a data processing system may be viewed as a subsystem (a part) of an overall information system.

Areas of Data Processing

Data processing may be business or scientific.

Business data processing (BDP) is characterized by the need to establish, retain, and process files of data for producing useful information. Generally, it involves a large volume of input data, limited arithmetic operations, and a relatively large volume of output. For example, a large retail store must maintain a record for each customer who purchases on account, update the balance owed on each account, and periodically present a bill to the customer for merchandise purchased. This type of record keeping requires reading a customer's account number, name, address, and previous balance. The bill involves a few basic calculations. The results are printed and mailed to the customer for collection. Tens of thousands of similar bills are commonly handled in the same way.

Scientific data processing. In science, data processing involves a limited volume of input and many logical or arithmetic calculations. Unlike business problems, most of the scientific problems are nonrepetitive, requiring a "one-time" solution. For example, in cancer research, data on cancer patients (collected over a period of time) are analyzed by a computer to produce a possible cure. Although a final cure is unavailable, computer analysis of the hundreds of variables suspected to be cancer agents has saved hundreds of man-years of computations. It has also brought us a step closer to the final answer to the cancer horror.

The Data Processing Cycle

Although scientific data may differ from business data, the processing pattern is quite similar. First, a system must be devised. Second, a problem must exist that can be represented in a form acceptable to the data processing system at hand. Thus, regardless of the type or size of system, the **data processing cycle** involves five basic steps:

1. origination,
2. input,
3. processing,
4. output, and
5. storage.

Figure 2–4 shows that the four primary steps are origination, input, processing, and output. The last step, storage, merely retains the results of the data processing operation for reference.

1. Origination. The initial capture of *raw* data on documents as transactions occur is referred to as **origination.** Source documents simply capture the data for input: Time cards, deposit slips, sales orders, and the like are all examples.

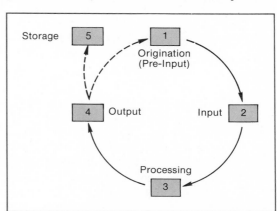

Figure 2–4. The key steps of a data processing cycle.

2. Input.　In the **input** step, source documents are collected and converted into a form acceptable for processing. Data recording requires that the available data be *edited* and *verified* for accuracy and format. When editing input data, you should code as much as possible, because coding reduces the volume of data. It is also a means of identifying and arranging data with like characteristics into groups or classes. For example, sales data may be classified by customer number, the salesperson's identification number, or the product sold.

3. Processing.　**Processing** consists of the actual operations performed on the input data. These operations include classifying, sorting, calculating, recording, and summarizing the data.

　　Classifying involves identifying and grouping data into distinguishable groups or classes. For example, bills may be classified by stamping them as "paid" or "unpaid" or time cards may be grouped by department; each employee's time card belongs in the group within the department where he or she works.

　　Sorting is the physical arrangement of data into an alphabetic or a numeric order. For example, employee time cards, may be sorted by the employee's last name or number for further processing.

　　Calculating consists of performing one or more arithmetic operations on data. It is a crucial phase of data manipulation, because the outcome of this operation becomes part of the output. For example, the hours on classified employee cards are used for computing the take-home pay (output) of each employee.

　　Recording relates to the documentation of intermediate figures and facts resulting from calculations. For example, in computing net pay, hours are multiplied by rate to arrive at gross pay. Net pay is then computed by subtracting all deductions from gross pay. Gross pay is an intermediate step which is retained temporarily for later use.

　　Summarizing is the presentation of data in a meaningful format. In business, summary reports are used for income-tax reporting, preparation of profit-and-loss statements, and other reports reflecting the activities of the business. Summarized data is printed and made available to the user for action.

4. Output.　The **output** step entails the preparation of processed information in a format acceptable to the user for analysis or as input for a second cycle. Communication is important in output preparation and dissemination. Failure to communicate the output clearly, completely, and accurately to the user is as wasteful as figuring out your income tax and then failing to file the return.

5. Storage and feedback.　The *storage* function is the retention of the results of processed data for future use or retrieval. Storage can be provided manually (such as in a ledger book), electromechanically (in punched cards), or electronically (magnetic tape, disk, main memory, and the like). The feedback function is the key to control in business. *Feedback* is the comparison of the output(s) and

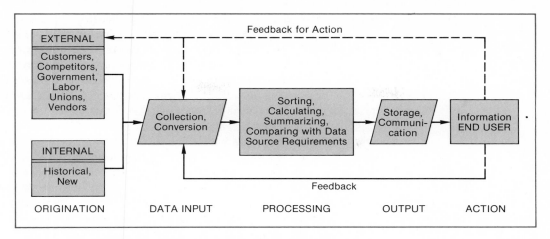

Figure 2–5. The data processing feedback cycle.

the goal set in advance; any discrepancy is analyzed, corrected, and fed back to the proper stage in the cycle. The *feedback* step permits businesspersons to follow up on essential information and to attain worthwhile goals.

In the recycling of data, the output of the previous cycle (machine run) often become the input data for a new cycle. This cycle is analagous to converting the ending (unsold) inventory at the end of a fiscal year into the beginning inventory for sale on the first day of the next year. Figure 2 – 5 illustrates the data processing cycle and its relationships with the user and the environment. Remember, however, that in a data processing cycle, the preparation of new data continues as previous data is processed, and vice versa. The steps in the illustration can be isolated for descriptive purposes but their operations in practice are constantly interlinked. You are looking at a stop-action photograph of a continuous process. Feedback makes the system dynamic, allowing each step to function in line with the functioning of the cycle as a system.

Modern-Day Business Applications

In the early days of computers, routine, accounting-oriented applications such as payroll and inventory accounting were the first to be computerized. These activities were well understood and documented, which made computerization easy. A computerized effort was also easily justified by savings through clerical staff reduction and through replacement of the more expensive (and slower) punch card system. These early systems processed data in "batches," handling transactions one by one, in a sequential order. They therefore required steady manual intervention, which limited the scope of most applications.

Today's applications are broader in scope and more responsive, serving many more users than the earlier applications. Earlier applications, handling one activity at a time, printed 100 percent of the transactions they processed. In contrast, current applications provide only the results that are important for management decision making. The results are printed out or displayed on a TV-like screen on a daily or hourly basis, when needed. The easy-to-use terminals also make it convenient for many users to access the computer regardless of distance. Airline reservation clerks can call a remote central computer to check customers' credit rating. They get the answer in a matter of seconds. The salesperson in a retail store can use the telephone to interrogate the computer whether a specific product is in stock, what branch it is available in, and if it is on sale. The computer-produced voice response is available almost instantly. These and other applications typify today's *man-machine* interface in business.

Still, not all applications are suitable for computerized processing. Many menial tasks can be performed more economically by noncomputerized devices. For an application to qualify for computerized handling, it must meet certain criteria. Given the cost of installing and operating computer systems, an application being considered for computerized handling must be viewed from at least three points of view:

1. *Definability.* The requirements of the user must be clearly defined and the objective achieved through a series of specific logical and arithmetic steps.

2. *Justifiability.* The end result (expected output, anticipated time or cost saving, or whatever results) must justify the cost of writing, testing, and executing programs to computerize the application.

3. *Size of application.* An application is expected to offer a large enough volume of data to warrant conversion to computerized processing.

Each factor must be weighed in light of the conceivably more economical alternative of the current processing method.

Stages of Applications Development

Characteristics of business applications correspond to changes in the development of computer systems. The three primary stages are:

Batch processing. Business applications were run through computer programs, one program at a time, processing transactions from sequential files on magnetic tape, punched cards, and other media. Batch processing is the simplest form of data processing. Later on, it expanded to handle more complex calculations, to perform limited analysis on summarized data, and to process transactions presented in random (nonsequential) order.

On-line processing. The term "on-line" refers to equipment or devices under the *direct* control of the central processing unit. This stage of development focuses on application systems that allow the user to transmit directly (by terminal) any records stored on disc.

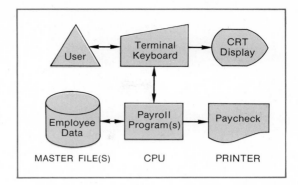

Figure 2–6. Distributed processing—an example.

MASTER FILE(S)   CPU   PRINTER

Distributed processing. The most complex level of computer processing, distributed processing generally consists of remote terminals linked to a large central computer system to help the user conduct inquiries about accounts, process jobs, or other data processing operations. In essence, computer power is "distributed" to accommodate the user at the operating level. As shown in Figure 2–6, an employee paycheck can be processed from the user's location, regardless of proximity to the central system. Payroll data (hours worked, job class, and other input) is transmitted to the computer via remote terminal. The payroll is computed and the payroll files updated in a matter of seconds. Payroll, format, and paycheck data is transmitted back to the user at the remote location.

Given the stages of computer development, therefore, business applications evolved also. Computers advanced from the handling of batch applications to distributed processing. In Table 2–1, you can see that business applications also evolved from simple, low-cost, *accounting-oriented* programs to complex, expensive, *user-oriented* systems. Thus, the potential benefits are bound to yield improved customer service, better managerial control, and lower overall cost.

Table 2–1. Stages of computer and application system development.

Stages of Computer Development / Application System Characteristics	SIMPLE ⟶ COMPLEX		
	Batch Processing	On-Line Processing	Distributed Processing
• Cost of development	Under $50,000	$50,000–$500,000	$200,000 to over $1 million (includes remote terminals, minicomputers, and large disc files.)
• Time span of development	Several man-months	Several man-months to two man-years	2–5 man-years
• Level of difficulty	Simple—within the framework of the data processing center	Relatively difficult— some technical and operational problems	Large operational and conversion problems

Table 2–1. (cont.)

Stages of Computer Development / Application System Characteristics	SIMPLE ⟶ COMPLEX		
	Batch Processing	On-Line Processing	Distributed Processing
• Response time to inquiry	Days-week(s)	Seconds-minutes	Seconds-minutes
• Organizational level involved	First-line supervisor or a department manager requesting EDP service	Vice president, assistant vice president	President, executive vice president
• User involvement in system operation	Virtually none	Average to above average (inquiry operation)	Above average—system is run through terminals
• Types of benefits expected	Clerical staff reduction	Improved management control, improved customer service	Improved management control at all levels, improved customer service, improved total cost reductions
• Magnitude of benefits	Small, but immediate	Relatively large, with noticeable benefits	Large, with gain measurable over time

The System's View

At first glance, you might get the false impression that a firm uses each application independently from others. Business applications, however, are closely interrelated. For example, accounts receivable, inventory control, order processing, and sales analysis are members of a group or of a system designed to serve the needs of the company's customers. As a system, the output of one application is the input to the next. For example, the source data from a sales invoice provides the basis for the shipping order. The shipping order becomes the input to the billing system. The bill produced by the billing system is the input to accounts receivable, inventory control, and sales analysis applications. Each application produces reports and information for various users to check on the size and state of the receivables, the available stock in the warehouse, the performance of salespersons, and other aspects of running the business. As shown in Figure 2–7, this linkage makes one application dependent on another and interlinked to ensure a continuing relationship.

Major Types of Business Applications

Business applications are classified by the functions they perform. Some applications are designed to handle accounting and financial activities; others focus on payroll, personnel, production, customer service, and managerial decision making. Each of these applications deserves a brief description.

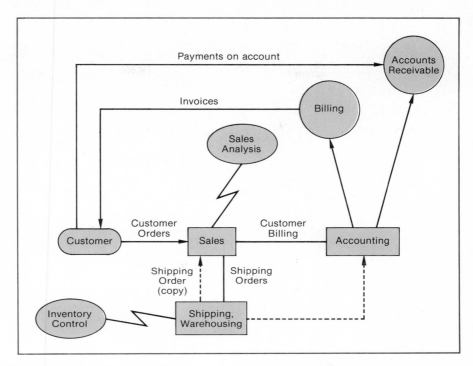

Figure 2–7. Interrelationships among selected customer-oriented applications.

Accounting and financial applications. As mentioned earlier, accounting-oriented applications were among the first to be computerized. Substantial enough clerical cost reductions justified the conversion. In spite of the routine nature of accounting and finance, several high-benefit applications have been developed. For example, large, diversified firms find cash management an extremely important task. The available cash must be invested and short-sighted investment decisions that force the company to borrow unnecessarily adds strain to financial resources. Computers have been used to collect, analyze, and produce information about cash reserves and cash requirements by user, department, or fiscal period. The outcome of such applications is shorter loan periods, lower interest rates, and higher total returns on short-term cash investments.

Financial analysis of selected proposals constitutes a major computer-based financial application. The financial analyst uses simulation[1] models to learn about the financial contributions of different proposals, such as building a new branch or acquiring a smaller firm. The information produced by these computerized models can be acted upon more quickly and expeditiously than on information from manual decision-making methods. Table 2–2 summarizes some of the traditional and high-level accounting and financial applications, with a trend toward the latter type.

[1]Simulation is explained in a later section in the chapter.

Table 2-2. Accounting and financial applications—selected examples.

Stages of Computer Development / Application	SIMPLE ————————————————————→ COMPLEX		
	Batch Processing	On-Line Processing	Distributed Processing
• General Accounting	Cost accounting ————————————————→		Cost estimating
	Budgetary accounting		
	Daily exception reporting		
	Check processing and reconciliation		
	Preparation of accounts payable registers		
• Purchasing	Purchase order preparation	Determining Economic Purchase Quantity (EPQs)	
	Purchase analysis—by vendor	Analysis of product quality, price, reliability, etc. by vendor	Produce or purchase decisions
• Finance	Financial statement preparation	Cash management, financial analysis	Analysis and decisions on financial proposals

*Adapted from Anthony Ralston, and C. L. Meek, (eds.), *Encyclopedia of Computer Science* (New York, N.Y.: Petrocelli/Charter, Inc., 1976), p. 31.

Payroll and personnel applications.   The highly repetitious and mechanical nature of payroll made it a logical target for automation. By the mid-1950s, many organizations had already prepared their payroll through a punched card data processing system. Later computerization of this application was relatively easy, since it meant storage of data files on magnetic tape rather than on punched cards. Thus, no major change was made in payroll applications other than in the type of hardware used.

In contrast to the mechanical nature of payroll, a number of high-level applications have been developed to manage human resources. In the personnel area, applications are designed to do the following:

1. automate basic personnel files,

2. prepare reports regarding sickness, leave of absence, vacations, etc., and

3. prepare performance evaluation notices.

Many large organizations have implemented complex personnel information systems designed to provide information for manpower planning and development. Figure 2-8 is a general model of a computerized personnel information system. The data base is established to include all data needs and meet all the legal and other report requirements of the organization. Other organizational systems are linked to the personnel information system model for information acquisition and feedback. Note that payroll and finance are interlinked with personnel for overall personnel functioning.

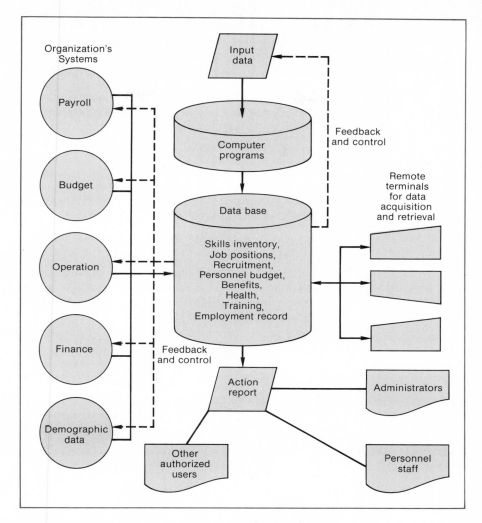

Figure 2—8. Personnel information system—a general model.

Production applications. Most production applications assist the planning and control of various aspects of production management. They include work order scheduling, work order status reporting, maintenance scheduling, and inventory updating and control. Because they involve a high degree of integration of information from several departments, these applications are often costly, requiring years to operationalize.

A widely computerized production application is inventory control. The procedure involves handling receipts, disbursement of inventory items on hand, and computation of their cost. A computer accounts for incoming and outgoing items, keeps regular track of the items on hand, and computes current stock levels, safety stock demands, and optimal order size. The outcomes are a reduction in the average inventory level and a substantial capital saving.

Inventory management faces constant functional changes that result from production, sales, and customer demands. These changes are met by:

1. developing centralized inventory control routines, with emphasis on statistical analysis for more accurate forecasting, and
2. establishing systems that aid in developing relationships between financial, marketing, production, and inventory activities.

Some systems are used in forecasting short-term variations in consumer demand, in determining economic order quantities, and in resource allocation. Simulating inventory levels, the system determines the location and number of additional warehouses required for a given time period.

Customer-oriented applications. Over one-third of the installed business computers are estimated to be committed to customer service. Such applications, designed to serve the needs of the company's customers, include programs for collecting receivables (owed by customers), processing customer orders, monitoring the availability of goods for sale, and analyzing sales. The recent development of sophisticated customer-oriented applications point out the importance placed on customer service. Table 2–3 summarizes the major applications and their level of complexity.

Table 2–3. Customer-oriented applications and their levels of complexity.

Stages of Computer Development / Application	SIMPLE ————————————————————————→ COMPLEX		
	Batch Processing	**On-Line Processing**	**Distributed Processing**
• Accounts Receivable	• Preparation of monthly statements • Preparation of aged trial balances	• Handling status of customer account	• On-line posting • Customer account update
• Inventory Control	• Periodic reporting of stock status	• Sales forecasting • Inquiry on status of goods on hand	• Multiple location balancing of stock • Complex Economic Order Quantity (EOQ) computations • Continuous update of inventory records
• Order Processing	• Preparation of customer invoices and other billing documents	• Check customer's credit • Check availability of stock • Compute freight charges • Direct order entry	• Conversational order entry • On-line billing

*Adapted from Anthony Ralston, and C. L. Meek, *Encyclopedia of Computer Science* (New York, N.Y.: Petrocelli/Charter, Inc., 1976), p. 25.

Management-oriented applications.   Applications that serve management fall into three major categories:

1. **Linear programming** is a quantitative approach for finding an optimum solution (either minimizing costs or maximizing profits) to specific problems. Given the resources, requirements, and their constraints, the relationship among these factors is expressed in terms of a set of linear equations. The equations can then be solved through a computer program to meet all stated requirements.

Linear programming is used in solving a wide range of problems. Industrial plants, for example, must schedule their machines or production lines to meet their share of the market demand. Bus lines program movements of buses and drivers according to predetermined bus schedules. In such problems, the primary objective is to attain the desired level of efficiency by minimizing the cost of meeting the demand. The more successful the company is in controlling cost, the more likely it will be able to survive its competition and pursue its growth objectives.

2. **Simulation** consists of a model (make-believe) representation of the essence of a project; the model can be physical (such as an airplane) or mathematical (a set of equations to study a given system). Simulation is necessary for many business problems that do not provide clearcut information with known cause-and-effect relationships. For example, building a steel plant or designing a jumbo jet requires knowledge about thousands of variables prior to actual production. A simulation minimizes the risk of failure or excessive losses.

Simulation by computer provides a wide range of answers to real problems that cannot be effectively worked out in real life. To list only some uses, it "constructs" on the computer projects ranging from railroads, to warehouses, and even to the production lines in many industries. Years of operation can be evaluated in a matter of minutes. Thus this technique offers a basis for "low-cost" decisions and wise planning for projects that often involve millions of dollars in potential investments.

To initiate a simulation routine, the problem is defined and the relationships among key variables are established. Since the designer is working with a model rather than with a real situation, certain assumptions governing the relationships incorporated in the model are spelled out. All possible factors, major and minor, are also considered. As the model approaches reality, the results become more accurate and reliable.

3. A **management game** is a small-scale simulation of the decisions made in a real-life business situation. In many business programs, students participate in a management game to develop an understanding of the interrelationships among key business functions (accounting, finance, marketing, production). Their better understanding leads to more effective decisions. Likewise, large organizations use the game as an effective tool in their executive-development programs for the same purposes. Complex games are normally played with the assistance of the computer for handling the required calculations.

To play the game, several teams represent the management of hypothetical companies. Each team is given information about its company, its assets, and production figures. The goal is to improve the competitive standing of the team's company in relationship to the other companies represented in the game. The decisions may relate to product pricing, volume of production, sales volume, and so forth. Each decision is fed into a program-controlled computer system, which prints out the results of the team's decision(s). Repetitive feedback helps each team improve its decision-making ability and competitive strategies.

Management information systems.   Advances in computer technology have caused managers to expect more from computers. In particular, **management information systems** (MIS) have already received widespread attention. An MIS is a computer-based man/machine system designed to provide the information that management needs for planning and control. The term "MIS," however, means different things to different people. Although this definition is technically accurate, it may not be universally accepted. Until industry agrees on the makeup and structure of an MIS, the controversy underlying MIS is expected to continue.

A management information system supports not only operations but also the management process. For MIS to be operational, data must be processed as received and in time to affect a decision. Its major characteristics are:

1. A *data base* that contains all the information and decision rules used by management in a format acceptable to all users and available when needed.

2. *Instant recording* of business transactions and related activities.

3. *Regular evaluation and monitoring* of the internal and external events, as well as of the elements that have a bearing on the existing data.

4. The *availability* of periodic reports and special informational reports when needed.

The major users and uses of MIS are:

1. *Upper management* — committed to policy making, resource allocation, strategic planning. Typical issues that the MIS deals with are: Should a new plant be built? Is a new product marketable? Should the company go international? Through modeling and other techniques, MIS assists in decision making analysis. It also improves response to inquiries and provides continuous (versus periodic) monitoring for the user.

2. *Middle management* — in charge of tactical planning and operational control. MIS answers questions relating to production scheduling, operational planning, identifying market trends, decision for correcting "out-of-line" conditions, or adjusting current operations to meet realistic goals.

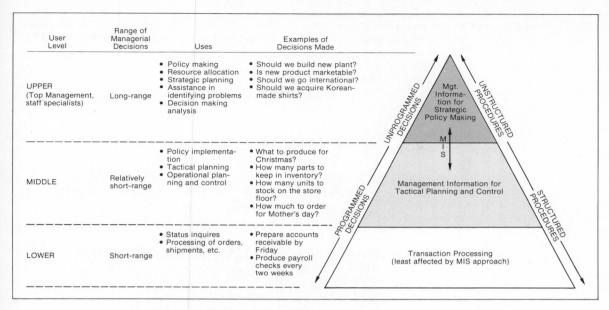

User Level	Range of Managerial Decisions	Uses	Examples of Decisions Made
UPPER (Top Management, staff specialists)	Long-range	• Policy making • Resource allocation • Strategic planning • Assistance in identifying problems • Decision making analysis	• Should we build new plant? • Is new product marketable? • Should we go international? • Should we acquire Korean-made shirts?
MIDDLE	Relatively short-range	• Policy implementation • Tactical planning • Operational planning and control	• What to produce for Christmas? • How many parts to keep in inventory? • How many units to stock on the store floor? • How much to order for Mother's day?
LOWER	Short-range	• Status inquires • Processing of orders, shipments, etc.	• Prepare accounts receivable by Friday • Produce payroll checks every two weeks

Figure 2–9. MIS and its uses.

3. *Lower management*—particularly the first-line supervisor, finds MIS-generated reports more meaningful and timely. Information retrieval is also greatly improved.

An MIS can be viewed as a pyramid structure (Figure 2–9) in which the bottom layer represents information for transaction processing. This bottom layer serves the needs of clerical personnel and lower managers who deal with structured procedures and programmed decisions. Consequently, it is least affected by an MIS approach. In contrast, the top MIS layer consists of information for operations and managerial decision making. It is oriented toward unstructured procedures and relatively unprogrammed decisions.

Special Areas of Computer Use

Education—Computer-Assisted Instruction (CAI)

A relatively recent innovation in instructional technology, **computer-assisted instruction (CAI),** is generating great excitement (Figure 2–10). The storage and memory capabilities of the computer provide the potential for true interaction with the learner. As an interactive learning environment, the computer tailors its information display according to communications and responses from the student. The student thus interacts independently with the computer on a self-paced basis. A major attraction of a CAI system is this individualized and highly interactive kind of instruction.

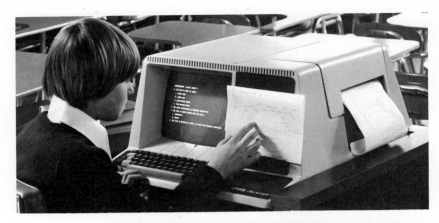

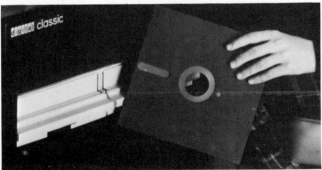

Figure 2–10. In January of 1975, DEC's Educational Products Group stated that its CLASSIC™ interactive computer system was the industry's first self-installable portable minicomputer system. *Courtesy: Digital Equipment Corporation*

Another important feature is comprised of the computer's consistent behavior and constant results. Unlike a human instructor, a computer interacts simultaneously with many students without any difficulty. It performs reliably in this manner — day after day, week after week — throughout the school year. It does not take coffee breaks, get sick, become impatient, or slip into moods. It does not even forget to do its lesson plans. Most significantly, it accomplishes all these tasks at a fraction of the cost of human instructor.

CAI interactions take several forms:

1. **Drill and practice** provide practice problems and proper information. The computer then submits a new problem, whose level of difficulty is set according to the student's past performance.

2. **Instructional games** help the learner apply concepts in a competitive (or cooperative) game played with the computer or with others through the computer. Children take to these games as adults do to electronic TV games. People spend hours competing with their TV sets! Using an attached microprocessor, they play tennis, hockey, tic-tac-toe, and other two-dimensional games. The TV's response in terms of scores have made it highly interactive.

3. **Computer-aided inquiry** is designed to help the student search for and retrieve information. Examples are finding books in the library through a computer terminal, programmed for that purpose.

4. **Modeling** focuses on concept learning. The learner applies problem solving through creating or controlling a "world" within which to solve the problem.

5. **Simulation** creates a make-believe model of the behavior of a complex system under study. The real world system is usually too dangerous, too time-consuming, or too expensive to learn in reality. For example, learning how to handle a jumbo jet in a crisis is better learned through a simulator than in a real jet.

6. **Tutorial programs** describe programmed instruction. The computer asks the student questions, grades the answers, and provides the right (or wrong) information based on the student's responses.

CAI advantages.   Among the major advantages of CAI are:

1. **Reduced student learning time.**   A substantial number of studies indicated that CAI requires less time than traditional methods to teach the same amount of material.

2. **Immediate feedback.**   Reinforcement is a real benefit to the learner.

3. **Reduced teacher staff.**   Savings in salaries are obvious.

4. **Availability.**   It is accessible whenever a proper terminal is free.

5. **Precisely even treatment.**   Equal treatment appeals especially to students who are disadvantaged learners.

CAI limitations.   The major limitations of CAI are:

1. **High start-up, acquisition, and operation costs.**   Huge outlays of funds are required for hardware. One study estimated $3.61 per student-hour for 10 hours per day for 24 days of use per month. Furthermore, as shown in Figure 2–11, you can spend more on developing and maintaining the course than on either the hardware or the programs used in the CAI effort.

2. **Specialized technical staff** is required to support a CAI system.

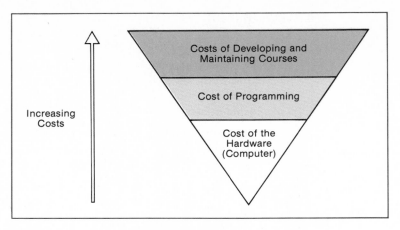

Figure 2–11. Major sources of CAI costs.

3. **Most adult students do not prefer to be taught exclusively by machine.** CAI tends to offer overly structured learning situations devoid of the open student-teacher interaction and discussion.

In regard to this last limitation, the computer does not "teach" in the *fullest* human sense, as CAI is presently conceived. Perhaps certain qualitative values and factors will never be easily reduced to the quantifiable form required for CAI. Despite this objection, the computer can now handle a wide variety of very important instructional duties that could otherwise be performed only by a human teacher. The continued effort to program the mechanistic phase of learning, coupled with the increasingly favorable computer cost/performance factor, provides the basis for growing optimism in the use of computers in higher education.

Medicine

Medicine is a major industry with a real need for the kind of services offered through computers. In 1970, less than 10 percent of the approximately 9,000 hospitals in this country had computers. They were used primarily for handling accounting and redundant applications. Today, it is rare not to find computerized activities dealing with medical care as well as with the business areas of health care management.

Medical research has also stressed computer technology. Significant models have been developed in respiratory behavior, the cardiac cycle, and the differential responses to drugs. Models of cell-life cycles have given specialists a better assessment of radiation treatments in cancer therapy.

Another area of prime importance is the monitoring of patients (Figure

Figure 2-12. The monitoring of patient. The IBM 3270 Information Display System enables this nurse to keep track of a patient's condition without ignoring other duties. *Courtesy: IBM*

2-12). Many medical applications use data acquired directly from such instruments as electroencephalogram recorders and electrocardiagram units. The data is analyzed for immediate treatment. Computerized systems replace the tedious, continuous bedside monitoring of the nurse, while storing vital data about the condition of the patient for later analysis. Other applications include the monitoring of vital signs during surgery and of the fetus during labor. The latter application can give the obstetrician advance warning of potential problems.

In clinical services, computers are used in radiation treatment planning. The purpose is to concentrate more accurate radiation intensity on tumors and to minimize it in other areas of the body. Other routine computer-based areas include quality control in clinical laboratories, test scheduling, and checking for possible interaction between a combination of drugs for a given patient.

In hospital management, most hospitals do their daily account processing on a computer. All daily transactions are entered into the computer, and the processed results are available by the following morning. To speed up the data gathering phase, on-line hospital information systems have appropriate terminals installed at the nursing stations throughout the hospital as well as in the pharmacy, the laboratories, and other service centers (Figure 2-13). Inquiries or orders are entered through the terminal as fast as the user can touch the

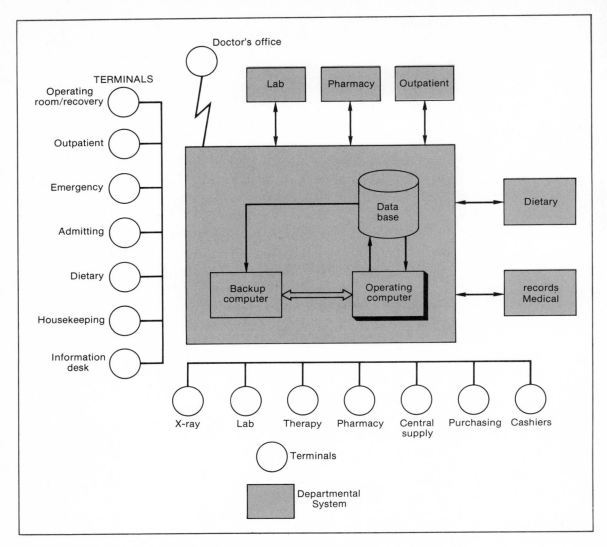

Figure 2–13. A hospital information system.

key(s). This technique eliminates paperwork and provides a means for transmitting orders (as well as other routine data such as laboratory results) to their proper destination.

Medical computing will obviously be a growing area of interest in the coming years. Computer-based systems are expected to play a major role in the development of health care as well as in the evaluation of activities that may have a bearing on the delivery of health care.

Government — of the People, for the People, by the Computer

The government, the largest single user of computer systems and the largest single employer of data processing personnel, is a pioneer in the development of computers. (Related statistical data on government's involvement in EDP is presented in Chapter 3.) According to the Legislature and National Security Subcommittee of the House Committee on Government Operations, annual spending on computer processing may exceed a staggering $15 billion — or roughly 4 percent of the entire federal budget. Already, eighty members of Congress have terminals in their offices to help them access information on subjects ranging from legislative data to energy statistics. Over two hundred Congressmen are making use of the $12,000-a-year computer allowance to perform their jobs.

Government applications are not limited to use in Congress. They range from budget control to aerospace and military intelligence. For example, the U.S. Civil Service Commission schedules more than 1 million applicants into 1,100 examination points throughout the nation. It computes the scores of those who took the nationwide exams and notifies them of the results. The Veterans Administration with over 200,000 employees, along with 22 other agencies of the government, has a computerized personnel system covering a total of 2,225,000 employees. The system, called PAID (Personnel and Accounting Integrated Data System) encompasses personnel management statistics, career training and development records, payroll information, and information on the authorized number of positions as compared with the number of employees on the rolls.

The computer's ability to search its memory and extract records of individuals with specific characteristics has been applied to the search for presidential appointee candidates. A computer-based file containing over 30,000 prospects for federal appointive positions are searched and evaluated electronically. This talent bank makes it easier and more effective for the president to make critical leadership selection decisions.

In aerospace, the role of the computer is obvious. The initial mathematical calculations for the space effort were phenomenal and would have required hundreds of man-years of manual effort. In fact, no space flight would have been possible without the split-second calculations necessary for maintaining a 25,000-mph spacecraft on course.

Conclusion

You have an idea by now that computers can store vast amounts of data, as well as perform arithmetic and logic operations at a speed measured in millionths of a second. As a result, many complex information systems have been developed to handle production scheduling, customer-oriented, accounting, and financial problems.

Despite their successes, it is incorrect to assume that computers can eventually automate all management information. By their very nature, some areas of decisions, analysis, and information are not amenable to efficient assistance by the computer. Furthermore, the higher levels of management activity have entirely different information requirements. In those areas, executives find it more appropriate to rely on manual analysis and human (versus computerized) judgment.

In the areas of decisions, analysis, and information that do lend themselves to efficient computer assistance, managers have made limited use of the computer. Some of the reasons are:

1. a defensive attitude by top managers regarding the threat the computer presents to their decision making functions,

2. a lag in the development of viable systems geared to assisting two managers in making decisions, and

3. a tendency for top executives to wait for other firms to incur the risk (and expense) of pioneering new areas of computer applications.

In another area, the computer has yet to make headway—the setting of corporate goals and objectives. Even with the tremendous advances in computer technology and the awareness of what the computer can and cannot do, it seems certain that personal managerial judgment will always play the dominant role in the making of major strategic decisions.

SUMMARY

1. This chapter summarizes the data processing cycle and the primary applications that are handled through computers. Management information is the output of a data processing operation. Users utilize information differently, depending on their level in the organization and on their assigned tasks. For example, upper management likely requires summarized information for policy making, while lower management expects detailed information for handling the day-to-day problems of their departments.

2. There are two areas of data processing. Business data processing involves a large volume of input data, a limited number of arithmetic operations, and a relatively large volume of output. In contrast, scientific data processing involves a limited volume of input and many logical arithmetic calculations. Most of the problems are nonrepetitive, requiring a "one-time" solution.

3. A data processing cycle performs five key steps: origination, input, pro-

cessing, output, and storage and feedback. The processing step centers around classifying, sorting, calculating, recording, and summarizing data. The feedback concept makes the data processing cycle dynamic. It allows each step to function in line with the functioning of the cycle as a system.

4. For an application to qualify for computerized handling, it must be definable, present easy justification, and offer a large enough volume of data to warrant conversion to computerized processing.

5. Characteristics of business applications correspond to three primary stages of computer development:
   a. *Batch processing.* Processing an application from sequential files, one program at a time.
   b. *On-line processing.* Allows the user to access application records on disc directly by terminal.
   c. *Distributed processing.* Allows computer power to be available at the user's location for conducting inquiries for action.

6. Business applications are viewed as systems, so that the output of one application is the input to the next. Applications are therefore interlinked to ensure a continuing relationship.

   Business applications are classified by the functions they perform. Some applications are designed to handle accounting and financial activities; others do payroll, personnel, production, customer service, and management decision making. An application may be handled through batch, on-line, or distributed processing; the latter is the most complex stage of computer development.

7. Special areas of computer use are worth noting. In education, CAI is making significant headway in individualized learning. CAI takes the form of drill and practice, instructional game, computer-aided inquiry, modeling, simulation, or tutorial instruction. Regardless of the form used, CAI generally lowers student learning time, gives immediate feedback, reduces teacher staff, and offers even treatment to all. Among its limitations, however, are high start-up and acquisition costs, the impersonal nature of the student-machine relationship, and the need for a specialized support staff to handle the system.

   In medicine, many applications use data acquired directly from medical instruments for further analysis and treatment. On-line, real-time systems provide professional, time-saving, and timely support to medical staff.

   The government is a heavy user of computers. Billions are spent each year to handle all kinds of applications at all levels. Even Congress is making regular use of computers to access vital records on a day-to-day basis.

TERMS TO LEARN

Batch processing
Calculating
Classifying
Computer-assisted instruction
Data
Data processing
Data processing cycle
Distributed processing
Feedback
Information
Input
Linear programming
Management games
Management information system (MIS)
Modeling
On-line processing
Output
Origination
Processing
Simulation
Sorting
Summarizing

REVIEW QUESTIONS

1. In what way is data processing important to management?

2. Give an example of how data processing can be used in a (a) church, (b) shoe repair shop, and (c) ice cream parlor.

3. How do the informational requirements of a university president differ from those of an instructor in your school? Explain.

4. Give an example of an information system that corresponds to the needs of upper, middle, and lower management.

5. "A data processing system is hardware-oriented, while an information system is user-oriented." Do you agree? Why?

6. In what way is the study of the man-machine interface important?

7. What is a management information system? How does it differ from an information system?

8. How is scientific data processing different from business data processing? What do they have in common?

9. Illustrate how the data processing cycle produces the final grades you receive at the end of the term.

10. Define in your own words the terms "origination," "input," and "processing."

11. Distinguish in your own words the difference between classifying and sorting.

12. Give two examples of the feedback you receive in your data processing course.

13. In what respect do today's business applications differ from earlier applications? Explain.

14. Describe in your own words the primary stages of application development. Which stage is descriptive of "decentralized" data processing?

15. Give an example of a business that can benefit from a distributed processing system.

16. Define in your own words "simulation," "linear programming," and "management game."

17. Illustrate how an MIS serves the needs of upper management. In what way does it help lower management?

18. Summarize the primary forms of CAI. Which form describes programmed instruction? Explain briefly.

19. Of the drawbacks of CAI listed in the chapter, which drawback do you consider most serious? Why?

chapter 3

Developments
and Trends
in Computer Technology

Learning Objectives

Past and present developments in computer technology help us understand the future impact of computer power. This chapter deals with such developments and looks into likely trends in the computer field. By the end of this chapter, you should know:

1. the primary developments in manual and mechanical calculations,

2. the introduction and makeup of a punched card data processing system,

3. the four major generations of computer growth,

4. the essence of distributed data processing,

5. the growth of computer manufacturers, and

6. specific developments of the 1970s and projections into the 1980s.

People have always sought better and more efficient ways to process information. While the processing of information is not new, the tools and techniques used in information handling have changed over time. Both past and present developments in computer technology help the user understand the future impact of computer power. This chapter deals with these developments and looks into likely trends in the computer field.

Manual and Mechanical Data Processing

Until the nineteenth century, people found business calculations a very complex job, because they had to be done "in the head." Writing materials were very scarce and therefore expensive to use for ordinary purposes. The first manual method of data processing was counting with the aid of the ten fingers. But finger-counting had its limitations, which were later overcome by using pebbles for basic arithmetic.

The first manual data processing device was the **abacus**, consisting of pebbles placed in grooves or of beads strung on a string. Figure 3–1 illustrates an abacus representing the number 528619574. Although still used in some oriental markets, the abacus gave way to manually written data processing tools. These written manual tools, summarized in Table 3–1, were developed for the basic multiplication of decimal numbers. Obviously, any manual method of calculation is tedious for companies that have complex informational requirements and a large volume of work.

Table 3–1. Historical developments in manual and mechanical data processing.

Date	Event	Origin/Inventor	Comment
Written Manual:			
1494	Book on arithmetic	Luca Paciolo (Venice)	Double-entry book-keeping
1500–1600	Grating method	Arabs	Used primarily in multiplication
1617	"Bones" method	John Napier (England)	Simplified multiplication of large numbers
1635	Sluggard method	Hindus	Basic multiplication tables
Written Mechanical:			
1642	Numerical wheel calculator	Blaise Pascal (France)	First decimal calculator
1673	"Four-function" machine	Gottfried Leibniz (Germany)	Mechanical multiplier
1820	Mechanical calculator	Charles Xavier Thomas (France)	Four-function arithmetic
1872	Calculator	Frank Baldwin (U.S.)	Beginning of calculating-machine industry in U.S.
1887	Comptometer	Dorr Eugene	Known then as the "Macaroni Box"
1890	Key-set adding-printing machine	W. S. Burroughs	Recorded, summarized, and calculated data
1911	Keyboard calculator	Jay R. Monroe	First commercially successful keyboard calculator

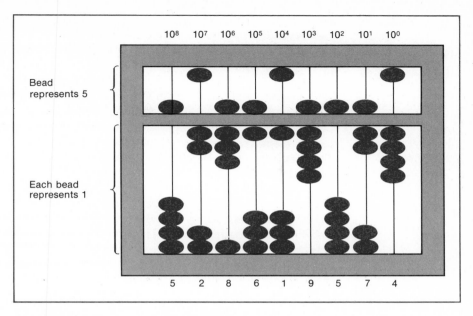

Figure 3–1. The abacus set for 528619574.

The inevitable alternative is a mechanized or automated data processing system. The written mechanical tools ranged from Pascal's original decimal calculator to Monroe's first commercially successful keyboard calculator. These developments provided the backbone for punched card and electronic data processing systems (Table 3–1). Although mechanical data processing provides greater response and accuracy than manual data processing, all adding machines, calculators, or accounting machines are "nonautomatic" equipment. They require human intervention in data entry and machine operation. Recently, computer technology made it possible to produce all-electronic calculators (Figure 3–2). A typical calculator has integrated circuits and a built-in memory to store data and accumulate totals when needed.

Figure 2–3. The Canon Palmtronic LC Memo is an ultra-thin electronic calculator with liquid crystal display readout. *Courtesy: Canon*

Punched Card Data Processing Systems

The history of punched card methods and machines dates from the late 1800s. It started when the U.S. Bureau of the Census demanded quicker and more accurate methods of handling census data. The 1880 census took 7.5 years to complete. By the time the information was ready for publication, it was old and useless.

During that year, Dr. Herman Hollerith, a noted statistician from Buffalo, New York, was hired to mechanize the census operations. He developed a punched card machine[1] in time to automate the 1890 census. The entire job was completed in 2.5 years, despite an increase in population from 50 to 63 million. Hollerith resigned in 1905 to form his own company which was later merged with today's IBM.

Dr. James Powers replaced Hollerith in the Bureau of the Census. His development of the *simultaneous punching* machine further advanced the efficiency of data processing. **Simultaneous punching** involves keying in all the data to be punched in a card. Then, depressing a certain key punches all the data simultaneously. In contrast, the *serial* method of punching causes a character to be punched in a column each time a key is depressed. The simultaneous method has the advantage of allowing the operator enough time to check on the accuracy of the keyed-in data prior to actual processing. Like Hollerith, Powers resigned in 1911 to form his own company. It was later acquired by Remington Rand which merged in 1927 with the Sperry Rand Corporation (Table 3–2).

Table 3–2. Developments in punched card data processing systems.

Date	Event	Origin/Inventor	Comment
1801	First punched card machine	Joseph Jacquard (France)	A loom to weave intricate design into cloth
1880	Beginning of punched card era	Herman Hollerith (U.S.)	Developed punched card machines to automate the 1890 U.S. census
1896	Tabulating Machine Company (serial punching principle)	Herman Hollerith	Absorbed by the Computing-Tabulating-Recording Company Name was changed to IBM in 1924.
1905	Simultaneous punching principle (Sorter and keypunch machines)	James Powers	Used successfully in the 1910 census
1911	Powers Accounting Machine Company	James Powers	Acquired by Remington Rand Corporation in 1927. The company later merged with the Sperry Rand Corporation.

[1] Also called the "keypunch," it is a keyboard actuated device that punches holes in a card to represent data. More on punched cards is illustrated in Chapter 6.

Punched card data systems were also referred to as unit record systems. "Unit record" means one record is handled at a time. Each record was recorded on the 80-column card that became known worldwide as "the IBM card." On the card, information was keypunched into specific, predefined columns. The unit record equipment consisted of the following machines:

1. The *keypunch* punched data into a card through a keyboard. The device could be "programmed" to duplicate, skip, or shift automatically. A verifier read the card to verify the original listing.

2. The *sorter* arranged a deck of cards in alphabetic or numeric sequence.

3. The *collator* intermixed similar data by merging, matching, sequence checking, selecting, or editing.

4. The *reproducer* duplicated data from one card into another card.

5. The *calculator* performed arithmetic functions through a wired control panel.

6. The *accounting machine,* also called the tabulator, summarized, printed, and summary-punched reports from the data on cards (Figure 3–3).

Figure 3–3. IBM 5424 punched card data processing device. *Courtesy: IBM*

Improvements in punched card systems continued until the late 1950s when they gave way to the electronic computer. Today the keypunch is the punched card machine used primarily as a data processing preparation device for computer processing.

**Calculator
or Computer?**

Readers often have the false impression that the work of Hollerith and Powers at the U.S. Bureau of the Census was computing. Yet Hollerith's operational unit record processor was actually a calculator — not a computer. Unlike computers, which solve complex mathematical problems, the punched card system was designed to read coded holes in cards that represented data, and then sort and count the cards.

Historical records attribute the origin of automatic computation to Charles Babbage of England. In 1812, he proposed the "difference engine" — a special-purpose machine capable of computing logarithmic tables automatically. In 1833, he proposed the "analytical engine," which was to be the first completely automatic, general-purpose digital computer. Its system of gears and cogs worked on the decimal system. It was capable of holding, executing, and modifying its instructions internally. Many believed this feature to be the beginning of the computer revolution which, one hundred years later, began to demonstrate its impact on business and society as a whole.

Actual computation did not surface, however, until the early 1940s when Dr. Norbert Wiener (MIT) was interested in using computers to emulate human communication. The principles he established moved our society from the lowly calculator to the sophisticated computer. Although they seem elementary to us, the five revolutionary principles require that a computer should (1) use electronic circuitry rather than mechanical relays, (2) use binary arithmetic, and (3) be free from human intervention. Further, programs, loaded internally in the computer, should (4) have a numerical central adding and multiplying unit, using registers for execution, and (5) contain a device to read, store, and read data. By the mid-forties, the ENIAC (the Electronic Numerical Integrator and Calculator) emerged as the first widely recognized computer.

The Father of the First Digital Computer

Modern computers originated in December of 1939, when Dr. John Vincent Atanasoff, Professor of Mathematics at Iowa State College, and a graduate student (Clifford Berry) developed a working model of the first electronic computer. Using vacuum tubes for the internal "thinking" circuitry and capacitors for main storage, the ABC (Atanasoff-Berry Computer) model had the characteristics and makeup of today's electronic computer. The ABC was the first true computer, although it is not popularly recognized as such.

The ENIAC

While the ABC was being developed, John Mauchly of the University of Pennsylvania visited Atanasoff. Using Atanasoff's basic principles, he and J. Presper Eckert of the Moore School of Engineering (University of Pennsylvania) began working on an electronic computer. In 1946, they built the ENIAC (Figure 3–4).

The ENIAC differed from many previous devices. For example, two years earlier (1944), Aiken of Harvard had developed the MARK I, under an IBM grant. Yet unlike the MARK I, which used electromechanical relay switches, the ENIAC was completely electronic. The ENIAC had no moving parts. It contained nearly 19,000 tubes for the electronic pulse-switching functions. It performed 5,000 additions in one second which outperformed electromechanical devices 300 to 1. It was programmable and had the capability to store problem calculations. The primary limitations of the ENIAC, however, were its size and batch processing drawbacks. It occupied 1,500 square feet of floor space and processed only one program or problem at a time.

After their success with the ENIAC in 1946, Eckert and Mauchly left the University of Pennsylvania to design commercial computers under the name Eckert-Mauchly Computer Corporation. In 1949, the company and the ENIAC patent were acquired by Remington Rand Corporation which developed the

Figure 3–4. The ENIAC. *Courtesy: Sperry Corporation*

UNIVAC computer. At the time, it was the only computer company in the U.S. IBM, GE, and Honeywell weren't convinced of the commercial potential of computers. IBM concentrated on electrical calculators and card sorters and collators, not at all interested in computers until 1951 when it began making its own.

An interesting historical sidelight is Atanasoff's ultimate recognition as a predecessor of Mauchley and Eckert. In October of 1973, U.S. district judge Earl R. Larson in Minneapolis handed down a decision that credits Dr. Atanasoff as the father of the electronic digital computer. Since 1950, Drs. Mauchly and Eckert were believed to have originated the concept for the electronic digital computer. In a $200 million suit, the 135-day trial convinced the judge that Atanasoff — rather than Mauchly and Eckert — fathered the computer.[1]

Computer Generations

The First Generation (1951–1958)

The introduction of the UNIVAC (UNIVersal Automatic Computer) I by Remington Rand Corporation in 1951 marked the advent of the first generation of computers. Also initiating this generation were the IBM 650 and the Burroughs 220. The sales figure for the IBM 650, originally set at 50, rose to 2,000. Its popularity set the tone for IBM's steady domination of the market from that point on

This generation utilized the vacuum tube as a means of storing data in memory. The addition of memory made the punched card systems and the calculators virtually obsolete. The wire board was replaced by computer programs written in a new language for processing. Early sales of the computer were relatively easy. Many salespeople became rich during these auspicious years. Computers of the first generation:

1. reduced processing time by a factor of ten,

2. were bulky and somewhat inflexible,

3. demanded strict observance of air-conditioning requirements,

4. were relatively unreliable due to electric current fluctuations and tube failure (in the IBM computer, the tubes burned out at the rate of one tube a day),

5. contained limited and primitive memory (main storage was made of a magnetic drum that stored approximately 16,000 characters),

6. leaned toward batch applications (the entire computer was dedicated to a specific application or a program until completed), and

7. required programs written for a specific computer (programs could not be run on another computer model).

[1]"Will the Inventor of the First Computer Please Stand up?" *Datamation* (February, 1974), p. 84.

When the first generation computer became available, no educational program precisely met the requirements of the new technology. The user organization was ill-prepared to implement the new system. A new breed of technicians appeared. They were the programmers, the computer operators, and the systems analysts. To determine qualifications, aptitude tests had to be administered by the manufacturer. He also evaluated the user's EDP staff, exerting a direct influence on hiring decisions.

The Second (Transistorized) Generation (1959–1964)

Transistorized circuits formed the basis for the second generation of computers in 1959. Typical second generation computers were the IBM 1401 and 7000 series, Control Data 3600, and Burroughs 5500. The IBM 1401 was the most popular computer by far. By the end of this generation of computers in 1964, there were more IBM 1401s than all other computers in operation.

The new transistor technology made the previous generation obsolete. The large-scale computers were marked by large memory banks, by faster millisecond processing speed,[2] and by more reliable operation. Other primary characteristics were:

1. The use of the transistor reduced the physical size of the computer.

2. Main memory capacity was improved by the use of magnetic cores. Large systems could store up to 1 million characters compared to the 16,000-character capacity of earlier computers.

3. Reliability improved through built-in error detection and correction features.

4. The transistor and magnetic core reduced the storage cost per character from $2.50 to $.85.

5. Versatility improved by accommodating multiple users to access the computer concurrently.

6. Data storage was improved through the introduction of the disc file. Data could now be written and read simultaneously and directly without having to go through the bulky tape files. Disc systems were capable of storing millions of characters. Data and programs from any disc could be retrieved within fractions of a second.

[2]The time required for a computer to do a calculation is measured by a special unit of time. A millisecond is one-thousandth of a second. In contrast, a microsecond is one-millionth of a second. Third and fourth generation computers calculate at the nanosecond (one billionth of a second) speed. To illustrate, a computer designed to calculate one multiplication in 100 nanoseconds is equivalent to 10 million multiplications in a second ($100 \div 1,000,000,000$), 10 multiplications in 1 microsecond, or 10,000 multiplications per millisecond.

7. Programs were written in symbolic language. Although it required special translating programs, it relieved the programmer of the details required in first generation computer programs.

8. High-level, machine-independent languages (Fortran, Cobol, and the like) began to appear. It made the programmer's life easier. He or she no longer had to have detailed knowledge of the computer.

The new languages, however, brought inefficiencies, which had an adverse effect on the escalating cost of computing. Data processing personnel costs increased in direct proportion to the increased cost of computer systems. As computers became more sophisticated during this generation, further job classifications had to be made. The traditional programmer became a systems programmer. Systems managers began to appear, to work with the new operating systems that controlled the computer. (An **operating system** is a set of programs or software, designed to control the computer and monitor its operations — details are discussed later in the text.)

Up to this point, computer manufacturers were developing high-level languages and software to accommodate the data processing specialist rather than the end user. While this strategy promoted a centralized facility, disregard for the real needs of the user prompted the end of the "mainframe" era and the dawn of the minicomputer in the late 1960s.

The Third Generation (1964–1971)

Typical of the so-called third generation computers introduced after 1964 were the IBM System 360, the Honeywell 200, the RCA Spectra 70 series, and National Cash Register Century series. The transistor was replaced by solid state technology and monolithic integrated circuits (Figure 3–5). Among the main features of third generation computers are the following:

1. Operating systems handled several jobs at the same time. Most applications could also be run in real time.

2. Time sharing systems emerged. Several users could use the computer facility at the same time.

3. Standardization developed among different computer models and on applications-oriented languages (Cobol, Fortran, and the rest).

4. While computational output per dollar was increased, main memory costs dropped to approximately $.25 per character.

5. Minicomputers increased in popularity and provided a vehicle for redistributing computer power to the user, when needed.

6. A wide range of input-output and direct-access devices (such as disk storage) sprang up, including special magnetic-ink readers and graph plotters.

Figure 3–5. Solid-state and monolithic integrated circuits.
Courtesy: IBM

7. Reliability and processing speed were improved. Internal computer errors were rare. The nanosecond speed became a reality.

A significant contribution of third generation computers was the remote (intelligent) terminal to permit geographically dispersed users to communicate with a central computer. Unlike the batch processing computer that handled one application at a time, the third generation computer handled many programs and responded to inquiries without delay. The on-line (direct), real-time (immediate) computer mode became a routine environment with most large systems.

In retrospect, the gains are remarkable. The ENIAC exhibited a processing speed 10,000 times faster than earlier computing methods. Twenty-five years later, through three successive generations, data processing speed gained 10,000 times—or roughly 100,000 times the speed of the ENIAC. Although these figures are approximate, they give us an idea about the direction and rate of development in business data processing.

The Fourth Generation (1971 – ?)

In 1971, a new line of controversial fourth generation computers was introduced. Although they offer users significant improvements over the third generation, they are considered more evolutionary than revolutionary. Typical computers are the IBM 370, Burroughs 700, and Honeywell 6000 series. Regardless of their brand name, their general features can be summarized as follows:

1. The miniaturization of circuits reduced hundreds of them to the size of a pinhead.

2. Breakdown diagnosis and error detection techniques increased. Most models have built-in automatic features that reprocess an error and record the occurrence in a log for analysis by the systems engineer.

3. **Multiprogramming** increased. Multiprogramming is the concurrent execution of two or more programs by a computer.

4. The CPU can operate in more than one mode to improve the system's overall performance.

5. Main memory cost was further reduced to $.05 per character.

6. Improvements in operating systems made **virtual storage** possible. This feature allows secondary storage devices (discs, tapes, and the like) to be treated as an expanded part of the computer's main memory, such that it gives the *virtual* appearance of one macromemory unit.

7. The implementation of special software for managing data bases gave rise to what is called "data base management systems."

With fourth generation computers, the user can now access files directly, schedule various production and other problems, and acquire authorized data, when needed. They consitute a step toward a truly user-oriented, interactive computer system.

One significant outcome of the evolutionary computers of the 1970s is a revolutionary effort to pack tremendous data processing power into minicomputers at a relatively low cost. As a result, minicomputers facilitate the decentralization of data processing, giving the system responsibility back to users. Users are more familiar with their particular problems and requirements than a remote data processing department that serves all company users. Thus the computer is getting back in line with the business at hand and cutting the escalating costs of business.

In line with the decentralization trend is the emerging concept called **distributed data processing (DDP)**. Such a system redistributes computer power back to the user, making authorized data immediately available. It also enables the people-oriented computer to assume a new position as a managerial tool rather than as a dehumanizing centralized controller of company operations. Distributed data processing is not the same as dispersed data processing. In distributed data processing, dispersed computers are interconnected to each other and to a central computer facility, allowing each end user to function as a part of a total system. In contrast, dispersed data processing represent semi-autonomous (stand-alone) mini- or microprocessors that are located at sites other than that of a central computer system. Little or no staff is committed on a full-time basis to data processing. Furthermore, few data processing professionals are required by the end user organization.

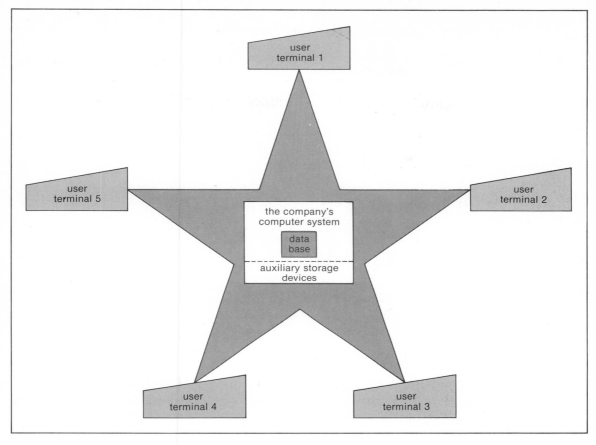

Figure 3–6. Distributed data processing structure—an example.

A basic DDP structure is illustrated in Figure 3–6. The company's computer data base is accessed on-line by terminals or by minicomputers. The terminals are distributed at the users' sites but tied into the computer through telephone lines. DDP's effectiveness rests on the fact that it shifts responsibility for data availability and data base to the user. It returns system control to the user and eliminates the need for the traditional centralized computer facility, even though the DDP system may have a central site.

Trends and Projections in Information Systems

The growing use of computers has been staggering and continues unabated. More and more users are relying on more and more computers to handle all types of problems—large and small. A great deal of the lure lay with the concomitant cost reductions and improvements (Table 3–3). Progress in information systems during the past three decades is characterized as follows:

1. a reduction in the physical size of storage and peripherals,

2. improvements in processing power and performance,

3. a reduction in hardware/software costs,

4. the continued growth in the number of computer installations and user organizations, and

5. improvements in reliability, human engineering, and user control.

Table 3–3. Cost reductions and other improvements during the seventies.

Item	Mid to late 1960s	1979
Processing power (million instructions/sec.)	2 million (for large-scale computers)	4.4 million
Cost of main memory	$2.00/byte	$.09 byte (reduction of 20 times)
Cost of on-line storage	$3,000/million bytes	$150.00/million bytes
Physical density of main memory	400 cu.ft. (early 1950s)	1/8 cu.ft. (reduction of 3,200 times)
Recording density on-line disc drives	100 bits/sec.	4,000 bits/sec.
Disc recording speed	1,200 rpm	3,600 rpm
Quantity of disc drive storage available for disc system	50 million bytes	50 billion bytes

Trends in Main Memory Size

The transition from magnetic core main memory to semiconductor memory is accompanied by continued attempts to pack more data into a single **chip**. A chip is an integrated circuit that is man-produced on a tiny piece of silicon. For example, in the early to mid-1970s, one chip had the capacity to store 1,000 bytes. An advanced chip of the mid-1970s was capable of storing 4,000 bytes. As shown in Figure 3–7, the chip of the late 1970s holds 16,000 bytes at 5 per-

Figure 3–7. The cost trend.

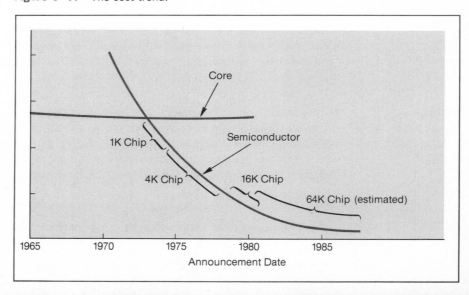

cent the cost of the magnetic core of the late 1960s. In 1980, the 64,000-byte memory chip (the densest chip to date) became a reality.

Improvements in auxiliary storage devices are also significant. For example, an early disc drive stored 100 bits per inch of track, with 20 tracks per inch of disc radius. The maximum capacity of one disc drive was 5 million characters. Today, disc drives have over 4,000 bits per inch of track, with over 370 tracks per inch of disc radius. Their total capacity is over 200 million characters. By the time the decade ended, the most recent disc drives had already doubled that capacity. The forthcoming **bubble memory** devices to supplant fast access disc files are expected to increase the file capacity to over one billion characters per drive by 1980. Bubble memory is explained in Chapter 5.

Computer Growth

Dramatic improvements in processing power, in the speed of calculations, and in the technological breakthroughs through the fifties, sixties, and seventies resulted in reduced computation costs and lower sale price of the computer. Table 3–4 stresses the following points:

Table 3–4. Computer growth and cost of computation.

	Number of Computers Installed	Average Sale Price	Percent of 1951 Sale Price	Average Cost per 1 Million Calculations	Total Cost of Designing and Programming/ Instruction
1951	10	$3,000,000	100.0	$250.00	$—
1953	50	2,750,000	91.8	250.00	4.00(est.)
1955	244	2,250,000	75.0	165.00	4.20
1959	3,000	1,225,000	41.8	20.00	4.50
1965	23,000	700,000	23.3	2.75	5.50
1969	59,500	400,000	13.3	.25	6.75
1971	82,000	375,000	12.5	.10	7.30
1972	100,420	350,000	11.7	.09	7.50
1975	155,000	300,000	10.0	.08	8.00
1980	300,000	265,000	8.1	.04	9.10
1985(est.)	500,000	210,000	7.0	.01	9.60

1. The number of computers installed has grown exponentially from 10 systems in 1951 to 82,000 in 1971, to 155,000 in 1975, to a staggering 300,000 in 1979, and to an estimated 500,000 computers in 1985.

2. The number of user organizations has also grown. For example, there were 95,000 sites in 1975 and 160,000 in 1980; 240,000 are estimated by 1985. At this rate, at least one computer installation should be available in every company with more than 50 employees by 1987. See also Figure 3–8.

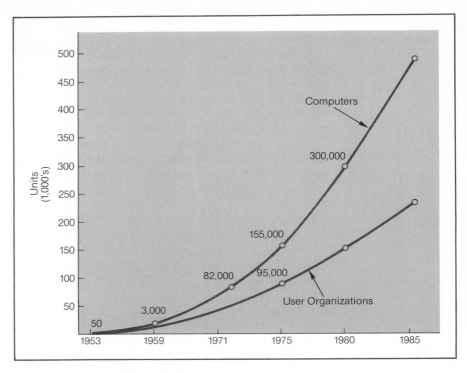

Figure 3–8. Computers installed and user organizations.

3. While the number of computer installations has increased, the average price of each computer has decreased. The price of computers dropped from $3 million in 1951, to $300,000 in 1975, and around $265,000 in 1980 — 8 percent of the price of the 1951 computer.

4. A decrease in computer price and a significant improvement in processing speed mean a substantial decrease in the cost of computation. For example, it cost around $250 per 1 million calculations on the 1951 computer, compared to $.04 on today's computer. For these calculations to be handled manually, it would cost over $10,000 — suggesting the tremendous cost-effectiveness of the electronic computer.

5. Although the average cost of computation has dropped, the total cost of designing and programming a computer instruction has steadily increased. As shown in Table 3–4, the total cost has increased from $4 in 1953 to an estimated $9.10 in 1980. It is expected to reach $9.60 per instruction by 1985. The primary causes of this increase are (a) the increased cost of professional talent, along with (b) the excess of demand over supply for qualified programmers and analysts to work with the latest systems.

6. The cost of programming and systems analysis will continue to rise unless improved software, better ways of using current technology, or more efficient systems analysis and design methods are developed. Such developments are likely to materialize during the early 1980s.

Inhibitors to computer growth.   Hardware performance has had an impressive growth record. However, software technology has not kept pace. So much hardware is beyond the ability of the user to put it to effective use. If this discrepancy continues, over 80 percent of the user's human resources will be devoted to the maintenance of old applications and less than 20 percent of new applications.

The two primary inhibitors to computer growth are the high costs of software and of qualified programmers and analysts. Currently, software costs outpace hardware costs. As illustrated in Figure 3–9, they represent over 80 percent of the total hardware/software cost figure. Although the picture is gradually improving, the lack of sufficiently trained programmers and analysts poses an additional constraint. In 1975, there were 1.2 million data processors[3] representing 1.5 percent of the total labor force. In 1980, the figure increased to 3.8 million, representing 2.9 percent of the total labor force. By 1985, it is estimated

Figure 3–9.   Hardware/software cost trend.

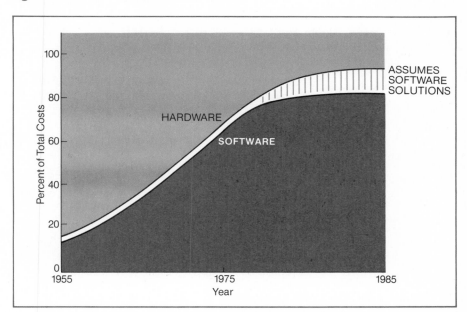

[3]This figure includes 200,000 programmers and 100,000 systems analysts.

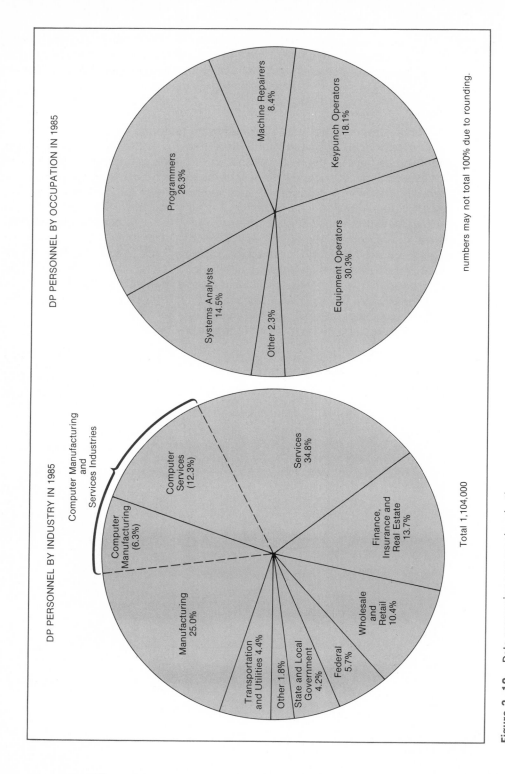

DP PERSONNEL BY OCCUPATION IN 1985

Machine Repairers
8.4%

Keypunch Operators
18.1%

Programmers
26.3%

Equipment Operators
30.3%

Systems Analysts
14.5%

Other 2.3%

numbers may not total 100% due to rounding.

DP PERSONNEL BY INDUSTRY IN 1985

Computer Manufacturing
and
Services Industries

Computer
Services
(12.3%)

Computer
Manufacturing
(6.3%)

Services
34.8%

Manufacturing
25.0%

Finance,
Insurance and
Real Estate
13.7%

Transportation
and Utilities 4.4%

Other 1.8%

State and Local
Government
4.2%

Federal
5.7%

Wholesale
and
Retail
10.4%

Total 1,104,000

Figure 3–10. Data processing personnel projections for 1985.

Source: Bureau of Labor Statistics, U.S. Dept. of Labor, 1977.

that close to 4.5 million (4.2 percent of the total labor force) will be employed in the computer processing area. Note that, in Figure 3–10, programmers and analysts represent the bulk of data processing personnel, regardless of industry.

Growth of Computer Makers

The phenomenal growth in the number of computer installations and sites was accompanied by a similar increase in the number of computer makers. With the advent of the mini- and microcomputers, the total number of computer firms is well over one hundred. However, a high degree of data processing revenues are concentrated in the largest companies. Of the top fifty companies in the data processing industry, Table 3–5 focuses on the top ten leading the field. IBM heads the list. Eighty-one percent of its total corporate revenues are derived from computer systems. The first seven companies have virtually all the general-purpose system revenues, about 78 percent of the minicomputer revenues, and 60 percent of the services revenues.

Table 3–5. Revenue profile of the top computer makers.

	DP revenues ($M)	DP revenues (% of total revenues)	1976 total revenues ($M)	1977 total revenues ($M)	Number of employees
1. IBM	$14,765	81%	$16,304	$18,133	310,155
2. Burroughs	1,844	87	1,902	2,127	51,295
3. NCR	1,574	62	2,313	2,522	64,000
4. Control Data	1,513	66	2,113	2,301	46,000
5. Sperry Rand	1,472	45	3,203	3,270	85,684
6. Digital Equipment	1,059	100	736	1,059	36,000
7. Honeywell	1,037	36	2,495	2,911	75,840
8. Memorex	405	90	345	450	8,823
9. Hewlett-Packard	402	30	1,112	1,360	35,100
10. TRW	350	11	2,929	3,264	87,152

Adapted from *Business Week* (May 30, 1977), pp. 61ff; *Datamation* (June 1978), pp. 88–94.

Such growth can also be described in terms of computer system shipments. One source[4] put the 1977 shipments of all computers at $6.5 billion and 1978 shipments at $7.5 billion. The projection for 1982 revenue from general-purpose computers is estimated to be $18–20 billion, with minicomputer shipments growing by 25 percent and microcomputer shipments also growing by 40 percent.

[4]*Computerworld* (March 6, 1978), p. 51.

Other Computer-Based Developments

Assessing the computer industry in retrospect, you can label the 1950s as *revolutionary,* the 1960s as *sensational,* the 1970s as *seething,* and the 1980s as *dynamic.* The advent of the computer in the 1950s brought revolutionary changes in business operations. It stabilized the "bread and butter" applications, such as payroll and receivables. The computers of the 1960s effected a sensational increase in the speed of computation and in the number of computer installations. It also signaled a dramatic decrease in the average price of most computers. The seething seventies ushered the entrance of the minicomputer and the microcomputer into all walks of life. The so-called "minis" and the **microprocessor**[5] provided the backbone for distributed data processing. Some of the unique developments of the 1970s are:

1. Magnetic bubble technology is appearing in terminals, word processing systems, and portable computers.

2. Electro-optical memories, made from a layer of thin rare-earth ferroelectrical crystalline material, are capable of erasing data and changing their condition at the speed of light.

3. The "talking computer" became a reality. Sometimes called a voice-response system or audio response, this unique technique is the answer to accurate and quick information retrieval. The speed of data acquisition is as fast as the human voice. The system consists mainly of a 12-button phone and a speaker which responds with a human voice to a dialed number. Banks use it for inquiring about the status of loans, checking accounts, and mortgage transactions. Retailers use it to provide a private response to slow-paying credit customers or misuse of credit cards. The job is done quickly, economically, and expeditiously.

4. Microcomputers have up to 16,000 words of storage on a single chip. Major progress has been made toward their development. Commercial applications are already in automobiles, personal computers, kitchen appliances, electronic games, and digital watches. They are programmed to monitor cleaning and maintenance chores, keep track of home improvement expenses, record tax-deductible bills, tutor children during specific periods, and answer telephone calls by voice-response touch-tone.

5. Although in its infancy, the electronic fund transfer (EFT) is here to stay. Electronic credit cards are designed to activate terminals that feed into electronic fund transfer computers. The computer has the customer's account number and other pertinent data. A customer is free to transfer money to pay a retailer whose account is in a different bank. The widespread acceptance of this arrangement would render today's clearing house methods obsolete.

[5]A microcomputer central processing unit on a chip.

6. Data is transmitted via satellite. A business firm may now exchange operating data with affiliating organizations and provide business and government reports (Figure 3–11).

7. Emphasis is shifting for the better from price/performance to people/performance, as computer systems are designed to make the user more productive. The user today is interested in system solutions—what a system can do, not how it does it. Thus computer languages are expected to be natural and simple to understand.

Figure 3–11. Future information transmission.

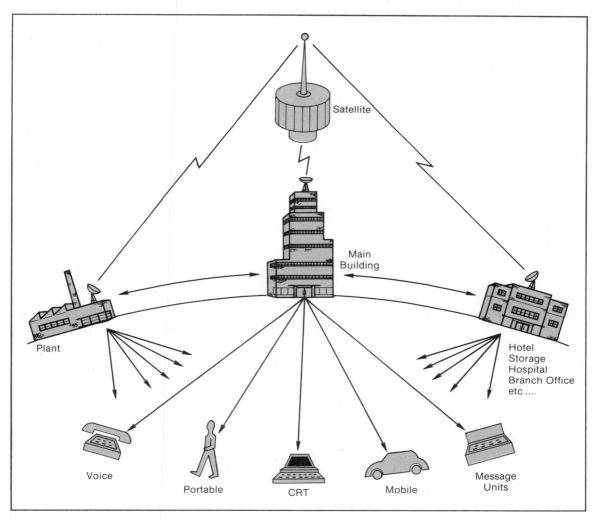

8. **Word processing (WP)** is developing intrinsic communication and data processing capabilities. The core hardware is the typewriter with a memory. The text (stored on disk, cards, or magnetic tapes) is reproduced more quickly than the traditional human typing. Stored information can be also edited, revised, or updated as necessary. Word processing is discussed in the appendix.

   With a stress on words and communications, word processing focuses on streamlining communication processes and on organizing a large volume of written work. For example, a law firm would find it more efficient to develop packages consisting of standardized paragraphs to be used in contracts or other legal documents. The savings resulting from this type of standardization is obvious. A detailed overview of word processing is contained in the appendix.

9. The trends in user attitudes toward more independence, more flexibility, and more communications are manifestations of a general trend toward distributed data processing. Very little occurs in the computer industry that can't be tied to the DDP concept. DDP systems locate the processing power, the data base, and the responsibility for them where they are most often needed — with the user.

   A possible reason for DDP is that more people now work in service-related jobs than in production-related jobs. More people do things than make things. For example, a salesperson for a distributor using an interactive order system can perform clerical and bookkeeping chores as a by-product of writing up the sale. This efficiency applies to the teller in a bank, the nurse in a hospital, or the cop in a police station.

The Future

What are the implications of these developments in information systems? The trends strongly suggest the following:

1. Data processing hardware will become more specialized and more modular than today.

2. Generalized computer systems will be *dedicated* to specialized applications or to distributed special-function units serving the end user. This orientation permits users to control their own local hardware. A central data processing staff will still be needed, though, to coordinate and maintain the company's data processing structure.

3. Distributed special-function units indicate that processing will move closer to the end user. If the processor at one site fails, the entire organization does not fail with it.

4. Computer systems will be simple to use and easy to access in this distributed environment. The end user will be trained to focus on problems and their solutions rather than on processing techniques.

5. Computers of the 1980s are likely going to be transaction-oriented, on-line, communication-oriented, and real-time computer systems ready to serve the user when needed. The system will dynamically adapt its resources to the current workload. It will provide dedicated resources for each task. The results will be better system balance, easier data access, and improved system security and integrity.

6. The on-line systems of the 1980s will rarely shut down. System breakdown is expected to be less than one hour every four years. Continuous processing means more work output per dollar of investment in the system.

7. The systems of the 1980s are also expected to minimize the need for human intervention so that the user's response time requirements are satisfied. Automatic error correction, retry techniques, and on-line failure analysis will also be operational.

These futuristic trends suggest two things: First, no individual or a group of individuals is in a position at any time to know what application the system is processing and for whom it is doing the processing. Computer manufacturers face the delicate task of safeguarding the user's interest against system failure caused by a possible mixup in programming or other software. To this extent, the challenges of the next computer generation to solve the "software bottleneck" will determine the dynamics and future impact of computer systems on society.

Second, there is no way to foresee the real meaning of these kinds of developments. When they're achieved, their potential is usually felt in successive stages. In the early stages, we realize that we're doing the things we're already doing better. Later on, we are able to handle new tasks that we didn't do before. Finally, the developments pervade our lifestyle and become a part of our societal makeup. The dynamic evolution of the forthcoming computer generation is just reaching the threshold of the final stage.

SUMMARY

1. Developments in computing and computations date back to the beginning of humankind. The first manual method of data processing was counting on the ten fingers. The first manual device was the abacus—tedious and slow by today's standards. The alternative was a mechanical data processing system. The first mechanical devices were Pascal's decimal calculator (1642), Baldwin's calculator (1872), and Monroe's first commercially successful keyboard calculator (1911).

2. The slow mechanical device gave way to the punch card data processing system. In 1890, Hollerith developed a punched card system to process

the 1890 U.S census. The company he formed was eventually absorbed by IBM. Hollerith's resignation brought Powers into the U.S Census Bureau. The simultaneous punching machine he developed helped in the processing of the 1910 census. The company he formed in 1911 was merged in 1927 with the Sperry Rand Corporation.

3. Actual computation surfaced in the early 1940s with Atanasoff's ABC computer. The model provided the backbone for Eckert and Mauchly's ENIAC in 1946. The ENIAC was completely electronic, programmable, and capable of storing problem calculations. Late that year, Eckert and Mauchly left the University of Pennsylvania to form their own computer company. Three years later, it was acquired by the Remington Rand Corporation which developed the UNIVAC computer. Not until 1951 did IBM begin to make its own computers.

4. The computer industry underwent four generations of computer growth. The first generation utilized the vacuum tube for data storage, and a new breed of technicians appeared. The wire board was replaced by the computer program. Processing time was reduced by a factor of ten. Their primary limitations were their bulky sizes and limited memories. Second generation computers used transistors, were less bulky, and large memories, and operated at the microsecond speed. The high-level languages made the programmer's life easier than before. The third generation computers are characterized by monolithic integrated circuits, multiprogramming and multiprocessing, improved reliability and processing speed, and a significant reduction in computation cost. The introduction of the minicomputer provides the basis for redistributing power to the user, when needed. Today's fourth generation computer reduces hundreds of circuits to the size of a pinhead, incorporates sophisticated breakdown and error detection techniques, and implements special software to manage data bases. Main memory cost is cut to $.05 per character.

   With today's computer, the user can now access files directly, schedule various problems, and acquire data when needed. The minicomputer, by packing data processing power into its circuitry, gives system responsibility back to the user. The emerging concept, distributed data processing, means that the people-oriented computer assumes a new position as a managerial tool for problem solving.

5. Progress in information systems during the past three decades is summarized in terms of:
   a. continued growth in the number of computer installations and sites,
   b. reduction in hardware/software costs,
   c. reduction in the physical size of storage,
   d. improvements in processing power and performance, and
   e. improvements in reliability and user control.

The primary inhibitors to computer growth, however, are the costs of software and of qualified programmers and analysts. Lack of sufficiently trained staff poses an additional constraint.

6. The primary developments of the 1970s include the application of bubble storage in terminals and in portable computers, the development of the microcomputer for personal computing, data transmission via satellite, and the application of word processing for organizing large volumes of written work. The trend in user attitudes toward independence and control provided the impetus behind DDP. Distributed special-function units mean processing will move closer to the end user.

7. The systems of the 1980s are expected to minimize the need for human intervention, provide automatic error correction and retry techniques, and make it possible for the user to focus on problems and their solutions rather than on processing techniques. The system will rarely shut down. If one site processor fails, the entire organization does not fail with it. These developments will pervade our lifestyle and become a part of our societal makeup.

TERMS TO LEARN

Abacus
Bubble memory
Chip
ENIAC
Keypunch
Microprocessor
Multiprogramming
Operating system
Simultaneous punching principle
Virtual storage
Word processing

REVIEW QUESTIONS

1. In what respect is mechanical data processing an improvement over manual data processing? What type or size of business could still use the mechanical method of calculation? Illustrate.

2. Distinguish between the simultaneous and the serial punching principle.

From the brief overview in the chapter, who introduced the serial method of punching data in cards?

3. Define in your own words the sorter, the collator, and the accounting machine.

4. If you were to design a punched card system, what would be the minimum components needed for a workable operation?

5. Is a punched card data processing system a calculator or a computer? Discuss.

6. In what way(s) does the ENIAC differ from the (a) MARK I, (b) UNIVAC, (c) punched card system?

7. Explain in your own words the improvements of the second generation computer over the first generation computer.

8. Distinguish the difference between:
   a. operating system and a computer program.
   b. multiprogramming and virtual memory.

9. Summarize the main features of third generation computers. Which feature had a direct bearing on DDP? Explain.

10. How do fourth generation computers differ from third generation computers?

11. In what respect is the minicomputer a contribution to the development of DDP? Explain.

12. What is DDP? Justify its operation in a business the size of Allstate Insurance Company.

13. From the material covered in the chapter, in which direction is computer growth heading?

14. How does the trend in memory size relate to a more effective computerized operation?

15. Given the accelerated increase in the cost of programming and systems analysis, what steps do you recommend to control this problem? Explain.

16. Name three applications of your own that can be handled by a minicomputer. Justify your answer.

chapter 4

The Classification of Computers

Learning Objectives

Key developments in computer cost and performance generated a new breed of computers and provided the basis for computerizing additional applications. The advent of the minicomputer and the implementation of distributed computing in business cast a new dimension to computer classifications. Thus, a fresh look at the categories of computers and an elaboration on their contributions would be helpful. By the end of this chapter, you should know:

1. the difference between general- and special-purpose computers,

2. the features of analog, digital, and hybrid computers,

3. the uses of microcomputers and personal computing, and

4. the types of distributed computing in business.

The Classification of Computers

General- and Special-Purpose Computers

General-Purpose computers
Special-Purpose computers

Analog, Digital, and Hybrid Computers

Analog Computers
Digital Computers
Hybrid Computers

Computer Capacity

Microcomputers

Typical Uses

Personal Computing

The Hobby Market

Minicomputers

Mini- Versus Microcomputers
Mini- Versus Conventional Computers
Definition
Advantages
Limitations
Basic Structure

Minicomputer Applications

Stand-Alone Applications
Network Applications

Distributed Processing

Types of Distribution

Medium-Sized Computers
Large-Scale Computers
"Super-" Computers

Since the 1960s, we have experienced a tremendous surge in the types and variety of computers in business. Over fifty computer manufacturers produce a wide array of computers, ranging from the super-computers to the microcomputers. The recent mass production of the microprocessor at a realistic price spawned the development of the personal computer for the single user at home, in school, and for business applications. Because of key developments in computer cost and performance, new and additional applications have been computerized. Microcomputers have also made it possible to decentralize computer power and distribute it to the user at the operating level when it is needed the most.

The distinctions among the various categories of computers has been subject to controversy. The layperson and the professional use terms that classify computers as analog or digital, general-purpose or special-purpose, or business or scientific. Others emphasize computer size, areas of usage, or periods of computer development. In this chapter, we attempt to define and explain these categories, as well as elaborate on the concepts of microcomputer processing and of personal (distributed) computing.

The Classification of Computers

Computer systems are generally classified by:

1. *purpose,* whether the system is general- or special-purpose;
2. The *type* of data it is capable of manipulating (specifically, whether the system is analog, digital, or hybrid); and
3. *capacity,* or the volume work the system can handle. The range of systems is from super- to microcomputer systems.

General- and Special-Purpose Computers

General-purpose computers. **General-purpose computers** are designed to handle a variety of applications such as payroll, accounts receivables, inventory control, marketing and financial problems. Although their versatility means a sacrifice in speed and efficiency of performance, they have the advantages of low-cost operation and long, extensive testing during production to eliminate "bugs."

Classification of general-purpose computers is determined by the speed of data handling and by type of data used. Processing speed is stated in terms of **milliseconds** (thousandths), **microseconds** (millionths) **nanoseconds** (billionths), and **picoseconds** (trillionths). The types of data used may be scientific or business. **Scientific** computers are designed to handle prolonged mathematical computations for the solution of a scientific problem. They do not have the capacity to handle large volumes of input and output, like business computers. In contrast, *business-oriented* computer systems have extensive input/output capability, but they lack the advanced, high-speed computational power of the scientific computer.

Special-purpose computers. **Special-purpose computers** are designed to solve specific types of problems. Usually tailored to the needs of a single customer, they lack the flexibility of the general-purpose computer. Many special-purpose systems have been successfully used for collecting highway tolls, air traffic control, satellite tracking, industrial process control, and airline reservations (Figure 4 – 1).

Figure 4–1. An airline's special-purpose system.

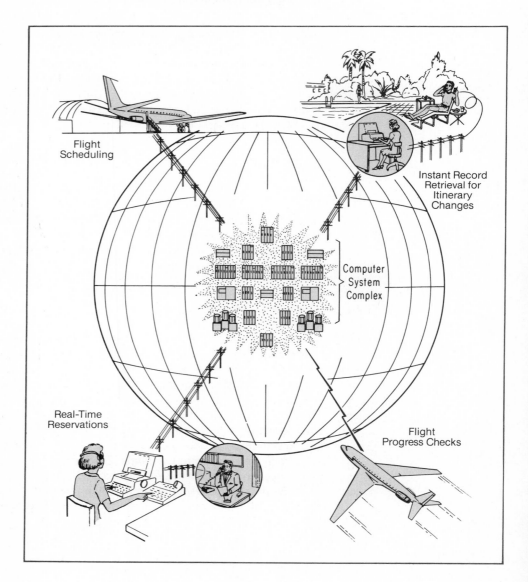

Analog, Digital, and Hybrid Computers

Analog computers. The name **analog** comes from the word "analogous," meaning "similar." The thermometer, for instance, records various mercury levels based on changes in temperature. In other words, changes in temperature are shown by analogous (or similar) changes in the level of mercury. The same principle is used by the analog computer to perform arithmetic functions. It converts data into voltages and computes by measuring the changes in voltage. Thus, as a measuring device, it represents values by continuously varying physical data such as the amount of pressure, voltage, or electric current. Computations are performed by combining these quantities.

Analog computers are commonly used in process measurements in industries, such as chemical and electric power plants and petroleum refineries. Their primary advantage is their prompt response to the handling of data generated by an ongoing physical process. The obvious drawback is the accuracy factor. Compared to the digital computer, an analog computer produces systematic errors which occasionally cause slight deviation from the true value.

Digital computers. In a **digital** computer, all arithmetic computations depend ultimately on counting. Unlike the analog computer, which receives data in a continuous form, the digital computer handles numbers in *discrete* form. It is capable of reading numbers in degrees of accuracy far greater than those reached by the analog computer. In addition to arithmetic operations, the digital computer is capable of storing data as long as needed, performing logical operations, editing input data, and printing out the results of its processing at high speed. Although the analog computer has similar characteristics, the method of accomplishing them is very different and cumbersome for business applications.

In summary, analog computers are ideal for scientific and engineering problems, when physical measurements are manipulated as data for arithmetic operations and when a high degree of accuracy is not critical. In contrast, digital computers are used in handling business applications, when repetitive routine arithmetic operations are involved and when 100 percent accuracy is demanded.

Hybrid computers. Although both analog and digital computers are extensively used and widely accepted in various industries, manufacturers have attempted to design a computer that combines the best features of both types. This special-purpose machine, called a **hybrid computer,** combines the measuring capabilities of the analog computer and the logical and control capabilities of the digital computer. It offers an efficient and economical method of working out special types of problems in science and various areas of engineering. Among the applications are space vehicle simulations and the training of space pilots, analysis of signals received from special sensors attached to humans and animals in laboratories, and the solving of differential equations for chemical reactors.

Computer Capacity

The term "capacity" refers to the volume of work the computer can handle. The capacity of first and second generation computers was determined by their physical size — the larger the size, the greater the volume. Today's miniaturization of most computer components made significant improvements in capacity. Capacity is currently measured by the number of jobs (or applications) that it can run rather than by the volume of data that it can process. With this criterion in mind, computer systems are classified as microcomputers, minicomputers, medium, and large computers.

Microcomputers

The mass production of silicon chips since 1971 has made it possible to put a "brain" into all sorts of machines. One such machine is the microcomputer. In less than eight years, the microcomputer chip has evolved from a piece of smart logic to a full-fledged, easily mass-produced component of established computer systems. It can be squeezed onto a 200-mil (fraction of an inch) square substrate requiring less than a few hundred milliwatts ($\frac{1}{1,000}$th watt) of power (Figure 4–2).

Figure 4–2. This microcomputer system is a "Deluxe Business 32K System" for a little over $4,000. *Courtesy: Radio Shack.*

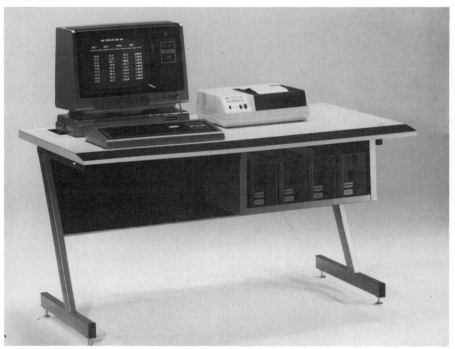

Sometimes called a "single-chip processor" or a "system-on-a-chip," the **microcomputer** is a digital computer system, under the control of a stored program, that uses a microprocessor, a programmable read-only memory (ROM), and a random-access memory (RAM). If allows great flexibility at low cost, and it requires minimal space and power.

The heart of the microcomputer is the microprocessor. The **microprocessor** is contained within a typical 0.16-inch square package (hence the "micro" label). It consists of an arithmetic-logic unit (ALU), the control circuitry that executes instructions, and general-purpose registers. There is typically one chip for each function, although the entire processor can be on a single chip (Figure 4–3). This chip is not a complete computer system, because it requires a device to link it with the outside world. When memory and input-output devices are added to the processor chip, they form a complete general-purpose microcomputer system. The microprocessor is a memory revolution that makes it possible for everyone to process data. With the microprocessor, we have a progammable device with all the capabilities of a computer. Yet the cost is less than $10, and a complete microcomputer using this microprocessor costs less than $1,500.

A general microprocessor design is illustrated in Figure 4–4. The **read-only memory (ROM)** defines the instructions to be executed by the computer. **Random-access memory (RAM)** is the functional equivalent of computer memory. The **arithmetic-logic unit** (ALU) performs arithmetic and logic operations. Its registers serve as the working memory for manipulating programs and data transferred from a magnetic tape or a floppy disc. (A **floppy disc** is a small-sized memory device used for storage and data retrieval; details on this and other devices are covered in Chapter 8.) This function is furnished by RAM, which in some cases may be a part of the microprocessor chip.

Figure 4–3.   A microprocessor chip. *Courtesy: Texas Instruments, Inc.*

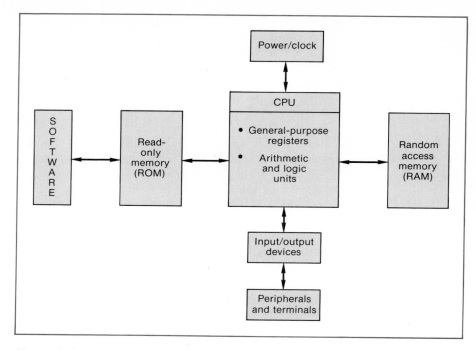

Figure 4-4. A general microprocessor design.

Typical uses. Microprocessor technology makes the small-scale commercial applications of computers feasible. Microcomputers have many uses in business: specifically, automobile ignition control, automatic car speed control, process control and logging, source data entry, word processing, text editing, small communication systems, among many others. As "intelligent" modules, they have also been used in programmable calculators, special-purpose terminals (badge readers, security card verifiers, and the like), and small accounting computers. Inventory control by a microprocessor-based system is now a reality. The operator can access any record on the disc of any item held in inventory. When an order is placed, the microprocessor calculates the invoice extension for each item ordered and immediately updates the inventory. In the event of a back-order, the customer is informed so that he or she can select an alternative item. At the end of the day, all totals are listed along with a reorder list for items below a minimum quantity. A separate list specifying slow-moving and fast-selling parts is also printed.

Continued progress in improving the performance of the microprocessor means more potential applications through the microcomputer. New chip fabrication techniques should increase chip storage densities by a factor of 100 or more. These improvements will eventually make it possible for one or two chips to emulate today's large CPU at a low cost. It is safe to predict that by 1982, a chip representing a microcomputer will sell for $1 to $10 each.

Personal Computing

The declining cost of the microprocessor and of memory has made it possible for the consumer to employ the computer for personal use. Personal computing is therefore consumer computing. It is a revolution in the availability of computer power for home and office use. The personal computer is not a "robot" for turning off microwave ovens or sewing machines. Instead, it is a microtool to aid the consumer in personal problem solving and in coping with an increasingly computerized society. The cost is so low that it can be used abundantly anywhere and anytime.

A *personal computer* typically consists of a microprocessor with 8,000 to 16,000 bytes of memory, a keyboard to feed in data, a TV screen for displaying the information keyed in or processed, two audio cassette drives, and a programming language interpreter.[1] The system can come as a kit or as a "turnkey" (that is, "plug-in-and-go"). Perhaps most important, it costs well under $1,000, although a system with the "bells and whistles" can cost up to $6,000. (Figure 4–5). The applications are wide and varied. A lawyer uses a personal computer as a word processor in preparing legal documents. A personnel office supervisor documents available positions and job applications on a personal computer. A Chicago dentist uses a personal computer to evaluate his fee structure. A Supreme Court judge in California relies on his home computer to store legal data during trials.[2] These and other examples show that computers will be at our fingertips in homes and offices. They will be available to solve even basic tasks at a nominal cost. As a new industry, however, personal computing suffers from two major handicaps: faulty software and incomplete documentation. Software documentation is confusing, because it lacks the necessary details for implementation. Some manuals don't even show how to turn the microcomputer on! As a result, some people are "turned off" by personal computers. Furthermore, the microcomputer industry has a number of fairly small companies with untested financial standings to warrant improvement in faulty software.

The hobby market. Personal computers nonetheless enjoy two major markets: the non-home and the home use markets. The *non-home use market* includes self-employed professionals, very small businesses, educational institutions, scientists, and industrial applications. The *home use market,* on the other hand, is dominated by the hobbyist and the general consumer. The strength of this area is illustrated by the phenomenal growth of computer hobby clubs, stores, and magazines. The first retail computer store opened in July 1975. Four years later, over 7,000 stereo and department stores carried computers. A dozen personal computing magazines cater to the hobbyist alone. Unit shipments for 1978 reached 300,000 from 42,000 systems shipped in 1977. The retail store

[1]Portia Isaacson, "Personal Computing," *Datamation* (October, 1977), p. 210.
[2]Don Muller, "Personal Computers in Home and Business Applications," *Computers & People* (December, 1977), p. 12.

Figure 4–5. A low-cost personal computer that evolved from Atari's line of video games. *Courtesy: Atari*

stocks equipment and software, offers maintenance contracts, and demonstrates systems for testing.

Statistics on the profile of the computer hobbyist reveals that over two-thirds have had prior exposure to computers in business or on the job. As shown in Figure 4–6, the hobbyist is a system builder, invests around $1,800 in the hobby, and spends about 15 hours each week on it.[3] As software documentation of computer specifications improve, more and more consumers are expected to invest in personal computers — more for home use than hobby only.

All indications point to the fact that microcomputers will appear in staggering numbers. In the next decade, they will become a part of everyday life. Children, growing with them to adulthood, will use them in the same way we use the telephone today. When future microcomputers — the $20–100 models become available, we will find them as necessary as an automobile is now. By then, the uses of these computers in our daily endeavors will have no limit. They will test our products, project our sales, control the atmosphere of our homes, operate our cars, act as our secretaries, and even prepare our meals. In general, they will serve as our alter egos.

[3]Alan Kaplan, "Home Computers versus Hobby Computers," *Datamation* (July, 1977), p. 72.

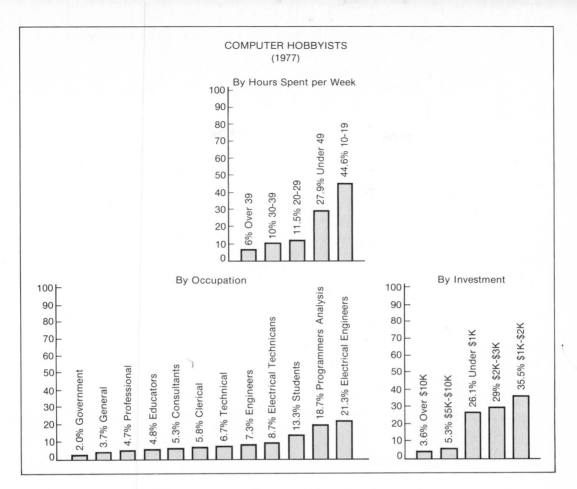

Figure 4—6. The microcomputer hobbyist — a profile.

Minicomputers

Minicomputers are one of the most talked-about systems in the computer industry. A product of the miniaturization revolution, they have become visible in almost every type of business application. They are performing many of the general-purpose functions that were once performed exclusively by large-scale computers. For example, a $50,000 minicomputer can do a good deal of the work at one time done only by computers costing $2 million.

Mini- versus microcomputers. Although the minicomputer and the microcomputer share similarities in function, architecture, and end user applications, their differences are substantial. Minicomputers use *discrete* circuit technology; in other words, each basic logic function is separate from the other. In microcomputers, most of the logic functions are *integrated* on to one or a few chips. Consequently, the overall price is roughly one-tenth the price of minis. Word size, main memory size, and software support are also different. The minicomputer has a 8- to 32-bit word size, 8,000- to 32,000-word memory, and a relatively established applications software. In contrast, the microcomputer has a 4- to 16-bit word size, a 500- to 4,000-word memory, and an emerging software. While 8- and 16-bit microcomputers have made great strides during the late 1970s, the minicomputer is still viewed as the "heavyweight" in terms of processing power, memory size, capacity, and implementation.

Mini- versus conventional computers.   Most minicomputers are capable of accomplishing what conventional computers do in business. At present, minicomputers utilize batch and real-time operating systems, along with both high-level and simple programming languages.

Again, however, the differences between mini- and conventional computers are significant (Table 4–1). Although the minicomputer is not as "powerful" as the medium or large computer, it is quite close, given the substantial price differentials. Other advantages of the conventional computer over the minis include better management of large networks (on which the mini is a distributed processor), more vendor support in system maintenance, more experienced technical talent, and higher user training.

Table 4–1.   Key characteristics of micro-, mini-, medium-, and large-scale computers.

Characteristic	Microcomputers	Minicomputers	Medium-Scale	Large-Scale
Hardware:				
Word length	8–16 bits	16 bits	32 bits	32 bits
Maximum memory size	64,000 bytes	262,000 bytes	524,000 bytes	8.4 mi. bytes
Processor architecture:				
CPU cycle time (how fast instructions can be carried out)	250 microseconds	300 nanoseconds	275 nanoseconds	80 nanoseconds
Memory cycle (how fast data or instructions can be retrieved from memory)	700 microseconds	850 nanoseconds	800 nanoseconds	480 nanoseconds
Software:				
Programming languages	Basic, micro-Cobol, Pascal	4 major languages Basic, Cobol, Fortran, RPG	8 languages	8 languages
Application packages (e.g., payroll, accounts receivable, etc.)	Dozens	Hundreds	Thousands	Thousands
Other considerations:				
Reliability	Very high	Very high (time to repair is brief due to relative simplicity)	High	High

Table 4–1. (cont.)

Characteristic	Microcomputers	Minicomputers	Medium-Scale	Large-Scale
Vendor support	Fair	Good	Outstanding	Outstanding
Operating requirements	None. The user learns system quickly. No special site preparation.	One good operator per shift No special site preparation Good systems Programmers required	Same as for large computers	Considerable preparation of space and air conditioning required Well trained programmers and analysts required
Purchase price	Under $6,000	Tens of thousands of dollars	Hundreds of thousands of dollars	Millions of dollars

Summarized from G. J. Burnett, and R. L. Nolan, "At Last, Major Roles for Minicomputers," *Harvard Business Review* (May-June 1975), pp. 150–151.

Definition.   The range of minicomputer classifications and their characteristics is summarized in Table 4–2. Broadly defined, however, a **minicomputer:**

1. is a physically small, digital computer with a stored program;

2. contains a main memory of from 4,000 to 32,000 words;

3. requires no special site or environmental preparation;

4. can be programmed in high-level languages, such as Basic, Cobol, or Fortran;

5. weighs less than 50 pounds and operates on standard home electric current; and

6. costs between $3,000 and $50,000, although many large minis cost upwards of $100,000.

Table 4–2. Classes of minicomputers—a summary.

Characteristic	Classes of minicomputers		
	SMALL————————————————————————————→LARGE		
	Micromini	Mini	Megamini
Main memory size	4K–16K*	16K–64K	Over 64K
Disk storage on-line	5–10 mi. bytes	10–40 mi. bytes	Over 40 mi. bytes
Operating systems	Single terminal	Multiterminal	Multiterminal
	Multiterminal	Multiprogramming	Multiprogramming
Programming languages	Basic	Expanded Basic	Extended Basic
	Fortran	RPG-II,	RPG-II
		Fortran	Cobol
			Fortran

Table 4–2. (cont.)

Characteristic	Classes of minicomputers		
	SMALL————————————————————————————————→LARGE		
	Micromini	Mini	Megamini
Printers	30–165 char./sec.	200–600 lines/min.	600–1,200 lines/min.
Card reader punch magnetic tape	Rarely used	Available (usually for backup and interface)	Available (for backup and interface)
Price range (full system, including software)	Up to $40,000	$40,000–$100,000	$100,000–$300,000
Representative system	Varian 620/f-100	DEC PDP 11/40	Hewlett Packard 3000

*Letter "K" represents 1,024 storage locations in memory. Thus, a "4K" memory means 4,096 storage locations of memory.

Advantages. Compared to larger computers, minicomputers offer several advantages:

1. *Adaptability.* The minicomputer is easily upgraded into a powerful system, since many compatible peripheral and memory-extension devices can be added as the firm's increasing volume demands. Thus, a minicomputer can grow as the business grows without the need for significant increases in clerical staff.

2. *Low cost and ease of operation.* Relatively low cost is a major attraction. Ease of operation makes an in-house time-shared system ideal for a company with multiple users. The people who use the data are the ones who use the computer. Since the files get updated directly, they are working with accurate information, instead of past history.

3. *Ease of installation.* The system doesn't require site preparation or expensive air-conditioning. It is also easier to maintain than the larger computer systems.

4. *Minimum technical personnel requirements.* The minicomputer is virtually operatorless. No special technical staff is required for operation.

5. *Making sounder decisions.* A minicomputer can handle many of the day-to-day and "what-if" questions that often overwhelm establish guidelines (such as credit limits, inventory reorder points, and the like). The computer alerts users when the guidelines are exceeded. This allows a business to manage by exception.

Limitations. Minicomputers have several limitations:

1. Memory size is more limited than in larger systems. Execution times are also relatively slow.

2. Many complex jobs (such as mathematical simulation) cannot be handled by a minicomputer.

3. The minicomputer's cost may well be less than the cost of its peripheral devices; that is, the total cost of the system is likely to be much higher than the basic computer.

Basic structure.   Minicomputers, like larger systems, consist of a CPU, input-output equipment, and peripheral devices. The CPU includes main memory, an arithmetic-logic unit, a set of registers, and one or more data buses for facilitating data transfer to the various CPU components. The basic CPU architecture is similar to that of the microcomputer (Figure 4–4). Minicomputers come with all the standard computer peripherals: printers, magnetic tape or cassette, CRT displays and keyboards, teletypewriters, and disc storage. The disc drives have a storage capacity of from 5 to 10 million bytes. Some units can even be increased up to 400 million bytes of storage. Figure 4–7 shows a representative minicomputer configuration.

Figure 4–7. A representative minicomputer configuration.

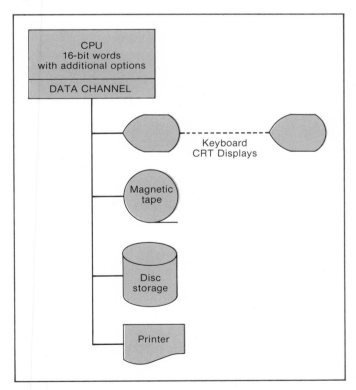

Minicomputer Applications

Minicomputers, the "blue-collar" computers of business, are everywhere. The representative applications emphasized in this section are classified as either stand-alone or network configurations.

Stand-alone applications.   A stand-alone minicomputer is used as the central computer system for small business and as a processor in a time sharing and remote job entry (RJE) environment. For example, a minicomputer can accept batch input data from geographically dispersed terminals, process the data, and transmit the output back to the remote user. A powerful minicomputer, can handle multiterminal real-time, time sharing, and batch activities simultaneously.

What small business is looking for in a minicomputer is simplicity of use, economy of operation, and production of information that has not been obtainable to date. It is expected to handle the following general business applications:
1. accounts receivable,
2. accounts payable,
3. general ledger,
4. inventory control,
5. invoicing,
6. order entry,
7. payroll, and
8. production and quality control.

In production, for example, a minicomputer may be programmed to (1) compare data with production schedules to determine if specific action is needed, (2) recognize events as they happen (real-time mode), and (3) provide periodic reports and answers to various inquiries. In quality control testing, the operator reads the program into the system's memory via a tape reader. The minicomputer, interfaced to testing devices, receives the testing data of a given sample and compares it to the testing parameters. If the data passes the test, the entire lot is accepted. Otherwise, the lot is tested, item by item for accuracy. The outcome of the testing operation is later presented in the form of a report to management for action.

Network applications.   The phrase, "computer network," is used here to refer to two or more computer elements linked together to provide optimal service to the end users. A minicomputer may be used in four types of networks:

1. *Hierarchical network.* Computers of different capacity and capability are related to certain levels in a business organization. For example, microcomputers may be used to control individual machine tools on the production floor. Each group of machines, in turn, is supervised by a minicomputer. The production department, as a whole, is monitored by a medium-sized computer that links to the company's large-scale central computer system.

Another view of the hierarchical network is categorizing computer systems as blue-collar (worker), supervisor, management, and corporate systems. The *blue-collar* minicomputer controls inventory, the supply of raw materials, and even monitors the production process, giving instructions when necessary. The *supervisor* (a small computer or large minicomputer) instructs the minicomputer to do various tasks. It supervises production schedules, raw materials, and prepares production reports for the management computer. The *management* (medium-sized) computer, in turn, uses the feedback to project the market, "decides" on the production rate, corrects one-time problems, and acts on any reported malfunctions. Finally, the *corporate* (large) computer plans the total organization. It handles mortgage loans and financing, projects corporate income and profits, pays stockholders' dividends, and generates information to help decide on future expansion in physical facilities and production.

2. *Resource sharing network.* This type of network focuses on the linkage of remote minicomputers with limited local capacity to a larger host computer for improving total service to the local end user. For example, in a bank's trust department, a minicomputer available to the trust officer performs data acquisition or processes daily activities relating to each estate and trust fund. At anytime during the day or week, the trust officer may call on the master computer system (located miles away) to produce a profile of certain trust funds or generate a report on the profitability of the trust accounts for the month. If the master computer shuts down, the local minicomputer can operate as a stand-alone system, collecting data and retaining it until the system is "up" again.

3. *Communications network.* Minicomputer control of a communications environment can be categorized into the following three basic areas:

a. *Remote data concentrators* take the data communication from low-speed terminals and concentrates them onto one telephone line by a special multiplexing arrangement. The minicomputer converts the transmissions into a format that makes the multiplexed transmission appear to the computer like the input from one high-speed device. Additional functions are editing, code conversion, and error checking.

b. A *front-end communication processor* is an intelligent user-programmable terminal that serves as an interface to the communication system. In an on-line system, the minicomputer may be used as a front-end processor to control communication traffic for the larger (host) computer. In effect, the central computer is not bogged down with interruptions in communicating with the remote terminals. The front-end minicomputer can perform such functions as code conversion, error checking, and control, while maintaining records of message traffic and poll and address terminals.

c. In a *message switching* system, a minicomputer is more like a traffic director. It is used to direct messages between terminals, routing them from point to point, and monitoring the total operation of the system. It also maintains a log of message volume and controls message priorities.

The fourth type of network application, distributed computing, is so significant that it deserves special treatment.

Distributed Processing

The premise of distibuted processing is the division of data processing "labor." A central "host" computer concentrates on the big applications, and minicomputers handle functions such as data entry, message switching, and talking to other terminals. It also includes the possibility of homogenous processing sites with a minimal central system. In either case, the minicomputer distributes computer power to lower levels of usage — to the warehouse, to the sales office, to the purchase order department, to all those places where the future of computer power lies. It represents a means of linking the user to information more easily and more quickly than ever before. It is a new extension of an established network of computer users.

A distributed processing network is illustrated in Figure 4–8. The multi-function minicomputer system incorporates and controls a number of terminals at the disposal of individual users. At the same time, higher-level interactive processing is made possible through the central computer system. This unique network:

1. returns the control of information to where it was before computers, to the data users;

2. permits more effective autonomous management at the operational level;

3. fosters the turnaround of orders and quicker problem solutions at a lower cost (faster solutions, mean the business is making capital gains more quickly);

4. maintains a uniform corporate system in a geographically dispersed environment;

5. allows the user to send in corrected data, not errors, and to transmit only when necessary;

6. improves reliability (downtime becomes a matter of reduced capibility rather than a total loss of computer processing);

7. enhances flexibility to meet changing demands; and

8. enables users to set priorities at work.

Distributed processing is not without drawbacks. Among the key drawbacks are:

1. the need for additional technical staff at the local level,

2. the potential duplication of data and the possible loss of control and security,

3. the necessity of cooperation throughout the data processsng areas within the company for successful control of the data processing function, and

4. the possibility of inefficient applications as an inexperienced user attempts to utilize the new local minicomputing power.

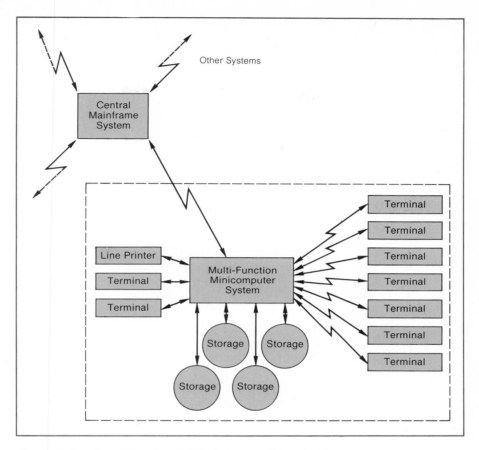

Figure 4–8. A multifunction distributed computing network

One way to minimize the problems is to centralize the development of standards, procedures, and application development. Such measures prevent local users to change key programs. Another method is to set up a joint programming staff to guide the local user through projects or to serve as a programming service resource. In addition, the firm can develop a data dictionary to be used in various business applications during local development efforts.

Types of distribution. A network structure is organized to support the goals and functions of the business. Three types of network organizations are possible with existing minicomputers:

1. the "star" hierarchical type,

2. the "hierarchical" type, and

3. the "ring distributed" type.

The first two types are similar to social organizations. In the star system, organized hierarchically, a powerful central computer acts as a kind of fuedal overlord of the entire system. In contrast, the ring concept is arranged anarchically, with the system consisting of a cluster of independent computers.

The *star network* is the simplest and most effective kind of network (refer to Figure 3–6 in Chapter 3). One computer plays host to a number of terminals or to peripheral devices located either locally or remotely. For example, each terminal might be in a different department in the organization. The network is economical, because it requires only one computer with terminals that are linked to the computer through a common telephone line and a device called a *modem.* The modem holds the telephone and facilitates the proper connection with the leased wire.

The hierarchical network implies the availability of minicomputers, tapes, files, and printers at remote locations. Each location transmits summary data (sales, inventory balance, and so on) or other kinds of data requested by the central computer. This network creates a hierarchy of users from the branch or division level to the corporate headquarters.

The *ring distributed network* is a series of at least two computers with neither computer dominating. The most obvious difference between the ring and the hierarchical organization is the absence of graded computer power in the ring network. Also, the computers in the ring network are interactive rather than batch-oreinted. This type of network is useful only in very large organizations such as the top Fortune 500 companies, in the military, and in the federal government.

In summary, distributed processing will have many positive effects. At the central site, top management will be able to monitor the activities of various branches more effectively. At the same time, corporate managers can delegate to lower management the authority to process whatever data directly supports local decisions. Thus local management acquires a powerful tool for local uses, while top management benefits from up-to-date summary reports and improved organizational control.

Medium-Sized Computers

Medium-sized computer systems surpass small computers or large minicomputers by providing greater operating speed, larger memory capacity, and high-speed input-output devices for efficient data handling (see Table 4–1). Among their features are:

1. *fast memory cycle,* measured in nanoseconds;

2. **multiprogramming** for increased productivity, easier handling of scheduling problems, and automatic manipulation of priority changes related to unscheduled tasks;

3. **operating system** (supervisory program) *control,* which synchronizes the system's operations for making best use of available processing power and programming efforts;

4. *language versatility,* which allows programming in all eight major languages, including Cobol and Fortran;

5. *design flexibility,* which meets the requirements of various-sized firms and services, to process in a batch, direct-access environment or in an on-line, real-time environment;

6. *expandable main memory,* which is time-shared between the individual channels and the central processor;

7. a unique feature, called *virtual memory,* by which main memory capacity is made to appear larger than the actual size. This feature allows the computer to handle programs that would otherwise be too large to fit in main memory.

A medium-sized computer can also support a management information system (MIS). Managers have terminals in their offices so that they can obtain information about customers or business activities through the data base. The data base is maintained on magnetic disk for fast access. Figure 4–9 shows a medium-size computer system with its input-output and peripheral devices.

Figure 4–9. A representative medium-sized computer system, the NCR Y-8455. *Courtesy: NCR Corporation*

Large-Scale Computers

Large-scale computers are the ultimate in system sophistication, flexibility, and speed. To be considered large-scale, a computer must have 1.5 million bytes or more of main memory and operating speeds in the low nanosecond range. A large system has a storage unit upwards of 8 million bytes and a CPU cycle time[4] of 80 nanoseconds (Figure 4–10). Most large computer systems have the following features:

1. a free-standing system console that features a keyboard and a CRT for conversation between the operator and the system;

2. multiple independent processors sharing a single operating system (each processor is capable of handling several input-output channels at data transfer rates over 8 million bytes per second);

3. data communication processors designed to relieve the central processors from handling line discipline routines;

4. a central exchange device employed to provide independent communication between memory modules, central processors, and input-output processors;

5. head-per-track disc-file memory systems (the direct-access memories have up to 600 million bytes) and

6. system software for continuous multiprogramming.

Such systems rent for approximately $200,000 a month. Such a large expense creates a problem for the user—the efficient utilization of computer time. The system must be employed efficiently during every second in all applications. Incompatibility of the peripheral devices accompanying the system often accounts for waste. While the tape drive is receiving or giving out information or while the printer is listing results, the arithmetic unit is idle. To make up for the slower operation of these peripherals, various programming enhancements have been developed. One is an "interrupt" connection, where magnetic tapes are used as intermediate data carriers, releasing the computer from dependence on card readers and line printers. Briefly, data is entered directly onto magnetic tapes (or magnetic discs), which in turn become the primary input medium. On output, the data from the computer is written onto magnetic tapes. The printer is then fed the required information for final printout from the tapes. In this approach, the magnetic tape performs the role of a buffer or a temporary storage to compensate for a difference in rate of flow of data.

Another way of maximizing the use of time on a large computer system is the "satellite" approach. Given enough work to do, one or more small com-

---

[4]CPU cycle time refers to how fast instructions can be carried out.

Figure 4–10. A representative large-scale computer system, the Burroughs' B 7800 series is especially well-suited for managing one-line networks with large-scale data bases. *Courtesy: Burroughs Corporation*

puters are situated around the large computer and constitute a satellite that prepares magnetic tapes for processing, testing, merging, and other tasks. This distributed processing approach has proved its effectiveness in many large installations.

Still another viable approach to utilizing the large computer's time is multiprogramming. This feature eliminates any slack in processing. For example, after a particular phase of one program is executed and is being handled by a peripheral device, the processor acts on a second program, processing it until a signal from the peripheral device indicates the peripheral's readiness for more output from the the first program. This signal causes the computer to revert to the first program, execute more instructions, and again activate the printer. The computer then returns to the second program and eventually to succeeding programs with virtually no waste of processing time.

Although efficiency systems are extremely expensive, large companies find them worth the expense. The larger firms can provide both skilled programmers and continuous applications, involving thousands of employees and hundreds of thousands of customer accounts on a daily bases. The computers responsible for such volume and such scope of operation are rightly included in the "millionaire" club.

"Super"-Computers

A computer system that works at a speed a hundred times faster than that of today's average large computer is being developed by scientists at NASA's Ames Research Center in Northern California. Although normal technological developments do not provide for the availability of such a machine before the year 2000, technology is being pushed to design a system for modeling aircraft in a wind tunnel and solving aerodynamic flows. The purpose is not to replace wind tunnels, but rather to substitute computer modeling for the early testing in a tunnel. The computer would have the capability to simulate the entire range of speeds, whereas no wind tunnels to date can test the entire spectrum.

A major computer manufacturer recently introduced a large-scale scientific system suited to the largest problem solving requirements of science, industry, and government. Numerical computations are carried out at speeds up to 50 million operations per second. Its secondary storage capacity is expandable to over 67 million, 56-bit words. Purchase prices range from approximately $3.8 to $6.1 million, lease rates vary from $128,000 to $175,000 per month (Figure 4–10).

What is the future for large computers? Almost all large users are beginning to require multiple processing or multimode environments. In other words, they have to mix the batch processing of certain applications and the on-line transaction processing of other applications for simultaneous handlings. High-priority needs also include:

1. time sharing for financial models or strategic planning;

2. greater system usability and 100 percent system availability in handling the high-priority jobs; and

3. ease of use.

Figure 4–11. The role of conversational diagnosers.

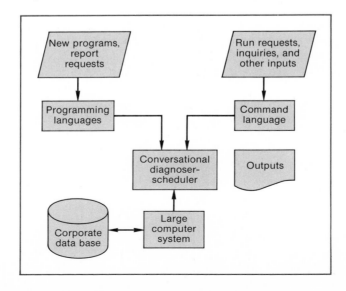

Ease of use will probably come about with the greater availability of conversational diagnosers, the trend of the future in production operation. As programmers enter their requirements for tests, a conversational diagnoser makes comments such as "You didn't close the last parenthesis" or "Your ID number is no good." When the dialog concludes, the program run is carried out according to plan. As shown in Figure 4–11, the production user makes inquiries to the data base through a command language. Once the user's needs are expressed to the conversational diagnoser, it provides the output when the need is verified and approved by the system. This conversational interface no longer requires the user to know what computer system is involved. The end user doesn't even have to know where the system is. With such a device, the system environment becomes virtual — it disappears from the user's sight.

SUMMARY

1. Computer systems are classified by purpose, by type of data, or by capacity. Special-purpose computers solve specific types of problems. They are tailored to the needs of a single customer. General-purpose computers handle a variety of applications. Some computers are scientific, in that they process mathematical computations of scientific problems. Other business-oriented computers have extensive input-output capability, although they lack the high-speed computer power of the scientific computer.

2. There are three types of computers: analog, digital, and hybrid. The analog computer represents values by continuously varying physical data. The digital computer measures and processes values by counting, for more accurate results. The hybrid computer combines the measuring capabilities of the analog computer with the logical and control capabilities of the digital computer.

3. Computer capacity focuses on the volume of work of the computer. Computers are classified as micro-, mini-, medium-, and large-scale computers. The microcomputer is a programmable system designed around a microprocessor, read-only memory (ROM), and random-access memory (RAM). It has many uses in business, programmable calculators, special-purpose terminals, and word processing. Its declining cost has made its use possible in personal computing. The strength of this area is signified by the phenomenal growth of computer hobby clubs, stores, and magazines.

4. A minicomputer is a small programmable computer. It contains 4 to 32K words of main memory. Although it is not as powerful as larger systems, it is capable of handling what conventional computers do in business. Minicomputers offer the advantages of adaptability, low cost, ease of operation

and installation, and minimum technical personnel requirements. Their main limitations are slower execution time and limited memory size, especially for complex jobs.

Minicomputer applications are classified as stand-alone or network configurations. A stand-alone minicomputer is used as a central system for small business and as a processor in a time sharing and remote job entry (RJE) environment. However, the minicomputer becomes a part of a network when two or more computers are involved. The network may be hierarchical, resource-sharing, communications control, or distributed processing. In distributed processing, network control over information is returned to the data user, permitting more effective autonomous management at the operational level. A drawback of this technique is the potential duplication of data and the loss of control and security over the data.

5. Medium-sized computers surpass small computers in operating speed, memory capacity, and high-speed input-output devices. Most systems can support multiprogramming, language and design versatility, virtual memory, and a management information system. In contrast, large computer systems are the ultimate in speed, flexibility, and system sophistication. A typical system has a storage unit capable of up to 8 million bytes, multiple independent and data communication processors, head per track disk file memory-bank subsystem, and system software for continuous multiprogramming and multiprocessing. Multimode environments constitute the trend of the future: time sharing for financial models or strategic planning, greater system usability, and conversational dialogue between the system and the user when needed.

TERMS TO LEARN

Analog
Digital
Floppy Disc
General-purpose computer
Hybrid
Microcomputer
Microprocessor
Microsecond
Millisecond
Minicomputer
Nanosecond
Picosecond
Random-access memory (RAM)
Read-only memory (ROM)
Scientific computer
Special-purpose computer

REVIEW QUESTIONS

1. Describe in your own words the difference between:
   a. general-purpose and special-purpose computers,
   b. analog and digital computers,
   c. microcomputers and minicomputers, and
   d. business and scientific computers.

2. Is a computer network used by a motel chain such as Holiday Inn a general-purpose or a special-purpose computer? Explain how such a system operates.

3. If you were asked to list four major characteristics of a microprocessor, what would you say?

4. Summarize the makeup of a microprocessor.

5. Think for a moment of the needs of small business for computerized information. List and briefly explain three applications which can be handled by a microcomputer.

6. What is consumer computing? Describe an application that the personal computer might aid the consumer in personal problem solving.

7. Compare and contrast the similarities and differences between mini- and microcomputers.

8. If you were to list five major characteristics of a minicomputer, what would they be?

9. What does small business look for in a stand-alone minicomputer? Explain.

10. In your own words, distinguish the difference between:
    a. hierarchical network and resource sharing network and
    b. star network and ring distributed network.

11. What is distributed processing? Summarize its key advantages and drawbacks.

12. In what way does a medium-size computer support a management information system?

13. Describe briefly the major features of a large-scale computer system. Illustrate one application that can be a candidate for such a system.

14. Based on the material in the text, what distinguishes a "super" computer from a large-scale computer?

part two

Internal Makeup and Structure of a Computer System

chapter 5

Main Memory and Data Representation

Learning Objectives

Without main memory, computation is not possible. Now that you know what a computer can do and the various categories of computers, the next step is to examine the types of computer memory, along with how data and programs are represented in main memory. By the end of this chapter, you should know:

1. the types of main memory,

2. how advanced memory systems function,

3. why core memory is losing ground to more advanced memories, and

4. how data is represented in memory.

Main Versus Secondary Memory

A computer system, regardless of its size, can be programmed to serve a useful function. It executes program instructions and acts on data stored in its main memory. Knowing the types of computer memory and how data is represented in memory are concepts that are helpful to programmers and systems analysts. They provide a framework within which programming languages and input-output operations can be discussed later in the text.

A *memory device* is any unit capable of retaining data until it is needed. Most computers have two types of memory: main and secondary. *Main memory,* a part of the CPU, holds data upon which the computer executes instructions. *Secondary memory,* a supplement to main memory, is generally used to store large data files needed for processing applications.

To illustrate the difference between main and secondary memory, let's examine the merchandising activities in retailing. Goods are ordered in quantities for a specified period. Seasonal price drops or price discounts for quantities over a minimum limit (say, 100 units) often induce the retailer to order in bulk. A common procedure is to stock the shelves on the sales floor and store the rest of the merchandise in the stockroom. Consider the storage area on the sales floor as the main storage (memory), while the stockroom represents secondary storage. As merchandise on the sales floor is sold, the salesperson calls for the transfer of additional units from the stockroom to meet customer demand. Maximum efficiency is realized when the merchandise is directly accessible for immediate turnover.

Like the retail store, the central processing unit must have direct access to certain data in main memory before performing any processing. Data is transferred from secondary and main storage through an input device, in the same manner that the salesperson on the sales floor receives merchandise via the stockroom as it is needed. The "stockroom" of the central processing unit can be an on-line device (such as a magnetic disc) that provides direct access to selected records; or it can be an *off-line* device (such as a punched card), where records are stored in sequential order for processing. The average time the computer requires to locate or to recall data from memory is called **the average access time.** Average access time is less for data in main memory than for data in secondary memory, because data in main memory is already within the computer.

In determining the computer's main and secondary storage requirements, the manager of the computer center should take into consideration such performance as speed (throughput), storage capacity, and data accessibility. If the processing speed, dependent on the company's requirements, is critical, main memory must be large enough to accommodate the programs and all vital data. Storage capacity should also meet the company's present and future needs. Many fourth generation computers offer over 4 million bytes of main memory. On-line secondary storage devices with much greater storage capacity are also available. Finally, data can be accessed by either a batch—sequential or an on-line solidus/direct-access method. In the final analysis, the manager must operate through a main memory that offers the most economical performance per unit of capacity.

Mass storage devices, such as optical and magnetic bubble memory, offer the type of performance very close to that of present-day main memories. Full-scale availability of such high-density, low-cost devices means that large data files can be stored and accessed as though they are stored in main memory. These and other devices are described later in this chapter.

Main Memory

The efficiency with which a computer performs calculations depends largely on the performance of its main memory. Three types of memory devices dominate today's computer: magnetic core, semiconductor, and bubble memory. They have the following characteristics:

1. Immediate Access to Stored Data. For arithmetic and logic operations, access time to data stored in main memory should be as close to zero as possible. Some processors access data in nanoseconds. Secondary direct-access devices (such as the magnetic disk) obtain stored data in microseconds.

2. Reusability. A main memory device permits the user to erase unneeded data and store new data in its place. In one respect, it is similar to a tape recorder, which erases previous data every time a new recording is made on the same tape. Most main memory devices have this characteristic.

3. Permanent Recording of Data Already in Storage. The computer's main memory unit is designed to retain stored data in the event of system breakdown. Loss of data should occur only at the command of the programmer or the console operator. Most main memory devices used in commercial computers retain data permanently.

4. Automatic of Self-Checking Ability. To verify the accuracy of the data in memory, a main memory device has an automatic self-checking feature, called a **parity check.** To make this check, the system counts the number of bits representing data in memory. The destruction or loss of a single bit is signaled on the console. The operator then evaluates the nature of the error and determines its location by manipulating certain switches. Many computers have special programs that handle such diagnostics.

5. Durability. Unlike punched cards, which wear out in time, main memory devices are built to last permanently in spite of repetitive use. Replacing or frequently repairing a main memory device would be inconvenient and costly.

6. Compact Size. Because space is always at a premium, a main memory device should be physically small, yet capable of storing a large volume of data.

Magnetic Core Memory

Each of the vacuum tubes in a first generation main memory represented only one bit of information. Their bulky size and storage limitations more or less necessitated the development of more compact memory, magnetic core, for second and third generation computers. Magnetic core memory was developed in the early 1950s by Dr. Jay Forrester of MIT who later sold the patent to IBM. This type of memory became the standard for second and third generation computers.[1] During the sixties and early seventies, core memory proved to be fast, reliable, and economical. Core memory has lost ground to other technologies.

A **magnetic core** is a tiny doughnut-shaped ring about the size of a grain of salt. Molded from ferromagnetic material, these cores are strung like beads in a matrix on intersecting wires to form a core plane. Magnetic cores can be polarized in one of two directions: on or off. Thus each core can represent either of the binary digits 0 and 1. Core planes are then stacked to form a core memory. As shown in Figure 5–1, cores in the same location in adjacent planes are used to represent numeric or alphabetic characters.

Addressing main memory. For the computer to access data, memory is divided into a specific number of areas called "locations." Each location is identified by a number called an **address.** For example, the address structure of a memory unit having 4,096 locations may be numbered sequentially from 0000 to 4095.

The assignment of the addresses is analogous to a coat checkroom. In a checkroom consisting of several racks, each rack is assigned a number (address). The number is printed on a ticket that is handed to the coat owner. Without this system of identification, the coat-check person would have difficulty retrieving the proper coat to its owner. Like the coat room structure, computer memory is referenced by its address, which remains unchanged and independent of the data it represents.

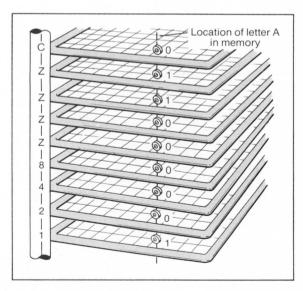

Figure 5–1. Representation of the letter "A" in memory.

[1]*Datamation* (March, 1976), pp. 161–164.

In magnetic core memory, core bits from each core plane are combined to represent a character (Figure 5–1). Such a structure is geared to individually addressable (*variable* word length) computers. Other computer memories have addresses designed to represent a fixed number of characters (or a word); this type of memory is found in *fixed* word length computers. Thus the amount of data represented by a given address depends on whether the computer uses a variable or fixed word length.

In a *fixed word length* computer, the number of characters making up a word is fixed in length, and the word is handled as a unit. Each word contains as many characters as *every* other word. For example, the numeric characters in Figure 5–2 make up two 8-character words. The first word is referenced by one address (1425), and the second word by another address (1426). The size of a computer word depends on the computer's design: It may range from 16 bits in minicomputers up to 60 bits in large systems.

In a *variable word length* computer, the size or number of characters making up a word is not limited. Each character is individually addressable; that is, each has a specific address. The character may be accessed or processed with other characters through proper programming instructions (Figure 5–3).

Variable word length computers perform arithmetic serially, one position at a time; fixed-word-length computers compute in parallel, handling any two data words in one cycle regardless of the size of each word. The relatively greater speed of fixed word length computers, however, requires more complex circuitry and a higher cost than variable word length computers.

Many third-generation computers accept fixed and variable words by *byte-addressable*[2] instructions. In a byte-addressable computer, a fixed word is made up of 8-bit bytes and is retrieved by the address of the first byte. Although certain instructions specify half a byte or a double byte, an instruction referencing this address causes the computer to retrieve four consecutive bytes automatically. The variable word length approach is accomplished through an instruction that references the address of the first byte and the number of succeeding bytes in a given word.

Figure 5–2.   Fixed word length memory structure.

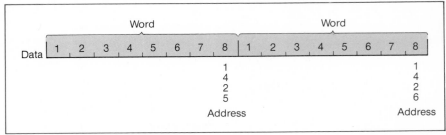

[2]*Byte* is a fixed number of bits (usually 8) representing a character in memory.

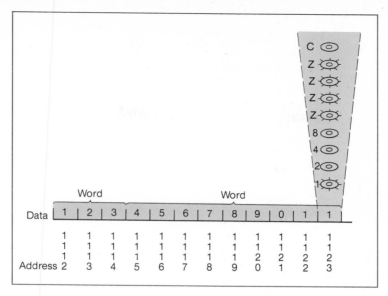

Figure 5–3. Variable word length memory structure.

Semiconductor Memory

As the internal speeds of processors increased from micro- to nano- to picoseconds, the access speed of main memory devices also had to improve at an equal pace. Semiconductor memory began to appear in fourth generation computer systems.

The semiconductor memory market continues to grow rapidly at the expense of core memory. Core memory is being phased out in all computer design, so that from 1980 on very little core memory will be in production. Hence, the "mating" of the processor with semiconductor memory. Today, semiconductors reflect the dominant memory technology in the computer industry.

A *semiconductor* is a microscopic, two-state electronic component used to form a computer's main memory. Thousands of these components are formed on a tiny silicon chip only a quarter of an inch square and quite flat. Most mass produced integrated circuits today consist of more than 3,000 components; the most advanced circuits contain upwards of 10,000 components! Semiconductor memory circuits are called *monolithic,* because the memory components are totally integrated on a single chip (Figure 5–4). Some of the primary advantages of semiconductor memory are:

1. low power usage (less than 0.02 watts), which means minimal heat dissipation,

2. high storage capacity and a reduction in the storage unit's physical size, and

3. increased memory access speed — less than 90 nanoseconds.

The main drawback of semiconductor memory is its "volatility." Unlike magnetic core memory, which retains the data with power failure, semiconductor memory loses the stored data when electric power is terminated. Core memory is considered nonvolatile, while semiconductors are volatile.

Another drawback is cost. However, recent mass production techniques have brought production costs down to a level that is competitive with that of magnetic core memory. For this reason, the high-density metal oxide semiconductor (MOS) has become the dominant type of computers' main memories.

What is a **chip?**[3] Under a microscope, it resembles an aerial view of a railroad switching yard. Made mostly of silicon (the second most abundant element on earth), the chip is cheap, easy to produce, fast, and extremely versatile. Approximately 250 chips are made from one razor-thin wafer of silicon 3 inches in diameter; a wafer is sliced from cylinders of 99.9 percent pure silicon. The wafer is first baked in a cylindrical oven filled with extremely hot oxygen (about 2,000° F), containing steam to prevent short-circuiting. Then it is imprinted with circuitry, baked again, and coated with an aluminum conductor. Finally, a computerized probe scans the wafer for defective circuitry. The good ones are then externally wired, sealed in plastic, and shipped off to the user.

The silicon can be either electrically conducting or nonconducting, depending on the impurities added to it. Thus, an area of a chip can be "doped" with impurities to give it a deficiency of electrons (electrically positive particles), while an adjacent area gets a surplus of electrons to create a negative zone. The positive zone can be used to represent a 1-bit, while the negative zone represents a 0-bit. The varying statuses of the positive and negative bits are used for data representation as the "doughnuts" were in magnetic core.

Advanced Memory Systems

Advances in memory technology over the past decades have resulted in steady decline in the prices of memory. As shown in Figure 5–4, the memory price in 1964 was $2 per byte. The price dropped to $1 in 1969 and to $.09 in 1979 — or 4 percent of the price in 1964. A leading vendor predicts the price to plunge to less than 2 cents per byte by 1985.

In pursuit of this trend, significant research was carried out in the 1970s to develop cheaper and more efficient memory devices. Memory techniques are underway that will respond to the picosecond speed of modern computers. Among such devices are the magnetic bubble, charge-coupled devices, laser, photodigital, and holographic memories.

Bubble Memory

In electronics, induced resistance to an electric current increases with increased wiring. The thousands of wires needed to interconnect the active logic components in core memories limit the maximum speed that can be achieved by

[3]For detailed coverage of the "miracle chip," refer to "The Computer Society," Time (February 20, 1978), pp. 44–45.

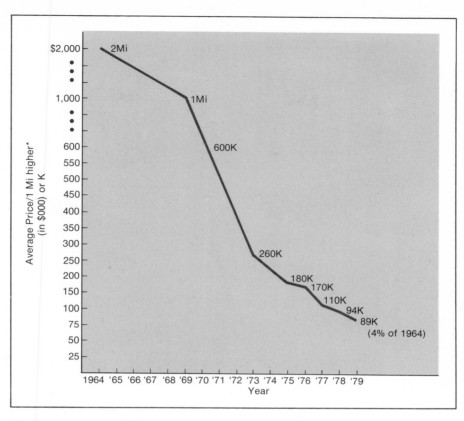

Figure 5–4. Declining memory prices.

the computer's electronic circuitry. Magnetic bubble memory is a revolutionary alternative to core memory. Since *no* wires are used, bubble memory would be easier to produce and miniaturize. It thus offers hope for greater reliability and longer life.

Bell Laboratories and IBM have been working on the application of magnetic bubble material in computer memories. Bell researchers have developed a method for growing a crystal substrate for the bubble; IBM has developed noncrystalline or amorphous materials and a way of sensing the bubbles. The new sensors are tiny strips of magnetoresistive material—the magnetization changes when a magnetic bubble is nearby. The presence of a bubble is transformed into an electrical signal compatible with the computer's electronic circuitry.

The bubbles (each measuring 3–5 microns[4] in diameter) are negatively magnetized cylindrical islands in a positively magnetized film made of amorphous material. They are formed on a garnet wafer by applying an external magnetic force. As shown in Figure 5–5, the wafer looks like a sandwich consist-

[4]A *micron* is 1/25,000 in.

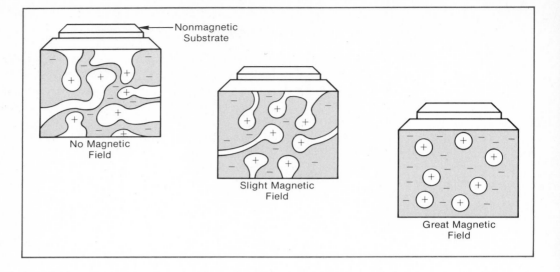

Figure 5–5. The magnetic bubble.

ing of a thin magnetic film garnet grown on a nonmagnetic substrate. In the absence of an external magnetic field, the magnetic film contains regions that can be magnetized in one of two directions: plus (or a 1-bit) or minus (0-bit). When an external field is applied, the magnetic regions magnetized in the opposite direction shrink until they form circular cylinders. When viewed from the top, they look like bubbles; hence, the term **magnetic bubbles.**[5] The appearance of a bubble represents a binary 1-bit, and its absence represents a binary 0-bit. The number of bubbles that can be created or erased in a given microscopic area is the "yardstick" for measuring computer storage beyond today's computer memories.

Among the attributes of bubble memory are:

1. an error rate of less than 1 in 100 trillion bits and the capacity to retain stored data for 100 years;

2. nonvolatility, which assures the retention of data during power loss;

3. nondestructive readout;

4. a 100-fold improvement in access time;

5. the capacity to operate at any speed for any length of time (virtually maintenance free) and to reverse the direction of data flow when necessary; and

[5]*Computerworld* (May 22, 1978), p. 75.

6. low operating costs, since very little electric power is needed to induce the magnetic field in manipulating the bubbles.

The value of bubble memory lies in add-on memory and high-volume data handling. It will allow manufacturers to put more storage into the computer itself and to eliminate the electromechanical devices that cause so many problems. An obvious use in data storage would be to replace the established storage media, such as the magnetic disc or tape.

The first commercial device to incorporate bubble memory was a portable data terminal developed by Texas Instruments. It contains up to 80,000 bytes of memory and weighs less than 17 pounds. The memory can access any index record in less than 15 milliseconds—more than 10 times as fast as the floppy disc. The "flubble" memory—a combination of the terms "floppy" and "bubble"—is a floppy disc drive whose entire track is stored in bubble memory. Such a combination would improve the total performance of data access and retrieval. (Floppy disc and other secondary storage devices are discussed in Chapter 9.)

The key to successful bubble memories is very high density. IBM scientists have been able to experimentally make magnetic bubbles one-eighth time the diameter of today's commercial bubbles. They demonstrated that a bubble as small as 0.4 micron in diameter can be formed. A square inch garnet with 3-micron bubbles can store 3 million bits of data. The same size garnet with 0.4-micron bubbles may be capable of storing 100 million bits of data. As the number of bubbles on a chip increases, the cost per bit on that chip decreases. Obviously, bubble memory could drive the cost of data storage for information processing to all-time lows.

Charge-Coupled Devices (CCD)

A **charge-coupled device** is a slower form of semicoductor memory. It employs the charges in a silicon crystal to store data. CCDs are completely electronic and very compact. Compared to bubble memory, they have similar density, but they are somewhat faster. Their main drawback, however, is *volatility* of storage; that is, the stored data is lost when the electric power is off.

The Josephson Circuit

Exploratory memory research conducted by IBM is based on a theory developed by a British graduate student named Brian Josephson. He theorized that at temperatures close to absolute zero (−459° F), an electric current can tunnel through barriers that would otherwise restrain it. Depending on the presence or absence of a small magnetic field, electrons would cross from one side of the barrier to another, requiring an infinitesimally small amount of current. Circuitry could be more tightly packed than even the magnetic bubble. By the 1980s scientists envision tiny computers refrigerated inside tanks of liquid helium, capable of processing data a hundred times as fast as today's computers.

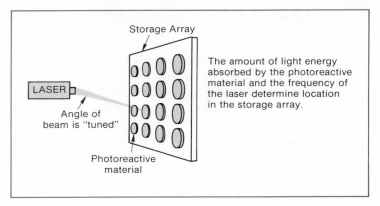

Figure 5-6. Tunable dye laser memory.

Tunable Dye Laser Memory

A major breakthrough in optical memory research is a technique for increasing the amount of data that can be packed into a given space. In this storage system, a bit is identified by its location in the laser frequency spectrum and in two- or three-dimensional space. Thousands of frequency-coded bits could be stored in a single, microscopically small space, measuring 1/25,000 of an inch, which is the diffraction limit of a laser beam. As shown in Figure 5-6, the direction of a laser beam pointed at an array of tiny blocks of photoreactive material can be varied for selecting the spatial addresses (or locations) of the blocks. Varying the frequency of the laser light also makes it possible to address different groups of molecules within each block.

Photodigital Memory

This memory technique employs an electron beam to record binary data on small film chips. The film is then developed by an internal automated "film laboratory," transported in plastic cells through a series of pneumatic tubes, and filed for future retrieval. However, the data is permanently recorded, which means that the chips cannot be reused.

Holographic Memory

The holographic memory system uses a special high-resolution photographic plate encased in a heat-sensitive plastic. A laser beam first passes through two electronically controlled crystals that are designed to deflect the beam in proportion to the frequency of sound waves also passing through them.

The deflected beam then strikes one of many different holograms (optical interference patterns) in a flat array called a *hololens*. The hololens splits the beam so that one part passes through, while the other part is made to fall on a flat plane composed of liquid crystal cells. The cells are tiny areas that can be made reflective (dark) or transparent (light). The cells introduce digital information into the laser beam in the forms of tiny dark areas and tiny light areas, which correspond to 1-bits or 0-bits of the binary code and which represent the data to be written into memory.

Data Representation

The 6-Bit Code

The next logical question is how data is represented in memory. To begin with, an internal coding scheme is developed so that each character (alphabetic, numerical, or special) is represented by a combination of 0- and 1-bit sets. The number of 0- and 1-bit combinations in a set is determined by raising 2 to an exponent equal to the number of 0 and 1 bits in the set. For example, a 3-bit set has 8 different 0 and 1 combinations; the "8" is the result of raising 2 to the power 3 ($2^3=8$). A 4-bit set (called **binary-coded decimal** or **BCD**) has 16 (2^4) different 0 and 1 combinations.[6] To represent 56 alphanumeric characters, then at least a 6-bit set (2^6) is required (Table 5–1).

The 6-bit coding scheme consists of the BCD (8 4 2 1) for representing numerical, or special) is represented by a combination of 0- and 1-bit sets. The bits to encode alphabetic and special characters. Any part of the 6-bit set that is not a 1-bit is set to 0.

Table 5–1. 6-bit coded data representation.

Examples		Zone bits		BCD 4-bit				Positional values — Binary digits (bits)
		B	A	(2^3) 8	(2^2) 4	(2^1) 2	(2^0) 1	
5		0	0	0	1	0	1	$(1 \times 4) + (1 \times 1) = 5$
9		0	0	1	0	0	1	$(1 \times 8) + (1 \times 1) = 9$
7		0	0	0	1	1	1	$(1 \times 4) + (1 \times 2) + (1 \times 1) = 7$
A		1	1	0	0	0	1	Zone bits 11 for coding letters A–I; digit bit 1 represents first letter (A)
.								
K		1	0	0	0	1	0	Zone bits 10 for coding letters J–R; digit bits 10 represent second letter (K)
.								
Z		0	1	1	0	0	1	Zone bits 01 for coding letters S–Z; digit bits 1001 represent last letter (Z)

[6]A 4-bit set is used in encoding each of the 16 hexadecimal (base 16) characters.

The 8-Bit Code

The 8-bit coding scheme, called a **byte,** allows the computer to handle up to 256 (2^8) characters. It forms binary-coded hexadecimals (base 16). The **hexadecimal** numbering system uses base 16 (positional values), unlike base 10 of the decimal system or base 2 of the binary system. Since the decimal system provides only 10 digits to represent the first 10 values of the hexadecimal system (0 to 9), the remaining six values in the hexadecimal system are represented by the letters A-F, respectively. As shown in Table 5–2, the hexadecimal set consists of 0, 1-9, and A-F. In this sequence, the letter A represents a decimal value of 10; B, a decimal value of 11; and so on to F which represents a decimal value of 15. Note that when the hexadecimal number exceeds 16, there is a carry to the next significant position. For example, in the hexadecimal notation 1F, 1 assumes a positional value of 16, just as it would assume a value of 10 in the decimal system. In effect, then, 1F equals 31 in decimal, or 15 (or F) + 16 (or the positional value of hex 1). In another example, 18 in hexadecimal equals 16 (the positional value of 1) plus 8 (the value of the first digit), or 24 in decimal.

Binary-coded hexadecimal (Table 5–3) simplifies the conversion routine for arithmetic operations. In problems involving only numeric digits, the 8-bit byte can be divided into two 4-bit (BCD) sets; the byte then packs two decimal digits and represents a hexadecimal digit in binary form (Table 5–3, Example 1). However, for encoding alphanumeric data, one 4-bit set codes the numeric digits, and the other 4-bit set codes the zone digits. In Example 2 of Table 5–3, the 8-bit byte represents a special character (%), but when it is handled as two 4-bit sets, it represents hexadecimal digits 6 and C in binary-coded form.

Table 5–2. Decimal, hexadecimal, and binary-coded hexadecimal equivalents.

Decimal digit	Hexadecimal digit	Binary-coded hexadecimal
0	0	0000
1	1	0001
2	2	0010
3	3	0011
4	4	0100
5	5	0101
6	6	0110
7	7	0111
8	8	1000
9	9	1001
10	A	1010
11	B	1011
12	C	1100
13	D	1101
14	E	1110
15	F	1111

Table 5–3. Special character byte representation.

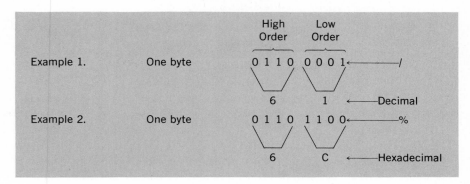

EBCDIC. A widely used 8-bit (byte) code in most modern computers is the **Extended Binary-coded Decimal Interchange (EBCDIC)**. Each byte of storage represents one character. As shown earlier, since 8 bits can be used to represent up to 256 characters, the EBCDIC coding scheme adequately represents the upper- and lower-case letters of the alphabet, 10 decimal digits, and many special characters. Table 5–4 shows the EBCDIC code and its hexadecimal equivalents. For example, the name J I M can be stored in a 5-byte (hex) code as follows:

$$D1 \ C9 \ D4 \ 40 \ 40 \quad \text{(Hex 40 represents a blank)}$$

Likewise, the decimal value 5432 can be represented in a 5-byte numeric EBCDIC field as:

$$F0 \ F5 \ F4 \ F3 \ F2$$

Note that an alphanumeric field is normally left-justified (aligned on the left), while a numeric field is right-justified.

Table 5–4. The EBCDIC code (for digits and uppercase letters) and the hexadecimal code.

Character	EBCDIC Zone Bits	Digit Bits	Hexadecimal Code	Character	EBCDIC Zone Bits	Digit Bits	Hexadecimal Code
A	1100	0001	C1	J	1101	0001	D1
B	1100	0010	C2	K	1101	0010	D2
C	1100	0011	C3	L	1101	0011	D3
D	1100	0100	C4	M	1101	0100	D4
E	1100	0101	C5	N	1101	0101	D5
F	1100	0110	C6	O	1101	0110	D6
G	1100	0111	C7	P	1101	0111	D7
H	1100	1000	C8	Q	1101	1000	D8
I	1100	1001	C9	R	1101	1001	D9

Table 5—4.   (cont.)

Character	EBCDIC Zone Bits	Digit Bits	Hexadecimal Code	Character	EBCDIC Zone Bits	Digit Bits	Hexadecimal Code
S	1110	0010	E2	0	1111	0000	F0
T	1110	0011	E3	1	1111	0001	F1
U	1110	0100	E4	2	1111	0010	F2
V	1110	0101	E5	3	1111	0011	F3
W	1110	0110	E6	4	1111	0100	F4
X	1110	0111	E7	5	1111	0101	F5
Y	1110	1000	E8	6	1111	0110	F6
Z	1110	1001	E9	7	1111	0111	F7
				8	1111	1000	F8
				9	1111	1001	F9

Representing numbers in EBCDIC is often referred to as **zoned decimal** form. The sign of a zones decimal value is coded by using the zone portion (or zone bits) of the byte (see Table 5–3). The number is positive if the zone portion of the byte is 1111 (hex F) or 1100 (hex C). The number is negative if the zone portion of the byte is 1101 or hex D. For example,

+ 5432 may be represented as: F5 F4 F3 C2
− 5432 may be represented as: F5 F4 F3 D2

Packed decimal.   As mentioned earlier, the 8-bit (byte) format offers the advantage of packing two decimal digits into each byte, since a decimal digit can be represented by a 4-bit code. In contrast to zoned decimal, the **packed decimal** format is designed to reduce storage requirements for decimal data. The leftmost 4 bits are used to represent the decimal digit and the right-most 4 bits are used for decimal digit or for sign designation. For example, −1234 is stored in 3 bytes as follows:

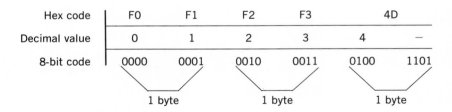

Parity check.   One of the interesting features of a computer is its ability to check the accuracy of the data represented in memory. The **parity check** performs this task. To do the job, a *check bit* (also called a *parity bit*) is added to each byte. For example, a 6-bit code takes 7 bits, and an 8-bit byte totals 9 bits. The error control mechanism counts the number of 1 bits representing a character and adds a check bit to the sum to make the total odd or *even*, depending on the computer design. For example, in computers specifying *odd parity*, the check bit is turned on (it is a 1-bit), when the total number of 1-bits representing a character is even. In *even parity,* the check bit is on when the total number of 1 bits is odd (Table 5–5).

Table 5—5. Examples of odd and even parity.

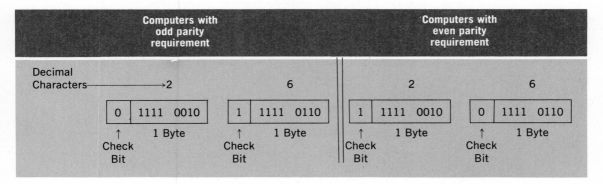

If a bit has been lost (or added) during processing, some computers turn on an error light and stop automatically. Other computers signal the operator for instructions regarding the error(s). Some computers have an automatic error-correcting device to correct the error without delay. In any event, the parity check function remains a crucial aspect of the computer to provide the accurate processing and transmission of stored data.

Data Structure and Organization

A *data structure* is an organized framework for storing data in memory. The data may represent any items that are related to one another. For data to be handled efficiently, it must be organized. There are four major levels of data organization: data items, data records, data files, and data bases.

1. Data items. One or more bytes are combined into a *data item* which describes some attribute of an object. For example, if the object is an employee, a data item may describe the employee's name, sex, age, or other characterisitc.

2. Data records. Data items relating to a common object are combined into a **record** for that object. For example, if the object is a business student, items such as the student's name, year in college, major, and advisor's name form the record for the student. Each record is identified by an identifier or a record key. The student's social security number could be an identifier for grade processing purposes.

Record designs are differentiated into logical and physical types. A *logical* record is a unit of related data items or fields that the computer program expects to manipulate. For example, an inventory record for the computer program is a unit that includes such data as "item code," "transaction code," or "number of units sold." In contrast, a *physical* record is a unit of one or more logical records handled by the system as a single entity. Either type of record may be fixed or variable in length. In general, processing fixed length is easier than processing variable length records. However, the potential savings in storage space through the variable-length records may more than make up for the difficulties of processing them.

3. Data files.   A data **file** (also called a data **set**) is a collection of logical records, spatially arranged for a particular pupose. It represents accumulated information available for processing. Each record must have an identifier (a key), which uniquely identifies the record. For example, a person's social security number is often used as a record key for a payroll file. Details relating to the types of files, file organization, and file maintenance are covered in a later chapter.

Figure 5–7.   A personnel information system.

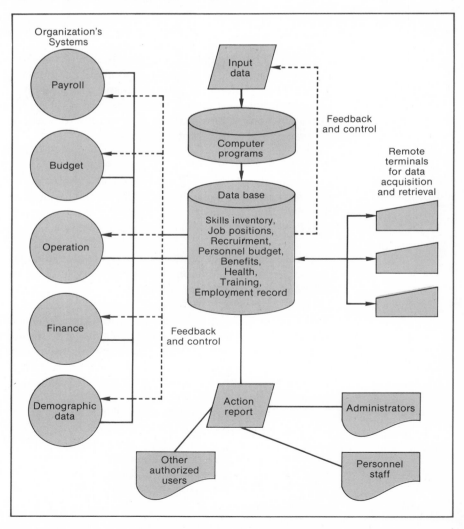

4. Data base.   The highest level in the data organization hierarchy, the **data base** is a "superfile" which consolidates and integrates data records formerly stored in several separate files. It is developed to improve the handling of files and to minimize data redundancy (duplication). *Nonredundant data* refers to information common to several data records, stored only once. For example, a personnel information system is designed with a single source of input data processed through a cluster of computer programs. As shown in Figure 5 – 7, the data base is established to include all data needs and to meet all the legal and other report requirements of the organization. Other organizational systems are linked to the personnel information system for information requisition and feedback.

Instruction Formats for Data Processing

Data must be structured and organized in memory for efficient data processing. A computer processes data by executing stored program instructions. An *instruction* specifies the operation to be performed, along with the address and lengths of the data to be operated on. The instruction may be two, four, or six bytes in length. Take, for example, the instruction format of an IBM 370 computer in Figure 5 – 8. The first byte specified in a unique code the operation to be performed. The second byte specifies the number of storage positions to be moved. The remaining four bytes represent two data addresses; they specify the location of each of the fields involved in the operation. Thus, if the length factor is binary 10, then 11 bytes of stored data beginning with Address 2 are moved to the 11 bytes specified by Address 1.

In an operational sense, a 2-byte address consists of two elements: The first half-byte has a **base address,** and the remaining one and a half bytes have the displacement factor. In an IBM 370 system, for example, binary bits 16-19 represent a general-purpose register (storage device) used as a base register.

Figure 5–8.   A general 6-byte instruction format.

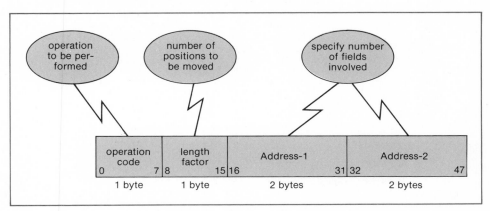

The actual address is derived by adding the address stored in the base register to the displacement factor. As shown in Figure 5–9, D2 is the hex code for the operation to be performed. Letter L is a code for the number of storage positions to be moved. B1 and B2 are each a half-byte address located in the general-purpose register. D1 and D2 are one and a half bytes each, representing a displacement factor.

To illustrate the use of the above instruction, a MOVE instruction requiring bytes 1410-1415 to be moved to 1450-1455 is represented in coded instruction format as:

Coded Format ⟶
Op. Code	L	B1	D1	B2	D2
D2	05	2	3AA	2	382

Instruction:

D2 is the operation code for moving data from one location to another. Hex 05 represents the 6 bytes to be moved. Address A-1 (B1) consists of register 2, which contains the base address plus a replacement factor of hex 3AA (or 938 in decimal). Likewise, address-2 consists of register 2, which has the base address plus a displacement factor of hex 382 (of 898 in decimal). For the actual movement of the data from one location to another, the base address (register 2) has to represent hex 200 (decimal 512). Thus, 512 is added to 938 in order to arrive at address 1 (or 1450). The same value (512) is also added to 898 to arrive at address 2 (1410). This form of decoding is performed with each instruction execution.

Figure 5–9. A coded version of a 6-byte MOVE instruction format in an IBM 370 computer.

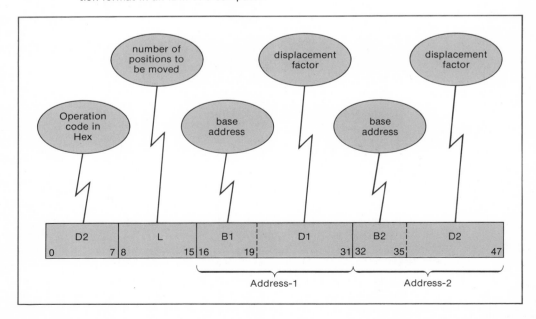

If this sort of instruction sounds complicated, it should not worry the newcomer. Programming in *machine language,* as this is called, is generally regarded as impractical. Instruction format and decoding are complex and extremely tedious. This brief exercise merely points out the desirability of learning symbolic languages in high-level languages such as Basic or Cobol. A chapter on each of these languages comes later in the text.

In addition to data movement instructions, the computer is capable of executing three other groups of instructions:

1. **Input-output (I/O)** instructions are generally executed by a **supervisor program,** which is a program designed to monitor the sequence and frequency of executing input or output instructions. An I/O operation prompts the supervisor to execute the appropriate instructions by *channels.* (Channels and overlapped processing are covered later in the chapter.)

2. **Arithmetic instructions** involve two data fields, with the result replacing one of the fields. For example, in an ADD instruction, the data in field 2 is added to the data in field-1. The sum replaces the contents of field 1. The same process applies to subtraction, multiplication, and division.

3. A *logical instruction* requires an evaluation of the fields involved on a collating sequence. Special characters, such as an ampersand, are treated as numerically less than alphabetic characters which, in turn, are valued less than decimal digits. Based on this rule, an ampersand (*) would be interpreted as less than letter A, and A is evaluated as less than 9.

Channels and Data Movement

For useful output, a computer system's components and peripherals must work together in a compatible and efficient manner. Today's computers execute instructions at nanosecond speed, but since most input and output devices are largely electromechanical, they still operate at slow speeds. The difference in operating speeds causes the CPU to be idle much of the time, waiting for the input and output devices to do their work. There is no compatibility, for instance, between a computer executing an instruction in 10 microseconds and a card reader reading data in 75 milliseconds, 7,500 times as slow.

"Overlapping" eases the delay between CPU and peripherals. Since the mid-1960s, most digital computers have had built-in features that overlap input and processing, input and output, or processing and output operations — to maximize the efficient use of the computer system. These features are referred to as **overlapped processing.**

Channels also facilitate the movement of data between relatively slow input devices and the high-speed central processor or between the central processor and output devices. A channel's main function is to accommodate the flow of information into and out of the central processor's main memory. This flow takes place over a data path or through a port in the CPU. A signal from the central processor allows the channel to operate independently of the processing routine of the CPU. When the peripheral's job is completed, the channel signals the CPU through an **interrupt** signal to indicate the completion of the input-output operation.

A channel may be a physically separate unit (linked to the CPU) or a part of the CPU accessible to input-output devices for independent action. A computer system that accommodates a number of I/O devices or terminals requires the use of an appropriate number of channels for efficient operation. Figure 5-10 shows the general relationship between data channels and the key input-output media and devices. (These devices will be covered in the next two chapters.)

Overlapped Processing

Overlapped processing can increase the CPU's efficiency (throughput) by overlapping input-output and processing operations. In earlier computers, **serial processing** performed a read-compute-print cycle in series, that is, one operation after another. As shown in Figure 5-11, the input, CPU, and output devices are idle for much of the time necessary to run a job. The system would be "input-output bound" if the CPU had to wait for the input-output devices to perform their tasks. On the other hand, it would be "process-bound" if the input-output devices had to wait for the CPU to perform its computational and other activities. Obviously, an input-compute-output cycle performed by serial processing is inefficient.

Today's computers are capable of performing **overlapped processing** (Figure 5-11). The total time for handling a transaction is reduced to the time it takes to handle the longest operation (that is, input, processing, or output). The total time in the overlapped processing of the three operations is therefore shorter than in their serial processing. As shown in the figure, nine time slices are used up in serially reading, processing, and printing (or writing) three records. In contrast, an overlapped system reads, processes, and writes seven records within the same time frame. Although the illustration assumes a fixed time interval for each processing phase, it serves to emphasize the obvious benefits of overlapped over nonoverlapped processing.

Channels and buffers play an important role in overlapped processing. Channels receive instruction signals (called *channel commands*) from the central processor to execute the I/O instructions, while the CPU executes the arithmetic, logic, and data movement instructions. I/O devices respond to the signals independently of the current operation of the CPU. While the CPU is processing, one channel may be controlling an input function, while another channel governs an output operation.

Buffers are high-speed units found as a part of the CPU or in some input-output devices. Input buffer storage accepts data from a relatively slow input device and releases the data at electronic speed. Output buffer storage receives information from the CPU at electronic speed and releases it at the slower speed of the output device. Channels control the data transfer between input-output devices and their respective buffer storage.

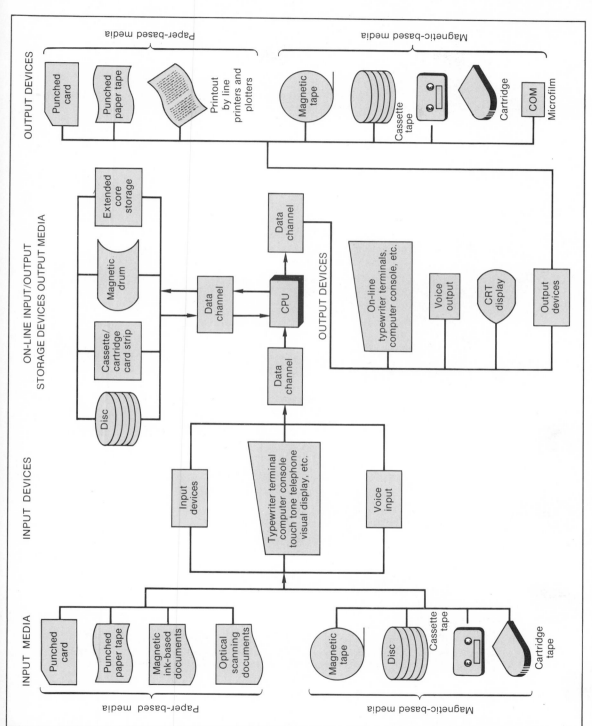

Figure 5–10. The use of channels in input-output CPU operations.

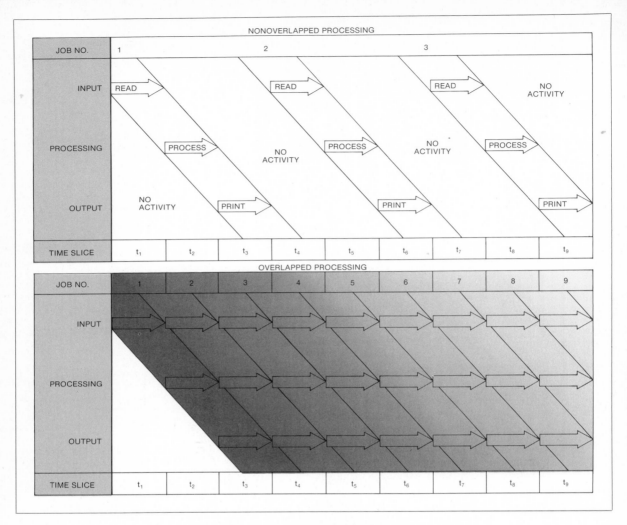

Figure 5–11. Serial (nonoverlapped) and overlapped processing.

Types of Channels

A channel, like a CPU, executes one operation at a time. In effect, the number of overlapped operations is limited by the number of channels available to the system. For example, a 1-channel system can overlap one I/O operation with the CPU for processing. Likewise, a 4-channel system can overlap 4 I/O operations with CPU processing. Channels that are active with only one I/O device at a time are called **selector channels.** The other two types of channels are "byte multiplexor" and "block multiplexor" channels.

A **byte multiplexor** channel is logically connected to several I/O devices at the same time, but it is electronically connected to a specific device only while that device is transmitting or receiving data. It is usually connected to low-speed

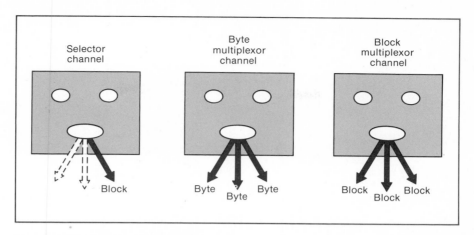

Figure 5–12. Primary types of data channels.

devices because a single high-speed channel can handle the activities of several low-speed devices. It handles only one byte at a time from each of the devices. In contrast, a **block multiplexor** channel accepts blocks (rather than bytes) of data and performs similar tasks as the byte multiplexor channel (Figure 5 – 12).

In Figure 5 – 13, a typical tape system consists of four tape drives and three slow-speed I/O devices — a console typewriter, a card reader/punch, and a line printer. A multiplexor channel is capable of receiving one byte (or block) from the card reader, sending one byte to the card punch and/or line printer, and then receiving another byte from the card reader — and so on. The ability to switch from one I/O device to another permits overlapping among these devices. The selector channel links only one of the four tape drives to the CPU at a time. So reading from one tape drive and writing on another cannot be overlapped with a single selector channel. Most computer system configurations consist of one multiplexor channel to overlap the slow-speed I/O operations and one or more selector channels for handling the tape (or disc) operations.

The switching of I/O operations and other routines associated with overlapped processing are all handled by the all-important **supervisor program.** This software item is available in main memory prior to actual computer processing. It initiates all I/O commands and manipulates the actual switching of I/O operations required for overlapped processing. The program remains in memory until all programs are executed.

Multiprogramming in Data Processing

Most computer programs are I/O-bound by one device or another. To make better use of the total system when it is running I/O- or process-bound programs, **multiprogramming** permits two or more programs to share the CPU in a time-interlaced manner. Thus it eliminates slack in processing. Some programs require substantial I/O time, but relatively limited processing time; others

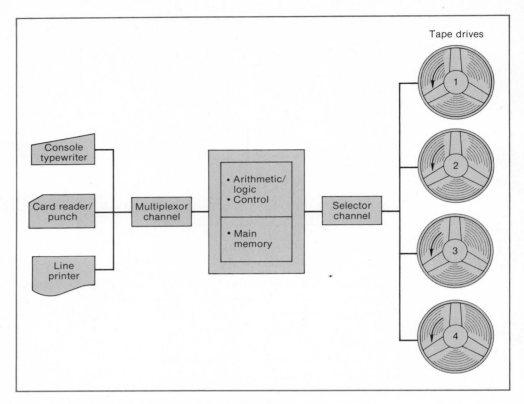

Figure 5–13. A representative tape system.

require little I/O time but considerable processing time. If both types of programs are seen simultaneously, their respective slack times complement each other. Both the CPU and its existing I/O devices are used—for two programs at the same time—as much as possible.

In multiprogramming systems, a supervisor program controls the central processor's switching from one program to another. It also makes sure that each processing phase is fully executed and handled in proper order. For example, after a particular phase of the first program has been acted upon and is being handled by a I/O device (such as the printer), the supervisor program releases one or more instructions of the second program for processing. When the I/O device sends an **interrupt** signal indicating the completion of its part of the first program, the supervisor reverts to the first program, releases more instructions for processing, activates the proper I/O device, and then resumes the second and eventually other programs in a similar manner.

The overall objective of multiprogramming, then, is to accommodate as many programs as possible with a minimum of wasted computer time. If enough programs are available in memory and if enough I/O devices are overlapped, CPU utilization can come close to 100 percent utilization. Although a computer system with extra channels, a large-size memory, and a supervisor program runs up a major initial cost, the total performance can well justify the investment. By minimizing CPU and I/O idle time, the EDP department can generate more informational output per dollar invested than in the case of a program-at-a-time system. The impact of multiprogramming is so profound that it is today's mode of information processing in most medium-sized and large-scale systems.

SUMMARY

1. A memory device is any unit capable of retaining data until it is needed. Main memory is part of the CPU that provides immediate access to stored data and the permanent recording of data already in memory. A self-checking feature ensures that stored data is always accurate.

2. Main memory may be magnetic core, semiconductor, or bubble memory. Semiconductor technology has already taken over magnetic core, which consists of a stack of core planes polarized to represent numeric or alphabetic characters. Data is identified by an address. The amount of data an address represents depends on whether the computer in question is a variable or a fixed word length computer.

3. A semiconductor is a microscopic, two-state electronic component. Thousands of these components are integrated on a tiny silicon chip only a quarter-inch square. It uses low power, has high storage capacity, is easy to produce, and has proved extremely versatile. Recent mass production techniques have brought production cost to a competitive level with that of core memory.

4. Magnetic bubbles are negatively magnetized cylindrical islands in a positively magnetized film made of amorphous material. The number of bubbles that can be created in a given area provides a basis for developing computer storage beyond today's computer memories. Among its attributes are an error-free rate, nonvolatility, nondestructive readout, and a one hundred-fold improvement in access time. Other advanced memory systems are IBM's Josephson circuit, tunable dye laser memory, photodigital memory, and holographic memory. The use of laser in main memory structure is now a reality.

5. Data is represented in memory by an internal coding scheme based on a combination of 0- and 1-bit sets. A basic 4-bit coding scheme represents numeric characters, while a 6-bit scheme is coded so that it represents alphabetic as well as numeric characters. Today, most data is represented by an 8-bit or a byte representation, which can be divided into two 4-bit

sets to pack 2 decimal digits. A widely used form of 8-bit code is EBCDIC, which is adequate to represent the upper- and lower-case letters of the alphabet, numeric, and special characters.

6. One or more bytes are combined into a data item that describes some attribute. Data items are combined into a record for a given object. A collection of logical records, spatially arranged for a particular purpose, form a data file. Data files, in turn, are organized into a data base for quick data access and retrieval.

7. Data is processed through program instructions. An instruction may be a MOVE, arithmetic, I/O, or logic instruction. It specifies the operation to be performed, along with the address and lengths of the data to be operated on. Learning to program in machine language is impractical, because instruction format and decoding are complex and tedious. The alternative is learning high-level languages such as Basic and Cobol.

8. Data movement between I/O devices and the CPU is facilitated through channels. A signal from the CPU allows the channel to operate independently of the processing routine of the CPU. Channels and buffers play an important role in overlapped processing. They execute I/O instructions, while the CPU executes the arithmetic, logic, and data movement instructions. Selector channels are active with only one I/O devices at a time, while multiplexor channels are logically connected to several I/O devices at the same time for maximum performance. The entire switching of I/O operations associated with overlapped processing are handled by a supervisor program, which remains in memory until all programs are executed.

TERMS TO LEARN

Average access time
Address
Base address
Binary-coded decimal (BCD)
Byte
Channel
Chip
Data Base
EBCDIC
File
Hexadecimal
Interrupt
Magnetic bubble
Magnetic core

Multiplexor channel
Multiprogramming
Overlapped processing
Packed decimal
Parity check
Record
Selector channel
Serial processing
Supervisor program
Zoned decimal

REVIEW QUESTIONS

1. What is main memory? Can a computer perform basic arithmetic without one? Why?

2. Distinguish the difference between:
   a. off-line and on-line devices,
   b. main and secondary storage,
   c. fixed and variable word-length computers,
   d. bit and byte,
   e. binary and hexadecimal system, and
   f. data file and data base.

3. What are the major characteristics of today's computer memory devices?

4. What are semiconductor memory circuits? Summarize their major advantages. Do they have any drawbacks?

5. How does a silicon chip store data?

6. What are the main attributes of bubble memory? How do you see the future use of this technology in large computer systems?

7. In three sentences or less, describe the features of the following memory devices:
   a. charge-coupled devices,
   b. the Josephson circuit,
   c. tunable dye laser memory, and
   d. holographic memory.

8. Illustrate the difference between:
   a. The 6-bit code and the 8-bit code,
   b. The 8-bit code and binary-coded hexadecimal,
   c. Zoned decimal and packed decimal,
   d. Data records and data files, and
   e. Byte multiplexor and block multiplexor.

9. Add the following hexadecimal numbers. Show the sum in hexadecimal:
   a. F + B
   b. 9 + D
   c. 1F + A
   d. A2 + 2B

10. Assume an even parity check system of data representation. Determine the presence of a parity check in each of the following:
    a. 1111 0111
    b. 1111 0001
    c. 1110 0111
    d. 1101 0111

11. What is a data base? Choose an application or an area in business where data base can be used to develop a management information system.

12. What groups of instructions is a computer capable of executing? Explain briefly each group.

13. How are channels used in input/output operations.

14. Evaluate the effect of overlapped processing on throughput.

15. How does multiprogramming improve the total handling of user demands? Explain.

chapter 6

Basic
Input and Output

Learning Objectives

Once you've learned the internal structure of the computer, the next logical step is to determine how input data is prepared and entered into the computer for processing. You also need to know what input and output devices are available for computer processing. By the end of this chapter, you should know:

1. the steps in the input-output cycle,

2. the key features of card input data preparation and recording,

3. how an 80-column card differs from a 96-card format, and

4. the makeup of computer output microfilm and computer micrographics.

How is input data prepared and entered into the computer for processing? Although the use of the computer is the trend in information processing, most small and minicomputer systems are card-oriented. They accept input data via the punched card and the card reader. Over 200,000 keypunch machines are still in operation. As an off-line data preparation device, the keypunch is expected to continue for sometime. In contrast, medium-sized and large-scale computer centers, have installed direct data-entry and preparation devices to replace the keypunch and the verifier. This chapter focuses on card-input data preparation and basic input-output devices.

The Input-Output Cycle

The central processing unit cannot function alone. Its performance depends largely on the design and capabilities of the input and output devices. *Input* devices transfer machine-readable data from input media to the CPU for processing. *Output* devices write processed information (output) for the user on request. Thus, to produce meaningful information, a computer system requires compatible input-output devices. These devices are manipulated by a control unit that decodes instructions from the CPU and activates a specific input output device. A channel connects the control unit to the CPU for on-line functioning. The sequence of steps for input entry is as follows:

1. The computer executes a program instruction to read a record held in an input device.
2. The control unit receives a signal to initiate the operation of the input device.
3. The input device reads the record. The record is converted into electrical pulses or signals.
4. The signals are checked by the control unit.
5. A data channel facilitates the transmission of data signals into memory for processing.
6. The CPU is activated to begin operation on the data received.

The six-step cycle also applies for output entry. If the output must be produced immediately, it is converted into "human" language by an output device called the line printer. On the other hand, if it is to be stored for future processing, it is stored in output media such as punched cards, magnetic tape, or magnetic disc.

Each type of computer has its own machine language and utilizes different input and output devices. Examining various devices will demonstrate the importance of system compatibility; it will also show the relevance of the "garbage-in"/"garbage-out" principle. The primary input-output devices, sometimes referred to as **peripheral equipment,** Table 6 – 1 and illustrated in Figure 6 – 1. The term "peripheral" means that although these devices are a part of the computer system, they are often located nearby.

Table 6–1 Key input/output media and devices.

I/O Device	Purpose	Medium Used	Typical I/O Speed Range	Storage Capacity and Characteristics	Nature of Use
Card read-punch	Input and output of transcribed data on 80-column or 96-column cards	Punched card	160–2,700 (I) cpm; 80–650 (O) cpm	80 or 96 columns per card; bulky	Low-volume applications in medium to small computer systems and turnaround documents-source data
Magnetic tape reader	High-speed I/O of large volume sequential files	Magnetic tape	15,000–1,250,000 cps	Up to 160 million characters per tape; compact and easy to transport	High-volume; batch processing applications such as payroll, receivables, inventory
Magnetic disc drive	Storage and high-speed I/O of large random access files	Magnetic disk	100,000–1,000,000	Up to $200 million characters per disc pack; almost unlimited storage for off-line storage; disc packs are portable, easy to transport	High volume, random access processing applications
Magnetic drum storage unit	Storage and high-speed I/O of data	Magnetic drum	230,000–3,000,000	Up to 200 million characters of storage; bulky and not mobile	
Line printer (output only)	Print out relatively low-volume output on paper	Special paper	200–18,000 lines per minute	High-speed printout function either serially or in parallel	For all applications requiring informational output for management reports or formal documentation of processed results
Card/strip storage unit	Input and output storage	Card/strip cartridge	25,000–50,000	Up to 150 million characters per on-line card/ strip cartridge	
Optical character reader	Source data automation direct reading of printed data from documents	Special paper	70–2,400		
CRT display	Keyboard entry of input data and inquiries, visual display of output on crt device	Cathode-ray tube	250–10,000		On-line inquiries and file updating; ideal in reservation and time-sharing systems

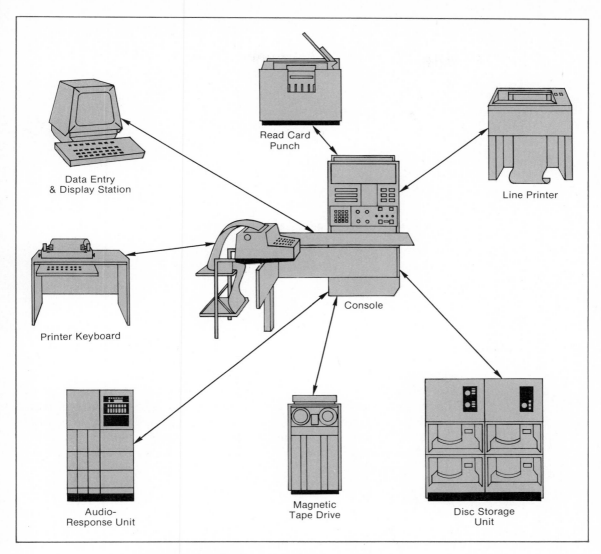

Figure 6—1. The CPU and peripheral devices.

Labels in figure:
Read Card Punch
Data Entry & Display Station
Line Printer
Printer Keyboard
Console
Audio-Response Unit
Magnetic Tape Drive
Disc Storage Unit

Card Input Data Preparation

The 80-Column Card

People who have not come into contact with punched cards are rare or nonexistent. These cards are used extensively for paychecks, time cards, soap coupons, gas credit cards, utility bills, Mastercharge or Visa, and even tickets on turnpikes. High schools, colleges, and universities use them as class admission cards. Most smaller-sized computers rely on punched cards for receiving input data or computer instructions for processing.

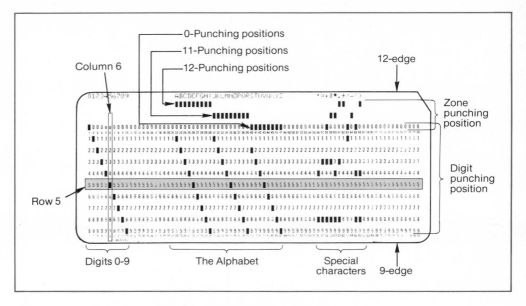

Figure 6–2. Punching positions of an 80-column card.

The *80-column card* is a rectangular pasteboard of high-quality paper designed to resist contraction or expansion caused by temperature or humidity. It is divided into 80 vertical spaces called **columns.** The columns are numbered (left to right) from 1 to 80. In each column, one or more holes can be punched to represent a letter, a digit, or a special character, for a maximum of 80 characters (Figure 6–2). For example, punching employee number 40875 in a card requires five consecutive columns. If we decided to reserve the first five columns for the employee number, digit 4 would be punched in column 1, digit 0 in column 2, and so on to digit 5 in column 5.

Besides showing all the characters punched in the 80-column Hollerith code, Figure 6–2 also shows two punching positions. The *zone punching position* consists of the 12, 11 (also called X row), and 0 rows, respectively. The *digit punching positions* are in the 0 through 9 rows. The 0 punch, then, is both a zone punch and a digit punch.

Data representation.   Data is recorded by key punching according to a coded arrangement of rectangular punched holes in 80-column cards. Once data has been punched, the card becomes a permanently stored reference, as well as a medium of communication between the user and the computer.

Numeric characters are recorded by punching *one hole* in a column for each character. In Table 6–2, digits 0 through 9 are punched in columns 1 to 10, respectively. In contrast, alphabetic characters require *two holes* in a column for each character. One hole must be in the *zone* punching position and the other in the *digit* punching position. For example, the combination of a 12-punch and a 1-punch represents the letter A, and the combination of an 11-

Table 6–2. Coding letters A–Z—with examples.

Letter	Zone	Digit
A	12	1
B	12	2
.	.	.
.	.	.
.	.	.
I	12	9
J	11	1
K	11	2
.	.	.
.	.	.
.	.	.
R	11	9
S	0	2
T	0	3
.	.	.
.	.	.
.	.	.
Z	0	9

punch and a 2-punch represents the letter K. Table 6–2 summarizes the coding scheme for the alphabet. The code is built into present-day keypunches. All a user must do is depress the proper keys on the keyboard, and the rectangular holes appear on the card as described.

The punched card is a **unit record;** that is, the data related to *one transaction* is recorded on each card. Each unit record, or card, can also be merged with other cards containing different information for calculating or summarizing data. Figure 6–3 illustrates how a particular invoice involves six transactions. One of the transactions, the one for the 50-watt amplifier, is used to demonstrate how each transaction is entered on a separate card. For this invoice, six such cards are required. Each transaction must be punched on a card in the same manner as for the one involving the 50-watt amplifier.

Card layout requirements.   The cards must be of a predetermined format so that each type of information occupies the same position on all cards. If the customer's number occupies columns 1 to 5, for example, it must always be punched in that location. The area should not be used for any other data. Standardizing the location of all data in a card is as important as standardizing the signature location to the bottom right side of a check or the location of a postage stamp on the upper right corner of an envelope. This standardization leads us to the concept of "field."

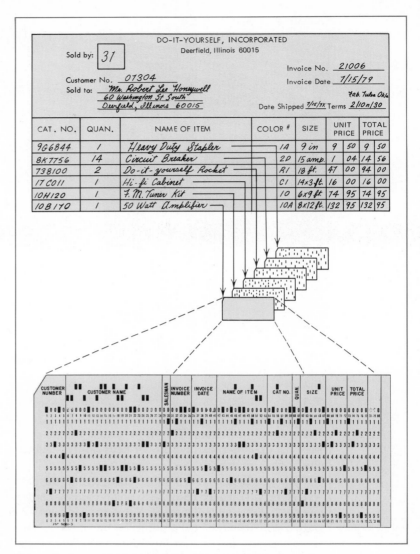

Figure 6–3. A partial invoice — the unit-record principle.

Each transaction contains certain details called *units of information*. A **field** is a group of consecutive card columns reserved for a specific unit of information. The length of the field is determined by the maximum anticipated length of the unit of information. The minimum length of a field is one column; the maximum is the size of the card, or 80 columns. In Figure 6–4, the punched card shows 11 fields which represent 11 units of information about the last transaction.

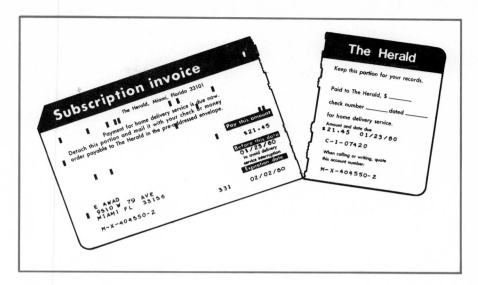

Figure 6–4. Stub card.

Identifying marks. A card may be identified by format, color, corner cut, horizontal color stripes, or control field. The *format* shows how the various fields are arranged on a card and distinguishes the card from others entered for computer processing. Similarly, a computer center uses different colored cards for various applications. For example, green cards may indicate payroll data, while brown cards may represent the transactions in a billing application.

A *control field* aids in locating and rearranging a group of cards that have previously been merged with other groups of cards for processing. You occasionally, hear of "X punch in column 80" or "X punch in column 27." The X punch is a distinctive code to extract the "coded" cards from a merged deck for processing.

Punched cards are still used in several key applications. Stub cards are specially adapted to situations in which the stubs substitute for a receipt (Figure 6–4). Utility billings, for example, use **stub cards.** Most bills (water, gas, mortgage payment) have a perforated card that may be torn off, leaving a 51-column card to be mailed back with the payment. The stub (a 29-column section with duplicate data) is retained by the customer. Banks have made wide use of this type of card for loan payments. The number of prepunched cards represents the installments a borrower agrees to pay. The set of cards is stapled on the left stub edge in booklet form.

Mark-sense cards have been traditionally used in reproducing small quantities of numeric data. In public utility data collection, the meter reader records the gas or electric meter reading with an electrographic pencil in designated locations on the face of the card. The card is later read by a special reader for processing the customer's billing.

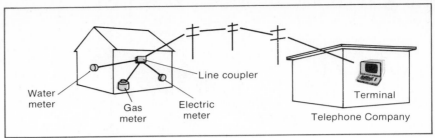

Figure 6–5. Schematic of a typical AMR system.

Today, automatic meter reading (AMR) is being installed in various sections of the country. This system requires no meter readers. Instead, prepunched cards containing the telephone number, the utility's accounting number, and a special "identity" for each customer's home are placed in one or more card readers. As shown in Figure 6–5, the code plus the last four digits in each subscriber's telephone number are transmitted through the regular telephone line. The meter reading binary data is converted to digital data and transferred to punched cards for use in utility billing.

The 96-Column Card

A unique departure from the 80-column card, the 96-column card was designed to meet the card-oriented computer systems for small business. Slightly larger than a standard wallet-sized credit card, the 96-column card holds 20 percent more data than the 80-column card. It provides greater efficiency in data storage and handling, having space for both punching and printing. Its coded data is also easily manipulated and converted by the computer for processing. The 96-column card permits the simultaneous punching and verifying of data, thus eliminating clerical errors caused by transcription.

Figure 6–6 shows a blank 96-column card with two areas: the print area and the punch area. In the *print area* are reserved four print lines to help the user read what is punched in the card. The first three print lines are numbered from 1 to 96, and 96 alphabetic characters can be printed to correspond with the 96 columns in the punch area. The fourth print line, numbered 97 to 128, does not correspond to any punched area, but may also be used for printing. The *punch area* is divided into three 32-column tiers. Since each column can be punched to represent one character, a maximum of 96 characters can be punched on the card.

Data representation. A character is coded in a card column by a fixed combination of round holes. Each tier has a 6-bit BCD format to represent any of the 32 possible characters. As indicated in Figure 6–6, the two topmost punch positions, B and A, constitute the zone punch portion, and the remaining four punch positions (8, 4, 2, and 1) represent the digit punch portion. In processing punched data, the computer distinguishes one character from another by the coded punch combinations.

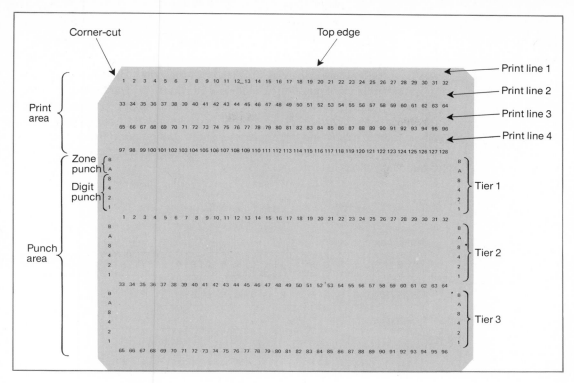

Figure 6-6. 96-column card

To code a numeric, the appropriate position or combination of positions in the digit portion of a column is punched; the punched positions add up to the desired digit. For example, digit 8 consists of a single hole in the 8 digit position; 7 consists of one hole in each of the 4, 2, and 1 digit positions. Table 6-3 shows the combinations of punches necessary for all the digits, 0 through 9.

Table 6-3. Numeric coding - the 96-column card.

| | | | \multicolumn{10}{c}{Numeric characters} |
Punch positions			0	1	2	3	4	5	6	7	8	9
	Zone	B										
		A	A									
	Digit	8									8	8
		4					4	4	4	4		
		2			2	2			2	2		
		1		1		1		1		1		1

Alphabetic and special character coding combines the zone and digit punch positions for each character. Refer right now to Table 6–4. The first 9 letters (A through I) are coded by holes in both the A and B positions, plus the appropriate hole configuration for digits 1 through 9. The second 9 letters (J through R) are coded by a hole in only row B and the appropriate hole configuration for digits 1 through 9. The remaining 8 letters (S through Z) are coded by a hole in only row A and the appropriate hole configuration for digits 2 (for letter S) through 9. Special characters are coded by various other combinations of the 6 punch positions in a column.

Table 6–4. Alphabetic and special-character coding—the 96-column card.

Alphabetic characters

Punch positions			A	B	C	D	E	F	G	H	I	J	K	L	M	N	O	P	Q	R	S	T	U	V	W	X	Y	Z
	Zone	B	B	B	B	B	B	B	B	B	B	B	B	B	B	B	B	B	B	B								
		A	A	A	A	A	A	A	A	A	A										A	A	A	A	A	A	A	A
	Digit	8								8	8								8	8							8	8
		4				4	4	4	4						4	4	4	4					4	4	4	4		
		2		2	2			2	2				2	2			2	2			2	2			2	2		
		1	1		1		1		1		1	1		1		1		1		1		1		1		1		1

Special characters

Punch positions			}	¢	.	<	(	+	|	!	$	*	)	;		-	/	&	,	%	—	>	?	:	#	@	'	=	"	b
	Zone	B	B	B	B	B	B	B	B	B	B	B	B	B	B	B														
		A	A	A	A	A	A	A	A												A	A	A	A	A	A	A			
	Digit	8		8	8	8	8	8	8	8	8	8	8	8	8	8		8	8	8	8	8	8	8	8	8	8	8	8	8
		4				4	4	4	4				4	4	4	4		4	4	4	4					4	4	4	4	
		2		2	2			2	2	2	2			2	2			2	2	2	2				2	2	2	2		2	2
		1			1		1		1		1		1		1		1		1		1		1		1		1		1	

As with the 80-column card, items of information are recorded in the 96-column card in groups of consecutive columns called fields. A **field** may vary in size from 1 to 96 columns, depending on the amount of data to be included in each group. When deciding on the length of a given field, make allowance for future expansion by punching present field data in the right-most columns. Any unused columns should be filled with zeros. Card layout forms are often helpful in planning the length and sequence of the fields related to the project under consideration.

Advantages and Limitations of Punch Card-Oriented Processing

Advantages.   The punched card in computer processing provides standardization of data for efficient handling. Although it stores only 80 to 96 characters, each character may be a code for the computer to perform a specific function. Other advantages include its ease of storage and assembly, its ease of reassembly for different applications, and its low cost (about one-tenth of a cent per card). It is also widely used as a communication medium (a turnaround document) for voting, opinion surveys, and consumer billing. It serves both as a source document and a data recording medium.

Limitations.   The primary limitation of the punched card is its physical make-up. It may not be folded, spindled, mutilated, or stapled at all, because any changes in the quality of the surface can jam the card reader. Its size is a further limitation: Only 80 characters can be stored per card. Finally, the requirement that data has to be punched in specified fields limits the number of characters that can be stored. In applications that involve thousands of customer accounts, this rigid standardization of data location results in much waste.

The value of the punched card has frequently been a subject of discussion. Yet card output in the form of turnaround documents (particularly invoice) is gaining in popularity. Computer-punched documents permit convenient, economical input with minimal need for rekeying and human handling. Its increased use of punched cards is based on economic and human-oriented considerations. As long as customers are invoiced by mail, the punched card is likely to remain a useful medium. Furthermore, applications using minicomputers and data terminals are likely to find the 96-column card a dominant form of card input. An overview of the functions and operations of the keypunch is available in the appendix.

Card Input and Output

Card Reader

Input.   The card reader, one of the more common input devices used in small-to medium-sized systems, is designed to read punched data and transfer it directly to the CPU for processing. Once it is read, each card drops into its respective stacker for later handling (Figure 6–7). The two types of punched card readers are the brush type and the photoelectric type. Figure 6–8 shows a *brush-type* punched card reader that reads one card at a time. A stack of cards is first placed into the read hopper. The first card in sequence passes underneath the first set of 80 brushes, called the *read-check* station (Figure 6–7). The brushes take a *hole count* to keep track of the number of holes in the card. The same card moves underneath the next set of 80 read brushes, which direct the data electrically into the central processing unit. The card then drops into the stacker. The second and all succeeding cards go through the same procedure in sequence, until the whole card file is read. The *photoelectric-type* card reader uses 80 pho-

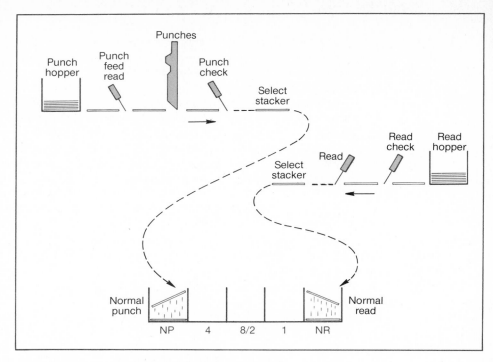

Figure 6–7. "Read" and "punch" schematic of brush-type reader. *Courtesy IBM*

Figure 6–8. Brush-type reader/punch. *Courtesy IBM*

toelectric cells rather than brushes to read the data in cards. Figure 6–9 presents a card reader that reads cards *serially* (column by column) by a light-sensing unit and that is capable of detecting invalid, off-punched, and mispositioned codes.

Output.   The left side of the reader (Figure 6–9) is used for punching output information from the CPU onto blank cards stacked in the punch hopper. A blank card moves automatically under the dies, and the output is punched. The punched card then moves under a set of 80 brushes, which check the accuracy of the dies. If they are correct, the card is ejected into the radial stacker below it. Otherwise, the machine stops, indicating an error.

Figure 6–9.   *Courtesy IBM*

Paper Tape Reader

A paper tape reader provides direct input to a computer by reading data prepunched on paper tape. It also provides output from a computer by punching output information onto the same medium. Paper tape systems are commonly used in applications where information is received over wire communication circuits and in scientific applications involving limited input and output. Many paper tape readers, punches, and combination devices are available. Some manufacturers also offer paper-to-magnetic tape converters (Figure 6–10). Although still comparatively less popular than other input-output media, paper tape is now being used more effectively than in the past.

Machines record on paper tape by punching data received by a direct connection to a typewriter or a keypunch. Other machines may then transmit the data punched into the paper tape over telephone or telegraph lines in order to produce a duplicate tape at the other end of the line, where the duplicate can be used for further processing.

Data stored on paper tape is recorded in patterns of round punched holes located in parallel tracks (channels) along the length of the tape. The number of channels on paper tapes varies; most tapes are either five or eight channels wide (Figure 6–11). A *channel* is an imaginary line that runs parallel to the edge of the tape. From the bottom, the channels are 1, 2, 4, 8, K, 0, and X. A numeric, alphabetic, or special character is represented by one or a combination of holes in a given vertical column.

Advantages. Punched paper tape has the advantage of easy and relatively compact storage. It takes less space for storage than the punched card. Light in weight, it is easier to handle and cheaper to mail. Also, it is more economical to use than punched cards because of the low cost of the tape and the transport units.

Limitations. Compared to more advanced media, however, punched paper tape has limitations:

Figure 6–10. Paper-to-magnetic tape converter. *Courtesy NCR Corp.*

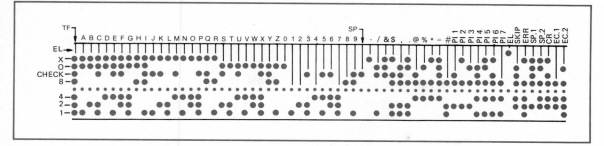

Figure 6–11. 8-channel code paper tape.

1. It is very slow and as impractical as the punched card.

2. The manual punching of coded information allows for considerable possibility of error. Because it is made of paper, tape is more likely to break during processing (giving rise to the expression a "torn-tape system").

3. Paper tape cannot be split apart for sorting, collating, and other related operations as can a set of punched cards.

4. Visual reading of punched paper tape is a problem for the untrained eye, although some machines interpret and print the characters from the paper tape in the same fashion that cards are interpreted.

Output information can be presented in many forms, depending on the output device or the user's requirements. One such device, the printer, is used in business applications to provide a permanent visual record of the information generated by the computer. Computers are designed to print out data in several ways. Some employ character-at-a-time (serial) printing, whereas others use line-at-a-time printing. Printing speeds vary, but printing output is up to 18,000 lines per minute. Normal speed, however, is around 2,500 lines per minute.

Printer Output

Character-at-a-Time (Impact) Printers

Typewriter. The electric typewriter is the simplest means of serial printing. It can be used either as a remote terminal or as a monitor printer when linked on-line to a computer console. It also allows the user to communicate with the computer: Through the typewriter, the user can "interrupt" the computer to disclose the balance of a specific account, to insert missing or new operating instructions into the stored program, to reset the system when an error condition causes the computer to halt, and to instruct the console to select different input-output devices. The usefulness of the typewriter as an on-line device, then, lies in the fact that the user can notify the computer of these conditions and exceptions (Figure 6–12).

Figure 6–12. An on-line typewriter. *Courtesy IBM*

Matrix printer. In the matrix printer, small wires are arranged in the form of a rectangle, usually in a 5 by 7 matrix (Figure 6–13). The matrix moves along the line of the paper to print alphabetic, numeric, or special characters. The ends of the selected wires are pressed by a hammer against an inked ribbon, resulting in the printing of the data on paper.

Chain printer. The chain printer is an electromechanical printer that utilizes five sections connected to form a chain. Each section has the capacity to print 48 characters (10 digits, 26 letters, and 12 special characters). See Figure 6–14. Positioned behind the inked ribbon, the chain revolves horizontally. The hammers, upon firing against the back of the paper, cause a character in the chain to press against the ribbon, which results in the printing of that character on the paper.

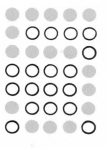

Figure 6–13. *Arrangement of wire-matrix printer—digit 5.*

Figure 6–14. A print chain (left) and a continuous-forms printer. *Courtesy, IBM*

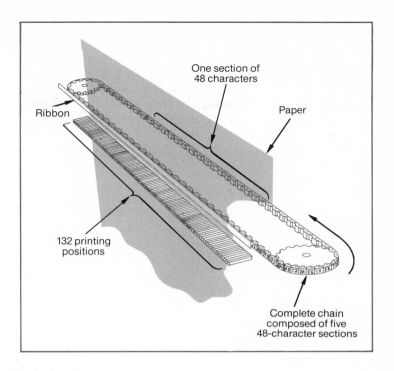

One section of
48 characters

Ribbon

Paper

132 printing
positions

Complete chain
composed of five
48-character sections

Unlike other printers, chain printers offer the features of accuracy and speed. Each line printer has an error-check indicator that stops and signals the operator when the data received from the central processing unit is inaccurately printed. The error indication is also signaled on the computer's console. In terms of speed, many line printers operate at 2,500 or more lines per minute. In other words, 1.5 million pages can be printed on a 3-shift, 600-hour-per-month basis.[1] Output of this scale serves as a warning to management of the obvious waste of a computer's time and effectiveness that occur unless proper planning and justification of computer use are made in advance.

The Nonimpact Page Printer

Although the impact printer still dominates the market, a variety of large, nonimpact page printers have become available. Not only are they an alternative for impact printing, but they also offer better quality, depend less on preprinted forms, and disseminate information throughout an organization with more flexibility.

The first nonimpact printer was introduced by IBM late in 1975. It prints at a top speed of 13,360 lines per minute, using laser and electrophotographic technology. A report required in multiple copies is simply printed the specified number of times. A year later, Honeywell developed an 18,000-line-per-minute page printer that accepts data from computer output tape containing print-image data. The data is processed by a built-in minicomputer. A buffer memory holds 93 lines of 132 characters each, corresponding to a full page of printing. Typical users are companies with print volumes of 500,000 pages per month or more. Some firms are using the system to print 3 million pages per month (Figure 6–15).

Special-Purpose Output Technology

Computer-Output Microfilm (COM)

In this "age of the instant" — jet planes, fast foods, and the computer — the slowest part of a computer system is the line printer. Bypassing this operation and eliminating the need to burst, decollate, bind, label, and distribute reams of printed output means savings in time, supplies, and labor. The mountain of computer printouts to which clerks had to refer in handling customer calls can be reduced, on microfilm, to a size that can be put at a clerk's fingertips. Microfilm also takes some of the load off computer memory and helps break the bottleneck of computer printout through **computer output microfilm (COM)**.

[1] The answer is derived as follows:
Size of paper form = 10 × 14 inches
Number of lines per inch = 6 (or 60 lines per page)
2,500 × 60 = 150,000 lines per hour
$$\frac{150,000}{60} = 2,500 \text{ pages per hour}$$
2,500 × 600 hours = 1,500,000 pages per month

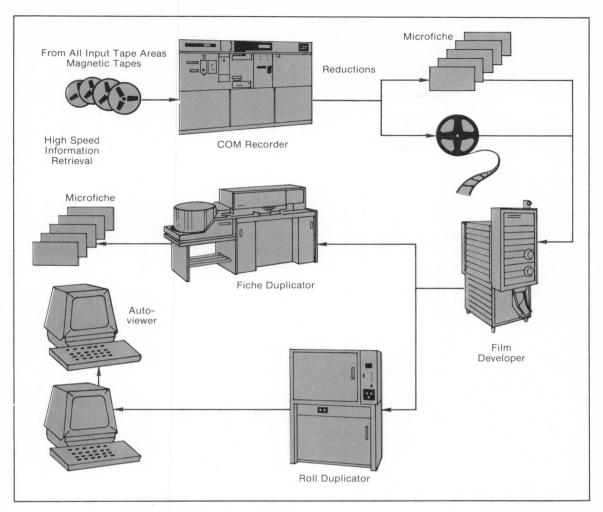

Figure 6–15. COM processing.

The concept of microfilm is not new. It found its first application in the military. When the Prussian Army laid siege to Paris in 1870, a man by the name of Dagron used carrier pigeons to fly microfilmed messages over enemy lines into Paris. The year 1920 marked the beginning of the microfilm industry, when a clerk in a New York city bank developed a device for photographing canceled checks. It gained immediate acceptance. Finally, V-mail during World War II relied on microfilm to handle correspondence to U.S. troops abroad. Letters were first microfilmed to reduce their weight and bulk before they were flown overseas. Upon arrival, they were enlarged to size, printed out, and delivered.

Microfilm allows us to retain necessary records in reduced size and in their correct sequence, protected from loss or accidental destruction. Although microfilm has been widely used in business for decades, the primary use in the past was as a record storage tool. Today, it has evolved into an integral information component, a development attributed to the development of computer output microfilm (COM).

COM brings together the best of two technologies — the computer and microfilm. It converts data generated by the computer and stored data on magnetic tape into human readable characters in microsize on film. It takes digital signals directly from storage on magnetic tape or a computer and converts them on a cathode ray tube (CRT). The CRT image is then reduced, photographed, and translated into 16-mm, 35-mm, or 105-mm microformats (Figure 6–15). The 105-mm rolls are converted into **microfiche.** A microfiche is a $4'' \times 6''$ sheet of film that holds 98 frames of $8\frac{1}{2}'' \times 11''$ pages reduced 24 times.

A COM can operate on-line from the host computer or off-line from magnetic tape drives. On-line COM systems produce data ten times as fast as printing, and they are less costly to run than off-line systems. In selecting a COM system, the user must first decide on (1) the type of microfilm storage (roll film, microfiche, etc.), (2) whether to operate on-line or off-line, and (3) whether to use an in-house or an outside system. Then COM vendors may be contacted for descriptive details and perhaps bids on the system that meets the user's specifications. The system chosen should be evaluated in terms of output quality, hardware integrity, reliability, and price. If an outright purchase cannot be justified, rental arrangements might be negotiated, or a service bureau might be a satisfactory compromise.

Advantages.   For medium- to large-scale data processing, COM offers;

1. *Compact storage.*   Microfilmed computer output occupies 2 percent of the space required for the equivalent paper printout. One hundred pounds of computer printout, for example, can be stored on only 60 microfiche. Through a process, called ultrareduction, the entire Bible can be reduced to a single, inch-square frame of film. The frame is so small, it is laminated to a 2-inch square for easier handling. Microfilm cameras can reduce 3,000, $8\frac{1}{2} \times 11$-inch pages to a film about the size of a 3×5 index card.

2. *Quick access and retrieval of records.*   By simple and inexpensive methods, the average microfilmed record can be retrieved in about one-ninth the time it takes to retrieve the same data on paper. A new system, built for Air Force personnel records, is capable of calling up any of 28 million pages on microfiche in about 15 seconds. A telephone directory service can store up to 120,000 directory pages on ultrafiche in a compact viewer and access any page within three seconds.

3. *Ease of distribution.*   Because microfiche is compact and light, cost and distribution time are much less than paper reports.

4. *Lower consumables costs.*   Because film costs less than paper, the cost of consumables for COM is 80 percent less than for an impact printer.

5. **Unlimited number of report copies.** The line printer can only make six copies from a single computer run. In contrast, a microfiche duplicating system can produce unlimited copies.

6. **Fast and simple reproduction.** COM eliminates the peripheral chores of bursting, decollating, and binding, replacing them with film-to-film duplication. The quality of the original is retained in all copies.

7. **Labor-saving.** Airlines, railroads, and some large rent-a-car agencies employ a microfilm retrieval system at their computerized reservation centers. They store thousands of pages of information on various tours, daily and special schedules, destinations, and special services. Eastern Airlines' microfilm system, for example, is reported to save over 900 agent-hours of telephone time each day. Through the use of computer-generated indexing, a COM system provides information retrieval nearly as fast as on-line, real-time computer retrieval, at a substantially lower cost.

Limitations. The primary limitations of COM are:

1. Microfilm cannot be read without a viewer. Stored data is not easy to search, and access to COM is limited in many systems.

2. Microfilm is not an acceptable medium for handling turnaround documents such as payroll checks, invoices, or utility bonds. In such cases, paper is a more efficient and economical medium than microfilm.

3. The initial and total costs of a COM system are quite high. They can be justified only in business firms handling high-volume documents on a regular basis.

4. Filming and film developing are new skills that require special training. Many users have experienced problems in training their personnel in the proper operation of a COM system.

5. A COM system is a poor choice for applications that require hard-copy output.

6. Unlike hard-copy output, a microfilm cannot be written on and provides no room for notes, which are often helpful in evaluating output.

System storage and technologies. In a computer system using COM, output information is produced in human-readable form by a microfilm process using a COM recorder. COM storage may be in the form of microfiche,[2] microfilm jackets, ultrafiche, roll film, or aperture cards.

Microfiche is a sheet of film, generally 4×6 inches with 98 frames (images) of $8\frac{1}{2} \times 11$-inch pages reduced 24 times. In EDP operations, it is used in-

---

[2]"Fiche" is derived from the French meaning "card."

stead of pages of printout for computer data. It usually contains a title and other identification, which can be read without magnification.

A *microfilm jacket* is made up of two pieces of clear plastic fused together with a series of ribs to form channels. These channels house individual strips of microfilm, which make it convenient for the user to update portions of a file quickly and at will. Microfilm jackets are ideally used in maintaining and updating personnel, medical, legal, or policy-holder files.

A microfilm becomes an **ultrafiche** when images are reduced more than 90 times, permitting thousands of images to be stored per fiche. When using ultrafiche, literally mountains of data can be reduce to "ant-hill" size. Large retail organizations, such as Sears and Montgomery Ward, use ultrafiche systems for referencing their catalogs or parts books. Banks also use them for recording customer transactions. A reduction ratio of 210:1 makes it possible to store 8,000 images on a 4×6 microfiche.

Roll film is normally a 100-foot reel of 16- or 35-mm film. A 100-foot 16-mm roll can store approximately 3,000 letter-size documents or record over 40,000 bank checks. It may be cut into single frames or into strips for inserting into microfilm jackets. The 35-mm films, widely used in engineering applications, is ideally suited for literary applications in newspapers and publications.

The **aperture card** is a standard 80-column card with a precut rectangular hole for holding a 35-mm microfilm, ideal for filming large engineering documents and drawings. Searching and refiling of an aperture card system may be carried out manually by reading the data on the top of the card (Figure 6–16).

The future of COM.   Compared to the impact printer, COM is gaining acceptance. According to a leading authority, it is threatening to replace everything except the central processor. Recently several improvements in COM technology have been reported. For example, some manufacturers have developed termi-

Figure 6–16.   CRT recording on microfilm.

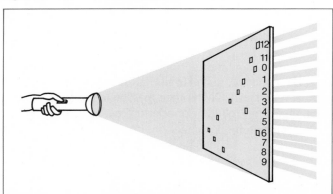

nal-display/microfilm-photography hybrids that permit the user to edit data on film from the terminal. A new concept under development employs a light pen with which the user adds or changes information directly onto microfilm. Some new COM units even produce hard copy from the display screen simply by pushing a button. Finally, research is being done on the possibility of allowing the user to sort or merge directly from microfilm to produce specialized reports.

Computer Micrographics

The tremendous output of the electronic computer has far outstripped the executive's ability to examine and use all the information generated in the day-to-day decision making. This imbalance between "man and machine" has been corrected through the development of computer **micrographics,** a medium that offers a new way of examining and communicating data. Graphics do not replace executives' judgment; they simply allow them to test their judgment that all possible alternatives have been considered before committing themselves to a course of action. Computer graphics is separated into two distinct areas: interactive graphics and plotting.

CRT display. *Interactive* computer graphics, a tool for business decision making, is the construction, retrieval, manipulation, alternation, and analysis of pictorial data using an on-line display console with manual input capability. An executive or manager creates and analyzes graphs relating to business decisions by interacting directly with a computer programmed to produce the information on a CRT screen. He or she portrays on the screen the desired information. Then by using a light pen, new values can be entered into the computer to obtain new graphs, charts, or tables. The response is available in a fraction of a second (Figure 6–17).

Figure 6–17. Interactive computer graphics. This Sanders graphics display rotates images in three dimensions. It also shows images in perspective, makes windows, zooms, maps, and projects images. Control is by either keyboard, "joystick," or many other types of input. *Courtesy: Sanders Associates, Inc.*

Plotters. Graph plotting produces free-form pictorial configurations under the direct control of the computer. A graph plotter consists mainly of a paper-holding drawing board with a mechanical pen suspended over it. When plotting begins, the pen is lowered to the surface of the paper to make various lines in different locations (Figure 6–18). Plotters are used in occupations such as civil engineering, drafting, and dress design. In medicine, they have been successfully used to plot human brains and skeleton with a high degree of accuracy. Much graphic output has also been made in oil, geophysical, and oceanographic applications.

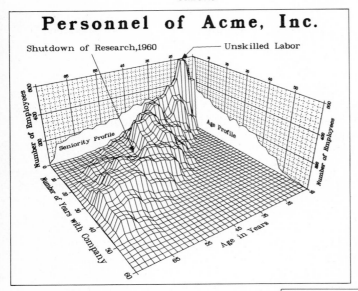

Figure 6–18. A graph plotter, with the proper software, can output sophisticated illustrative detail, as shown here. *Courtesy: Integrated Software Systems Corporation*

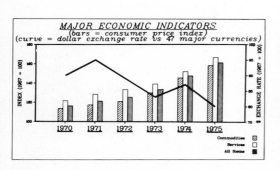

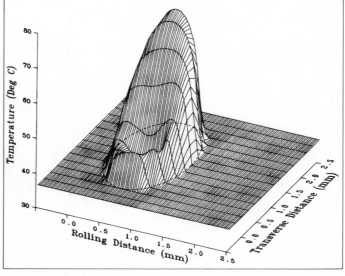

Voice Response

In addition to computer micrographics and COM, voice-response devices have been popular in various industries. Generating the human voice from a prerecorded set of words stored in computer memory, the devices have become common fixtures in such places as brokerage houses, banks, and airline and bus terminals. Their appeal is primarily due to their ability to project immediate output regarding the desired information. Details on these devices are covered in Chapter 10.

SUMMARY

1. The CPU cannot function without input and output devices. The devices are manipulated by a control unit that coordinates the order and frequency of the data flow during processing. The most commonly used media in card-oriented computers are the 80- and 96-column cards. Either type is designed to store in coded form a transaction or a program instruction. The stored data may be alphabetic, numeric, or alphanumeric; but it must be in predetermined format so that each unit of information occupies the same position on all the cards in the deck. Among the types of cards in use are the stub, aperture, and mark-sensed cards.

2. The punched card offers the advantages of data standardization for efficient processing, ease of data storage and assembly, and low-cost storage per unit of information. Among its limitations is its physical make up: It cannot be spindled, folded, or stapled. Its size further limits the amount of data that it can store. Compared to the 80-column card, the 96-column card offers the advantages of easier physical handling, greater information capacity, and the use of simpler and more reliable equipment at lower cost.

3. Each type of card uses a separate keypunch for data recording. The 80-column keypunch has a keyboard for data entry. Automatic keypunching is achieved through a program card that guides the keypunch to do such jobs as skipping, punching, or duplicating data. In contrast, the 96-column data recorder has a buffered input-output area. After all data has been keyed and verified, it is read electronically from the verifier and punched into the card serially.

4. The punched card reader is a popular input device in small- to medium-sized installations. The card punch section of the reader is activated when a program instruction calls for punching output information onto a set of blank cards. A paper tape reader performs a similar function, except for reading punched data in paper tape.

5. Compared to the punched card, paper tape offers the advantages of compact storage and easy handling. It is also cheaper to use and mail than the punched card. Compared to more advanced media, however, paper tape is as slow and as impractical as the punched card. It breaks easily and cannot be visually read by the average operator, when necessary.

6. A line printer is strictly an output device. Impact (character-at-a-time) printers include the console typewriter, matrix, and chain printers. Although impact printers still dominate the market, a variety of nonimpact (page) printers have become available. They offer better quality, less dependence on preprinted forms, and more flexibility in disseminating information throughout the organization. The top printing speed is 18,000 lines per minute. Typical users are companies with printing volumes of 500,000 pages per month or more.

7. A viable approach to combating output bottlenecks is computer output microfilm (COM). It offers the advantages of reduced storage space requirements, quick record retrieval, lower cost of supplies, high recording speed, and unlimited copies of original data with reproduction quality that cannot be matched by the impact printer. However, it is a poor choice for applications that require hard-copy output.

8. COM storage may be microfiche, microfilm jackets, ultrafiche, roll film, or aperture card. In selecting a COM system, a decision has to be made on the type of microfilm storage, whether to operate on-line or off-line, and whether to use an in-house or an outside system. The system chosen should be evaluated in terms of output quality, hardware integrity, reliability, and price.

9. Micrographics, a new way of examining and communicating data, allows executives to ascertain whether all possible alternatives have been considered before committing themselves to a course of action. Computer graphics may be interactive graphics or plotting. Each area serves a unique set of applications and users.

TERMS TO LEARN

Aperture card
Computer output microfilm (COM)
Field
Microfiche
Micrographics

Peripheral equipment
Stub card
Ultrafiche
Unit record

REVIEW QUESTIONS

1. Explain how a computer receives input data for processing.

2. What media are used for input data preparation? Explain briefly the format or procedure used for each medium.

3. Summarize the requirements for an 80-column card layout.

4. How is data represented in a 96-column card?

5. Describe the operation of the card reader.

6. What are the functions, uses, and methods of recording data on punched tape?

7. In your own words, explain the difference between impact and nonimpact printers.

8. In what way does COM bring together the best of the computer and microfilm? Explain.

9. Distinguish between:
   a. microfilm and microfiche,
   b. punched card and aperture card, and
   c. interactive graphics and plotters.

chapter 7

Magnetic Tape
Input and Output

Learning Objectives

Recording data on magnetic tape constitutes a major departure from card input and output. The most common and the oldest of media, computer tape is ideally suited for processing sequential files. This chapter focuses on:

1. magnetic tape characteristics
2. data representation on tape,
3. the primary functions of the tape drive, and
4. processing sorting tape files.

Computers are not designed to store all the transactions and volumes of data in their main memories while performing the processing function. Despite improved access time, the cost of such a massive memory system would be prohibitive. Thus, secondary and mass storage media and devices are essential. Once such medium, magnetic tape, constitutes a major departure from card input and output. In a tape-oriented system, magnetic tape is widely used as secondary storage and as high-speed input-output. In this chapter, we focus on the characteristics and make up of magnetic tape as an alternative input-output medium and on its use in data processing.

Tape Characteristics

The most common and the oldest of all media products is computer tape. A continuous strip of plastic wound on a reel is called the *file reel*. A typical tape reel is a half-inch wide and comes in lengths from 200 to 3,200 feet. A common version is a 2,400-foot roll on a 10.5-inch tape reel (Figure 7–1). Data on tape is read at a typical speed of 320,000 characters per second—the equivalent of 4,000 punched cards. In addition to high speed, a tape's main attribute is its ability to pack thousands of characters on one inch of tape. Since it may be erased and reused reptitively, it is one of the most economical and versatile forms of storage.

Today's computer tape is manufactured to meet rigid specifications. Wide rolls of polyester film are coated with an oxide mixture, which looks like light brown paint. The coated roll is then slit into one-half inch wide tapes, which are then wound into individual reels. The oxide can easily be magnetized, retaining its magnetism indefinitely. Bits of data in the form of magnetic spots are recorded on the oxide side of the tape by the read-write heads of the tape unit. The spots, which are invisible to the human eye, are placed across the width of the tape on parallel tracks running along the entire length of the tape. Each track is assigned a read-write head for recording or writing data.

Magnetic tape is a *sequential* file storage medium. "Sequential" means that the first record written on the medium is read or scanned before the second record, the second before the third, and so forth. Sequential file storage is ideal when regular updating of applications such as accounts receivable is required.

Figure 7–1. A magnetic tape reel.

The computer does not waste time, because it does not have to search for a specific record; each customer's account is in sequential order. In applications that require the reading of records scattered throughout the tape, access is slower, and magnetic tape is impractical.

Advantages

The primary advantages of magnetic tape are:

1. **Compact storage.**   A single reel of tape can store from 1 million to 156 million characters (the equivalent of 1,950,000 cards) depending on tape density, the size of the gaps that separate records, and the length of the tape.

2. **Ease of handling and recording.**   Tapes are less bulky and more convenient to handle than punched cards. Data recording is also easier than cards because each card must be handled separately by the machine or by a human operator.

3. **Flexible record size.**   A record stored on tape can be as long or as short as desired. In contrast, a record stored on cards is limited to 80 characters.

4. **Error correction.**   Errors on tape can be erased and replaced with the correct data. No other data on tape is rewritten or duplicated, as is the case in punched cards.

5. **Cost and speed.**   The packing density of tape makes it a low-cost storage medium. A tape recorded at 1,600 bits per inch could contain as much information as a whole disc pack (explained in the next chapter) and cost as little as 10 percent of what a disc pack costs. At approximately $10 to $15 a reel, tape is what Consumer Reports might call a "best buy" in magnetic media. In terms of speed, tape is the fastest form of input-output medium for sequential file processing.

Limitations

Among the limitations of magnetic tape are:

1. **Tape breakage and handling.**   Because of the high tape recording density, tape breakage inevitably means loss of vital data, regardless of how carefully the tape is spliced. Also, accidental dropping or careless handling of a tape reel often causes nicks or kinks. In time, handling affects the recording or reading quality of the data. A damaged tape is as inferior as a chipped phonograph disc.

2. *Environmental factors.* Magnetic tape is generally vulnerable to extreme temperature change and humidity, which affect its oxide coating and the quality of data recording. New tapes should be acclimatized to the computer room at least 24 hours before use. They should be stored in an environmental range of from 60°F to 80°F and from 20 percent to 80 percent relative humidity. Finally, environmental contaminants resulting from impact printers, smoking, and high-speed rewinding of a tape drive should be controlled for successful tape care and handling.[1]

3. *Access time.* Magnetic tape input-output is ideal for sequential data processing, but it is slow in applications requiring direct access to random records. In this case, direct access devices such as magnetic disc are recommended.

Data Representation

Data is recorded on magnetic tape in seven or nine parallel tracks or channels. The pattern of magnetized spots across the tape is a coded representation of the stored data. The spots are polarized in one of two directions, indicating either a 0-bit or a 1-bit to correspond to the pulse received from the computer. In the *seven-channel code,* the first six tracks across the width of the tape (the bottom six in Figure 7–2) represent one column (frame) of data or a character. The seventh (top) is a parity check bit. As shown in Figure 7–2, a dash stands for the presence of a magnetized spot (1-bit), and a blank represents a 0-bit. The 1- and 0-bits are used together to code alphabetic, numeric, or special characters.

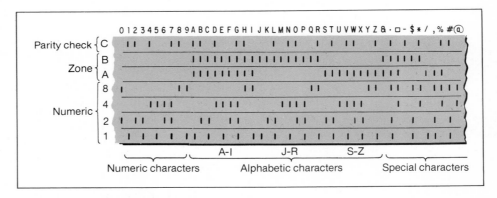

Figure 7–2. Seven-bit alphanumeric code.

[1]Graham Magnetics manufactures a new "super tape" that can be used for applications in temperatures ranging from 65°F to 400°F, compared to operating temperature ranges from 50°F to 90°F for the previously best available tape. While it will appeal most to space or geographic applications where extreme temperatures are found, the new tape could be used for business applications where extra cost is justified as a form of insurance against natural disaster such as fire. The cost of a 1,000 feet of half-inch tape and reel is $125, over five times the price of the commerical tape.

Most modern computers use a *nine-channel code,* or the **extended binary-coded decimal interchange code (EBCDIC),** as shown in Table 7–1. The code uses four numeric tracks (1, 2, 4, 8), a parity check, and four (versus two) zone positions. The additional two zone bits are used in coding lowercase alphabetical and other special characters. Note that the arrangement of the tracks is not in sequential order. The most frequently used tracks are clustered toward the center of the tape to protect the data from dirt, dust, or physical damage to the outer edges of the tape.

Table 7–1. Nine-channel code.

Track no.	Equivalent 7-track tape code position	0	1	2	3	4	A	B	. . .Z
9	8								|
8	2			|	|			|	
7	added zone	|	|	|	|	|	|	|	|
6	added zone	|	|	|	|	|	|	|	|
5	B	|	|	|	|				|
4	check (odd)	|			|	|			
3	A	|	|	|	|	|			
2	1		|	|	|		|		|
1	4					|			

Other computers use a **packed-decimal** design in a ten-track format, which utilizes two BCD numeric bits and two check bits (Table 7–2). In contrast to the seven-track tape, two digits can be recorded in a single column, doubling the use of available storage space.

Table 7–2. Ten-track coding — packed format.

Check bits	{ CO { C1
Numeric bits	{ 8 { 4 { 2 { 1
Numeric bits	{ 8 { 4 { 2 { 1

Accuracy Check

Magnetized spots can be erased accidentally or obscured by dust, dirt, or cracks in the oxide coating. To ascertain the accuracy of data during parity check tape reading or recording, tape drives have one or more safeguards:

1. parity check,
2. dual recording, and
3. the dual gap read-write heads.

Parity check.   In **parity check,** the number of 1-bits representing a character is counted. In odd parity, if the number of 1-bits representing a character is even, the check (C) bit is turned on to make the total number of 1 bits odd. Thus each character is represented by an odd number of 1 bits (Table 7 – 1).

Other types of error are possible, of course. Two bits could be reversed in a single frame and remain undetected under a system that uses only vertical parity check. Thus a tape operation further employs a **longitudinal check character** at the end of each tape record. If the check is for even parity, an extra 1-bit is added to each channel that contains an odd number of 1-bits to make it even. The opposite is true in the case of odd parity.

Dual-recording systems.   In such systems, a character is written twice in each frame across the width of the tape. The recorded data is compared for equality when it is written and again when it is read. This method is used only on tape systems that have enough channels to record two characters side-by-side.

Dual-gap read-write heads.   To insure the accuracy of data recorded on tape, *dual-gap read-write* heads are also used. A character written on tape is immediately "read" by a read head to verify its validity and readability. If the character is not readable, an error signal is given. Under the direct control of the computer, the tape can be backspaced and instructed to rewrite the proper data. Even then, the dual-gap feature checks the accuracy of the rewrite before any further recording continues.

Tape Density and Format

Data may be packed (recorded) on tape at a density of 200, 550, 800, 1,600, or 6,250 characters per inch. *Packing density* refers to the greatest number of columns of data that can be recorded on a specified length of tape, usually one inch. At 6,250 characters per inch, for instance, the data from seventy-eight 80-column punched cards can be stored on one inch of tape, resulting in a total storage capacity of 156 million characters (or 1,950,000 cards) on a 2,400-foot tape. The capacity of single tape reels ranges from 1 million to 160 million characters, depending on tape density, the size of interrecorded gap, and the length of the reel.

Data is stored on tape as groups of characters (or bytes) called *records.* There are no addresses to identify the location of records on tape. Therefore, **interrecord gaps (IRGs)** are used to separate one record from another. An IRG varies from three-tenths to three-quarters of an inch, depending on the type of tape drive and whether the tape is seven- or nine-track. The three-quarter-inch gap is the most common (Figure 7–3). The gaps are created automatically when data is written on tape. During program execution, all the data between two IRGs are read by a single read instruction. The IRGs also allow space for the tape drive to come to a stop after reading or writing a block of data and gain speed to read (or write) the next block.

In many cases, single records are too small in size to warrant individual separation. An alternative is *blocking* or grouping a number of logically related records into one physical record between IRGs. Blocking saves tape and speeds data input since the tape drive accelerates and decelerates less frequently. All the recordings in a given block are read before the unit pauses. In Figure 7–4 the blocking factor is three, and the IRG is referred to as **IBG (interblock gap).**

Figure 7–3. Example of interrecord gaps and single record format.

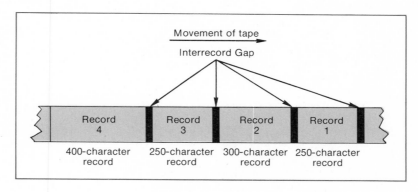

Figure 7–4. Blocked records and IRGs.

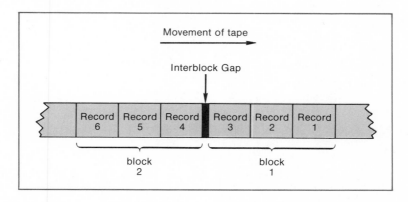

The Tape Drive

The tape drive, operating as an input or output drive, is used to read records from or to write records onto tape (Figure 7–5). In preparing either operation, the operator mounts the supply (data) reel on the left side and an empty (take-up) reel on the right side. The tape from the left reel is threaded past the read-write head to the take-up reel. When the tape is mounted, the operator pushes the start button. The tape drive locates the first sequential record by looking for the **load point marker,** a reflective spot that indicates the beginning of the readable portion of the tape. Tape records are then read one after another under the direction of a stored program.

Because of the high speed involved in starting and stopping, a loop in the tape drops (floats) into each vacuum tube acting as a buffer against tape breakage. The resulting slack absorbs tape tension during the sudden burst of speed generated by a read instruction from the computer. When the tape loop in the right vacuum tube begins to reach the bottom, an electronic eye actuates the take-up reel to absorb the slack automatically. As the tape in the left vacuum tube is drawn by the take-up reel, it is replenished by the file reel immediately above it (Figure 7–6).

When the tape is processed, the operator rewinds the tape and stores it on the original reel, leaving the take-up reel empty for the next application. Some tape drives are capable of reading the tape in the reverse direction so that no rewinding is necessary. Most tape drives can be programmed to rewind a tape, backspace one block (or record) at a time, skip over a bad portion of the tape or correct errors without interruption of processing.

Figure 7–5. Magnetic tape drive: IBM 3420
Courtesy IBM

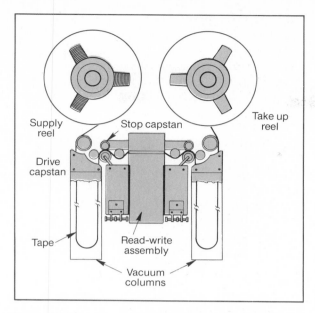

Supply reel

Stop capstan

Take up reel

Drive capstan

Tape

Read-write assembly

Vacuum columns

Figure 7–6. Schematic drawing of a tape drive showing read-write assembly.

When a reading error is detected, the system branches to a programmed error routine. The tape is then backspaced to read one block again. If, after a specified number of backspacing and reading attempts, the data is not read correctly, the computer operator is alerted to the error for further handling. A similar procedure is also available when an error is detected in writing data on tape.

In tape control, some form of visual identification is made. A typical computer center might have hundreds of tape reels related to various applications. Since one reel of tape looks the same as any other reel, an external label is used to describe the data recorded on the tape. The label contains the tape serial number, reel number, data of application, type of application (payroll, accounts receivable, accounts payable, etc.), the number of times the tape has been passed through the machine, and the name of the programmer who made up the stored program. An index can also be made (by serial number or by type of application) of all the reels available. When a processing run becomes necessary, the librarian or the operator merely reads the label for proper identification of the correct reel.

In addition to the outside label, a special **header label** preceding the first data record is checked by a programming routine. It contains such items as file name and the date when processing continues. If all is well, processing continues. Otherwise, the program prints out an error message and terminates processing.

The accidental destruction of recorded data on tape is avoided by placing a plastic "ring" on the back of the tape before mounting it. The saying, "no ring,

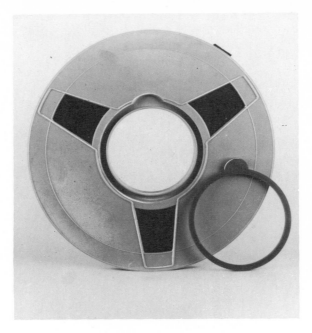

Figure 7–7. A protective file ring.

no write," simply means that the tape drive always reads data on tape unless a plastic reel is inserted into its groove (Figure 7 – 7).

The end of a tape file is detected by a special record called a **trailer label,** located after the last data record on the tape. The trailer label contains the number of blocks in the total file so that a check of the accuracy of the processing can be made at the end of the run.

Tape Speed and Capacity

The speed of a tape operation is measured by the transfer rate of the tape drive. *Transfer rate* refers to the number of characters (or bytes) that can be transferred from the tape drive to storage per second (or vice versa). Most tape drives have speeds that range from 5,000 to 400,000 bytes per second. For example, a transfer rate of 160,000 bytes per second is equivalent to reading two thousand 80-column cards per second.

As mentioned earlier, a tape drive stops and starts everytime it encounters an IRG or IBG. The effective transfer rate, then, has to account for such delays. To illustrate, suppose we have a tape file of 10,000 records, each consisting of 100 bytes of data. At 100,000 bytes per second, it would take a tape drive 10 seconds (1,000,000 ÷ 100,000) to read the file. However, the tape drive stops and starts 10,000 times between records, at an average time of 5/1,000 second per stop/start. Hence, 50 seconds (10,000 × 0.005) are used up. Thus, it takes 10 seconds to read the file and 50 seconds to start and stop the tape. The effective transfer rate, in this case, is 60,000 (versus 100,000) bytes per second.[2]

Blocking records is an effective time-saving procedure in tape file processing. Using the same example, with a blocking factor of 40 (4,000 bytes of data per block) the 10,000-record file is blocked into 250 blocks. Reading the file still takes 10 seconds. However, the stop/start time is reduced from 10 seconds to 1.25 (250 × 0.005) seconds. The total time for reading the file is then reduced from 60 seconds to 11.25 seconds. Blocking obviously has a great impact on the speed of tape file processing.

Calculation of file capacity is important in system planning and file design. Tape file capacity is calculated as follows:

1. Determine the number of blocks required by the file.

2. Compute the length of the record block by multiplying the number of bytes per block by the number of blocks of the file.

3. Determine the physical space requirement (inches per block) by dividing the block length by the tape drive's recording density.

4. Add the IBG length to the block length to arrive at the total physical space (in inches) occupied by each block.

5. Multiply the total block length (in step 4) by the number of blocks making up the file (in step 1) to arrive at the total file capacity in inches.

6. Divide the total file capacity by 12 to represent the file capacity in feet.

Once file capacity is calculated, approximately 30 feet of tape is allowed for header and trailer label considerations. The total linear footage represents the total tape file requirements.

Processing Tape Files

For files to be kept up-to-date, they have to be periodically processed and maintained. Updating can be facilitated or obstructed by the way files are classified, and they may be classified in many different ways according to the wide diversity of applications. Files are generally classified as follows:

1. *By content.* The contents of files can be considered as master files or transaction files.
   a. A **master file** is a relatively permanent set of records containing historical, statistical, and identification data. A personnel file is an example. It may be of fixed length (such as in personnel records) or of variable length records (as in sales ledgers). It is used as a source of reference or for information retrieval.

[2]Reading and stop/start times are 10 + 50 = 60 seconds. Transfer rate is 60 ÷ 1,000,000 bytes = 0.00006 second per byte or 60,000 bytes per second.

b. A **transaction** file is a collection of records about specific activities that have some effect on a master file. Thus, it is used to update a master file.

2. *By methods of processing.* The primary methods of processing files are sequential and direct access. In sequential processing (as in magnetic tape), files are created by sorting records in sequence according to their keys. Input transactions are grouped and sorted into master-file, control-number sequence. The resulting arrangement is then processed against the master file. In contrast, direct access processing (as in magnetic disc) handles transactions against a master file regardless of the order in which they occur. Records are retrieved without the need to examine intervening records.

3. *By storage devices.* The primary storage devices are serial access and direct access. Serial (or sequential) access devices are characterized by magnetic tape. Serial access means that a record cannot be accessed until the record(s) preceding it have been scanned. Direct access storage devices (DASD) are represented by magnetic disc. Any records in the file are directly accessible and can be replaced anywhere in the existing file, without regard to the sequence in which the file is arranged.

In file design, an important rule of thumb to remember is that, on the average, accessing a record at random from a tape file takes roughly one-half the time that reading the entire file on that tape does. Random or direct-accessing on tape, then is quite inefficient. This means that a better alternative is to organize and process tape files sequentially.

Tape file processing is characterized by sequencing a suitable batch of transactions in the same order as the master file before processing. Master records are processed against transaction records by a series of comparisons: The computer compares a master record with a transaction record for equality. Master records having the same identification number as the transaction records are updated and rewritten on a new tape. Unaffected master records are merely copied. Any out-of-sequence records are individually handled before further processing is made. The old master file and transaction tapes are kept until the processing cycle is completed. During the next processing cycle, the updated master file is used as input with a new batch of transactions, as shown in Figure 7 – 8.

To illustrate a tape processing run, assume that the master record tape consists of four logical records identified as M(01), M(02), M(03), and M(04). Assume also that the transaction record tape consists of four logical records identified as T(01), T(03), T(04), and T(04) (Figure 7 – 9). Processing these records requires preparation of a computer program similar in general form to the one shown in Figure 7 – 10.

When the program is loaded and the processing cycle begins, the following steps take place:

1. T(01) and M(01) are read and their identification numbers are compared for equality. Since they are equal, the transaction is processed and an output record of it is written.

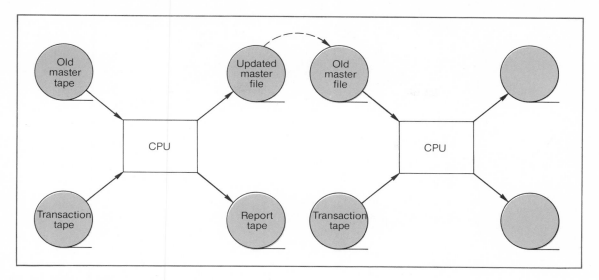

Figure 7–8. Processing magnetic tape files.

Figure 7–9. Processing magnetic tape files—an example.

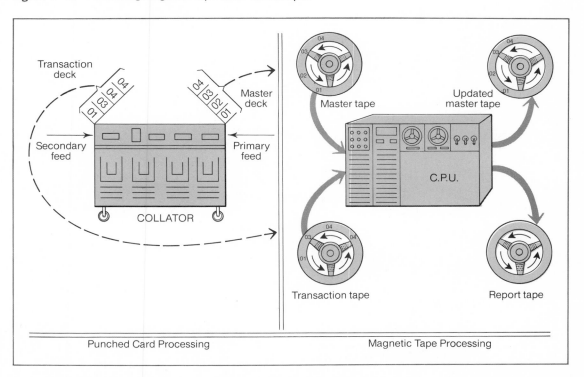

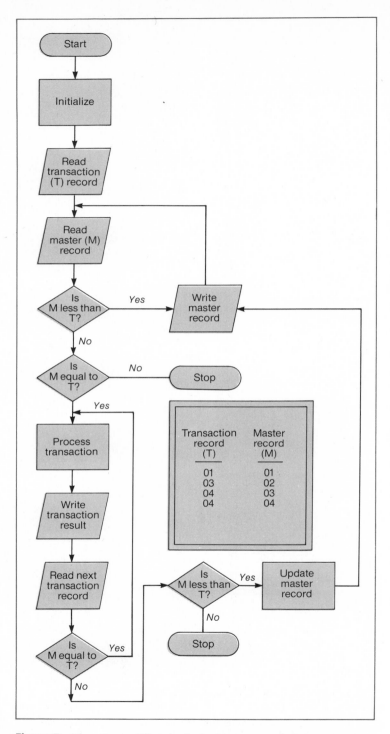

Figure 7-10. General flowchart of a tape processing run.

2. T(03) is read and, having an identification number greater than M(01), causes M(01) to be updated, and master record M(01) to be written on the output tape.

3. M(02) is read, and T(03) is compared with M(02). M(02), having a smaller identification number than T(03), is copied onto the output tape, and M(03) is read next.

4. T(03) is equal to M(03). Therefore, the transaction is processed and an output record of it is written.

5. T(04) is read and, having an identification number greater than M(03), causes M(03) to be updated. The master record M(03) is copied on the output tape.

6. M(04) is read, and T(04) is compared with M(04). Since they are equal, the transaction is processed, and an output record is written.

7. The last T(04) is read. T(04) and M(04) are again equal, so the transaction is processed and an output record of it is written. Since it is the last transaction and the end of the operation, M(04) is updated, and master record M(04) is written on the output tape.

Today's output tape becomes tomorrow's input tape for file processing. Today's input tape is filed away for future reference.

Sorting Tape Files

As mentioned earlier, a magnetic tape file must be in sequence before processing. Because tape records cannot be physically sorted, the computer is used for that purpose. Records written on magnetic tape are sorted by interfiling blocks of sequential records into longer blocks until one large block (or sequence) of logical records is achieved. To illustrate this method, suppose we have a magnetic tape containing 20 records. The identification number of each record is shown in Figure 7–11. Sequencing the 20 records involves the following passes:

Pass 1. Break input tape A into two tapes (B and C), as shown in Figure 7–12. Note that the first five records, the next six records, and the remaining nine records are in sequence. Pass 1 involves writing the first batch of five sequential records onto tape B and then switching to tape C for writing the next batch of six sequential records. The next nine sequential records are switched to tape B, completing the first pass. In an operation involving many batches of sequential records, switching from one tape to another continues until the last batch has been written.

Pass 2. Before pass 2 begins, tape A is removed and stored for future reference. A new tape (referred to as tape C) replaces tape A, and an additional tape

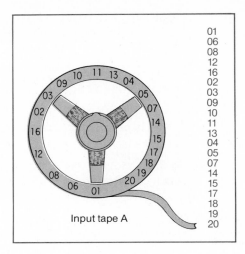

Input tape A

Figure 7–11. Block of 20 records on tape A, before inter-filing.

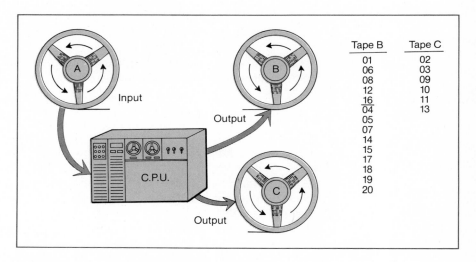

		Tape B	Tape C
		01	02
		06	03
		08	09
		12	10
		16	11
		04	13
		05	
		07	
		14	
		15	
		17	
		18	
		19	
		20	

Figure 7–12. Sorting tape records — pass 1.

(tape E) is also mounted. In this pass, tapes B and C are the input tapes and tapes D and E are the output tapes (Figure 7–13). The first batch of eleven sequential records on tapes B and C is merged and written onto tape D, followed by writing onto tape E the second batch of nine merged sequential records. In other words, the first batches of tapes B and C (01, 06, 08, 12, and 16 of tape B and 02, 03, 09, 10, 11, and 13 of tape C) are merged in ascending sequence and written onto tape D (Figure 7–13). The second batch (in this example, the remaining nine records of tape B in Figure 7–12) is copied onto tape E.

Pass 3. A third pass is needed to merge the two sets of records on tapes D and E into one sequence. Tapes D and E now become the input tapes, and a new tape (tape F) becomes the output tape. Since only one batch of sequenced records is on each tape, it is merged in one final pass and is written on tape F (Figure 7–14).

Figure 7–13. Sorting tape records—pass 2.

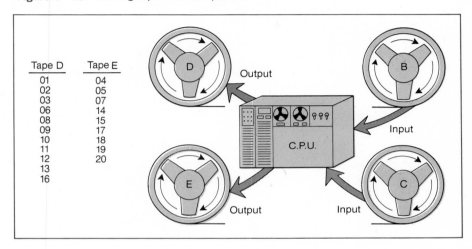

Tape D	Tape E
01	04
02	05
03	07
06	14
08	15
09	17
10	18
11	19
12	20
13	
16	

Figure 7–14. Sorting tape records—pass 3.

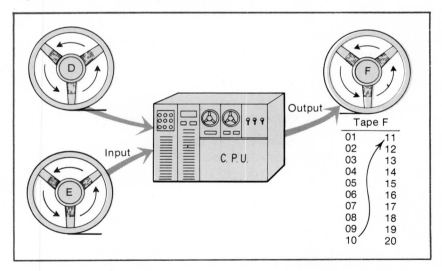

Tape F	
01	11
02	12
03	13
04	14
05	15
06	16
07	17
08	18
09	19
10	20

Are Magnetic Tapes Vulnerable to Magnets?

For over a decade, various data processing journals published articles on the vulnerability of magnetic tape files to magnets. Here are some of the claims:

1. An entire tape library is erased by a dime-store magnet.
2. The tape inside a metal file cabinet is erased by a magnetic flashlight placed on the side of the cabinet.
3. Thousands of tapes are destroyed within minutes with magnets the size of a quarter.
4. A thousand tapes are destroyed with a small hand magnet.
5. Data tapes are endangered by metal detectors at airline gates.

The Stanford Research Institute began to look into these claims by testing various versions and sizes and magnets against data files stored on tape. Some of the results of their experiments show the following conclusions:

1. Even a high-strength, heavy magnet poses little threat to tapes properly stored in double-walled, fire-resistant, tape filing cabinets.
2. The airline's present metal detectors, by themselves, do not disrupt the validity of the stored data on tape.
3. A computer malfunction can take place if small magnets are brought into direct contact with data throughout the length of the tape. Thus in a 9,000-tape library, the time taken to alter existing data would be substantial.
4. A large magnet in excess of 20 pounds and with a magnetic intensity of about 3,000 gauss at the poles could alter recorded tape data if it could be moved along tape reels in an open file rack.

Among the steps recommended to protect data from possible damage are:

1. a thorough investigation of the backgound of data-processing personnel,
2. maintenance of copies of the active tapes in a separate, security proof, and fireproof cabinet, and
3. the development of an effective computer-room-access control system so that it is always known who is using what tape, when, and for how long.

Depending on the particular installation, both management and outside consultants should work together on designing and implementing the plan that best provides maximum security for critical and other tape files of the system.

SUMMARY

1. Magnetic tape represents a major departure from card input-output. Magnetic tape is a sequential file storage medium. It comes in lengths from 200 to 3,200 feet, and it runs at a typical reading speed of 320,000 characters per second — the equivalent of 4,000 punched cards.

2. The primary advantages of tape are compact storage, flexible record size, low-cost storage, and high-speed sequential file processing. For direct-access applications, however, magnetic disc is a better choice than tape.

3. Data is recorded on tape in seven- or nine-channel code. The nine-channel code uses four numeric tracks, a parity check, and four zone positions. Other computers use a packed-decimal design in a ten-track format, which utilizes two BCD numeric bits and two check bits.

4. Accuracy of data recording is checked by a vertical parity check and a longitudinal check character at the end of each tape record. The dual-gap read-write head features further checks on the validity and readability of stored data.

5. Data may be packed at densities of up to 6,250 characters per inch, stored on tape as groups of characters (or bytes) called records. Records are separated by interrecord gaps (IRGs). When records are blocked, interblock gaps (IBGs) are also created to separate one block from another.

6. A tape drive locates the first sequential record by looking for the load point marker, which marks the beginning of the readable portion of the tape. Records are read one at a time under the direction of a stored program. Most tape drivers can be programmed to rewind a tape, backspace one block (or record) at a time, skip over a bad portion of the tape, or correct errors without interruption of processing.

7. A tape is identified by an outside label and a header label, which precedes the first data record. The end of the tape file is detected by a trailer label, which is located after the last data record on the tape.

8. The speed of a tape operation is measured by the transfer rate of the tape drive. Most drives have speeds ranging from 5,000 to 400,000 bytes per record. Blocking records is an efficient way of maximizing the speed of tape file processing.

9. Files are classified by content (master or transaction files), by methods of processing (sequential or direct-access), or by storage devices (serial or

direct-access). Tape file processing is characterized by collecting a suitable batch of transactions and sequencing them in the same order as the master file before processing. Tape records are sorted by interfiling blocks of sequential records into longer blocks until one large block (or sequence) of logical records is achieved.

TERMS TO LEARN

Header label
Interrecord gap (IRG)
Interblock gap (IBG)
Load point marker
Longitudinal check character
Master file
Trailer label
Transaction file

REVIEW QUESTIONS

1. In what respect is magnetic tape a sequential file medium?

2. What is the difference between EBCDIC and the seven-channel code?

3. Explain the difference between:
   a. packed decimal in 10-track format and packing density,
   b. trailer label and header label,
   c. interrecord gap and interblock gap, and
   d. access time and transfer rate.

4. Assume the following: (a) recording density of 1,600 characters per inch; (b) 2,400-foot tape; and (c) no restrictions on the use of the entire tape.
   a. What is the total amount of data that can be written on tape?
   b. If the tape moves at 500 inches per second, what is the total time required to write the data on the tape?
   c. Suppose the data recorded on tape are in blocks of 500 characters per block, how many blocks would we have on the tape?

5. In your own words, describe how tape files are classified.

6. Do you believe that magnetic tapes are vulnerable to magnets? Why?

chapter 8

Direct-Access Data Processing

Learning Objectives

Magnetic tape is known for two major limitations. It is ill-suited for processing selected records without scanning preceding records. Because its records must be processed in sequence, a tape file often requires several sorting time-consuming steps. With these limitations, tape is obviously not suited to direct-access processing; magnetic disc is a more efficient alternative. By the end of this chapter, you should know:

1. the characteristics and attributes of magnetic disc,

2. disc layout and data transfer,

3. file organization basics, and

4. the major features of magnetic drum storage.

Tape Versus Disc for Direct-Access Processing

Direct-access processing is a form of data processing in which any record in the file may be accessed directly, updated, and/or replaced anywhere in the file, regardless of the file sequence. File sorting requirements are eliminated. The time taken to update the file depends on the number of records to be updated rather than on the number of records in the master file.

Magnetic tape is not as well suited to direct-access processing as is magnetic disc. A magnetic tape system is used primarily for processing large amounts of sequential data at high speed. However, magnetic tape poses two major limitations. First, except in applications where each and every record is updated sequentially, tape processing is time-consuming and therefore inefficient. The average time required to access a record at random from a tape file is roughly one-half the time that reading the entire file on that tape takes. Second, because the records to be processed must be in sequence, a tape application often requires several sorting steps. For example, a master file must be in the same sequence as the transaction file before it can be properly updated. During updating, all the records from the old master tape are read and written onto a new tape. So if 1,000 records out of a 10,000-record tape are updated, 9,000 records have to read from and written as a matter of routine. With these limitations, tape is obviously not suited for direct-access processing.

Magnetic disc is a more efficient alternative than magnetic tape; and magnetic disc storage is therefore the most commonly used type for direct-access processing. It is extremely efficient in applications requiring large volume of data with immediate accessibility. Like magnetic tape, a magnetic disc may be re-used indefinitely. Once recorded, the data can be read or rewritten as often as necessary.

The Characteristics of Magnetic Disc

Discs[1] include disc cartridges, disc packs, and data modules. A disc *cartridge* generally consists of one disc inside a sealed plastic housing. A disc *pack* has a stack of from three to as many as twelve discs (platters). Data *modules* are the latest generation of disc packs. Read-write heads and access mechanisms are built into the unit. In contrast, disc packs are just stacks of platters. The read-write heads and the access mechanisms are a part of the disc drive unit (Figure 8–1).

A **magnetic disc** is an on-line mass storage medium that works in much the same way as a phonograph record. If, for example, you want to hear one line of a song that is in the twentieth groove, you place the tone arm right into that circular groove and play it. Now picture a stack of six records bolted together with an inch of space between the records. Also imagine this assembly on an odd-looking record player with seven tone arms, each with two needles top and bottom. This player, called the *disc drive,* can play any of the records simultaneously.

[1]The word "disk" may be spelled as "disk" or "disc." The root word is the Greek *dikein* to throw. From *dikein* came the Greek *diskos,* which was associated with the game of quoits. The Greek *diskos* eventually became the Latin *discus.* Since English borrows from both Greek and Latin, the word is spelled either with a "c" or a "k." In terms of meaning, however, a *disc* means "a phonograph record," while *disk* means "any thin, flat, circular plate." Since "disc" (a phonograph record) thus connotes storage of information and "disk" does not, the preferred word is "disc."

Figure 8—1. Disc pack. *Courtesy IBM*

     Earlier disc modules had one large access arm that served a stack of twenty-five or fifty fixed discs. Since just reaching the record location required some time, designers later introduced the two-access arm model: One arm processes a specific transaction at a given storage position, while the other arm moves toward the next record.

     Most of today's disc drives have a read-write head for each disc, to reduce the average access time to a minimum. As shown in Figure 8—2, the head-per-track disc system couples the recording economies of magnetic discs with the programming simplicity of main memory storage. With no moving read-write heads or access arms, no time is lost in positioning a read-write head over the track containing the data to be accessed. Read-write heads are permanently positioned over each information track on the disc surface. The discs spin at a constant speed under the heads, and the heads are air-flown to within a few millionths of an inch of the vertical disc surface (Figure 8—3).

Figure 8—2. Head-per-disc design. *Courtesy IBM*

Figure 8–3. Head-per-track design. *Courtesy IBM*

The Disc Pack

A *disc pack* is a compact device that weighs between 8 and 20 pounds and that contains a stack of magnetic discs handled as a unit. For example, the disc pack in Figure 8–4 consists of 10 recording discs, each 14 inches in diameter. Together, they provide 19 surfaces for recording 100 million bytes of data. The disc pack is mounted in a disc-drive unit, which accommodates up to 8 disc packs rotating at a constant speed of 3,600 revolutions per minute.

Disc packs can store tremendous amounts of information, accessible in fractions of a second. The largest disc pack can store 300 million bytes, compared to the disc cartridge's capacity of from 500,000 to 3 million bytes. A 100-million byte pack, for instance, can store the names and addresses of the entire population of New Hampshire — and any address on the pack can be retrieved in less than 0.03 seconds.

Users who rarely change disc packs on their disc drive facility find fixed disc drive a more efficient alternative to mass storage. For example, the system shown in Figure 8–5 has 8 spindle drives, each with a storage capacity of 317.5 million (or 317.5 megabytes), for a total capacity of 2,540 megabytes. A system of this magnitude cuts the storage cost per byte in half. Considering purchase and maintenance costs, however, such a system is most appropriate only for large-scale computer systems.

As capacious as disc packs are, their efficient use can enhance their value to the user, whose files often exceed the disc pack's capacity. A common solution is to organize the data by priority and to store it in as many removable disc packs as needed. Active data that is used daily can be stored on one disc pack, while relatively inactive data can be stored on separate disc packs. Although the access time may not be as fast as having the entire file on one unit, a substantial

Figure 8–4. Disc drive unit. *Courtesy IBM*

Figure 8–5. Large-scale fixed disc-drive system. *Courtesy IBM*

cost saving can be realized. The final choice depends largely on the access requirements of the data, on the overall characteristics of the existing computer system, and on the deadlines imposed by management in obtaining the results.

Disc Layout and Data Transfer

Each disc surface has 200 concentric circles called **tracks** (Figure 8–6). Data is recorded on these tracks in bits that are strung together so that eight bits make up one byte. In the figure, a partial track is blown up to show the data "A12" represented by three bytes in EBCDIC code (see Figure 5–12).

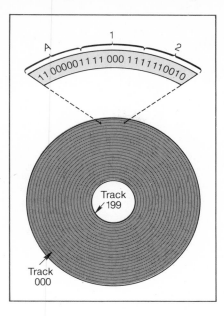

Figure 8–6. Disc tracks and data coding.

Data is addressed on magnetic disc by disc number, track number, and sector number. A **sector** is a segment of the track, normally fixed in length and accommodates one or more records. The number of sectors per track and the number of tracks per disc surface differ with various manufacturers. Generally, you can figure the capacity of a given disc pack by multiplying:

1. the *number of disc surfaces* in the pack,

2. by the *number of tracks per surface,*

3. by the *number of sectors per track,* and

4. by the *number of bytes per sector.*

(Additional details on disc file capacity are covered at the end of the chapter.)

Some discs do not have sectors; instead, data is addressed by disc face and disc track only. A physical record may occupy an entire track; but since a track is much too large for one record, several records are normally stored on it. A record can be stored in either of two track formats:

1. count-data format or

2. count-key data format.

In the *count-data format,* each record (or *data area*) on a track is preceded by a **count area.** In Figure 8–7, four data areas are preceded by four count areas. Each count area contains the disc address of the record following it. Thus, a disc address identifies only one record on a disc for direct access or for processing.

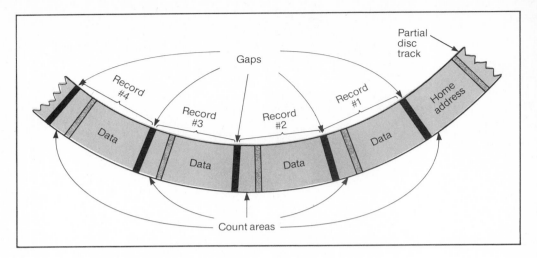

Figure 8–7. Layout of variable-length records in a count-data format.

In addition to the count and data areas, the count-data format includes a *home address,* which identifies each track on the disc. The home address is located immediately before the first count area on a track. So there are as many home addresses as there are tracks on a disc pack.

The *count-key data format* also has a home address at the beginning of each track. In addition, it has a key area between each count area and data area. The *key area* represents an employee ID number, a part number, a control field, or anything that identifies a record in a file. In contrast, the count area holds a disc address which identifies the location of a record on the disc (Figure 8–8). As we shall see later, both count and key areas can be used to locate records directly on disc.

Figure 8–8. Layout of variable-length records in a count-key data format.

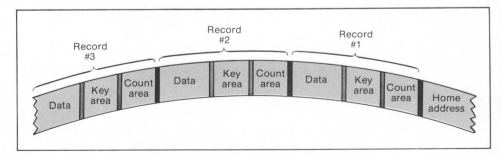

Data Transfer Time

Data transfer time is the time that data takes to transfer from disc to main memory. Four factors bear directly on data transfer speed:

1. *Access-motion (seek) time* is the time the read-write head takes to position itself over the track containing the record. If the head is fixed, the access-motion time is zero.

2. *Head-activation time* is the time required to select electronically the proper read-write head of the access mechanism. This time is generally considered to be negligible.

3. *Rotational delay* is the time required for the desired data to reach the read-write head so that the actual reading or writing may begin. Rotational delay ranges from no movement to one complete revolution of the disc. Rotational delay depends on how fast the disc is rotating and on the location of the data in relation to the read-write head.

4. *Data-transfer time* is the time required to transfer the data from the storage device to the main memory of the computer. It is a function of the rotational speed and the density of the recorded data. It is usually expressed in thousands of characters (or bytes) per second.

File Organization

A *file organization* is supposed to make records available for processing, file creation, and file maintenance. Files used primarily for data processing applications are arranged in one of three major ways:

1. sequential,
2. direct, or
3. indexed-sequential.

Sequential Files

In **sequential file** organization, the simplest type, records are stored in sequential order by record key. A *record key* may be an employee name, special ID number, social security, or some identifying element. To locate a given record, the system starts at the beginning of the file and compares each record key to the record being sought. Although sequential files commonly use magnetic tape, they may also be stored on direct-access storage devices such as discs. In a sequential disc file organization, records are stored in control number sequence so those with successively higher control numbers have successively higher addresses.

Other than a sequential search procedure, the file can locate a record also by a *binary search procedure*. Essentially, the system goes to the middle record in the file and compares the record key there with that of the record sought. If the record is in the first half of the file, the key of the middle record of that half is compared with the key of the record sought. This halving procedure is continued until the record is located.

Direct Files

In direct files any record can be read without reading the records preceding it; this system's directness is its major advantage. In its simplest form, a direct file uses the record key as the address of the disc number and track where the record is stored. The key is subjected to a programming routine that produces the address. In one such routine, called **randomizing,** a uniformly distributed set of addresses map the record keys into an assigned storage area as uniformly as possible.

A common arithmetic procedure for producing addresses by randomizing is to divide the record key by a prime number.[2] The prime number is approximately equal to the number of available addresses; the remainder of the division represents the address locator. For example, 100 tracks are required for a given file, and 97 is a prime number close to 100. The key is divided by 97, and the remainder (0 through 98) becomes the relative track address. If the key is 12,442, then $12,442 \div 97 = 99$ with a remainder of 67. The remainder (67), representing the address locator or the relative track address, is added to the beginning track of the file to arrive at the actual track address. If the program fails to locate a given record at the generated address, it goes to a special overflow area, which is searched sequentially.

Indexed-Sequential Files

Although sequential and direct file organizations have their advantages, they also have limitations. In a sequential file, updating or inserting records and data into the middle of the file is difficult. The entire file has to be rewritten in order to add one or more records to the file. On the other hand, while direct file organization can update a file anywhere in the file, figuring out the record addresses is required for processing.

Indexed-sequential files combine both sequential and direct-access possibilities. In this type of file organization (also called ISAM for "indexed-sequential access method"), the following features are important (Figure 8–9):

1. A prime area is available where records are formatted in sequence with the key.

[2]A prime number can be evenly divided by no other whole number than itself and 1, such as 1, 2, 3, 7, and 11.

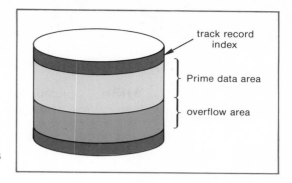

Figure 8–9. The prime features of ISAM.

2. One or more indexes enables the system to locate records individually without reading the entire file.

3. A separate overflow area provides room for the subsequent storage of records displaced from the prime data area.

To create an indexed-sequential file, records must be in sequence by record key (Figure 8–10. After placing the keys in the prime area, an index is automatically created by the operating system for each cylinder on which records are stored. In the case of blocked records, the index contains the highest record key within the block and the block's storage address. The records can be accessed sequentially by starting with the first block and proceeding with the operation in sequence. They can also be accessed directly by scanning the index to reference

Figure 8–10. Indexed-sequential file organization—an example.

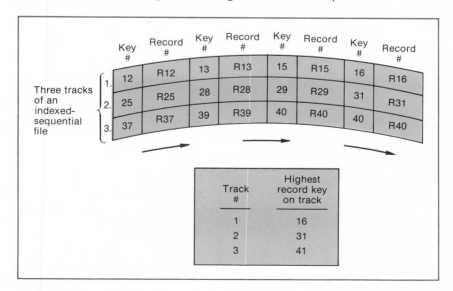

the block number that contains the record. Then, each of the records in the block is searched sequentially to locate the desired record. Blocks are organized with extra locations so that records can be added or updated without having to recognize the rest of the file.

Example. Of three consecutive file tracks, each contains four fixed unblocked records, as shown in Figure 8–10. Each record is in order by a unique key. To access record number 29, one way is to read the records sequentially until record 29 is located. A more direct alternative is to go to the track index, which lists the highest record key of each track. To locate the track that has record 29, the system locates the track with a record key greater than 29. In the Figure it is track number 2, whose highest record key is 31. Therefore, record 29 (if it is on the track) must be somewhere on track 2.

Indexed-sequential organization combines the best features of the sequential and direct-access file organization methods by means of the index. It reduced the magnitude of sequential searching and provides quick access for sequential as well as for direct processing. The primary drawback, however, is that extra storage room must be allowed for the index and for insertions into the file. Compared to direct file organization, it takes longer to search the index for data retrieval. For a highly volatile file, excessive time can be expected as overflow storage locations are filled.

Disc File Capacity

The following general-capacity formula may be used in computing the number of physical records per track:

Physical records/track $= 1 +$
$$\frac{\text{(Quoted track capacity)} - \text{(Bytes for last data record)}}{\text{(Bytes required from remaining data record)}}$$

Track capacity is calculated in two steps: First figure the byte capacity for all key-formatted records except the last. Then calculate the byte capacity of the last record.

1. Total byte capacity (except last record) $= \dfrac{150 + 2,100(KL + DL)}{2,025}$

2. Last record bytes $= 50 + KL + DL$

Where:

150 $=$ the estimated number of bytes needed for track areas reserved for identification;

$KL =$ key length;

$DL =$ data length;

$\dfrac{2,100}{2,025}$ = a fraction that allows for the possible change in the location of a record; and

50 = the gap between the key area and data area.

Example. A disc has a quoted track capacity of 8,000 bytes. A file, consisting of key-formatted records, has the following characteristics:

1. The data area consists of 10 logical records.
2. Each (blocked) record is 20 bytes in length.
3. The record key (a customer account number) is 5 bytes in length.
4. Each area preceding the data area is a 5-byte key.

Track capacity is computed as follows:

1. Byte capacity $= 150 + \dfrac{2,100(5 + 200)}{2,025}$
   $= 363$ bytes

2. Last record $= 50 + 5 + 200$
   $= 255$ bytes

3. Physical records/track $= 1 + \dfrac{8,000 - 255}{363}$
   $= 22$ physical records (rounded to the nearest digit)

The calculations specify that the disc tracks have the capacity to store 22 physical records.

Considerations in the Use of Magnetic Disc

Magnetic disc storage is most appropriate in applications, such as billing systems, that require the processing of a relatively limited number of input transactions against a very large master file. The direct-access capability of the magnetic disc—as opposed to tape—allows the retrieval of any single record without having to "rummage through" other records in storage. Disc storage is also effective in a high-activity application, such as a 5,000-employee payroll, which involves the frequent updating of a comparatively small percentage of records. Direct-access magnetic discs also eliminate the need for batching, unlike tapes which require records to be sequentially organized prior to processing.

Since 1970, magnetic disc has become a more and more popular medium for secondary storage. Except for some minicomputers, most digital computers can now be obtained with magnetic disc storage. Although the total amount of hardware ordered still favors tape, comparing the sales figures for reels of tape to those for discs shows a more rapid growth rate for disc.

Several factors affect the decision between magnetic disc and magnetic tape:

1. the applications involved,
2. the required data-access speed,
3. storage-size requirement, and
4. cost.

The application.   Direct-access applications are best processed through magnetic disc, whereas sequential processing is routinely handled on magnetic tape.

Data-access speed.   In disc file processing, a computer system is programmed to locate and process a specific record stored in a predetermined disc file address. The record is located immediately and almost immediately read into main memory. Although the speed factor depends on the model, magnetic disc units have generally surpassed magnetic tape in data transfer speed. (Tape mobility is also an important benefit, especially to users who regularly transfer large volumes of data from one location to another or who want to run a job on one computer but print it on another.

Storage-size requirements.   Disc storage is quite durable, and is becoming as popular a medium for bulk data storage as is magnetic tape. However, in a tape-updating routine, a new tape is created, leaving the old, unaltered tape for reference and backup. In magnetic disc processing, the record is read, updated, and written back onto the disc; most, if not all, of the original data is erased.

Cost.   Finally, the cost factor can be crucial. Magnetic disc is costs more than magnetic tape. A removable disc pack, for example, is at least twenty times more expensive than a reel of tape of the same storage capacity.

Magnetic Drum Storage

Magnetic disc storage devices are potentially powerful and efficient devices for a great many applications. However, in some applications, accessing a smaller volume of data very quickly is necessary or desirable. In such situations, magnetic drum storage is probably most suitable.

The **magnetic drum** is a high-quality metal drum coated with magnetically sensitive film on its outer surface (Figure 8–11). The surface is divided into a number of bands or tracks around the circumference of the drum. Each track has single or multiple read-write heads, depending on whether data transfer is *serial* (bit-by-bit) or *parallel* (multiple bits at a time). The presence of one or more read-write heads for each track eliminates access-motion time completely. Since the only time factors pertinent to drum operation involve head-selection (which is negligible), rotational delay, and data transfer, the magnetic drum provides faster and more efficient operation than other direct-access storage devices.

Figure 8–11. A magnetic drum unit.

Most current magnetic drums are high-speed, low-capacity devices, generally used as on-line storage devices when fast response is of greater importance than large capacity. For example, they may be used to store mathematical tables or program changes that are frequently needed during processing. One particular magnetic drum transfers data at over 1 million bytes per second — a rate unmatched by any other similar device to date. One advantage of the drum is the absence of acceleration problems, since it rotates at constant speed. In contrast, acceleration problems often occur in magnetic tape during reading and/or writing operations. Unless periodically checked, media with such problems could cut into the efficiency of data transfer. On the other hand, the magnetic drum poses a basic limitation: It cannot be removed from one unit and used elsewhere. It does not come in "drum packs" like the magnetic disc. In a sentence, what the drum device surrenders in storage it makes up for in speed.

Direct Access in General

A business firm integrating direct-access devices into its system must maintain an efficient balance between storage volume and unit costs of storage. Direct-access devices hold large volumes of data at a reasonable cost and in the necessary form for processing. Compared to magnetic tape, however, direct-access devices have certain control disadvantages and comparatively higher costs. As cost is reduced, direct-access devices are likely to become the most popular form of secondary storage in the future.

The type of secondary storage device chosen depends on some trade-off among storage capacity, speed, and price. Extended main memory, which two or more computer systems can share, offers large systems the accessibility characteristics (fast access time and transfer rate) at a fraction of the cost. In terms of hardware costs, magnetic tape storage is relatively inexpensive, but it is not as efficient as direct-access memories. For random processing of large-sized files, removable disc packs can be acquired at a relatively reasonable cost. For smaller files, drum memory or the conventional disc memory unit might be the best choice.

SUMMARY

1. This chapter describes direct-access processing as a way of updating records at random. Unlike sequential file processing, the file does not have to be in sequence prior to processing. Thus, the time it takes to update the file depends on the number of records to be updated rather than on the number of records in the master file.

2. A magnetic disc is an on-line mass storage medium. It may be a disc cartridge, a disc pack, or a data module. Each type serves a useful purpose in various systems. Data is recorded on or read from the disc by read-write heads that are a part of the disc drive. The latest drives have a head-per-track design that offers maximum efficiency during data transfer.

3. Discs can store tremendous amounts of information. They are stacked in a unit called a disc pack. The largest disc pack can store over 300 million bytes (300 megabytes) of data. Each disc surface normally has 200 concentric circles called tracks. The data recorded on a track is strung together in bytes. It is addressed by disc number, track number, and sector number. The number of sectors per track and the number of tracks per disc differ with various manufacturers.

4. A record can be stored in count-data format or in count-key data format. In the count-data format, each record (data area) on a track is preceded by a count area, which contains the disc address of the record following it. The latter format has a home address at the beginning of each track and a key area between the count area and the data area. The key area contains a control field, which identifies the record in a file. Both count and key areas can be used to locate records directly on disc.

5. Files used for data processing applications may be arranged in sequential, direct, or indexed-sequential manner. In sequential file organization, records are stored in sequential order by record key. In direct file organization, the record key is generally the address of the disc number and track

where the record is stored. Indexed-sequential file organization combines both sequential and direct-access capabilities. Records can be accessed sequentially by starting with the first block and proceeding with the operation in sequence. They can also be accessed directly by scanning an index to reference the block number that contains the record. Then each record in the block is searched sequentially to locate the desired record.

6. Another direct-access device is the magnetic drum. Like the magnetic disc, the drum is divided into a number of tracks. Each track has a read-write head for data recording or transfer. Magnetic drum is used as an on-line storage device in systems requiring fast access and transfer speeds. What the drum offers in terms of speed, however, it falls short of in terms of storage capacity.

TERMS TO LEARN

Count Area
Data Transfer Time
Indexed-Sequential File
Magnetic Disc
Magnetic Drum
Randomizing
Sector
Seek Time
Sequential Files
Track

REVIEW QUESTIONS

1. What is magnetic disc? Compare and describe briefly the three types of discs.

2. Illustrate the basic layout of disc and how data are coded.

3. Distinguish the difference between:
   a. disc pack and data module,
   b. count-data format and count-key data format,
   c. access-motion time and head-activation time, and
   d. sequential and indexed-sequential file organization.

4. Files used primarily for data processing applications are organized in three major ways. What are they? Explain each briefly.

5. What are the major advantages and drawbacks of sequential file organization?

6. Explain briefly the randomizing procedure in random file organization.

7. How is an indexed-sequential file created?

8. What considerations are given regarding the use of magnetic disc? Explain.

9. What is a magnetic drum? When is it used? How does it compare to other storage devices in terms of fast response?

chapter 9

Card Replacement
and Data Entry Devices

Learning Objectives

Keypunching and verifying are manual steps. They require constant physical handling, they consume time, and they run up costs over the long run. Consequently, other approaches to data preparation and entry had to be developed. These approaches are classified as keypunch replacement devices, pattern recognition devices, and source data automation. Their common objectives are to find a way around the keypunch bottleneck and to prepare data efficiently and on time. By the end of this chapter, you should know:

1. the features and capabilities of data entry devices,

2. pattern recognition data entry devices with a focus on MICR and optical character readers,

3. the uses and impact of intelligent terminals and point-of sale transfers in banking and retailing, and

4. the characteristics of bar code for data entry.

Introduction
Data Entry Devices

Tape

Key-to-Tape Devices
Key-to-Cassette/Cartridge Devices
Tape Systems in General

Disc

Key-to-Disc Data Entry
Floppy Disc System

Pattern Recognition Data Entry

Magnetic Ink Character Recognition (MICR)
Optical Character Recognition (OCR)

Optical Readers
Applications

Source Data Automation (SDA)

Intelligent Terminals
Electronic Funds Transfer (EFT)

Pay-by-Phone
Direct Deposits
Automated Teller Machines (ATMs)
Point-of-Sale Transfers

Point-Of-Sale (POS) Systems in Retailing

POS Systems by Application
POS Systems by Type

Bar Code for Data Entry

Conclusion

Introduction

Data entry is the weakest link in a data processing system. Besides being time-consuming and error-prone, it amounts to between 30 and 50 percent of the total processing costs. The objective, then, is to minimize "bottlenecks" at the input stage so that the high-speed, electronic computer runs efficiently and expeditiously.

As a data entry medium, the punched card did well as long as no alternatives were available. For almost three decades, the punched card was the traditional medium for preparing input data in remote batches.[1] It has proven its worth as a viable input medium. To the small user, it is the most versatile multimedia, lowcost vehicle for data entry and for turnaround data entry methods.[2] The keypunch has also earned its reputation as a rugged, reliable, and relatively economical data entry device. However, because keypunching and verifying are manual steps, they require constant physical handling, consuming both time and costs over the long run. Because they are a primary source of delay at this stage, keypunching and verifying have often been referred to as the "keypunch bottleneck."

To bypass this bottleneck, alternate methods of data entry had to be devised. One alternative is to use the punched card as a **turnaround document** in the form of a telephone bill, insurance premium notice, and the like (Figure 6–5). However, to benefit from this technique, the company must count on a high percentage of full payments returned with the bills or notices. Without full payment by the customer, the document cannot be used as direct input for computer processing. Partial payment requires human intervention. Obviously, the turnaround document is not the ultimate solution to the bottleneck. Other approaches are needed.

During the 1970s, replacements for the keypunch made much progress. Today, most input systems rely on direct data entry devices, grouped under three categories:

1. *Keypunch replacement devices.* The key-to-tape, key-to-disc, and key-to-floppy diskette devices.

2. *Pattern recognition devices.* Magnetic ink and optical character recognition devices.

3. *Source data automation.* Each device offers unique features and is designed to meet certain data entry specifications.

---

[1]The term "batch" refers to the preparation of input data in batches before they are ready for processing. "Remote batch" implies that data can be prepared in locations other than at the computer center.

[2]Over 400,000 businesses in the United States with fewer than 150 employees have yet to install their first computer system. These companies include 200,000 retail firms for cycle billing and inventory control, 125,000 production firms for payroll, job costing, work-in-process, loading, and accounts receivable, as well as 20,000 banks and savings and loans for processing savings accounts, mortgages, trust accounting, and escrow analysis. The common theme in these industries is a requirement for processing turnaround documents. The 80-column card provides the small computer system user with the most cost effective turnaround document and data entry method. It is not too small for manual handling and mailing, large enough to represent adequate information.

Data Entry Devices

Tape

Key-to-tape devices. The first attempt to replace the keypunch and the verifier was the data recorder, pioneered in 1965 by Mohawk Data Sciences (Figure 9–1). On this device, source data is keyed in and verified directly onto magnetic tape. The unit consists of:

1. a keypunch-type keyboard,
2. a control panel that links the keyboard to the tape drive,
3. a small magnetic tape memory and logic, and
4. a handler for the magnetic tape.

The key-to-tape device's primary functions are data entry, data verification, and data search.

Figure 9–1. Key-to-tape data recorder. *Courtesy MDS*

1. **Data entry.** As source data is entered into the recorder's memory, the written record is automatically backspaced by the unit and read to check for parity. Each complete record is extracted from memory and written onto tape (Figure 9–2).

2. **Data verification.** When a batch of records already on tape must be verified, one record at a time is read from the tape into memory. The operator then keys in the source (original) record. If no error is detected, the recorder reads in the next record; this procedure continues until all records are verified. However, if an error is detected, a red indicator flashes. The

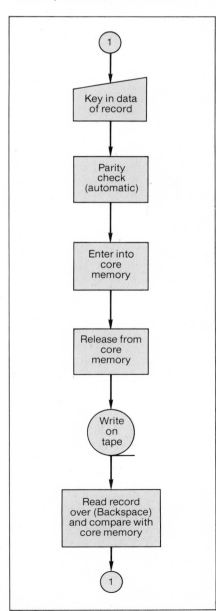

Figure 9–2. Sequence of primary steps in the data entry mode.

operator has three tries to key in the correct character(s) into memory. Once corrected, the record is rewritten back on tape (Figure 9–3).

3. **The search mode.** This step is used to locate records on tape. When a particular record is located, the operator makes the necessary changes in the record.

Besides these basic functions, some key-to-tape devices have attachments that perform auxiliary tasks, such as poolers, communicators, or card readers. The *pooler* combines, or "pools," the outputs of several keying stations onto a single tape for entry into the main computer. The *communicator* has an adaptor for transmitting data either between two devices or to a remote computer center over a leased voice-band line. Remote data entry allows the user (such as a salesperson) direct access to the computer facility from the data source.

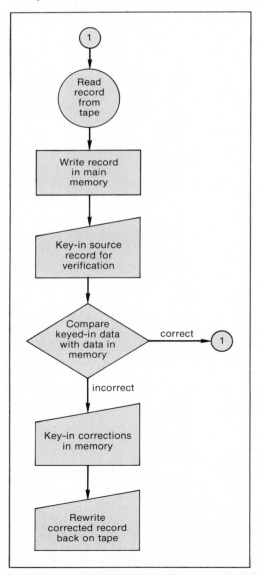

Figure 9–3. Primary steps in data verification.

The key-to-tape features therefore offer several advantages over the key-punch:

1. A key-to-tape device is faster than the keypuch because it is electronic, whereas the keypunch is electromechanical.

2. It has greater flexibility in input format with transactions that exceed the 80-column card limit.

3. Backspacing provides for error correction. While keypunching requires replacing the whole card to correct an error, an error on tape requires only backspacing to the error's location and then inscribing the correct character. Error handling at the source means the elimination of future problems and of additional costs.

4. The tape drive encounters fewer reading problems than the card reader does with cards that might be mutilated, stapled, or spindled. Furthermore, a key-to-tape machine performs the functions of both the keypunch and the verifier in one operation.

5. The replacement of punched cards with tape means a reduction in manual handling along with approximately a 25-percent increase in productivity. The saving becomes more obvious with larger volumes of source data for entry and with a better organized overall data entry process.

6. On tape, recorded data cannot get out of sequence.

A major drawback of key-to-tape systems is their limited record display; that is, not all of the record can be displayed on a screen at once, due to the sequential nature of tape. This limitation makes "eyeball" verification impossible and also makes error correcting while keying more difficult.

Key-to-cassette/cartridge devices. A key-to-cassette/cartridge system records source data directly onto a small magnetic cassette tape or cartridge. The stored data is later converted to a full-sized magnetic tape for computer processing (Figure 9–4).

Basically with a key-to-tape medium, these devices generally offer the same advantages and involve the same limitations as key-to-tape equipment. Their unique advantages, however, are the simplicity of their operation and their ability to capture data anywhere it originates. In large organizations, for example, district or regional offices record locally originated data on cassette or cartridge. Later, either the data is transmitted over telephone lines, or the cassette/cartridge is mailed to high-level offices for processing. Compared to traditional magnetic tape, cassettes or cartridges have these other advantages:

1. *Economic storage and easy handling.* No spooling or tape loading is necessary, since these steps are automatic.

Figure 9–4. Tape cartridge and reader (left) and tape cassette.

2. *A convenient method of maintaining batch control.* In a banking application for processing rejected checks, the average batch of 250 records of 80 columns each is easily stored on one cartridge.

3. *Protection from dirt.* Each cartridge or cassette is placed in a plastic housing to protect stored data from dirt or human mishandling.

Tape systems in general. The performance and reliability of any tape system depend largely on its packing density (bits per inch) and data transfer rate. Closer packing densities create a higher probability of error due to dust particles and tape quality. Given these and other factors, the cartridge has an edge over the cassette. IBM, Bell Telephone, and the U.S. Navy have adopted the cartridge as their standard data storage medium, probably for the following reasons:

1. The cartridge has a 1,600-bit/inch recording density on multiple tracks, compared to the cassette's maximum 800-bit/inch density—a two-fold advantage in storage capacity for the cartridge.

2. At a 1,600-bit/inch density and a 30-inch/second tape velocity, the cartridge provides a data transfer rate of 48,000 bit/second. In contrast, a cassette operates at a maximum speed of 8 inch/second and with its 800-

bit/inch density, providing a data transfer rate of only 6,400 bit/inch. This means an eight-fold advantage for the cartridge without losing reliability.

3. The data cartridge has major mechanical advantages over the cassette. Its built-in tape guides eliminate skew and ensure error-free operation. The data cassette does not have such assurances.

Disc

Key-to-disc data entry. Unlike the tape or cassette/cartridge devices, the key-to-disc (or **shared processor**) system is a pioneering step toward data input automation. First developed in 1967 by the Computer Machinery Corporation, the system consists of a magnetic disc, a set of key stations (ranging from 8 to 64), a mini-sized computer, a control package, and a tape unit. The keyed-in input data is edited by the minicomputer prior to storage on the disc. In output, the "loaded" disc is read out on computer-compatible magnetic tape for processing (Figure 9–5).

Several features are unique to the key-to-disc system. Compared to key-punching, key-to-disc systems offer the following advantages:

1. *Improved data entry input format flexibility.* As the input data is keyed in, it is arranged in predetermined formats. The stored format concept is a time-saving feature compared to the keypunch, which requires changing a program card for each format.

Figure 9–5. Key-to-disc method of data input.

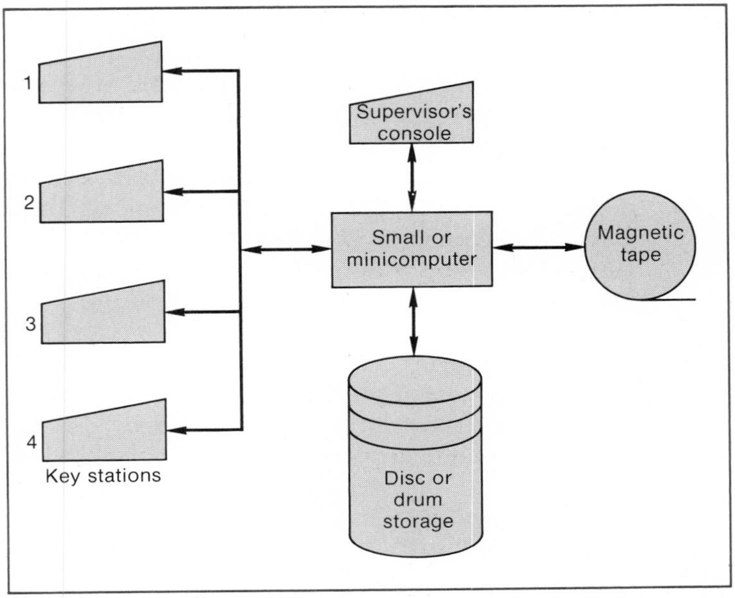

213

2. *Reduced error rates.* The character display panel on most systems is useful for sight verification. Depending on the make, the panel displays the last character or even the entire record entered or verified. This feature reduces verification strokes and improves the system's total efficiency.

3. *Greater responsiveness.* An experienced keypunch operator produces about 8,000 strokes per hour with about a 1-percent error rate. A key-to-disc operator produces an average of 13,000 strokes per hour with as high as 21,000 strokes per hour, virtually error-free.

4. *Better editing and data control.* Most key-to-disc systems provide, as a byproduct, production figures for each key station operator. The system maintains a file on the number of keystrokes made and the jobs processed by each operator. Some systems even count the number of errors made and the time it takes the operator to enter and verify the source data. The computer can easily determine the operator's efficiency and effectiveness for feedback to management.

5. *A productivity gain of 20 to 30 percent.* A disc system eliminates handling necessary in the tape or cassette systems or on the keypunch.

6. *Reduced hardware requirements.* In one installation, a 9-station key-to-disc system replaced 16 keypunch machines.

7. *Easier operator acceptance.* The disc system provides total operator-system interaction at a mental level that has been shown to increase productivity. Operators now work in an enhanced working environment with a quieter and neater system than the keypunch.

Given the benefits of key-to-disc data entry, applications involving preparation and entry large amounts of data easily justify conversion from a keypunch to a key-to-disc system, because the cost savings are usually great. For example, one organization had 16 operators committed to 12 keypunches and 4 verifiers. They used an average of 75 million cards per month. The "sweat shop" operation occupied 700 square feet. A key-to-disc conversion resulted in a 30-percent cost saving, including a 22-percent reduction in personnel and a 9-percent reduction in media cost. The new work environment alone has been credited for a significant reduction in labor turnover and for an improvement in employee morale in the shop. More and more organizations are therefore pursuing such benefits.

Floppy disc system. The advent of the minicomputer and the demand for low-cost data storage provided the basis for the development of a unique peripheral—the floppy disc system. Also called "diskette," the **floppy disc** is a compact, flexible data storage medium. It resembles a 45-rpm phonograph record enclosed in a plastic jacket (Figure 9–6). Ever since their introduction in 1970, "floppies" have been replacing punched cards, cassettes, and cartridges in minicomputer systems, calculators, and word processing systems. They con-

Figure 9–6. A floppy disc or diskette. *Courtesy Verbatim Corporation*

stitute an advance in remote data capture for a decentralized data entry environment, as well as an excellent load medium for remote terminals and distributed processing.

A basic key-to-diskette system consists of an operator key station and a data converter for transforming the diskette output to a 9-track magnetic tape for processing. The key station includes a keypunch-like keyboard, a display screen to show the status of data, a controller, and a diskette. The diskette is a round disc (7.5 inch in diameter), with concentric tracks of data storage and a moving read-write head for direct access processing. One floppy disc has the capacity to store three-thousand 80-column punched cards.

Data is organized and retrieved according to the disc's equal-sized pie shapes, called *sectors*. The disc tracks cut across each sector to form addresses for locating stored data. A sector can be identified by a magnetic code written onto the diskette, and the beginning of the track can be signaled by an index hole in the diskette.

A summary of alternative methods of data entry is illustrated in Figure 9–7.

Pattern Recognition Data Entry

As the cost of input preparation steadily increases, direct data entry devices — although a major improvement over the keypunch — do not completely eliminate the bottleneck. Ideally, the key-in should be eliminated completely. Turnaround source documents accomplished this ideal goal to some extent: Data,

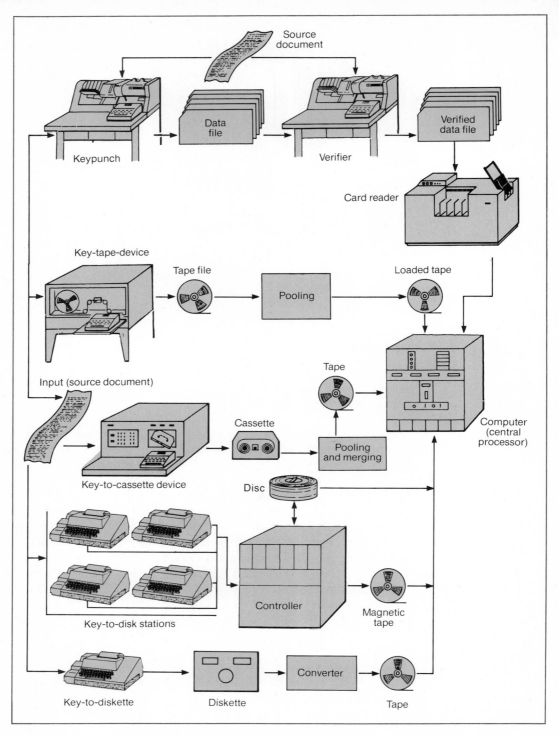

Figure 9–7. Alternative methods of data entry.

represented by magnetic flux patterns are recognized by the computer for processing. Along the same line, another alternative is to automate the direct entry of source data. This technique focuses on electronic funds transfer (EFT) and point-of-sale (POS) data entry in retailing.

Magnetic Ink Character Recognition (MICR)

Magnetic ink character recognition (MICR) is an automated data entry technique in which data is pre-inscribed on the check (the source document) for reading into a computer via a special reader. The amount of the check is later inscribed by bank personnel just prior to final processing. The banking industry pioneered magnetic ink character recognition (MICR) to automate check processing through the computer. After the use of checks increased at a phenomenal rate over the years, in 1955 the American Bankers Association (ABA) recognized the need to automate the paperwork. Either the check or a new document had to be developed as input to an automated system. In 1959, the Association adopted a standard type font to be used in coding all checks. A year later, the encoding of checks with magnetic ink was finally standardized throughout the banking industry. As an original document, the check can now be used directly as input to the computer.

Check processing begins with the blank check. A customer who opens an account is issued a book of checks, each of which is similar to the sample in Figure 9–8. Precoded near the bottom of each check are the bank number, routing data, and the account number. Because each character is printed in magnetic

Figure 9–8. A MICR encoded check—an example.

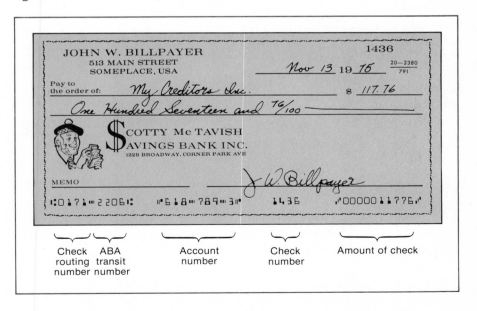

ink, the check can be read by a MICR reader-sorter[3] that is connected directly to a computer. Once the data is detected, the pattern is converted into electronic signals to be used by the computer for updating the customer's account. The MICR sorter-reader and the 14 MICR characters currently used in magnetic character recognition are shown in Figure 9–9.

The only data that cannot be pre-inscribed is the amount of the check. Therefore, when a filled-out check is deposited by a customer, a bank employee encodes the amount of the check on the lower right on a MICR inscriber (Figure 9–10). Since someone must use the inscriber's keyboard, the key-in step still requires human intervention.

The primary function of the MICR reader-sorter is to read the data from the checks and transfer it to the computer. As a secondary task, it also physically sorts checks by account number so that they can be returned to the customer with the monthly statement. In an on-line system, the MICR unit, physically hooked to a computer, reads the checks for direct processing. Otherwise, in an off-line operation, the data is stored on magnetic tape for later processing. Among the advantages of MICR are:

1. ***High check reading accuracy.*** Some systems have less than a 2-percent reject rate.

2. ***An easily readable type font.*** The user generally has no problem reading the inscribed data when necessary.

Figure 9–9. The Burroughs' B9138 high-speed MICR reader-sorter (left) and magnetic ink character identification chart. *Courtesy Burroughs Corporation*

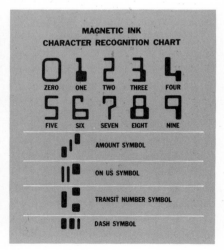

[3]The reader-sorter is the final judge of the proper coding of documents. Unreadable data goes to a separate reject pocket for manual handling.

Figure 9–10. MICR inscriber. *Courtesy NCR Corporation*

3. **Reduced error rate.** Encoding checks with the customer's account number and the issuing bank's coded number minimizes the chance for error.

Optical Character Recognition (OCR)

In *optical scanning,* the computer searches (or scans) a form for marks, bars, or characters, converting the reflected optical impulses to electrical signals that represent characters. *Recognition* is the computer's comparison of these electrical signals with matched sets of stored signals to determine their identity. **Optical character recognition (OCR)** is a step in the man-machine interface by which a form understandable to humans is converted to a form acceptable to a computer. Like other direct input devices, OCR reduces the cost of capturing source data, but it also offers the following benefits:

1. It eliminates redundant keypunching and transcription errors;

2. it increases equipment utilization;

3. it reduces the need for highly skilled employees; and

4. it reduces turnaround time.

OCR readers have a history dating back to the early 1800s, when similar devices were used to help the blind. In 1870, an image transmission unit was developed that used photocells. Around 1890, a sequential scanning device was built to analyze the image one line at a time. In 1912, a machine was invented to read a printed set of characters and convert it into telegraph code.

The first commercial OCR device, developed in 1951 by Intelligent Machine Research Corporation, was the optical reader. Since then, these readers have been acclaimed as the panacea for data entry woes and as finally "coming of age." Today, among the major OCR users are credit card organizations, airlines, banks, health care institutions, retail stores, insurance companies, government, and utilities. In oil company credit card operations, for instance, OCR devices are widely used to read carbon imprints of customer card numbers and the amount charged for billing purposes. The OCR system proved to be the answer to the "input bottleneck."

Optical readers.   Optical readers are classified into three categories:

1. *Optical mark sense readers (OMRS)*   have been used traditionally for test scoring, inventory control, and other "mark-the-correct-box" applications. Turnaround documents, such as utility bills, are also processed the same way. Mark sense readers may interface directly with a computer or may operate off-line, feeding data read onto magnetic tape for later computer entry.

2. *Bar or line code readers*   accept card-size documents imprinted with special bar or line codes. Major applications of bar coded documents are in credit card data entry, logging and routing of packages, and in point-of-sale (POS) retail systems. (Details on POS systems are presented later in the chapter.)

3. *Optical character readers (OCRS)*   offer the most efficient reading and translating of typed, printed, or handwritten characters into machine language. They identify each character by comparing its features with features stored in memory. The OCR reader consists of a transport unit, scanning unit, and recognition unit (Figure 9–11). Characters are converted into a "picture" through a photoelectric eye. Internally stored reference patterns guide the recognition unit to verify (match) the patterns held by the scanning unit. The matching process is made on the basis of the line formation of each charater (called *stroke analysis*) or, in the case of handwritten characters, the outline of the character (called *curve tracing*). Unmatched character patterns cause a rejection of the document.

OCR readers (category 3) are differentiated on the basis of the physical size of the documents and on the class of type fonts. The three document classes are:

a. *Journal tape readers*   are designed to read cash register and adding machine tapes in retailing.

b. *Small document readers*   scan turnaround documents, such as utility bills or preprinted credit card stubs. The data is used later for entry into the computer system for processing.

c. *Page readers*   are capable of reading multiple lines of typed or printed material from a normal page layout. The document size ranges from 6×8 to 12×14 inches.

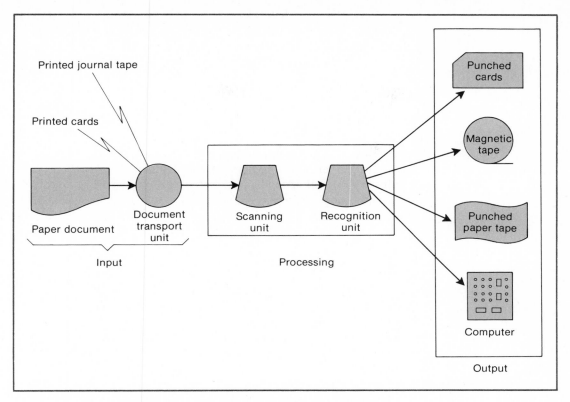

Figure 9–11. The primary elements of an OCR reader.

The three classes of OCR font capability are:

a. **Mark readers** were already explained. Mark sensing is the machine reading of pencil marks placed in predefined positions on special forms. Each position is preassigned a value which remains fixed for that type of document.

b. **Single-font** and *multifont readers* are capable of reading a single style of type and several printed fonts (upper and lower case), respectively.

c. **Hand-print readers** read block-printed characters. Each character must be clearly printed with no open loops, disconnected lines, or linked characters (Figure 9–12). The reader, tracing the outline of the hand-printed character, accepts the character if it fits within tolerance configurations. Employees who have to hand-print numbers are usually trained in advance. Proper training can take as long as two days. Although the reject rate runs as high as 10 percent among new users, the average reject rate among established users is less than 1 percent.

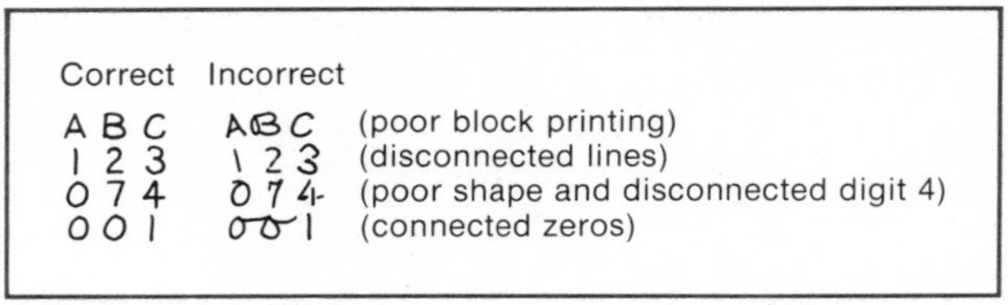

```
Correct   Incorrect
A B C     A B C    (poor block printing)
1 2 3     1 2 3    (disconnected lines)
0 7 4     0 7 4    (poor shape and disconnected digit 4)
0 0 1     0 0 1    (connected zeros)
```

Figure 9–12.

Applications.   OCR readers are widely used by companies with large volumes of billing requirements. A typical installation handles over 100,000 documents per hour; this kind of speedy input contributes to rapid billing and to a more available cash flow. Although the oil industry was the first major industry to adopt OCR on a large scale, OCR users now include insurance companies, utilities, department stores, petroleum companies, mail order houses, airlines, and publishing firms.

The *utilities* industry uses optical mark readers to process turnaround documents returned (with payment) by customers. Information handwritten by meter readers is read by an OCR device and written directly onto magnetic tape. The data is later used as input for processing. This system simplifies the chores in billing and accounts receivable.

Large *mail order* houses use OCR systems to process tens of thousands of turnaround documents from customers every day. A mail order house in Chicago, for example, uses a large OCR system to process over 115,000 customer account statements every day.

The *Social Security Administration* in Baltimore uses an optical page reader to scan the name, Social Security number, and quarterly earnings of 80 million reported wage earners. Punching the data onto cards for conventional reading takes over 3 months. The OCR system is reported to have saved the bureau over $3,000,000 as of 1979.

Airlines also find much use for the OCR system. United Airlines, for example, operates a reader that processes over two million coupons per month by scanning each coupon's 14-digit ticket and coupon number at an effective throughput rate of 490 documents per minute. Rejects resulting from agents' errors are estimated at 1.5 percent. Print quality and the reader's scanning errors account for another 1.5 percent of the rejected documents.

Other industries using OCR include insurance companies, industries using credit cards, the food industry for controlling inventory, breweries, telephone companies, banks, and the postal system. In each case, justification for the use of OCR is based on the economic benefits derived from processing large volumes of data at a speed unmatched by alternate data entry methods. In one installation, going to OCR meant a reduction from twenty three data entry operators to three fulltime and three part-time operators, along with net annual savings of $100,000.

Insofar as key-to-tape/disc/diskette/cassette terminals do not eliminate the labor-intensive keying operation, regardless of any computer assistance, they cannot be characterized as source data automation (SDA) systems. **Source data automation** is the automatic capture of the data at the source. It is the conversion of information about a transaction into machine-readable form when and where the transaction occurs.

Intelligent Terminals

In an SDA system, data capture and entry devices are usually "intelligent" terminals. An **intelligent terminal** is a specialized, operator-oriented, single-key entry station. In intelligent terminals, the data is entered, validated, and edited in connection with a stored program format. The data remains stored on a medium (such as a floppy disc) until it is transmitted in batches to the central processor. The terminal has the following features:

1. a processor and high-speed memory for data and/or program storage,

2. communication capability for transmitting and receiving data from a "host" or master computer,

3. a CRT display for presenting data to the operator, and

4. programmability.

A programmable intelligent terminal offers several advantages. By editing, refining, and consolidating information before passing it on to the host computer, its unique role is handling basic data processing and formatting tasks independently of the computer. This capability saves costly computer processing time; it also provides temporary local storage, reduces operator errors at the point of entry, and enables the user to program the device for other chores. Some intelligent terminals can even maintain and access their own data base files of customer numbers, thus turning information around quickly without wasting computer time. The major drawback, is that intelligent terminals cost more to buy and to operate than "dumb" terminals. The equipment cost is higher, and operator training is more extensive.

The decision to use intelligent terminals depends largely on the application's needs and limitations. For example, if turnaround information is not critical, a remote batch terminal might be adequate to gather and buffer data during the day. Otherwise, for faster turnaround, an intelligent terminal is a better choice. The final decision must balance specific objectives with acceptable trade-offs. For example, if a company needs a sales order entering system for a remote sales office that will match the orders with customer numbers in the data base file, three types of terminals are eligible:

1. *A "store-and-forward" batch terminal* collects, edits, and for-

mats data, then stores it on floppy discs or magnetic tape for transmission to the host computer at the end of the day. Although equipment and transmission costs are low, turnaround performance suffers because the terminal is not on-line to the files of the master computer.

2. *An on-line, interactive terminal* is directly linked to the data base for entering invoice information. The terminal operator is "coached" by the host computer to enter the correct information and access and receive the proper files. The turnaround performance in this case is high, although communication costs and the host computer's processing time are excessive.

3. *A distributed (intelligent) terminal* stores and accesses its own local data base files of customer numbers for quick turnaround time without wasting host computer time. A company with personnel expertise and established data security measures is likely to choose the distributed terminal over the other two listed.

SDA breaks down into three areas:

1. electronic funds transfer (EFT),

2. point-of-sale (POS) systems, and

3. bar code entry.

Electronic Funds Transfer (EFT)

Electronic funds transfer (EFT), generally, is a system that enables banks to deliver deposits, to make withdrawals, and to perform other customer services — all electronically — where and when the customer needs the services. No paperwork is exchanged. One bank's computer tells another bank's computer to credit a customer's account by a certain amount. The account is updated instantly without writing, depositing, or clearing a check.

EFT takes many forms. The earliest form took place in 1962 in Indianapolis. Several local banks received payroll information on magnetic tapes from a local firm. The tape was exchanged among the banks, and payroll funds were credited to employees' checking accounts. In 1968, the Federal Reserve Banks were linked by a telegram system, permitting any Federal Reserve Bank and its member banks to "wire" money in multiples of one hundred dollars. In 1974, a bank in Lincoln, Nebraska, successfully set up an EFT system in collaboration with two local supermarkets. Within 45 days, the bank's electronic branches at the supermarkets had secured 650 new accounts and $650,000 in cash deposits. In general, four major types of EFT services are available today:

1. pay-by-phone,

2. direct deposits and automatic payments,

3. automated teller machines, and

4. point-of-sale transfer.

Pay-by-phone.   Such systems allow an individual to telephone his or her bank and order either payments to third persons or transfers between accounts. Bridging the gap between the plodding paperwork of the present and the electronic blips of the future, the customer punches coded numerals through a Touch-Tone™phone; the numerals hook up the customer to a computer. Then, the customer uses the phone again to punch in the information regarding the transaction—how much money goes to which merchant. Customers without Touch-Tone™phones call tellers who feed the information into the cumputer. A check is then sent to the merchant or utility, representing payments of all customers who utilize the service.

Direct deposits.   This system automates transactions within an account. The deposit of a customers' wages or Social Security benefits— or the deduction of utility bills or insurance premiums from the account—is all done automatically with little or no paperwork. Big banks are busy persuading corporate customers to pay employees by electronic transfers rather than by checks. By 1985, one-half of the people in the country will likely be paid by electronic transfer.

Automated teller machines (ATMs).   These machines permit a variety of banking transactions 24 hours a day, every day. Also referred to as "vending machine" banking, ATMs allow customers to make mortgage payments, loan payments, cash withdrawals from savings or checking accounts, cash advances from a credit card, and fund transfers from one account to another—all at the command of a plastic transaction card (Figure 9–13). The major steps in operating an ATM are:

1. The customer inserts a magnetically encoded card into the terminal, to initiate the transaction.

2. He or she enters another secret security code to verify the card and to identify the customer.

3. The customer selects a transaction (such as a cash withdrawal).

4. He or she enters the transaction amount to update the account record and to indicate the amount withdrawn.

5. In an on-line ATM, the computer verifies the record. Two receipts are generally printed: one for the customer and one to be retained for an audit trail. The receipt shows the time, type, and amount of the transaction and other pertinent information.

6. The card returns to the customer.

7. The terminal dispenses a printed receipt and the amount of cash withdrawn.

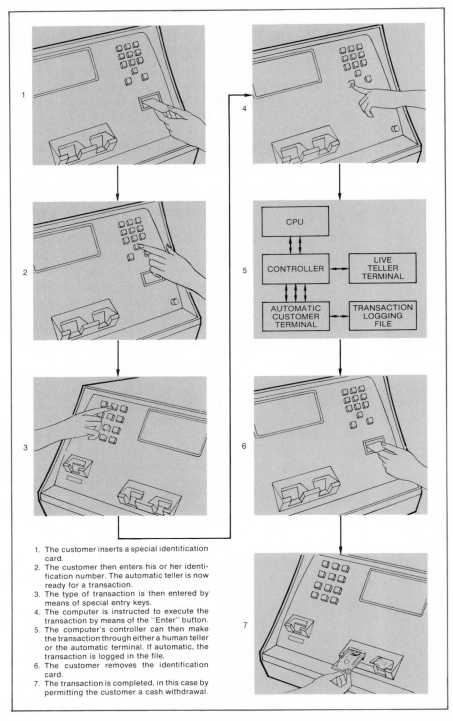

1. The customer inserts a special identification card.
2. The customer then enters his or her identification number. The automatic teller is now ready for a transaction.
3. The type of transaction is then entered by means of special entry keys.
4. The computer is instructed to execute the transaction by means of the "Enter" button.
5. The computer's controller can then make the transaction through either a human teller or the automatic terminal. If automatic, the transaction is logged in the file.
6. The customer removes the identification card.
7. The transaction is completed, in this case by permitting the customer a cash withdrawal.

Figure 9–13. The automatic teller/customer interface.

ATMs have both advantages and drawbacks. Among the advantages are:

1. For the retailer, they increase security, because less cash need be on hand. They also relieve employees from cashing customers' checks.
2. Teller and operating costs are reduced.
3. Financial transactions can be initiated at convenient locations.

The primary drawbacks are:

1. Customers prefer tellers over ATMs.
2. The customer loses personal contact.
3. Customers react adversely to machines that are out of service or cash.
4. Customers are afraid of being robbed if cash is withdrawn from isolated ATM locations.

Overall, vending machine banking is gaining momentum. ATMs are now being installed through-the-wall to extend banking hours. Eventually, banks will install machines in airports, bus depots, train stations, and merchants' sites — all electronically linked to the bank's data base. As automated services become more prevalent, however, banks will have to improve their personalized services, such as financial counseling and packaged services, because a bank's primary objective is the continued and improved service to its customers.

Point-of-sale transfers.   This kind of transfer enables a customer, through a retailer's computer terminal, to transfer money instantly from his or her checking account to the merchant's. The customer presents a plastic card to the sales clerk, who places the card into the terminal. The card is read electronically, and the debit-credit cash transfer is done instantly. Only a dozen big banks now offer versions of POS electronic banking. The main problem at present is security — maintaining the customers' privacy and protecting them against fraudulent access by an employee.

Point-of-Sale (POS) Systems in Retailing

A **point-of-sale** data collection system collects transactional data automatically at the time and at the place of the transaction. Such systems date back to the early 1950s, when machine-readable tags were used to encode inventory information. When an item was sold, the tag was saved. They were later sent in batches to a data processing center where they were converted to a faster input medium for processing. POS terminals are superior to the batch method, since they handle tag reading directly. Most systems handle information related to such items as discounts, uneven trades, and down payments on merchandise sold. Such capabilities simplify the clerk's functions and allow him or her to concentrate on the needs of the customer.

Although the majority of POS systems share similar characteristics, the approach they use in capturing the data may be electromechanical, optical, or magnetic. The *electromechanical* approach involves a hand-held device or a reader for reading the traditional perforated tape. The *optical* and the *magnetic* approaches use a portable "wand" reader, which scans the price and stock number on the tag with foolproof accuracy. When the optical wand reads the data, it emits a "beep" with each wave of the wand to tell the salesclerk that the data is entered correctly (Figure 9–14). This procedure minimizes data entry errors and allows various levels of authorization for selected transactions. Some systems visually display the sequence of operator instructions, while other systems visually light up each key in its proper sequence. Both systems are rated highly accurate.

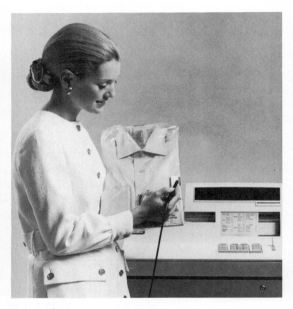

Figure 9–14. Examples of leading POS systems. *Courtesy NCR Corporation*

Over 75 percent of the information required by retailers can be captured at the point of the sale. The retail industry has already begun using a new source data collection system, which collects business data at the point of the transactions and records it in computer-usable form. Capturing sales data on a real-time basis means that the retailer can now more effectively control inventory, more promptly react to customer needs, and more efficiently reduce cash losses and receivables. Likewise, the customer doesn't have to wait long on checkout lines. Some POS systems have wand-type readers that eliminate keyboard data entry; other systems provide credit authorization that reduces the credit approval time to seconds.

POS systems are located at the checkout counters of retail stores, usually operated by the employees. Among the benefits are:

1. *More effective personnel utilization.* Salespersons can handle each transaction at the time it occurs quickly and expeditiously.

2. *Better control over customer credit.* Credit authorization is handled through an automated phase of the POS system.

3. *Better cash control.*

4. *Better inventory control and reductions in inventory personnel.*

5. *Improved customer service.* Tax calculations, discount calculations, group pricing, and the like are all automatic. This means faster checkout time.

POS systems by application. POS systems are classified as *general merchandise, supermarket-oriented,* or *fast food-oriented* systems. All systems share similar basic functions, although they are designed to meet different requirements. Systems designed for the general merchandise (department) store or retailer are designed to handle a large number of items per customer. Since department stores sell mostly on credit, the system must run credit authorizations. Since it is also product-oriented, the store's products are department-assignable; that is, one or more terminals must be installed in each department.

Like general merchandise systems, POS systems for the supermarket handle many items per customer, and they are designed for use by unskilled clerks. However, they differ in that, since the supermarket is a "cash-and-carry" operation, credit authorization is less important than in the department store system. Furthermore, a supermarket operation is "nonstop shopping," requiring uninterrupted operation. The rapid inventory turnover and the high volume of checkout counter activity require that the system must never fail.

Systems in fast food stores (such as MacDonald's, Kentucky Fried Chicken, and the like) handle a limited number of menu items, but they traffic a large volume of business each day. For productive operation, most terminals have a separate key for each item. They also carry out automatic tax calculations and price extensions.

POS systems by type. POS systems in retailing may also be categorized as:

1. local recording,
2. centralized, or
3. remote on-line, interactive systems.

The *local recording system* consists of a group of stand-alone terminals with built-in processors for collecting and storing the data for later use by the store manager. The data may also be stored on tape cassettes or cartridge for later transmission or for delivery to a processing computer center.

With a *centralized (in-store)* configuration, a number of terminals are linked through a controller or a minicomputer. At the end of the day, all data is collected onto one tape instead of onto different cassettes, as is the case with local recording terminals. The centralized in-store system is the most widely used POS system today.

The *remote on-line POS system* is an extension of the centralized system. Terminals in the store(s) are linked to the company's computer center through one or more controllers. The controller edits and formats the data, prepares the data for transmission, and acts as a communication link to the computer system.

Bar Code for Data Entry

A **bar code** consists of a series of lines (or bars) that vary in thickness and spacing (Figure 9–15).When the differing light reflections are detected and converted into electronic signals, each code thus represents a product. In 1973, for example, the grocery industry adopted as its standard Universal Product Code (UPC), a bar code. Although different industries use various versions, the basic one is shown in Figure 9–16. Code symbols are expected to meet certain requirements. They must:

1. be machine- and human-readable,
2. be readable omnidirectionally,
3. be readable by hand-held wands as well as by fixed scanners,
4. have a scanning reject rate of less than 0.01 percent, and
5. have a scanning process not measurably affected by dirt and other environmental factors.

First used to identify freight cars, the bar code has come into use in a variety of applications in production, warehouses, hospitals, department stores, and supermarkets. Bar codes appear on storage bins and shelves as part of an inventory control system. A hospital uses a bar code at a terminal to facilitate the entry

Figure 9–15. A bar coded label—an example.

of a patient, a requested service, or the operator's identification. In grocery stores, all canned and frozen products have bar code labels as a part of an inventory control system (Figure 9–15).

Recently, the unit prices of items are included in bar codes; as a result, the price of items can be on the shelves rather than on each item. The wand at the checkout counter reads the bar code on each item and records the price and inventory specifics. In addition to arithmetic operations, the POS terminal displays the scanned items on a panel for the customer to check, at the same time generating a hard copy detailing the items sold.

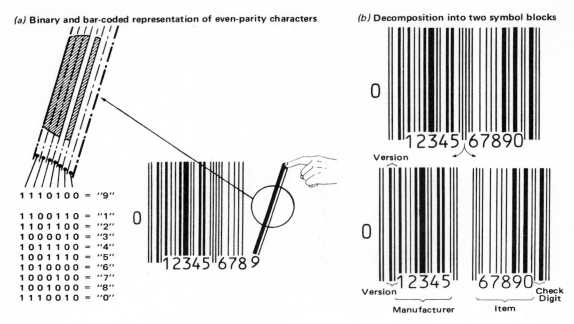

(a) Binary and bar-coded representation of even-parity characters

1110100 = "9"
1100110 = "1"
1101100 = "2"
1000010 = "3"
1011100 = "4"
1001110 = "5"
1010000 = "6"
1000100 = "7"
1001000 = "8"
1110010 = "0"

(b) Decomposition into two symbol blocks

Version

Version   Manufacturer   Item   Check Digit

Figure 9–16. The UPC structure.

Conclusion

SDA does not deal with a single product line but rather involves a broad range of devices. These diverse systems have several purposes in common—to speed data capture, to reduce response time, and to save money for the user. The development of specific SDA techniques are spurred by the interest of major industry groups such as retail merchants, grocers, bankers, and insurance firms. The proliferation of SDA systems gives strong evidence that the benefits outweigh the risks in most systems. It is fair to assume that this trend will continue.

SUMMARY

1. Data entry is the weakest link in a data processing system. The keypunch has earned its reputation as a reliable and economical data entry device. The problem, however, is that the physical handling of the decks of cards and the data verification process are time-consuming. Consequently, three major alternatives have been introduced to replace the keypunch: the key-to-disc/tape/floppy disc, pattern recognition devices, and source data automation.

2. Direct data entry devices surpass the keypunch in several ways. While they offer improvement in operator throughput, they also reduced the cost of media and personnel, make data verification and correction routines more efficient and easier, and measure operators statistically for performance. In determining which data entry device best suits a given application, users who need to translate source documents into computer input from remote locations will find a key-to-diskette system appropriate. For users with source documents in one location, key-to-disc data entry is a proper choice. However, users with high volume, fast turnaround requirements will find optical character recognition (OCR) equipment the ideal choice.

3. MICR was developed primarily to automate banking paperwork. The process involves encoding checks with magnetic ink, which is later read by a special reader-sorter for updating a customer's checking account.

4. OCR is designed to reduce the cost of capturing source data, to eliminate the need for keypunching, to increase equipment utilization, and to reduce mandatory employee skill levels and turnaround time. OCR readers identify each character by comparing its features with features stored in memory. The matching process is made on the basis of stroke analysis or curve tracing. Unmatched character patterns cause a rejection of the document.

5. Source data automation (SDA) refers to the capture of the data at the source. In intelligent data entry, the data is entered, validated, and edited with an intelligent terminal under a stored program format. For fast turnaround, an on-line, interactive, or distributed terminal is a must.

6. SDA is classified into three groups: electronic fund transfer (EFT), point-of-sale (POS), and bar code entry. EFT makes it possible for banks to electronically deliver deposits, make withdrawals, and perform other services where and when the customer needs these services. The account is updated instantly without a check being written, deposited, or cleared. The types of EFT services are pay-by-phone, direct deposits and automated payments, automated teller machines (ATMs), or point-of-sale (POS) transfer. The latter system is unique to retailing.

7. The bar code system is adopted by the grocery industry to automate data gathering and processing. A wand at the checkout counter reads the bar code on each item and records the price and inventory specifics. A POS terminal performs arithmetic, displays the scanned item(s) on a panel for the customer to check, and produces a hard copy detailing the items sold. The proliferation of SDA systems gives strong evidence of the net benefits in most systems.

TERMS TO LEARN

Bar Code
Electronic funds transfer (EFT)
Intelligent terminal
Magnetic ink character recognition (MICR)
Optical character recognition (OCR)

Point-of-sale
Shared processor
Source data automation
  (SDA)
Turnaround document

REVIEW QUESTIONS

1. Compare and contrast the uses of key-to-tape and key-to-disc system.

2. What unique features does key-to-cassette have? When would one decide on using the cassette over the key-to-tape?

3. How does the key-to-disc system differ from the floppy disc?

4. In view of the latest developments in direct input and other data entry devices, what is your assessment of the future of the floppy disc?

5. What is MICR? How does it help banks process information? Explain.

6. In your own words, describe the functions and benefits of OCR. Who uses it? Why?

7. Distinguish between:

   (a) stroke analysis and curve tracing,
   (b) bar code reader and hand print reader,
   (c) batch and remote batch processing,
   (d) MICR inscriber and MICR reader-sorter, and
   (e) intelligent and dumb terminal.

8. Explain the major types of electronic funds transfer. Illustrate.

9. Discuss the pros and cons of automated teller machines.

10. Visit a local supermarket chain and report on the type of POS system available. If none are used, explore the feasibility of a POS installation.

chapter 10

Communicating with the Computer

Learning Objectives

Telecommunications, an integral aspect of virtually every computer-based network, is a system of communication channels that originates and terminates at user nodes through terminals. The transported commodity is data. Without telecommunications, distributed networks, time-sharing, and on-line/real-time environments are all impossible. Therefore, we must understand telecommunications, explore its basic structure, and evaluate its contributions to decision making. By the end of this chapter, you should know:

1. what application categories are in operation,

2. the concepts and modes of transmission,

3. the different types of telecommunication terminals used for data transmission,

4. how telecommunication equipment interconnects with networks, and

5. the major common carriers and the varieties of services they offer.

Introduction

Telecommunications permeate virtually every aspect of our society. Business, finance, education, police, the retailing of merchandise, and the wholesaling of entertainment — all are embedded in the offerings and enmeshed by the constraints of telecommunications. Today's demand for this technology in business attests to the viability of the interrelationship between data communications and data processing. Telecommunications link the computer with companies in dispersed locations by transmitting processed data. Computers, on the other hand, process the data received and direct the demands of various centers into an organized set of communication channels.

The saga of telecommunications began on May 24, 1844 when Sam Morse (a New England portrait painter) tapped out the world's first telegram 40 miles over an iron wire linking the Chambers of the U.S. Supreme Court in Washington with the Baltimore & Ohio Railroad station in Baltimore, Maryland. Interestingly enough, the decoded message read "What hath God wrought!" Thirty-two years later, Alexander Graham Bell's famous message to his assistant — "Mr. Watson, come here, I want you" — proved that the telegraph could transmit "the timbre of a sound." Bell's telephone was here to stay. In 1897, Marconi sent the first wireless telegraph signal across the English Channel, using a standard Morse code. A few years later, radio telegraphy was transmitting messages around the world. From Bell and Marconi came the first enterprises we know today as Western Union, AT&T, and many others. Others contributed to the advancement of data communications. Thomas Edison produced the Quadruplex in 1894, which transmitted four messages in each direction over a single wire. Sam Colt (inventor of the revolver) tested submarine telegraphy when he directed the laying of a cable in 1845 across the East River in New York.

The key channel used in telecommunications today is the telephone line. In 1918, the *carrier* concept was implemented when 12 voice channels were carried over one wire pair. By the mid-1940s, a large number of voice channels could be carried over coaxial cables. Ten years later, microwave chains were developed to carry many more channels. Today's telephone cables and microwave chains carry over 21,000 voice channels. In the 1970s, cross-country helical wave-guide channels, carried 100,000 or more voice channels, thus accommodating virtually any request for commercial data transmission.

Such steady growth in the types and capacities of telecommunication systems was necessary to keep pace with today's exponential information growth. Acceptance of telecommunications is due in part to the birth of more conglomerates and to the expansion and diversification of many corporations and government agencies. The need to quickly process data between the headquarters and branches becomes paramount. The earlier conventional batch processing of vital information can now be accomplished on-line, providing management with up-to-the-minute reports on request. On-line control of operations means savings in the form of better customer service, increased efficiency, and more effective use of facilities.

Since the role of telecommunications is vital, we shall discuss its key elements and structure, simplifying the technical detail and presenting an overview of the field and supportive devices.

Telecommunication (also referred to as *data communication*) is the movement of information by an electrical transmission system among multiple sites. Whereas the data entry user usually operates a main computer system at one site, the telecommunication user might work with networks of thousands of miles of telephone transmission lines and hundreds of data sets (modems), as well as with many terminals and computers. To put telecommunications into its proper perspective, three terms must be defined:

Communication: The exchange or transmission of information orally or in writing.

Telecommunication: A set of functional units designed to transfer data in computer-readable form between two or more terminals through private or public networks.

Telecommunication **network:** A system of communication channels or other elements (called *nodes*) that are interconnected in some way. In a basic computer network, the transported commodity is data. It origniates and arrives at user nodes consisting of terminals. It is transported through a maze of interconnected links provided by the network carrier. The full computer network less the computer(s) and terminals is commonly called **subnet.**

The purpose of telecommunication networks is to:

1. reduce the time to transfer data from its source to the computer and back to user,

2. reduce the overall costs of conducting business,

3. provide the required information when needed,

4. facilitate business expansion at a reasonable cost, and

5. contribute to more effective management control of the operations.

A telecommunications network offers the following features:

1. *Channel input-output operations.* Incoming data is channeled directly into computer memory at predetermined locations. Once the desired amount of data is available, processing commences automatically.

2. *Fast, efficient, built-in interrupt subsystems.* The computer system is designed to handle any interrupt, whether it stems from an incoming message or from a processing error. A switching center performs like a traffic policeman, funneling the many interrupts continuously without trouble.

3. *Low operating costs.* An electronic telecommunications network is ideal in high-speed transmission. It requires only a nominal operating expense for the physical handling of transmitted data.

4. *Maintenance of low-cost transmission.* Systems that use multiple channels are monitored by a transmission control device that allows simultaneous transmission from many lines and requires no particular stored-program unit. The lines link terminals, inquiry displays, and audio-response units to the system.

5. *Space flexibility.* Incoming messages can be temporarily allocated to specific areas in main memory for processing. When they are no longer needed, another incoming message is stored instead. Thus, the storage-segment feature eliminates the need for reserving an entire area for incoming data.

6. *System modification.* More applications can be handled by the CPU simply by adding one or more modules as needed. In this respect, the original system design and its peripheral devices remain undisturbed.

Telecommunications combines the benefits of two technologies. On one hand, computers offer communications several benefits:

1. *Automatic error handling.* Computers can be programmed to halt the transmission of input messages once an error has been detected.

2. *Message buffering.* The buffering feature in computers means that the sender can send messages at all times. During peak periods or if the receiver's line is busy, the message is temporarily stored and transmitted later as lines become available.

3. *Multiple-transmission capability.* The sender who wishes to transmit a message to several receivers submits the message with a list of the receivers. The computer transmits the message to each station as its line becomes available.

4. *Flexibility in routines.* A computer can control the rates, sequence of message transmission, and other routines with minimum delay.

The communications industry, on the other hand, offers computers two important benefits:

1. *Implementation of time-sharing systems.* Users from various locations are provided direct access to the computer.

2. *Remote data acquisition.* Through remote terminals, hundreds of users can access and receive information stored in a centralized location. Data can also be fed into a centralized computer system from such points as warehouses and distribution centers.

To bring computer power to the maximum number of users, serious attention should be given to the "human-computer" interface. Since this interface differs from one person to another and from one computer to another, a wide variety of telecommunication networks has been designed. Some networks are on-line; others are off-line. Some are interactive; others are noninteractive.

In an *on-line system,* telecommunication data goes directly to the computer from some point of origination, and output data is, in turn, transmitted directly to the user. Most transmission from terminals is interactive, since a response is generally received from the computer. Some on-line systems, however, are noninteractive, such as when the computer merely receives a batch transmission requiring no response.

In an *off-line system,* input data is first either written onto magnetic tape or disc or punched into cards or paper tape for later processing. Off-line systems are noninteractive, since the computer and the input data source are not directly linked and the computer cannot provide a response to the source.

Application Categories

Telecommunications is used in a wide range of computer processing acitivities. The major application categories are:

1. conversational time-sharing,

2. information inquiry and retrieval,

3. remote job entry (RJE),

4. message switching, and

5. source data entry and collection.

Conversational Time Sharing

This usage typically involves communication links between a central computer facility and a number of remote input-output terminals. In some cases, two or more computers may be linked together for sharing the workload. Typical applications are engineering design, text editing, and general problem solving.

Information Inquiry and Retrieval

This type of linkage allows extensive interaction between the terminal operator and the computer. In inquiry processing, remote devices are linked to central data files for direct access. In a real time setup, files are kept up-to-date at all times.

Data retrieval is basically one-way transmission from the computer to the terminal operator: Stored data is retrieved but not changed (Figure 10–1).

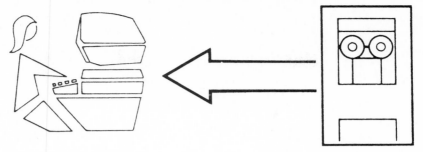

Figure 10–1. Data retrieval application.

Among the data retrieval applications are credit checking, bank account status, airline and hotel reservation systems, and brokerage firms that handle thousands of transactions each day.

Remote Job Entry (RJE)

In **remote job entry,** transactions are normally batched and require processing times ranging from minutes to hours. Input or output for each transaction may take several seconds or minutes to complete. A typical RJE application consists of remote high-speed card reading and printing.

Message Switching

Message switching is a method of handling messages over telecommunication networks in which the entire message is transmitted to an intermediate point (a switching computer), stored for a short time, and then transmitted to its destination. Some companies use a message-switching mode for handling large volumes of messages between their geographically dispersed locations and a central computer facility. By two-way communication, a message switching center receives messages from designated terminals and transmits them to others, storing them in between if necessary. Delivery time requirements range from minutes to hours. A typical application is company memo distribution.

Source Data Entry and Collection

A data entry system transmits data from remote terminals directly to a central computer. The computer acknowledges receipt of the data and outputs the data entry display to the terminal operator. Examples of data entry applications are order entry, production data collection, and account updating (Figure 10–2).

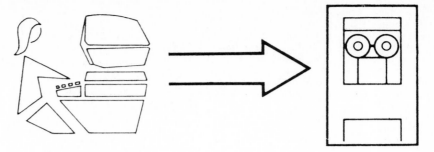

Figure 10–2. Data entry application.

Although terminals do not provide every type of computing capability, they offer a remote user the convenience of computer access and eliminate the need for an on-site installation. Direct data transmission also cuts down on data handling, manual processing, and human errors. In business applications, remote batch processing is applied in gathering payroll data, inventory control, production control, market and sales analysis, and labor cost distribution.

Fundamental Communications Concepts

Primary Elements of a Telecommunications System

Understanding data processing systems necessitates a study of the elements responsible for data flow or communication. In a general communications system, source data is converted to an organized set of symbols or electrical impulses in the form of a coded message. The encoded message is next transmitted over a transmission facility, such as the telephone line, to relay the message to its destination. Before reaching its destination, a receiver converts the message into a human language. The decoded message is error-checked before it is finally released to its proper destination. For effective communication, data must be transmitted and received without distortion or alteration.

A telecommunication system is similar to a general communications system. As illustrated in Figure 10–3, it consists of the following elements:

1. *Source.* The originator of the information, the source is the point from which data is transmitted through known channels such as the telephone and telegraph. Industry also uses television channels especially designed for data transmission systems. The transmitted data is later relayed to another person or device located elsewhere.

2. *Message.* A set of symbols that represents the transmitted data. The message can be expressed in oral form, in written form, or as a digital signal. Like a business letter format, a message element must be formatted in the proper sequence and in a manner prescribed by a set of rules. Further-

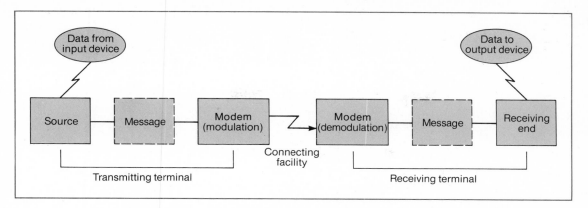

Figure 10–3. General telecommunications system — data flow.

more, the text of the message should be relayed in such a way as to give a true and clear interpretation to the sender.

3. *Channel.* A *medium* or a circuit over which the data travels, a transmission channel facilitates the communication of source data between two or more transmission points. The line is leased from a "common carrier" such as the Bell Telephone system. The carrier is a company licensed by the Federal Communication Commission (FCC) or a state agency to provide communication service to individual subscribers or organizations.

4. *Receiver-transmitter.* This is a device or a center capable of receiving, retaining, and transmitting data to a predetermined person, device, or destination.

5. *Terminal.* A terminal, often alternating as a source and a receiver **(sink),** is an area in a data transmission system where messages can enter or exit.

6. *Modems.* A modem is a device that converts digital signals from the terminal into wave-like signals suitable for transmission over a voice line. At the receiving end, another modem converts the signals back into digital pulses for processing. Details on modems are covered later in the chapter.

7. *Switching centers.* Much like traffic policemen, switching centers funnel incoming messages from the line to an outgoing channel.

Data transmission assumes various forms. It may take place between two computers, between a human and a computer, or between a computer and input-output devices. For example, a computer may be connected to another computer by a telephone line and programmed to transmit data to the other computer as though it were an output device. Some computers are even assigned coded (telephone) numbers that other computers can dial for data acquisition or transmission. People can also "talk" to computers through special tele-communications devices. However, the more common data transmission approach is between input-output terminals and a computer center connected remotely by a private telephone line or by a dial system much like that of the ordinary telephone.

Modes of Transmission

Telecommunication terminals are classified by their mode of transmission: asynchronous or synchronous. **Asynchronous** (also called *start/stop*) transmission is used for low-volume, low-speed requirements, because data comes over the transmission line only *one character at a time.* Each character is "framed" by the sending device, which signals where the character's bits begin and end. As shown in Figure 10–4, each character is preceded by a start bit which signals to the receiving terminal that a character is being transmitted. At the end of the character transmission, the line is returned to a mark condition and made ready for the beginning of the next character by a stop bit. This procedure is repeated, character by character, until the entire message has been sent.

Synchronous transmission is used for high-volume, high-speed requirements, because it transmits a whole block of data at a time. Upon sensing the start bits, the receiving equipment is put into "sync," thus allowing data to be transmitted in a continuous stream without the intervening start and stop bits (Figure 10–5).

Asynchronous transmission is not only superior when transmission is irregular, but it is also cheaper because of the simpler terminal interface logic and circuitry. Synchronous transmission, on the other hand, makes far better use of the transmission facility by eliminating start and stop bits on every character speeds throughput; it also allows higher transmission speeds. However, the cost is greater because of the more complex circuitry needed for the operation.

Figure 10–4. Asynchronous transmission.

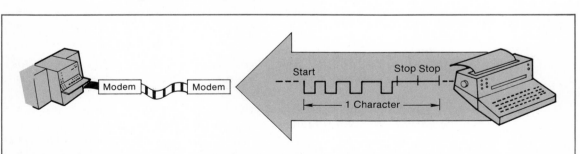

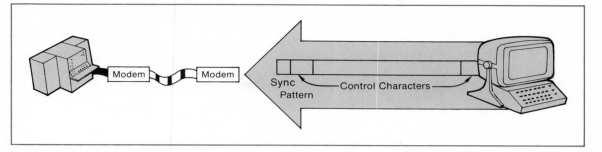

Figure 10–5. Synchronous transmission.

Line sharing among terminals. Terminals and computers communicate by **protocol,** which is a formal set of procedures governing the format and timing of message exchange between two communicating devices. It defines:

1. how to begin and terminate a transmission,

2. how errors are detected

3. how to retransmit when an error is detected,

4. the message layout, and

5. how the dialog on the line proceeds.[1]

Any line sharing requires a protocol to distinguish which message block was sent by which terminal. The most common method of line sharing is by polling and addressing from the central computer. In the **polling** mode, the central computer "polls" a terminal by sending the address of that terminal, asking, "Do you have a message block to send me?" If the message block is ready, it is sent in response. The computer also uses the addressing technique to transmit a message to a terminal. The telecommunications central control decides on a certain terminal by sending that terminal's address. The message is transmitted the moment the terminal signals its readiness to receive.

Although no manufacturer supports another's data communication protocol, several protocols are available, with IBM's System Data Link Control (SDLC) the dominant force. SDLC is a discipline for the management of information transfer over telecommunication lines. Its main control functions include:

1. the detection and recovery of transmission errors,

2. synchronizing the transmitting and receiving terminals, and

[1]Dean, Phil, "Data Comm Concepts Dictate Terminal Selection, Network Cost," *Data Management* (December 1978), p. 10.

3. controlling the sending and receiving between stations. Virtually each protocol is derived from SDLC through specified standards.

The three other known telecommunications protocols are as follows:

1. NCR's Binary Synchronous Communications (also called BISYNC), a discipline that uses a defined set of control characters for synchronized transmission of data between telecommunications stations;

2. Burroughs Data Link Control (BDLC); and

3. Honeywell Data Link Control (HDLC).

Coding Technology and Structure

Information in telecommunications is normally transmitted serially over a transmission line or channel. The codes representing the information vary with the bit group representing a character and in the assignment of the bit patterns to that character. For example, the character "A" may be represented by 1000001 in the USASCII coding scheme; in another coding scheme, the bit group would be different. In most cases, both the sending and receiving terminals must be programmed to use the same code used by the telecommunications network. The major telecommunications codes, all of which can be used in asynchronous or synchronous modes, are as follows:

1. *United States of America Standard Code for Information Interchange (USASCII).* This is a standard 7-level code for most communications equipment. It has provision for a compatible 8-bit code; the eighth bit is for parity check. The 8-bit code contains 128 (2^7) characters, 94 graphic characters, and 34 control symbols.

2. *The **Baudot** 5-bit code.* Used by older teletype units, this code uses 5 bits to represent each character. Since its coding structure allows for only 32 characters (which is not enough for 26 alphabetic and 10 decimal characters), the Baudot code assigns two characters to a few of the 5-bit codes.

3. *Data interchange code.* This 8-bit code uses 7 bits to represent the characters and 1 bit for parity. It is primarily used on the slower-speed subvoice-grade lines utilizing teletype equipment since the early 1960s.

4. *The BCD 6-bit code.* With 64 valid character combinations this code is used primarily in low-speed lines.

5. *The 4-of-8 code.* This IBM code uses only 4 of the 8 bits of data. If allows only configurations that have four 1s and four 0s to accomplish an accuracy check by ensuring the presence of only 1s or 0s. This code detects errors better than codes that use a single parity check. It is used primarily on low-speed line.

6. *The Extended Binary Coded Decimal Interchange Code (EBCDIC).* This IBM code has 256 (2^8) valid character combinations.

Obviously, the number of bits used to represent a character depends on the code used. Each code may have a different number of characters and unique error detection system. For example, the Baudot code has 56 characters but no error detection. In contrast, EBCDIC has 256 characters and a separate parity bit for error detection. In the design of an information system, the different forms and codes of information that may be needed must be considered. Information that appears in different media (cards, paper tape, and so on) may require code conversion devices or routines for proper handling.

Methods of Transmission

A **channel** (also called a *line,* a *link,* or a *path*) is a path for electrical transmission between two or more points. Telecommunications lines employ three major methods of transmission:

1. **A *simplex*** transmission channel transmits in one direction only; that is, it does not allow an interchange between the message source and the receiver. A simple telegraph system is an example of a simplex arrangement: It is useful only for transmitting data from a remote location (Figure 10–6).

2. **A half-duplex** channel transmits in either direction but in one direction at a time. In a half-duplex telegraph, for example, closing either signal key causes both receivers to react and makes it possible to send messages only one way at a time (Figure 10–7).

3. **A full-duplex** channel transmits in both directions simultaneously. It is equivalent to two simplex lines or to one half-duplex line used in opposite directions. It is available in systems in which sending and receiving stations must send messages to each other at the same time (Figure 10–8).

Figure 10–6. Simplex transmission.

Figure 10–7. Half-duplex transmission.

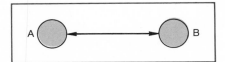

Figure 10–8. Full-duplex transmission.

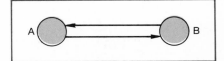

Types of Transmission Media

The transmission rate depends on the bandwidth of the transmission medium. Transmission speed is measured in **bauds,** which are not the same as "bits per second." The *baud rate* is a figure indicating the number of times (per second) that a signal changes. *Bits per second* is a figure that indicates the true bit data transfer rate. Thus wider bands can carry higher frequencies and faster transmission rates. There are several types of transmission media:

1. *Wire cables* are twisted in pairs and laid under the streets of cities. Each wire is capable of carrying one *voice grade* telephone channel for human voice transmission.

2. *Coaxial cable* can transmit at much higher frequencies than a wire pair. It can also handle up to 18,740 telephone calls at a time.

3. **Microwave transmission** can carry several thousand voice channels at a time, requiring no cables. Microwave transmission requires special towers spaced approximately 30 miles apart for "line-of-sight" transmission. Each tower picks up the signal, amplifies it, and transmits it to the next tower.

4. *Communication satellites* provide a special form of microwave transmission. Commerical satellites are placed in a 22,300-mile orbit so they travel at the same speed as the rotation of the earth. This makes the satellite appear to be standing still, more like a very high microwave tower. Because of the curvature of the earth, only three satellites are needed to relay data communications around the world.

5. *Laser transmission* is a new technology in telecommunications and the world's first lightwave communications to carry data on pulsating beams of light. The light is funneled through hair-like super-pure glass fibers called light-guides. The lightguides are bundled into slim cables which connect office building or data centers to telephone companies switching centers.

    A solid-state laser transmits 100,000 times as much data as microwave transmission. It flashes on and off 44.7 million times a second. At such a high frequency, two fibers can carry 672 simultaneous two-way conversations or data transmission. In contrast, four copper wires carry a maximum of 48 telephone conversations or a reduced mix of voice and data signals.

Telecommunications Hardware

Central Computers

A telecommunications network requires a suitable computer to accomplish the transmission and processing functions. Telecommunication configurations may be stand-alone, general-purpose, front-end computers. In the **stand-alone** configuration, the central computer is designed to handle all the communication

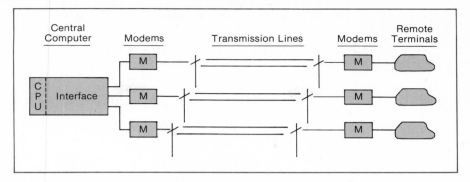

Figure 10–9. Stand-alone communication configuration.

protocols. The architecture provides interaction in a real-time mode, with emphasis on communication rather than on data processing (Figure 10–9). In contrast, a *general-purpose* computer handles a small telecommunication interaction capability but high volume data processing. As the number of terminals increases, the system approaches a point of performance "degradation" due to its inefficient handling of the communication part of the job (Figure 10–10).

The third telecommunications configuration is the **front-end processor,** a programmable data handling device that controls data transmission between a central computer and remote terminals (Figure 10–10). Specifically, it performs the following functions:

1. polls terminals to determine if they have a message to send or if they are in a position to receive a message;

2. assigns serial numbers or similar identification to all messages that it handles;

3. checks the accuracy of the received message(s);

Figure 10–10. Central computer in a front-end configuration.

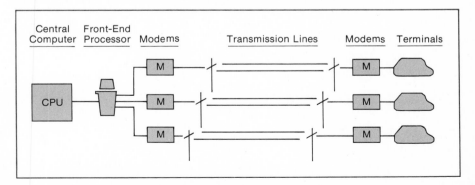

4. logs all inbound and outbound messages on a special log;

5. handles a message priority system to assure that certain transactions of higher importance are handled first;

6. edits message content and form;

7. decides on alternative paths through which data must be transmitted; and

8. correlates message traffic density and circuit availability.

Many of these functions are assigned to the front-end communications processor to free the central computer to handle the actual processing of the various messages.

Modems

Terminals transmit signals in digital form, whereas telephone lines use analog transmission. A transmission medium accommodates several independent data paths. Each path links a remote terminal to a central computer. A **modem** (short for *modulator-demodulator*) serves as the interface between remote terminals and the central computer. In modulation, it converts constant-level direct-current pulses or digital signals into analog or wave-like signals suitable for transmission over a voice line. At the receiving end, another modem demonstrates the signal; that is, converts it back into digital pulses for processing and printout (Figure 10–11).

Modems, then, are used to modify data signals so that they can be properly transmitted and, later, processed. They use four methods of modification.

1. *Amplitude modulation (AM)* involves changing the amplitude or strength of the carrier signal. Transmission is accomplished by a sequence of tone bursts when used with a device like the Data-Phone. Amplitude modulation, then, varies the tone bursts. The peaks of one amplitude represents 1 bit; the peaks of another represent 0 bits (Figure 10–11).

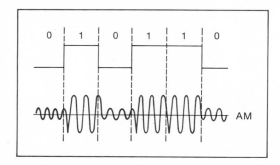

Figure 10–11. Amplitude modulation.

2. *Frequency modulation (FM)* is the most common form of modulation at speeds up to 1,800 bits per second (bps). It refers to the number of times a signal is repeated over a given period. The carrier signal is modulated to different frequencies (cycles per second) without affecting amplitude (Figure 10–12).

3. *Phase modulation (PM)* is unique to high-speed transmission (above 2,000 bps). This kind of modulation refers to the *duration* of the signal in time. It jumps along the carrier wave, past a point, to a fixed reference point. Phase modulation is used only with digital transmission systems, since phase-change detectors can sense only large, abrupt changes, such as those produced by digital signals (Figure 10–13).

4. *Pulse code modulation (PCM)* is a digital technique for transmission. Data is converted into a stream of bits looking like computer data. The characteristics of pulses within a pulse train is modified by varying the amplitude, width, or position, to convey the information. It is the most noise-free technique of the methods described in this section (Figure 10–14).

Conditioning and equalization. Medium-speed modems are almost entirely synchronous. They operate between 2,000 and 3,600 bits per second over dial-up or leased lines. High-speed synchronous units operate at speeds ranging

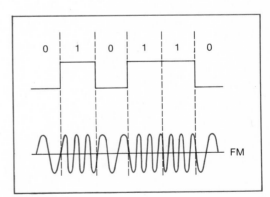

Figure 10–12. Frequency modulation (the cycles per second varies).

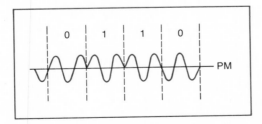

Figure 10–13. Phase modulation (the wave form is shifted).

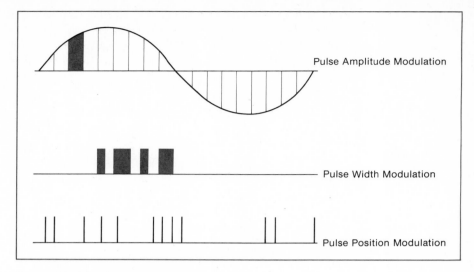

Figure 10–14. Pulse code modulation.

from 4,800 bits per second on voice-grade lines to 9,600 bits per second on leased circuits. Such high speeds are maintained either by conditioning or by equalization.

Conditioning is the process by which the telephone company maintains the quality of a privately leased line to a predetermined standard of performance and clarity. In this context, **equalization** is the process by which the modem itself accomplishes this task. Lower-speed modems attached to a leased line do not normally require equalization, since minimal line conditioning is adequate. However, conditioning and equalization are required when higher-speed modems are attached. Modems used for high-speed transmission over the dial-up net require equalization because it is never known in advance which unconditioned telephone line will be used. Modems in these categories are typically used for multiplexing applications.

Multiplexers

Because of rising charges and the increasing need for telecommunications, many computer users with multiple locations can realize substantial savings and greater operating efficiency through multiplexing. Multiplexing expands the capacity of the line by concentrating the signals from several terminals on to a single line for transmission to a distant computer. At the other end, a similar unit separates the discrete data inputs. By definition, **multiplexing** *is the simultaneous transmission of several messages over a single channel through the use of predetermined frequencies within the full bandwidth.*

A multiplexer[2] queries each input line (or device) in some sequence to check the readiness of the device to transmit. When the line is found ready to transmit, the multiplexer connects the line to the device until transmission is complete. Then the multiplexer proceeds to examine the remaining lines in sequence and without delay. In such a system, if a second device is ready to transmit while the first one is transmitting, it must wait until the first device has completed its message. If several activities occur simultaneously, the last one in line could be forced to wait for an extended period of time. This delay makes this type of multiplexing satisfactory generally only for connecting manual-entry devices to a computer.

Telecommunications Terminals

In the design of a telecommunications network, the terminals must be compatible with the network. The five categories of telecommunications terminals include:

1. teletypewriter,
2. audio,
3. remote job entry,
4. transaction, and
5. visual display.

Teletypewriter terminals. These are nonprogrammable, typewriter-like terminals that have a keyboard and a line printer. They print one character at a time at less than 150 characters per second. Some of these terminals have punched paper tape readers and punches that are functionally related to the terminal. They are still used for certain dial-up situations, although video terminals have steadily overtaken this segment of the market.

Audio terminals. Most computer systems provide facilities for voice communication channels, as compatibility between data processing and data communication is already a reality. A breakthrough in computer technology has been the development of the computer's ability to "talk" with the user. The user transmits a coded message to a central computer. In return, he or she receives a voice reply. To reply, the computer must have access to a prerecorded vocabulary,

[2]There are two types of multiplexing: The older *frequency-division multiplexing* (FDM) and the later *time-division multiplexing* (TDM). An FDM multiplexer combines the signals it receives by slicing the bandwidth of a voice-grade channel and assigning each signal its own portion of the frequency band. A TDM multiplexer, on the other hand, is more flexible; it slices up the available transmitting capability according to time elements.

which is used in giving out an answer. In some systems, a sizable number of human voice words can be stored on active files in recital form.

Audio terminals are used in applications such as banking and retailing. A major department store in Chicago has a voice-response system that employs more than one thousand Touch-Tone™ phones at the main store and its twelve branches. When a charge card is presented for a purchase, the clerk dials a special number to the computer. If the account is in good standing, the computer authorizes the sale and issues a special number to the audio-response unit. A "voice" then gives the approval number to the clerk by telephone to authorize the sale. In the meantime, the computer automatically subtracts the amount from the customer's credit limit. The balance is ready to be used for checking on future credit purchases.

The Touch-Tone™ telephone has been used effectively in various telecommunication applications. Unlike the ordinary telephone, it allows both voice and data transmission. It can therefore be used with any electronic data processing system that is linked by telecommunications channels (Figure 10–15).

The Touch-Tone™ system consists of 12 standard keys—10 numeric and 2 special-character keys for data transmission. The special characters can be used to indicate the end of transmission or the end of message for control of carriage returns or for other predetermined control codes. When depressed, each key generates a unique transmittable tone that is recognized by a receiving unit. Transmitting coded messages is as easy as keying in a telephone number. Figure 10–16 summarizes selected Touch-Tone™ commands.

One type of Touch-Tone™ device, called the *card dialer*, reads prepunched holes in a plastic card at 8 to 9 characters per second. This combination of the card and dialer is ideally used in information retrieval and in applications requiring entry of fixed information, such as the account number punched in a gasoline credit card (Figure 10–17).

Figure 10–15. Telephone Data-Phone. *Courtesy AT&T.*

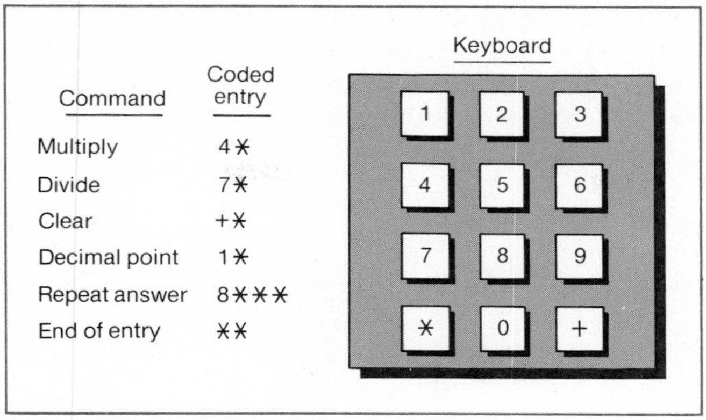
Keyboard
Command
Coded entry
Multiply
4✱
Divide
7✱
Clear
+✱
Decimal point
1✱
Repeat answer
8✱✱✱
End of entry
✱✱
1
2
3
4
5
6
7
8
9
✱
0
+

Figure 10–16. Selected Touch-Tone™ devices and an example.

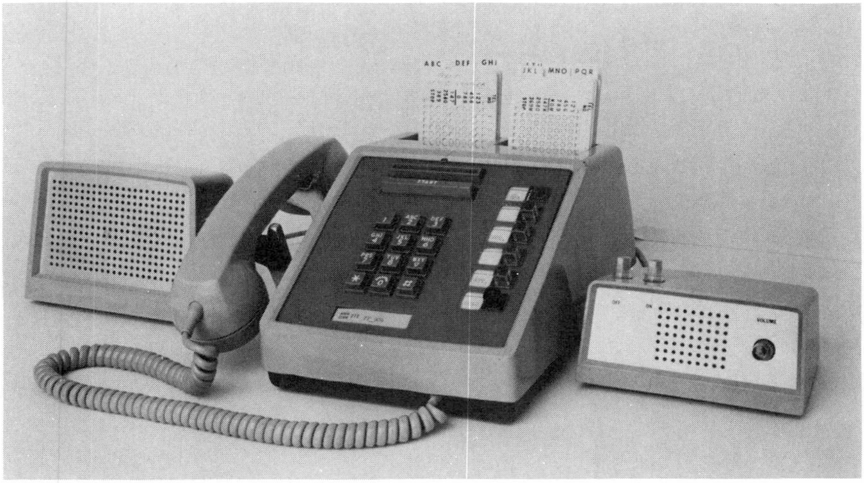

Figure 10–17. The card-dialer. *Courtesy AT&T*

Figure 10–17. An RJE station.

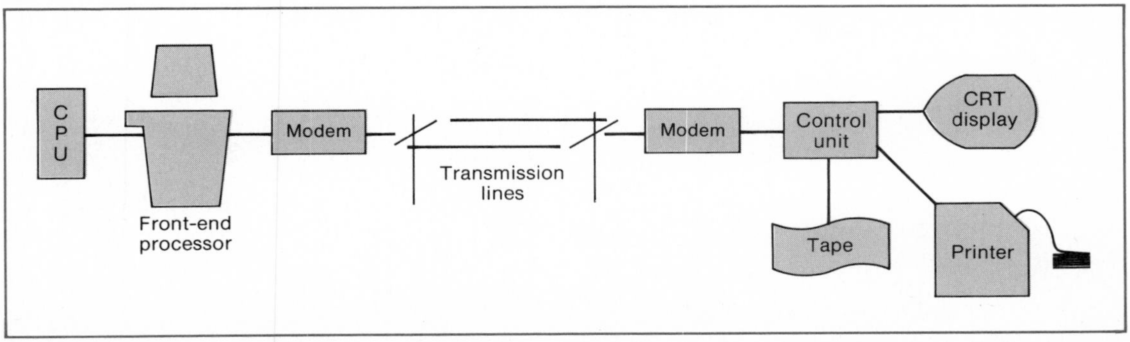
CPU
Front-end processor
Modem
Transmission lines
Modem
Control unit
CRT display
Tape
Printer

Another Touch-Tone™ device is the *Call-A-Matic*. It stores on-line several hundred entries on a magnetic belt by the telephone dial. To read the information into the telephone network, the user depresses a button after verifying the entry, which is displayed at the window. A summary of other Touch-Tone™ device features is presented in Table 10–1.

Table 10–1. Summary of Touch-Tone™ device features.

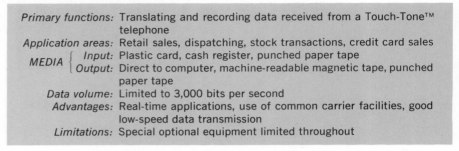

Primary functions:	Translating and recording data received from a Touch-Tone™ telephone
Application areas:	Retail sales, dispatching, stock transactions, credit card sales
MEDIA { *Input:*	Plastic card, cash register, punched paper tape
Output:	Direct to computer, machine-readable magnetic tape, punched paper tape
Data volume:	Limited to 3,000 bits per second
Advantages:	Real-time applications, use of common carrier facilities, good low-speed data transmission
Limitations:	Special optional equipment limited throughout

Remote job entry stations. An RJE station generally consists of a control unit, a card reader, a line printer, and a CRT. Most of the sophisticated stations are minicomputers that handle basic data processing. They pass on to the central computer only the work that they cannot handle. Figure 10–17 shows the makeup of a basic RJE station.

Transaction terminals. These are low-cost devices, usually driven by a mini-computer located in the same area. For example, in a retail store, a terminal is placed in each department. It can be used as a point-of-sale register and/or for credit checking. Supermarkets use them as checkout terminals (Figure 10–18).

Figure 10–18. Transaction terminals.

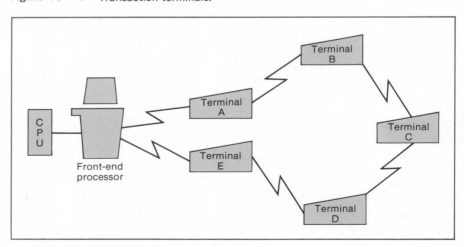

Visual display terminals.   The increasing need to automate business applications caused the search for a substitute for conventional keyboards and printers. In addition to being slow, they were not a satisfactory human-machine interface. The logical substitute is a visual display device, which can interact with the operator by means of the keyboard and display. Like a television screen, the display device is a cathode ray tube (CRT) that flashes graphs, numbers, or messages on the screen. This type of terminal is useful in applications that require direct operator interaction with a centralized computer system. Information generated by the operator is displayed and edited on the screen prior to transmission to the computer. Table 10 – 2 is a summary of CRT device features.

Table 10–2.   Summary of CRT device features.

Primary functions:	Displaying data received from remote computer or keyboard entry; transmitting to computer for storage or other media output
Application areas:	Text editing, computer input, file maintenance, stock quotations, air traffic control
MEDIA { *Input:*	Computer keyboard, punched tape
{ *Output:*	Video display, punched paper tape, direct to computer
Data volume:	Limited by message length and transmission facilities
Advantages:	Real-time file, minimal training, quick response time
Limitations:	Common carrier facility costs, limited character set and display capacity

Types of visual display.   Digital data displays fall into one of three categories: alphanumeric, graphic, or large-screen. The *alphanumeric* display unit (commonly used on telephone lines) has a 5- to 10-inch screen and a typewriter-like keyboard with which the user can operate the system, modify existing data, or key in new data. A visual display unit without a keyboard functions as an output terminal with incoming data displayed on its screen. These units can be commonly found in bus and air terminals where up-to-date information on arrivals and departures is displayed. On terminals with keyboards, an input message interrogating the system is often very short, but the response could be a screenful of meaningful data provided in less than 5 seconds (Figure 10 – 19).

Alphanumeric display terminals are either buffered or unbuffered. *Buffered* displays include a memory for storing the message. They perform editing and other required operations on the message before it is relayed to or received from the computer. *Unbuffered* displays have no such memory. Keyed messages are sent directly to the computer for further processing.

Graphic display devices display graphs and line drawings, as well as alphanumeric data output, on an 8- to 20-inch screen. Today's plotters offer a new way for management to look at data via graphs. The computer, programmed to respond to the executive's changes from a light pen applied to the screen, updates the curves of the graph instantly. In the privacy of an office, an executive can use a computer-based display with operating graphs that represent decisions relating to sales, prices, inventory, and other matters. Other business uses are for real estate development, location of manufacturing facilities, and the study of tourist attractions (Figure 10 – 20).

Figure 10–19. CRT display—alphanumeric device. *Courtesy NCR Corporation*

Figure 10–20. Graphic display. *Courtesy IBM*

Likely to be in demand in the future, *large-screen* display units are usually custom-built to accommodate six or more viewers. The computerized management control room in large business could feasibly include a wall-sized display screen and a number of individual consoles where each executive could communicate directly with the computer.

Applications. Applications for data display are primarily for information retrieval and direct data input. Information retrieval-based applications deal with:

1. *management problems* for presenting a picture of financial reports, competitive position, program milestones, inventory status, deliveries, and product development;

2. *services* in banking, insurance, and information industries to answer customers' requests, to centralize records, to monitor and simplify work flow, and to deploy personnel; and

3. *file inquiry* for providing immediate presentation of retail credit or inventory status, medical case histories and references, and library applications.

Direct data input provides simplified file maintenance, because a data base can be updated in real time so that subsequent inquiries can be made immediately. It also simplifies new data entry, since new input data can be taken directly from the source. Direct entry eliminates several entry steps and minimizes human errors.

In deciding on a visual display system, the prospective user should first evaluate the display requirements and distinguish among the routines that are display-dependent, those that are computer-dependent, and other processes with questionable dependence. Once the user's display requirements have been determined, the next phase is to evaluate the capabilities, the data-handling capacity, and the data processing ability of the available displays. Determining the capacity of graphic displays is probably the most difficult task. It depends on hard-to-figure factors, such as the average time it takes to access data stored in memory and the total time required to process all details related to a given operation.

Network Configuration and Control

Once the facts about equipment have been acquired, the next question is how the equipment interconnects with networks. **Networks** are systems of communication channels. Telecommunications networks are classified as switched or non-switched. **Nonswitched** networks consist of two building blocks: point-to-point and multipoint ("multidrop") lines. **Point-to-point** lines have two end points—a computer and a terminal (Figure 10–21). To reduce the cost of a communications network, two or more terminals are attached to a single line. Thus, a line with several "drop points" is called a **multidrop** line (Figure 10–21). In a multidrop configuration, only one terminal can transmit at a time,

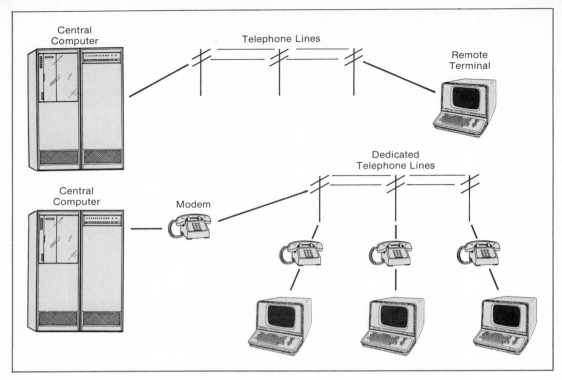

Figure 10-21. Point-to-point (2) and multidrop configurations (b).

except when multiplexing is incorporated into the network. Each terminal "listens" on the line for its own address. When the designated terminal senses a message sent to its address, it receives the message. Other terminals ignore it.

A **switched network** provides an economical interconnection arrangement between any two stations that wish to communicate with each other. In this approach, all sending lines funnel into a switching center that links the desired station until the message has been transmitted. *Line switching* of this type is a one-to-one relationship. Only one connecting line is required for each receiving station. In direct-line (nonswitched) configuration, more connecting lines are required than the number of stations involved—equal to $n(n-1)/2$. As shown in Figure 10–22 and in Table 10–3:

1. The number of connections in a direct-line system increases by more than one for each additional location. With three locations, three direct lines are needed. With a fourth location, another three lines (a total of six) are required, and so on.

2. In line switching, only one connection is required for every location in the communications network. The net saving becomes more significant as more locations are included in the network.

3. With a line-switching system, then, there are fewer connecting lines and, therefore, a less costly system is realized than would be the case in a direct-line system.

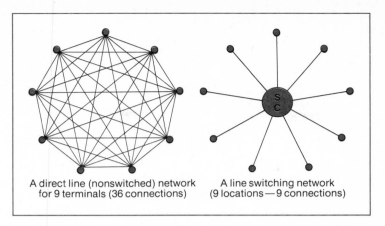

A direct line (nonswitched) network for 9 terminals (36 connections)

A line switching network (9 locations—9 connections)

Figure 10–22. Direct line (nonswitched) and line switching networks.

Table 10–3. Relationship of locations to lines.

| No. of locations | Total number of connections | | No. of lines saved with line switching |
	Direct-line $n(n-1)/2$	Line switched	
3	3	3	0
4	6	4	2
5	10	5	5
6	15	6	9
7	21	7	14
8	28	8	20
9	36	9	27
10	45	10	35

As an alternative to line switching, a **store-and-forward** switched network is designed to store messages temporarily for later transmission to their proper destination. This type of switching makes better use of the communications network, since it does not require the sender or receiver to stay on the line until the message has been transmitted.

Network Control

The objectives of network control are to ensure the orderly exchange of information, to synchronize data flow to and from the computer, and to define the procedure to restart the network in the event of disruption. Control on a point-to-point system is relatively simple. The sender's request for permission to transmit readies the receiver. Upon receiving the request symbol, the receiver acknowledges the request. The sender then begins with a "start-of-message" signal and proceeds to send the message. When finished, the sender notifies the receiver with an "end-of-message" signal. Once acknowledged, both terminals revert to idling again.

Control on the multipoint-line system includes the following steps:

1. A signal at the beginning of each message identifies the terminal to which the message is transmitted.

2. Another signal indicates the beginning of the message and the protocol for acknowledgment by the receiver. Once this is performed, other terminals can ignore the message transmission.

3. A third signal indicates the end of transmission and also notifies other terminals that they should become "alert" again.

Another method of network control, called *contention,* allows the computer to sense a bid from and authorizes the terminal to begin transmission. The computer has pre-established queuing procedures to handle the request. That is, it knows which terminal should be served next. The contention method offers the advantage of involving the computer only during the stage when data is ready to be transmitted from a terminal.

The most popular method of network control, called **polling,** emphasizes the computer's constant control over the total network. It allows the computer to determine the order in which each terminal can transmit data. Two types of polling are used:

1. *Roll-call* polling allows the computer to make inquiries from a list of all the existing terminals to check on their send status.

2. *Hub* polling passes an inquiry from the computer to the farthest terminal. If it is not found in a sending mode, the terminal relays the inquiry to the next farthest terminal — and so on until all available terminals are polled. The purpose of this procedure is to do away with the turnaround time between the computer and its terminals.

Common Carriers

The concept behind the common carrier is to provide communication transport for a fee. The American Telephone and Telegraph (AT&T) company is the largest of the common carriers. Two other large companies that offer a wide range of telecommunications services are General Telephone and Western Union. The communication services offered are classified as *switched, leased,* and *hybrid.*

Switched Services

Switched services allow the subscriber to make a connection to another subscriber by dialing a regular home telephone. The major offerings are:

1. *Direct distance dialing (DDD)* involves using the dial telephone for data communication. The user calls a distant station, a terminal, or a

computer by using the regular switched telephone system. Rates are based on the distance between the stations and the amount of time the line is used.

2. *Wide Area Telecommunications Service (WATS)* is a special bulk rate service offered by AT&T for direct dial, station-to-station calls on the public dial telephone network. The service is available for data as well as voice transmission. The continental United States is divided into six regions or bands. The first band consists of the states that border on the one in which you are contracting for service. The second band consists of the states that border on the first band and so on. WATS service equipped with telephone channels is ideal for transmitting a large volume of outgoing data.

3. *Teletypewriter Exchange Service (TELEX)* is a teletypewriter to a teletypewriter communication network offered by Western Union. Each subscriber has a private dial-up line and a conventional telephone with a number. It is an alternative to the voice telephone system, but it provides hard copy transmission between subscribers.

4. *TWX* is similar to TELEX, except that the subscriber may provide the terminal instead of leasing it from the common carrier. TWX is most appropriate for users with low-volume requirements. The service is set up by the telephone companies using leased telephone wires. Each user has his or her own wire, and the wires can be addressed by other TWX outlets. Also available is a directory listing the users of these wires and their access numbers.

Leased Services

Leased private line services are lines that are dedicated to the subscriber. The primary services are:

1. *Low-speed* lines are used basically for teletypewriter data transmission up to 150 bits per second (bps).

2. *Voice-grade* lines are the most prevalent form of communication service. Voice-grade channels allow transmission speeds up to 9,600 bps.

3. *TELPAK* lines, used for wide-band applications, constitute a group private pricing arrangement of voice-grade private line services. They consist of separate voice-grade lines usable up to the specified maximum.

4. *Wide-band services* are used for high-speed data transmission, for facsimile transmission, or for simultaneous voice and data transmission on up to 12 voice-grade lines.

5. *Digital service* is employed for transmitting synchronous data signals.

It contains diagnostic features for error detection and correction. The digital network is available in approximately 200 of the large metropolitan cities in the U.S.

6. *Satallite service* is a point-to-point communication facility for data and voice applications. Voice-grade satellite channels are available only to major cities such as New York and Chicago.

Hybrid Services

Hybrid services have both switched and leased characteristics. They include:

1. *The common control switching arrangement (CCSA)* is a private long-distance dialed system consisting of intercity telephone circuits purchased by large companies to interconnect several bus operations. Each operation must be physically connected to it.

2. *The hot line* is designed to directly connect two telephones in distant cities. When either receiver is lifted, the other telephone rings immediately. This service is available only to certain cities within the United States.

3. *Packet switching* (also called a "value-added network" or "VAN") is a shared intelligence network that brings the benefits of telecommunications to the widest possible audience. All information is passed through the switching network in the form of discrete units called *packets*. The network facilities are paid for only when the packets are actually being transmitted.

   As shown in Figure 10–23, the packet switching **nodes** (usually programmable minicomputers) accept streams of packets from several sources. They interleave the packets on digital high-capacity inter-nodal trunks. This means a more efficient use of transmission network and a reduction in costs.

With any of these services, a company that needs to communicate over short or in-house distances ought to own its own telecommunication lines. However, when a great enough volume of data has to be communicated between two or more locations, leased (nonswitched) lines are more practical; leased lines are permanently connected to the user's terminals for direct service. No dialing is required. The lines may be leased for any period of the day and may be used for any mixture of voice communication, written messages, and data transmission. Rental charges depend on the quality of the line and the distance covered.

In cases where the volume of transmission between any two points is too small to justify leased lines, dial-up facilities may be more practical. Data is routed and transmitted over the normal telephone switching network, and the connection is dialed and paid for as is a long-distance call. A continuous data

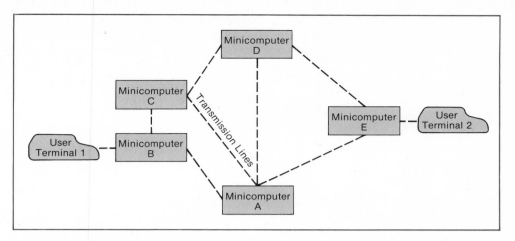

Figure 10–23. Packet switching network.

path is established for only the period of time during which transmission is to take place. Although the leased line is more expensive than the switched line, it is available at any moment. Its transmission quality is superior to that of the switched line, which must be connected for each dial-up.

SUMMARY

1. Telecommunications involve the movement of information by an electrical transmission system between multiple sites. In a basic network, data originates and terminates at user nodes consisting of terminals. The data is transported through interconnected links provided by the network carrier. Computers offer communications automatic error handling, message buffering, and flexibility in transmission routines. On the other hand, communications offer computer users fast access to the data files when needed. The major applications are conversational time sharing, information inquiry and retrieval, remote job entry, message switching, and source data entry and collection. Each category has its unique contributions and design for information processing.

2. A general telecommunications system consists of a source, a message channel, a receiver/transmitter, two or more terminals, and switching centers. Terminals are classified by their mode of transmission. They may be asynchronous (transmitting one character at a time) or synchronous (transmitting a whole block of data at a time). Protocol governs the format and timing of the message exchange between terminals and the computer.

3. Information is transmitted in codes. The major codes are USASCII, Baudot, Data Interchange, BCD, 4-of-8, and EBCDIC codes. Each code has a different number of characters and a unique error detection system. Telecommunication lines employ three methods of transmission: simplex (one direction only), half-duplex (either direction, one direction at a time), and full duplex (both directions simultaneously). Among the major media used for telecommunications are microwave, satellite, and laser transmission — the world's first light wave communications medium to carry data on pulsating beams of light.

4. Telecommunication configurations may be a stand-alone, general-purpose, or front-end processor. The front-end processor polls terminals, logs messages, and edits their content and form. These functions free the central computer for handling message processing. Each configuration also uses modems to modify data signals for transmission and processing. Modification may involve changing the carrier signal's *amplitude, frequency* (cycles per second), *wave form* (or phase), or *pulse code*. A configuration with multiple locations generally uses multiplexing, which allows the simultaneous transmission of several messages over a single channel. The outcome, a definite saving, improves the operating efficiency of the system.

5. Telecommunications terminals may be teletypewriter, audio, remote job entry, transaction, or visual display. Each category serves a unique set of applications in business and industry. For example, audio terminals are used in banking and retailing applications. Transaction terminals are employed as a POS register for credit checking. Supermarkets use them as checkout terminals.

6. Applications for data display, whether data or graphic display, are primarily for information retrieval and direct data input. Direct data input simplifies new data entry and minimizes human errors. In deciding on a visual display, evaluating the user's requirements is extremely important. Once determined, the capacity and capabilities of the available displays are analyzed for a selection decision.

7. Telecommunication networks are classified as switched or nonswitched. In a switched network, all sending lines funnel into a switching center during message transmission. Nonswitched networks are desgined as point-to-point or multidrop configurations. Each configuration has its own structure and constraints.

8. Common carriers provide switched, leased, and hybrid services. A switched service is similar in operation to the regular home telephone. The major offerings are DDD, WATS, TELEX, and TWX. Leased services are

lines that are dedicated to the subscriber. They include voice-grade, TEL-PAK, wide-band, digital, and satellite services. Voice-grade is today's most prevalent form of communication service.

Finally, hybrid service has the characteristics of switched and leased services. They include the Common Control Switching Arrangement, hot line, and packet switching. Leased (nonswitched) services are practical when there is a sufficient volume of communication between two or more locations. Rental charges depend on the quality of the line and the distance covered.

TERMS TO LEARN

Amplitude modulation (AM)
Asynchronous
Baud
Baudot
Channel
Conditioning
Equalization
Frequency modulation (FM)
Front-end processor
Full-duplex
Half-duplex
Microwave
Modem
Multidrop line
Multiplexor
Network
Node

Nonswitched network
Packet switching
Phase modulation (PM)
Point-to-point line
Polling
Protocol
Pulse code modulation (PCM)
Remote job entry (RJE)
Simplex
Sink
Stand-alone
Store-and-forward network
Subnet
Switched network
Synchronous
Telecommunications

REVIEW QUESTIONS

1. What is telecommunications? In what respect does it combine computer technology into its design?

2. Distinguish between:
   (a) modems and multiplexers,
   (b) synchronous and asynchronous transmission,
   (c) stand-alone and front-end configurations,
   (d) conditioning and equalization, and
   (e) amplitude and frequency modulation.

3. In your own words, briefly describe the major application categories in telecommunications.

4. List and briefly comment on the major elements of a telecommunication system.

5. If you require transmission of high volume data at high speed, what mode of transmission would be suitable? Why?

6. What is meant by "protocol?" How does it relate to polling terminals in telecommunications?

7. What is the difference between half-duplex and full-duplex transmission? Which method is used for transmitting data?

8. "Wider bands can carry higher frequencies and faster transmission rates." Do you agree? Explain.

9. In your own words, explain three types of media in data handling.

10. How does performance degradation occur in a general-purpose communication configuration?

11. What functions does a front-end processor perform?

12. Summarize the features and uses of the various categories of telecommunications terminals.

13. Distinguish between:
    (a) switched and nonswitched networks,
    (b) point-to-point and multipoint lines,
    (c) line switching and store-and-forward switched network,
    (d) roll-call polling and hub polling, and
    (e) leased services and hybrid services.

14. Describe the three major communication services offered by common carriers.

part three

Systems
Applications
Development

chapter 11

Systems Analysis for Information Processing

Learning Objectives

After you learn the basics of computers, the next question is, "How is an application or a problem converted for computer processing?" Converting a business application requires analysis of its elements to determine whether conversion is feasible. The role of the systems analyst is to evaluate existing applications in an effort to design better ones. The design's major objective is computerized information. When you complete this chapter, you should know:

1. why companies decide on converting applications,

2. the major areas in systems analysis,

3. how a systems analyst gathers and organizes data for analysis, and

4. what constitutes a systems proposal.

Prerequisites for Systems Analysis
Major Areas in Systems Analysis
    The User's Objectives
    The System's Environment and Constraints
    Output Requirements
    Operations

        The processing performed
        Input requirements

    Control Measures
    Feedback

Documentation of the Present System
Data Collection for Analysis

    Procedure Manuals and Forms
    Participant Observation
    Interviews and Questionnaires

        Relative Merits
        Construction

Data Organization

    Charts
    Primary Tools for Data Organization

        Flowcharts
        Supportive charts
        Decision tables

Cost Analysis and the Systems Proposals

    The Elements of Costs
    Categories of Costs
    The Systems Proposal

Since management relies on current and timely information for making day-to-day decisions, computerizing applications relieves the manager from handling problems that can be solved by the computer. Computerizing business applications or improving computerized systems requires analysis. Hence the system analyst constantly evaluates existing applications and designs better ones. Analysis is a field that has become crucial for successful information processing.

A computer application goes through a kind of "life cycle," a planned process involving systems analysis, systems design, and systems implementation. This chapter focuses only on systems analysis; Figure 11–1 summarizes the general steps carried out in systems analysis. The next chapter explains systems design and implementation. When you complete these two chapters, the

Figure 11–1. General steps in systems analysis.

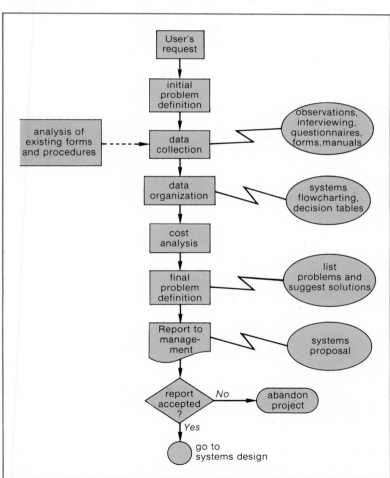

field of information systems will begin to make sense. You should understand:

1. why companies decide on certain applications to be run by the computer,

2. how the analysts determine whether an existing application should be computerized, and

3. how they design and implement the system under study.

Prerequisites for Systems Analysis

A **system** is an organized group of components or elements linked together according to a plan to achieve an objective. In systems work, the analyst must be aware of the elements of the system, the linkages that bind them together, and the system's objectives. **Systems analysis** is the separation of a system into its key components and the study of each component independently and in relation to the other components. The result of analysis is the definition of a problem area as a basis for designing a more efficient system.

A major prerequisite for systems analysis is a problem facing the user. First, the user fills out a request form (Figure 11 – 1), which states the problem and the reason for reporting it. The report is then submitted to the systems department or to an analyst for follow-up. *The success of systems analysis depends on how real the user's problem is.* Distinguish carefully between *symptoms* and *facts:* What appears on the surface to be a problem often turns out to be only a symptom. In one consulting experience in a paper cup plant, a sudden high reject rate of the 6-ounce paper cups was labeled by the user as the problem. Further analysis showed that the *real* problem was the poorly trained substitute help doing the work of experienced employees who were on vacation. In this case, the symptom was a high reject rate, but the real problem was poorly trained help.

Major Areas in Systems Analysis

Systems analysis involves careful evaluation of:

1. the user's objectives,

2. the system's environment,

3. output requirements,

4. operations,

5. control measures, and

6. feedback.

The User's Objectives

The first step in systems analysis is clearly to understand the user's objectives and how the present system meets these objectives. Objectives may be primary or secondary. For example, in an accounts receivable application, the *primary* objective is to control the flow of cash coming from credit sales. The system tells management how much cash is coming in or how much is likely to become available in the next 30 days. This information helps in deciding whether or not to authorize additional purchases of merchandise, expand a product line, and so forth. The *secondary* objective is to obtain information on the billing cycle — the number of "repeat" customers and the highest-volume product line, for instance. Although such information is only a byproduct of the accounts receivable system, it does contribute to achieving the user's primary objectives.

Besides primary and secondary information, the personnel operating a system require different types of information for handling job-related tasks. In addition to understanding the user's objectives, therefore, the analyst must also determine whether or not the existing system satisfies the informational needs of its operating personnel. Their comments and cooperation are often helpful in systems design and implementation.

The System's Environment and Constraints

The systems analyst needs to define the type of information exchanged between the system and other systems, as well as the interface it maintains with much systems. The interface aspect is important because a system depends on other systems to provide the required input for successful operation.

In addition to the operating environment, the analyst must also study the present system's physical, financial, and legal constraints. *Physical constraints* relate to the limitations of what the present computer system can do in handling applications. *Financial constraints* refer to specific funds in the user's bedget to be spent on short-term improvement of the present system. *Legal constraints* related to formats, reports, or procedures that cannot change because of state or federal requirements. For example, the employer's annual federal unemployment tax return has to be used according to the instructions that accompany the form. The analyst is constrained by the format and the sequence of stated information.

Output Requirements

Evaluation of output precedes the evaluation of input and processing. Without prior knowledge of the output requirements, the analyst is in no position to change either input or processing.

Operations

The processing performed. Once output requirements have been defined, the analyst establishes the processing to be carried out and evaluates ways of improving the processing. Evaluation includes such considerations as revising the existing programs or training the staff to handle changes in hardware or software. Thus a change in one aspect of processing may be a positive step in updating the total processing picture for an improved systems output.

Input requirements.   This step is an evaluation of the current inputs used in producing the output. Input media may be punched cards, punched paper tape, magnetic tape, magnetic disc, or diskette. Each medium must be evaluated in terms of its capabilities, limitations, and efficiency of data capture.

Control Measures

A control routine is designed to maintain the accuracy and reliability of the required output. It determines whether the output produced is as accurate and reliable as the data input fed into the system. For instance, one control measure, **validity check,** verifies the reasonableness of the value of a given computation. To illustrate, suppose that a programmer earns between $10 and $15 an hour and works a maximum of 40 hours per week. In processing payroll, a maximum gross pay of $600 (40 × 15) is reasonable. If gross pay exceeds the "reasonable" limit, a built-in control measure is available to discontinue the process, pending a validity check.

Feedback

Before output is utilized, a comparison is made between the initial objectives and the output. Discrepancies are analyzed and fed back to the proper phase in the cycle. Without feedback, it is difficult to determine to what extent the available output represents reality.

Documentation of the Present System

Documentation, a collection of copies of all records and reports used in the present system, enables the user to coordinate the procedures, design, and implementation activities of the system. After evaluating output documentation, the analyst takes a look at the processing and input activities of the present system. Data from job manuals, along with interviews with the user or staff, is recorded and later sorted for future use.

Data Collection for Analysis

The collection of data relevant to the system under investigation is a major aspect of systems analysis, because it uncovers any areas in which performance could be more efficient. As shown in Figure 11–2, the primary data collection methods are:

1. study of procedures *manuals* and *forms,*

2. participant *observation,*

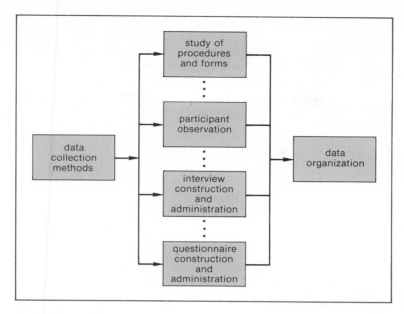

Figure 11–2. Data collection methods.

3. *interviewing* the user, and

4. *questionnaire* construction and administration.

Although each method serves a unique purpose, most systems projects require two or more data collection methods. Regardless of the method(s) used, data must be collected in the proper perspective, under the right conditions, and in the appropriate sequence for effective analysis. Data may come from the outside through vendors, through other organizations, through governmental documents, through newspapers, and through professional journals. Internal sources of data stem from financial reports, personnel staff, the user, or current system documentation or manuals. Both sources of data are carefully checked and evaluated for systems analysis.

Procedure Manuals and Forms

Systems analysts begin collecting data by reviewing the existing procedures manuals and forms, which provide information regarding the format and functions of the present system. Up-to-date manuals save hours of interview time and provide much of the data needed for analysis. If they are not available or up-to-date, the analyst may resort to gathering data by interviewing or observing the present system in action.

Included in the review of procedures and manuals is a close look at existing forms. A *form* is a carrier of information. For example, a purchase order has information on the name of the vendor, date of delivery requirements, the quantity, names of the units ordered, unit price, and total price of merchandise. In evaluating the form, the analysts asks:

1. Who uses the form?

2. Does the form include all the necessary information? How can it be improved?

3. How many departments receive the form? Why?

4. How readable and easy-to-follow is the form?

5. How does the information in the form help other users make better decisions?

These questions help the analyst map out a better form, if necessary. The outcome is better information and more efficient data communication.

Participant Observation

Participant observation refers to the collecting of data through direct observation. The purpose of this technique is to get as close as possible to the "real" system being studied. During observation, the analyst does more listening than talking. He or she avoids giving advice, withholds judgment, and asks the following questions:

1. What kind of system is it? What does it do?

2. Who runs the system? Who are the important people in it?

3. What is its formal function? Is it a primary or a secondary contributor to the organization?

4. Is it fast-paced or is it a leisurely system that responds slowly to the needs of the user?

Participant observation is a difficult data collection method. Since it requires intrusion into the user's area, it can cause adverse reaction among the staff if not handled properly. Furthermore, it can be very time-consuming, especially in situations when the analyst has a limited amount of time for analysis.

Interviews and Questionnaires

Relative merits. Systems analysts spend a large proportion of their time interviewing people at all levels. Whereas information obtained through a questionnaire is limited to written responses to predefined questions, an interview provides an opporutnity for greater flexibility in eliciting information. The primary advantages of the interview are as follows:

1. The interview offers a better opportunity than the questionnaire to evaluate the validity of data gathered. During the interview, the analyst can observe the subject's responses and determines how consistent the responses are.

2. It is a more appropriate technique for eliciting information about complex subjects.

3. It yields more cooperation than the questionnaire. Many people are willing to cooperate in systems study when all they have to do is talk.

By its very nature, a questionnaire also offers several advantages:

1. It is less expensive and requires less skill to construct and administer than the interview.

2. Unlike the interview, which generally questions one person at a time, a questionnaire can be administered to large number of individuals simultaneously.

3. The respondents feel greater confidence in the anonymity of a questionnaire than in that of an interview.

4. The standardized wording and order of the questions ensure uniformity of questions. In contrast, the interview situation is rarely uniform from one interview to the next.

Construction. Interviews and questionnaires vary widely in form and structure. Interviews range from the highly **structured,** in which the questions and the alternative responses are fixed, to the highly **unstructured,** in which neither the questions nor their responses are specified prior to the interview. The following are examples:

Structured question: As senior vice president of this bank, do you belong to the American Banking Association?
Yes _____
No _____

Unstructured question: Now that you have been a user of this on-line computer system for six months, I wonder if you could tell me how you feel about it.

In either case, interviewing is an art. For the respondent to offer complete and accurate information, the analyst must create a permissive situation and a friendly atmosphere in a neutral location and at a convenient time. With a proper introduction to the interview, the analyst is expected to ask the right questions, in the right sequence, within the time allotted for the interview.

Questionnaire construction also requires the formulation of sound, pertinent, and error-free questions. To do a satisfactory job, the analyst must focus on question content, wording, and format. Once it is completed, he or she should pilot-test the questionnaire in advance of full administration.

Gaining rapport with users and their staff is also an art. During the data collection phase, analysts should not mislead, become personally involved with, brag to, or use up the time of the staff. They should neither promise what they cannot deliver nor behave in ways that might be viewed as a threat to the subjects.

Many systems investigations fail due to poor data collection. Take care that data is properly recorded and identified as to the source, the time of collection, and the surrounding circumstances. The notebook should contain copies of all notes taken during the investigation and the instruments used in data collection. The method of organizing material is also important. A well organized notebook or file can help in the hectic period when the systems study is drawing to a close.

Data Organization   Data collection alone is inadequate for a clear understanding of the present system. All data must be rearranged and organized for a complete picture of the system's elements. This overall picture is achieved through special charts and tools designed for this purpose.

Charts

If a picture is worth a thousand words, a chart is probably worth even more. In systems analysis, a *chart* is a pictorial means of presenting data; it helps the systems analyst display the information needed for all personnel concerned. Other uses of charts are to:

1. illustrate present systems,
2. depict the sequence of operations,
3. describe a proposed system to the user, programmers, or operators, and
4. delineate personnel relationships, as in organization charts.

Primary Tools for Data Organization[1]

Systems analysts use a number of tools. The three primary tools are:

1. flowcharts,
2. supportive charts, and
3. decision tables.

[1]Tools for data organization describing flowcharts and decision tables are covered in Chapter 14.

Flowcharts. The most widely used tool is the flowchart. A flowchart is drawn vertically or horizontally from left to right of a page. The use of standard symbols is approved by the American National Standards Institute (ANSI): Some symbols are used primarily for program flowcharting, others for systems flowcharting, while still others are used for both types. These symbols are drawn from templates, obtainable everywhere. (Details on flowcharting symbols and procedures are covered in Chapter 14.)

Five major types of flowcharts are emphasized:

1. *A systems flowchart* shows the overall data flow and operations of the system. It specifies the inputs, the stages through which inputs will be processed, and the outputs using a variety of symbols (Figure 11–3).

Figure 11–3. Christmas club—daily run.

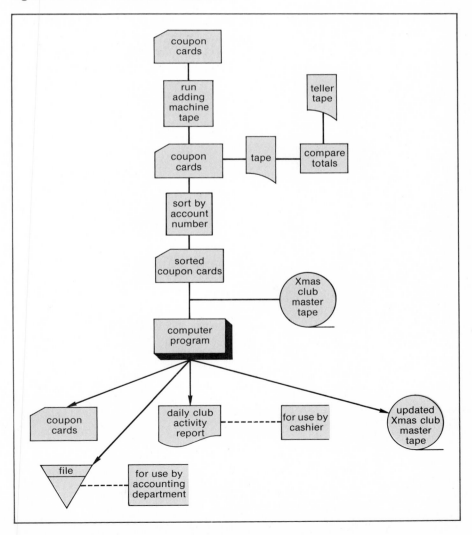

2. *A program flowchart* is a detailed outline showing *how* each step of the systems procedure is actually performed (Figure 11–4).

3. *A process flowchart* is used for breaking down and evaluating the steps in a procedure or a system. In systems analysis, it can be used to trace the flow of a report or a data form. Figure 11–5 shows the sequence of steps for requisition of petty cash.

4. *A layout flowchart* is designed to help in planning the physical layout of a work area or showing the flow of paperwork, location of storage areas, and the like.

5. *A forms distribution flowchart* shows the activities related to paperwork. Figure 11–6 presents the basic flowcharting symbols used in forms distribution flowcharts and an example.

Supportive charts. These special-purpose charts, designed to provide additional input for analysis and design, fall into two major types: organization charts and scheduling charts. An *organization chart* is a map of the formal positions in an organization, along with the authority relationships of these positions. Each position is indicated by a box connected to other boxes by a straight line. Overall, the organization chart identifies the levels of authority from top to bottom,

Figure 11–4. A program flowchart.

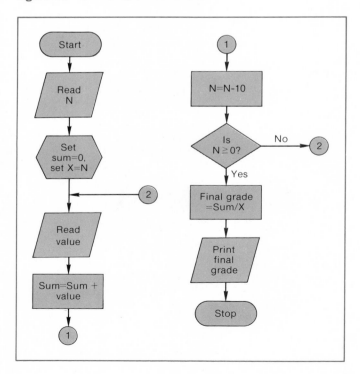

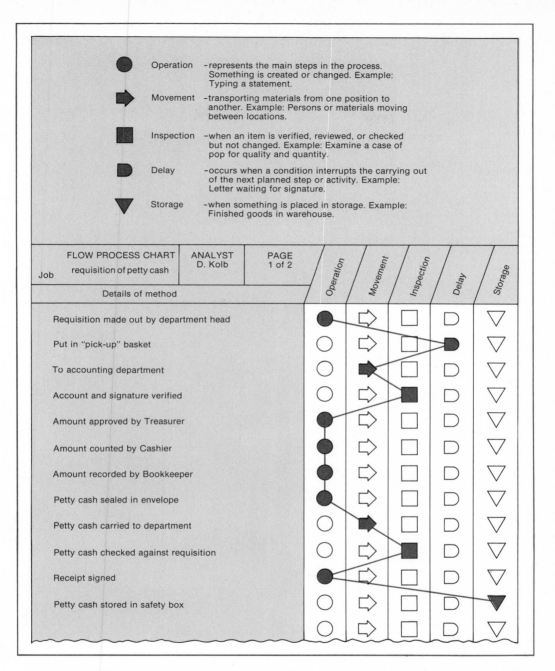

Figure 11—5. Process flowcharting symbols and an example.

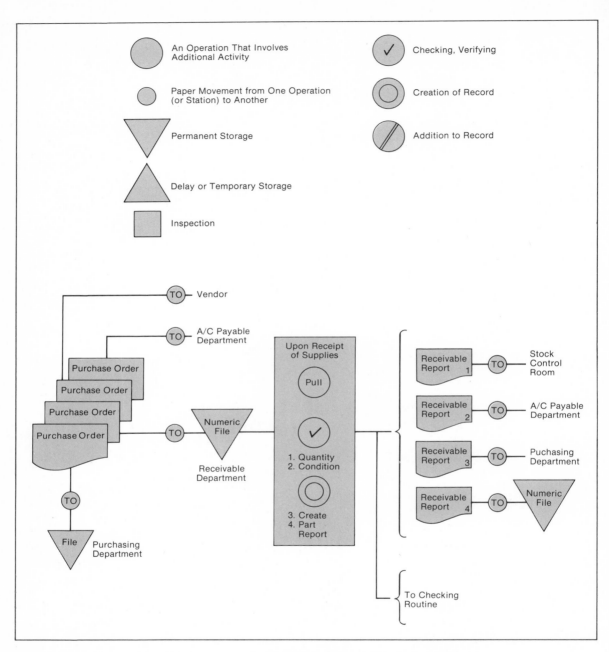

Figure 11–6. Forms distribution flowcharting symbols and an example.

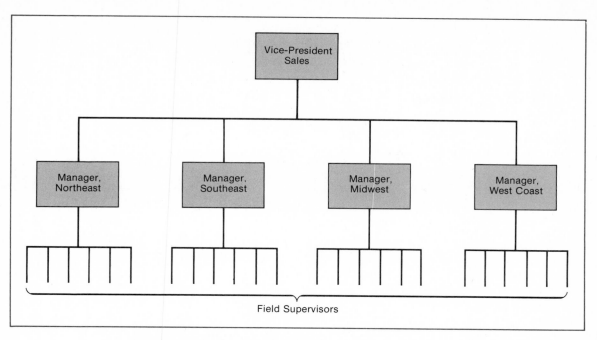

Figure 11–7. An organization chart—an example.

indicates the pattern of formal communication channels, and specifies the names and status of the employees occupying each position (Figure 11–7).

A *scheduling chart* maps out the use of physical and human resources, as well as other activities of the organization. The scheduling techniques available to the systems analyst range from the appointment book to advanced programming models. Two widely used scheduling charts are the **Gantt chart** and PERT (Program Evaluation and Review Technique). In Figure 11–8, information is provided on the production schedule of an assembly plant by measuring progress against the schedule. The light line indicates the length of time it takes to complete a job (specified by the work order number). The heavy line represents the cumulative time schedule for each department. The dotted line indicates that the Stamping Department is two days behind schedule. The arrowhead specifies the date (May 1) when the chart is to be in effect.

Decision tables. In addition to flowcharts, a systems analyst often uses decision tables for organizing the data collected for analysis. A *decision table* is a documentation format or a table of contingencies to be dealt with in defining a problem and the actions to be taken. Compared to the flowchart, it offers a more concise documentation tool and a simpler form of data analysis. Designed around the programmer's logical thinking, it is verbally oriented for managers. It is easy to learn and continues to function once the logic is developed. (Details on the makeup and design of decision tables are also covered in Chapter 14).

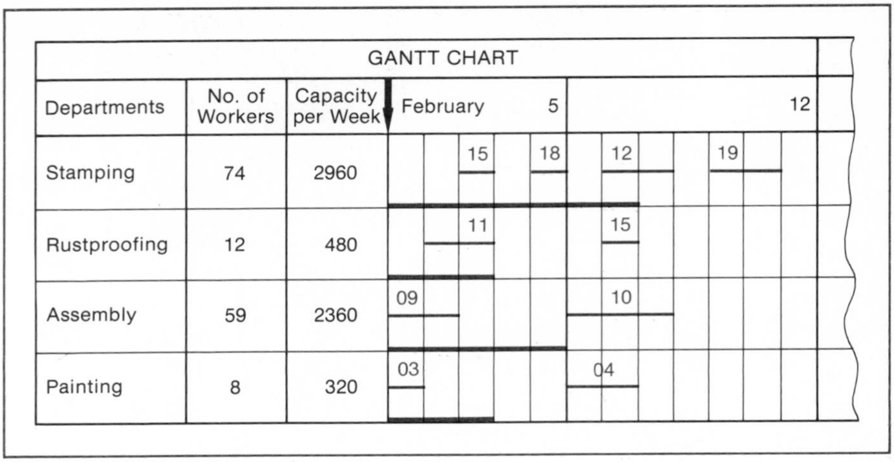

GANTT CHART								
Departments	No. of Workers	Capacity per Week	February		5			12
Stamping	74	2960		15	18	12		19
Rustproofing	12	480		11		15		
Assembly	59	2360	09			10		
Painting	8	320	03			04		

Figure 11—8. A Gantt Chart—an example.

Cost Analysis and the Systems Proposals

In all phases of systems analysis and design, cost is a consideration, a factor in determining major problem areas. After the system has been analyzed from a cost standpoint, a formal problem definition report is presented to management for approval. In determining systems costs, the analyst is expected to understand both the elements and categories of costs.

The Elements of Costs

Cost elements relevant to systems analysis comprise the following:

1. *Equipment and related hardware.* This element includes the cost of all data processing equipment, such as key-to-tape terminals, card readers, and intelligent terminals.

2. *Labor.* The major components of labor are the wages and salaries of employees, as well as fringe benefits such as profit sharing, health insurance, vacations, and sick time.

3. *Materials and supplies.* This cost element includes the cost of disc packs, magnetic tape, and consumable supplies such as paper tape, punched cards, paper forms, and the like.

4. *Overhead.* The cost of utilities, maintenance, and expenditures for creating a pleasant working environment must be included in the cost analysis.

A *cost advantage* is a step that eventually reduces or eliminates expenditures of one or more of these cost elements. However, some savings provide no direct relief from existing costs. To illustrate, in one consulting experience, a medium-sized bank installed an on-line teller system with fourteen new remote terminals. No reduction in personnel is immediately planned. However, the following benefits were anticipated:

1. A savings in tellers' time to update accounts,

2. reduction of errors in handling transactions,

3. easier access and retrieval of customers' account balances,

4. higher employee morale and increased employee stability, and

5. the capability of absorbing an additional volume of business of 35 percent.

Categories of Costs

From a cost accounting viewpoint, costs fall into four categories:

1. **Direct costs** are those normally applied directly to the operation in question. For example, the purchase of a magnetic tape for $20 is a direct cost because we can associate the tape with the dollars spent.

2. **Indirect costs** are allocated costs or overhead. They include protection of the computer facility, insurance expense, maintenance service, heat, light, and power.

3. **Fixed costs** are one-time or "sunk" costs. Examples are depreciation of computer equipment, insurance, and similar costs that do not vary with the volume of processing or with the number of shifts of the computer facility.

4. **Variable costs** are incurred in proportion to the volume of work processed. For example, printed forms are used up in direct proportion to the number of jobs and the length of each application that requires printed output.

Table 11–1 illustrates the use of various costs. This schedule shows the costs associated with a present banking system and the savings expected to offset existing costs through a proposed system. Personnel and equipment costs are fixed. The cost of supplies is variable. The supplies cost figures are average amounts based on actual usage over the past year. The third category is overhead, which includes insurance expense, janitorial service, heat, light, and power expenses prorated for the operation of the present system.

Table 11-1. Costs and savings in computerized banking.

	Summary of costs and savings A computerized teller system		
Present system costs	*Totals*		
Teller department			
Personnel			
Collection tellers (14)	$100,040		
Savings tellers (5)	30,500		
Supplies	5,400		
Equipment (teller machine rental)	10,200		
Overhead	2,020		
Subtotal		$148,160	
Bookkeeping department			
Personnel (bookkeepers) (6)	40,000		
Supplies	1,380		
Equipment	2,700		
Overhead	1,140		
Subtotal		45,220	
Proof department			
Personnel			
Proof operators (4)	28,880		
Proof supervisor (1)	7,500		
Supplies	4,140		
Equipment (machine rentals)	11,000		
Subtotal		41,520	
Total present system costs			$234,900
Positions eliminated			
Teller department (6)	$ 45,020		
Bookkeeping department (3)	18,000		
Proof department (1)	6,720		
Total		$ 69,740	
Equipment eliminated			
Bookkeeping department			
(3 calculators)	$ 1,810		
Proof department			
(1 MICR unit)	4,500		
Total		$ 6,310	
Supplies eliminated		3,600	
Total displaceable costs (savings)		$ 79,650	
Less: Online processing charges		41,000	
Net displaceable costs			$ 38,650
Total nondisplaceable costs			$196,250

Both cost categories and elements point out the importance of cost as a consideration. In analyzing a given system, the analyst needs to measure the cost advantage and resultant savings in labor, supplies, and equipment. Remember, however, that during analysis most cost figures are only estimates, even though based on documented records. Only when the system is in operation can the analyst determine the actual cost of the application.

The Systems Proposal

When the problem area has been thoroughly evaluated from every point of view, the systems analyst prepares a final report containing the major findings and recommendations. Generally called a **systems proposal** or a problem definition report, the proposal is a detailed summary of the investigation carried out on the present system. It is the "legal" document used by management to decide if a new system should be designed. Unless the systems analyst is unable to justify the cost of a new or an improved system, management can generally be expected to approve implementation of the new design. The systems proposal includes the following sections:

1. *Cover letter.* The letter briefly indicates the nature, general findings, and recommendations that make up the report.

2. *Table of contents.* This section lists the pages of the report headings and the page numbers where they can be found. It is a quick reference to the parts of the report that concern particular readers.

3. *Introduction.* This section summarizes the purpose and function of the present system, the person who requested the study, and the crucial problems facing the system.

4. *Summary of findings.* This section, a summary of the study's findings, helps management take a quick look at the major issues and the evidence surrounding the study.

5. *Details of findings.* The findings arrived at by the systems analyst are detailed in this section. In addition, a discussion of the system's efficiency and effectiveness, as well as its operating costs, is included. In many reports, a description of the objectives and general procedures of the proposed system is also included.

6. *Economic justification.* This section includes a point-by-point economic and cost comparison of the current and the proposed system. In essence, it is a comparative evaluation of the pros and cons of both systems.

7. *Recommendations and conclusions.* The analyst concludes the report with recommendations about the operations of the current system

or for the acceptance of the new one. Following the recommendations, any conclusions reached during the analysis should also be included.

8. *Appendix.* All data received during the course of the investigation is included in the appendix for reference.

SUMMARY

1. Systems analysis is a procedural evaluation of a problem or an operation. It focuses on the user's objectives, the system's operational environment, output requirements, the processing performed, input requirements, and the system's controls. The analyst's judgment should be geared for practical goals and achievable results.

2. A major aspect of analysis is an evaluation of the interaction among input, processing, and output. This is necessary for determining how well the present system meets its objectives. Much of the analyst's time is spent collecting data through a study of procedures, manuals and forms, observations, interviewing, and questionnaires. Observations are directed at understanding events as they occur. Interviews offer greater flexibility in eliciting information than questionnaires. On the other hand, questionnaires are less expensive and require less skill to conduct and administer than interviews. Interviews range from the highly structured to the unstructured. In either case, interviewing is an art that requires sensitivity to the interviewee and skill in asking the right question, in the right sequence, within the time allotted for the interview.

3. Data collected for analysis must be organized through specialized tools. The major tools are flowcharts, supportive charts, and decision tables. The flowchart is the most widely used tool. The major varieties of flowcharts are system, program, process, layout, and forms distribution flowcharts. Supportive charts are used for providing additional inputs for analysis; they include organization and scheduling charts.

4. Compared to the flowchart, decision tables offer more concise documentation and an easier form for system analysis. They are designed around the programmer's logical thinking and are verbally appealing to managers. They are also easy to learn and construct.

5. Cost analysis is an integral part of systems analysis. Cost elements include hardware, labor, materials and supplies, and overhead. Costs may be fixed and variable. Costs that are removed once the new system is implemented are displaceable costs.

6. After costs have been estimated, the analyst presents a final report to

management. Also called a systems proposal, the report outlines the existing system and provides a profile of the proposed system. This report represents the conclusion of the systems analysis phase.

TERMS TO LEARN

Direct costs
Documentation
Fixed costs
Gantt chart
Overhead
Participant observation
Program flowchart
Structured interview

System
Systems analysis
Systems flowchart
Systems proposal
Unstructured interview
Validity check
Variable costs

REVIEW QUESTIONS

1. What is systems analysis? How does it differ from systems design?

2. Briefly summarize the major steps in systems analysis.

3. Distinguish between the user's primary and secondary objectives. How do they relate to systems work?

4. What primary data collection methods are used in systems analysis? Explain.

5. Define the following terms:
   (a) form
   (b) participant observation
   (c) caption
   (d) validity check

6. Compare and contrast the use of interviews and questionnaires for data collection.

7. Under what circumstances or for what purpose could a systems analyst use an interview over other data collection methods? Explain.

8. Distinguish the difference between structured and unstructured interviewing. Given an example of a structured question – an unstructured question.

9. What is a chart? Summarize the major types of flowcharts.

10. What cost elements are considered in systems analysis? Explain.

11. In your own words, distinguish between:
    (a) direct and indirect costs
    (b) fixed and variable costs
    (c) displaceable and nondisplaceable costs

12. Briefly explain the format and contents of a systems proposal.

Case Situation

The vice president of the trust department of a local bank is considering the feasibility of upgrading the quality of the trust accounting service. He asked an outside systems analyst to look into the matter.

The analyst first reviewed the costs of operating the present trust accounting activities. Four trust officers and the vice president earn a total of $64,000 a year. Supplies averaged $400 last year. Trust account statements and other reports are produced on an outdated machine at an annual cost of $400. Overhead relating to air conditioning, lighting, power usage, and maintenance average $2,165 a year.

The next step the analyst took was to evaluate three available software packages designed for trust work. Since the packages were comparable in terms of capabilities, he chose a software package at a cost of $13,980. When implemented, payroll will be reduced by $8,000 — the salary of a junior trust officer. This means that under the proposed system, officers' salaries are expected to be $56,000 per year. Supplies were estimated at $1,900. Overhead was computed at $2,450 for air conditioning, lighting, power, and maintenance.

After the information was gathered, a report was submitted to the vice president, incorporating the facts and the figures pertaining to the cost of a computerized trust package in comparison with the existing operation.

Table 11–2.

Operation Costs		
	Proposed system	Present system
Salaries	$56,000	$64,000
Supplies	1,900	400
System charges	14,000	450
Overhead		
Air conditioning	700	540
Lighting	850	710
Power	650	400
Maintenance-janitorial	250	240
Total	$74,350	66,740

An additional point in the report was worth noting. Should the trust department generate its reports through a computer, a brokerage house with which it regularly deals agreed to underwrite 30 percent of the system charges of $14,000, or $4,200 each year. So, the actual charges of the proposed system, per se, is $9,800.

Questions

1. Did the analyst present the correct salary costs for both systems? Explain.

2. Did the analyst present all the costs pertaining to the proposed system? What about the costs for the present system? Elaborate.

3. Based on the above cost figures, can the vice president cost-justify the introduction of the proposed system? Why?

chapter 12

Systems Design and Implementation

Learning Objectives

While systems analysis is the first step, the next step is design. The new system must more effectively meet the requirements of the user. System design therefore involves developing the mechanics for a new system, based on the requirements stated in the systems proposal. The details provide the basis for programming, testing, and putting the new system into operation. When you complete this chapter, you should know:

1. the major steps in systems design,

2. how files are classified and organized,

3. the basics of forms design,

4. the steps taken in system testing, and

5. what procedure is followed in system conversion.

Following approval of the system proposal, a system must be designed to more effectively meet the user's requirements. In essence, **systems design** *is the development of the mechanics for a new system based on the requirements set in systems analysis.* Systems design must be done in detail, because it provides the framework for programming, testing, and implementation. This chapter deals with the basics of systems design and the steps taken to implement the new system. Specifically, we shall briefly cover file design, input-output and forms design, system testing, and system implementation.

Prerequisites for Systems Design

Systems design is conducted after a careful evaluation of the *user, hardware,* and *systems* requirements. Each requirement, in turn, is examined in conjunction with the financial, material, and human resources available to the analyst (Figure 12–1). User requirements must be within the financial constraints and the cost estimate of the proposed system. Knowing the capabilities and limitations of the computer system at hand, the requirements of the new system must be within the guidelines set in the problem definition report. Furthermore, the new system should be flexible in accommodating changes that are reliable, economical, and acceptable to the users. Although it is difficult to achieve, any system design even approximating the ideal is considered a success.

Figure 12–1. Prerequisites for systems design.

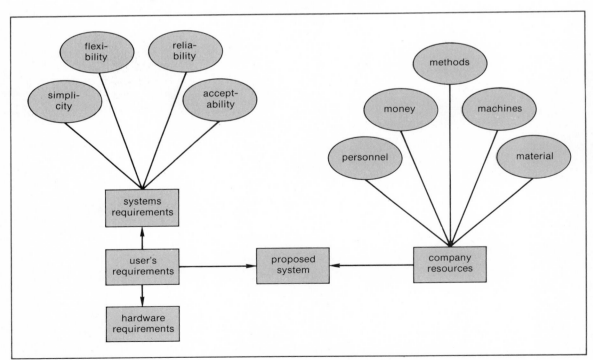

Major Steps in Systems Design

Similar in procedure to systems analysis, **systems design** focuses on the following steps (Figure 12-2):

1. review systems objectives,
2. evaluate systems constraints,
3. output design,
4. processing design,
5. input design,
6. installation planning, and
7. cost analysis.

Review the System's Objectives

The system's objectives are normally specified in the problem definition report. The analyst checks to clear any conflicts or misunderstandings relating to the stated objectives of the new system.

Figure 12–2.   Major steps in systems design.

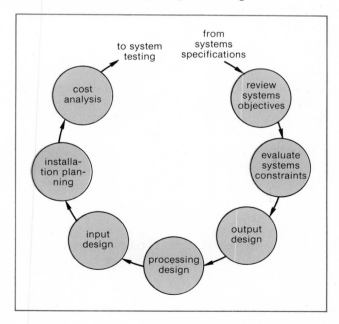

Evaluate the System's Constraints

Although constraints imposed by the law, time, finances, and hardware tend to limit systems design, they often serve as a control over unnecessary changes in the new design. Overall, the analyst must design the system around these constraints in a balanced and efficient way. Success in accomplishing this tricky task is the mark of a true professional.

Output Design

This major step focuses on the importance of producing the new reports in a readable, organized, and attractive manner. The content of each report should also be accurate, reliable, and comprehensive, providing every relevant bit of information to the user. As a matter of good practice, the analyst should design a sample form for the user, showing representative information in the intended format. At that time, the user may recommend changes, where necessary.

Processing Design

The next logical question is, "How should the input be processed?" In an operational sense, processing design includes the following:

1. specifying the calculations and hardware needed for updating final reports,
2. establishing schedules for producing the output reports, and
3. determining the frequency with which the output must be produced and reported to the user.

Input Design

This step determines the nature of the new system's input files and the input forms that are compatible with the output. In designing input forms, file layouts serve to display the codes used in input preparation and the records making up an input file. Joint user-analyst participation in creating the layouts promotes a harmonious relationship and successful system implementation.

Installation Planning

Planning the installation of the new system requires detailed schedules for system testing and personnel training. System testing includes program debugging and producing test copies of output reports. Sample data is prepared for a "dry" run. A successful test paves the way for the user to take over the operation of the new system.

Cost Analysis

Management has to be convinced that the savings from the new system are substantial enough to justify replacing the old system. The final report to management therefore not only details the capabilities of the new system, but it also compares the cost of the present system with that of the new one. Approval of the report is a prerequisite to final system implementation.

As a part of systems design, the analyst should provide controls to ensure the proper functioning and routine auditing. Systems controls are maintained through an audit trail. An **audit trail** is a routine that allows the analyst, the user, or the auditor to verify a process in the new system. In a computerized system, transactions pertaining to a file can be recorded on a journal tape, which can be an input to an audit program. The transactions of certain accounts can be available to the auditor for tracing the status of the account(s) in detail. An audit trail contains error-control points, which are evaluated on the basis of error frequency, cost of error detection, and the timing of error detection. Audit considerations must be incorporated at an early stage of the new system development so that changes can be made at a reasonable cost.

File Design

In systems design, the analyst must be knowledgeable in file processing and file organization. File data is arranged in a hierarchy, ranging from the smallest element (the bit) to the largest structure (the data base). The elements making up a file, from the smallest to the largest, are:

1. A *bit* is the smallest unit of data. Bits are organized in sets of 6 or 8 to represent alphabetic, numeric, or alphanumeric characters.

2. A *byte* is a set of eight bits used to represent either a character or a pair of decimal digits.

3. A **data item** consists of one or more combined bytes. It describes an attribute of an object, such as name, sex, or Social Security number.

4. A **record** is a combination of data items that relate to a common object. For example, a hospital patient's record includes name, health insurance policy number, name of next of kin, and other related information.

5. A **file** is a collection of related records. Each record has a key (a number) that identifies it during processing. The key could be Social Security number, employee number, or the like.

6. A **data base,** a collection of logically related files, is the highest level in the hierarchy. In computerized systems, a magnetic disc normally has more than one file, although a large file sometimes requires more than one disc pack for storage.

Classifications of Files

Files are classified in a number of ways:

1. by *content,* either master or transaction file;
2. by *method of processing,* either sequential or random processing; or
3. by *storage devices,* either serial-access or direct-access storage.

Content. Files can be either master or transaction files. A *master file* is a relatively permanent record of historical and identification information. A *transaction file* is used to update a master file. It is a collection of records about specific transactions that have an effect on a master file. Examples of transaction files are sales invoice and purchase order files. Each transaction file is created in the order of occurrence and sorted later for processing.

Method. File processing methods are either sequential or random. In **sequential processing,** files are created by storing records in sequence according to their keys. In contrast, **random processing** retrieves and updates any records without examining intervening records (Figure 12–3).

Storage devices. This type of classification includes serial-access and direct-access storage. In **serial-access processing,** each record is handled in the order that it is stored. **Direct-access processing** acts directly on any record with no particular regard to the sequence in which the files are arranged. Unlike serial-access devices, direct-access devices are very efficient sequential processors as well as random processors. They make it possible to choose the best method to suit the application.

File Organization

A file has to be organized to facilitate the availability of records for processing. Files used primarily for data processing applications are arranged in sequential, random, or indexed-sequential order.

Sequential. Sequential file organization is the simplest. Records are stored in sequential order by record key (such as ID number, Social Security number, and the like). Locating a record requires only knowledge of the sequence key. The system simply starts at the beginning of the file, comparing each record key to the record key sought.

Random. In **random** file organization, any record can be read without reading the records preceding it. A record can be obtained directly if the address of that record is known. The record key is generally the address of the disc number and track where the record is stored. The key is subjected to a calculation routine that produces the address.

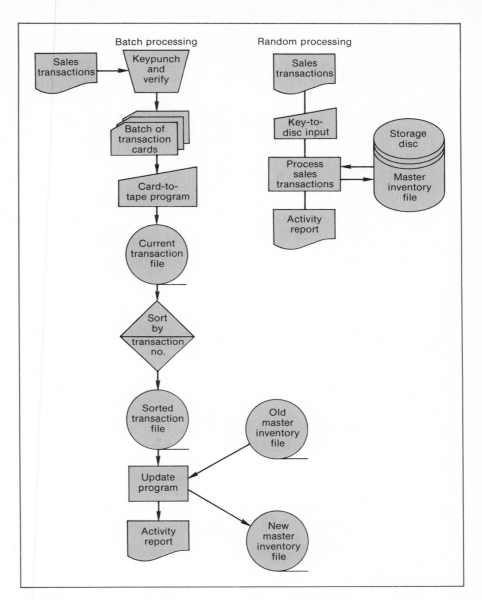

Figure 12–3. Sequential and random processing—examples.

Indexed-sequential. Combining the best features of the sequential and direct-access types of organization, the **indexed-sequential file** uses an index to store records in sequence by record key. The index is automatically created by the operating system for each disc cylinder on which records are stored. The records can be accessed sequentially by starting with the first block and continuing with the operation in sequence. They can also be accessed directly by scanning the index to reference the block number that contains the record. Then, each record in the block is searched sequentially to locate the desired record.

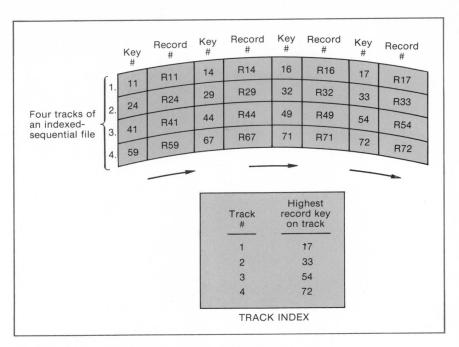

Figure 12—4. Indexed-sequential file organization—an example.

Figure 12–4 is an example of indexed-sequential organization. On each of four tracks, there are four fixed records. Each record has a unique key and is in order by key. To access record 49, you can either read records sequentially up to record 49 or go to the track index that lists the highest record key of each track. To locate the track with record 49, look up the track with a record key greater than 49. In this case, that track is number 3, which has record 54 as the highest record key. So record 49, if it is on the track, must be somewhere on track three.

Input-output and Forms Design

A major step in systems design is the preparation of the required input and the design of output reports, both on forms acceptable to the user. Forms design is therefore a prerequisite for successful information handling and system implementation.

Input-Output Design

Input data, whether prepared in batches or entered directly into the system, must be designed to conform to the requirements of the new system. In input design, analysts must consider input content and format, the method of input, the frequency of its receipt, and the sequence of receipt. In addition, they must determine the recording medium (magnetic tape, card, and the like), the speed of capture, and the type of entry into the computer. For example, magnetic tape may be suitable for batch sequential processing, while punched cards may be unsuitable for on-line processing, because much time is required for this type of processing. Table 12–1 summarizes various methods of data capture and entry.

Table 12–1. Selected data capture methods.

Methods	Types of processing
Punched cards	Batch, sequential
Punched paper tape	Batch, sequential
Magnetic tape	Batch, sequential (or random)
MICR devices	Batch, sequential (or random)
OCR devices	Batch, sequential (or random)
Remote terminals	On-line, random (or batch)
On-line terminals	On-line, random

In output design, decisions have to be made in a number of areas:

1. the type of output device:
   a. line printer,
   b. card reader,
   c. MICR reader,
   d. computer output microfilm,
   e. cathode ray tube device,
   f. graph plotter, and
   g. audio response device.

2. output format, and

3. editing, which ranges from the suppression of unwanted zeros to the merging of selected records to produce new figures.

Forms Design

A **form** is the physical carrier of data — of information; it also carries the authority for action. For example, a purchase order says "buy," and a customer's order says "ship." There are three types of forms:

1. *Action* forms are designed to order, instruct, or authorize action. Examples include an application form, sales slip, and purchase order.

2. *Memory* forms consist of historical data and serve as controls on certain details. Examples are journal sheets, purchase records, stock ledgers.

3. *Report* forms are a summary picture of projects, used by managers with the authority to effect change. Examples are the balance sheet, profit and loss statement, and trial balance.

Forms design, following forms analysis, focuses on evaluating present documents and creating new forms that offer management useful information for action. Some of the requirements for good forms design are as follows:

1. The form's title must be clearly indicated to identify its purpose.

2. The form must be legible, intelligible, and uncomplicated. Ample writing space must be provided for the insertion of data. It should provide room for signatures and for any handwriting.

3. The form's composition, color, layout, and paper stock should lend themselves to easy reading.

4. The form must be easily stored and filed.

5. The form must be cost-effective. It should allow clearly divided columns for data items and include printed captions for posting information in the right location.

Types of Forms

Of the several types of forms, each offers unique features and format.

1. *Flat forms* are single-copy forms or forms that have no carbon copies.

2. A *snapout form* has an original and several copies with carbon sheets interleaved between each sheet. The whole set is glued together (Figure 12–5).

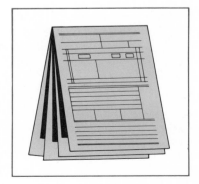

Figure 12–5. Snapout form.

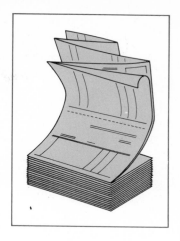

Figure 12–6. Continuous strip form.

3. *Continuous strip/fanfold forms* are multiple unit forms joined in a continuous strip with perforations between each pair of forms. One-time carbon is interleaved between copies (Figure 12–6). Continuous forms cost more initially than the flat forms, but they eliminate the need to align forms manually and the messy job of inserting and removing carbons between copies.

4. *NCR (no carbon required) paper* is chemically treated paper that does not require carbon for carrying impressions from the top form to the copies underneath.

Any type of form is designed by a combination of captions, rules (lines), and column headings. A **caption** consists of a word or a group of words, printed on the form itself, that specifies the information to write into the spaces provided. Simply stated, a caption tells the user what to write on the form. In contrast, a **rule** is a technical term for a line. It is used to make boxes and separate zones on the form. Rules and captions go together: *Rules guide and separate, while captions guide and instruct.*

Forms can be printed on paper of different colors, grades, and weights. *Color* is used to distinguish between copies. For forms design, *paper* is classified as onionskin, bond, duplicator, ledger, or card stock. Its *weight* (thickness) is expressed in pounds. Onionskin is the lightest weight (9 pounds), while card stock is the heaviest (over 140 pounds). In deciding on the kind of paper to select, the forms designer must evaluate the factors of appearance, longevity, and handling. All these factors are considered in light of the cost constraint.

Finally, a company's forms must be centrally controlled. Some planning and organizing must precede putting forms into full operation. If handled successfully, **bootleg** (illegal) **forms** should be eliminated.

System Testing

System testing is a prerequisite for system implementation. Although testing an application can be a tedious and stressful task, it is mandatory for user satisfaction. Prior to actual testing, a test plan should be developed. As shown in Figure

12 – 7, an activity network for system testing follows a set of overlapping test plan stages. Test plan activities center around the following steps:

1. Prepare a test plan in accordance with established design specifications.

2. Specify the conditions for a user acceptance test plan.

3. Program or encode the logical elements affecting the new system.

4. Prepare test data for program testing.

5. Develop test data for testing the path of each transaction from origin to destination.

6. Prepare a user training plan to handle job training, development of training materials, job outlines, and other documents.

7. Compile or assemble all programs that will be used for testing.

8. Develop a test bundling package for testing the individual components of the system's software and hardware problems.

9. Develop job performance aids, such as a posted instruction schedule for mounting and removing a tape reel and other routines.

10. Develop operational documents to familiarize the user with the various apsects of the new system.

Once a test plan has been developed, system testing can begin. A system test identifies **clerical** and **logic errors** within the system's performance criteria: turnaround and backup, file protection, and human considerations (lighting, air conditioning, and so on). Testing proceeds step by step from a single program module, to bundled modules, to successively larger bundles — until you build up to the system test level. The choice of test data (artificial or live) is extremely critical. In most cases, acquiring sufficient amounts of live data is difficult. The alternative is to develop artificial data that meets the program requirements under all conceivable conditions.

System Implementation and Maintenance

The term "implementation" can mean as little as a basic conversion of a computerized application, or as much as a complete replacement of one computer with another. For the purpose of this discussion, *implementation* refers to the process of converting a systems design into an operational one. The primary areas of consideration are:

1. *conversion,*

2. *post-implementation review,* and

3. *system maintenance.*

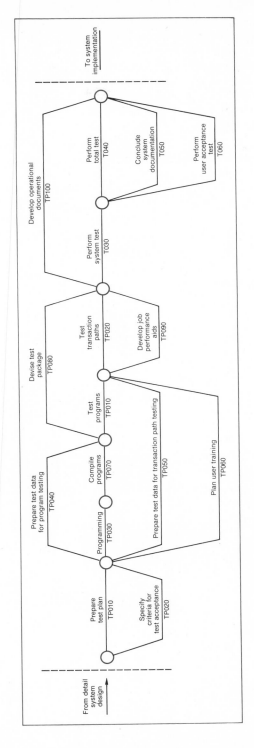

Figure 12–7. Activity network for system testing.

Conversion

Conversion is the process by which a user changes from one system to another; the objective is to put the tested system into operation. It involves creation of new computer-compatible files, training operating staff, installing new terminals or hardware, and implementing new procedures. A critical aspect of conversion is that it must be handled so as to permit the organization's ongoing operation to function without a serious setback.

Procedures for conversion. Several procedures are unique to conversion. As shown in Figure 12–8, conversion begins with a review of the project plan. It then proceeds with a system test documentation, and implementation plan. After the conversion portion of the implementation plan is approved, first file conversion is performed, then parallel processing. The results of the parallel computer runs are logged on a special form. Barring any discrepancies, the end of parallel processing marks the completion of conversion.

Figure 12–8. Procedures and documents unique to conversion.

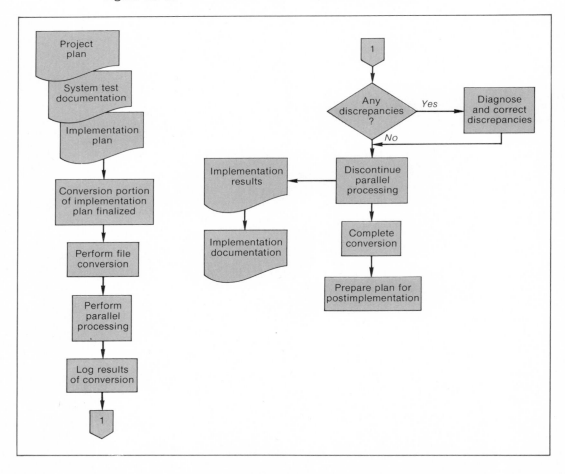

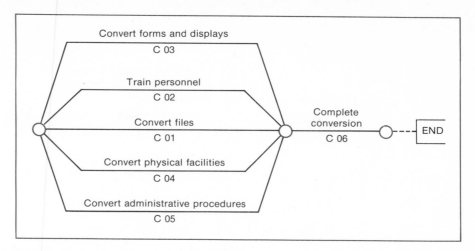

Figure 12–9. Activity network for conversion.

Other specific activities are relevant to conversions (Figure 12–9):

1. *File conversion* focuses on data capture, clerical procedure design, and program specification. To convert a file, the file data is first recorded onto designated input media and verified. A special conversion program reads the recorded data. The new file then becomes the output by the user program. Controls are maintained until the final "cutover" when the new system is "up" and on its own.

2. *Personnel training* may be general training for management, focusing on the objectives and overall benefits of the system, or it may be specific training for the user in the operation of the new system.

3. During *forms and displays conversion,* old displays and/or forms are replaced with new ones.

4. With the *conversion of physical facilities* (offices, lights, work flow, etc.); the environment is transformed to meet the specifications set in the new systems design.

5. *Conversion of administrative procedures* is last. As an administrator, the user of the new system is trained in handling various emergencies, such as procedures when the system is "down" or when hardware or software breaks down temporarily.

Post-Implementation Review

Every system, large or small, requires periodic evaluation after implementation. Post-implementation review is designed to determine how well the system continues to meet performance specifications. The information it provides enables the user to decide whether a major redesign is necessary.

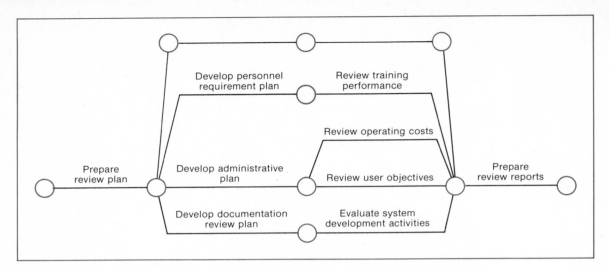

Figure 12—10. Post-implementation review.

Post-implementation review begins on the first day after conversion and continues throughout the life of the system. Primary responsibility for ongoing reviews lies with the user organization, which assigns special staff to determine the nature and causes of problem areas and the action to be taken. The activity network for this phase of system development is shown in Figure 12–10.

System Maintenance

Systems wear out and grow more mature over time. System maintenance therefore becomes increasingly important in keeping systems up-to-date for the user. The best way to reduce maintenance costs is to discourage unnecessary system modifications and to minimize system maintenance. These goals can be accomplished through system modularity and modification procedures. Each maintenance project must be justified and carried out by the system staff with the support of the initial requester. The basic activities of a maintenance project are flowcharted in Figure 12–11.

System Documentation

One of the critical tasks in systems work is adequate documentation. From a system manager's point of view, documentation is an important element in human communication, because it defines the relationships between the computer system, the programs, and the user's environment. From the analyst's point of view, documentation means a well-managed assembling, coding, and dissemination of relevant information during system development. From the user's viewpoint, documentation takes the form of recorded information, produced as output, which supports the department's operations. No matter how it is viewed, documentation is obviously essential to systems analysis and design.

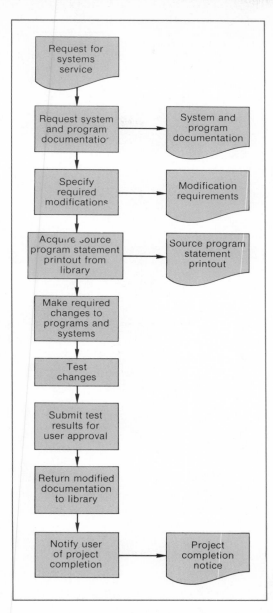

Figure 12-11. Basic activities of a maintenance project.

Documents are originated during various phases of the life cycle of a system. The origin and sequence of document preparation are illustrated in Figure 12-12. Note that documents are generated in the system study phase and terminate with system conversion. Depending on its point of origin, documentation assumes four forms:

1. *Project initiation* documentation pertains to the statement(s) of the nature and objectives of the work requested by the user. The primary docu-

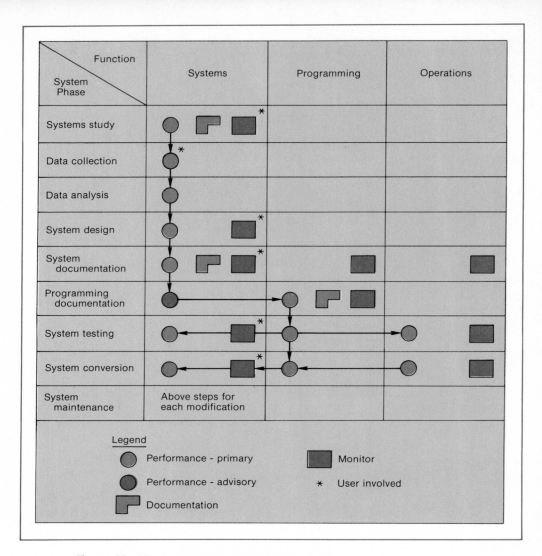

Figure 12—12. Origin and sequence of documentation.

ments are the user's request form, the system's proposal, and a description of the proposed system.

2. *Project development* documentation specifies data for programming, testing, and implementation in the form of a system specifications report. The report is a permanent record of the structure, flow, and procedures of the new system. Its completion marks the termination of systems design. The approval of the report represents the last "go/no-go" decision before actual programming, testing, and conversion begin. Figure 12–13 summarizes the content of a system specifications report.

3. *Program documentation* represents the routines necessary for a program

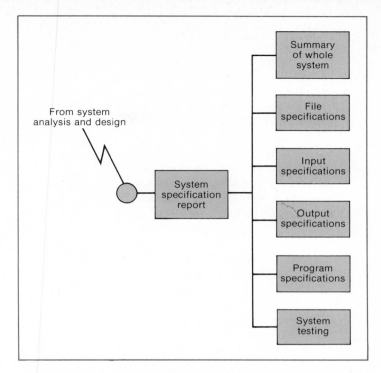

Figure 12–13. The makeup of a system specifications report.

manual and for conversion. The primary functions include coding, program assembly, program testing, and operationalization.

4. *Operations documentation* instructs the operator on how to run a program test. The program test manual, prepared by the programmer, lists the steps that specify the operating requirements of the system.

The effectiveness of a document depends on its organization, appearance, format, completeness, clarity, illustrations, and reliability. Supportive information should be pertinent, clear, and in a language suitable both to the nature of the document and to the level of the user.

Finally, documentation should be secure against unauthorized disclosure by company officials. In order to secure classified documents, only authorized personnel should be allowed access. Overall, to maintain secure system documentation, responsibility must be assumed by specialized project personnel in the systems area.

The Role of the Systems Analyst

The primary job of systems analysts is to find solutions to business problems. To do a satisfactory job, they must know the user's business, goals, and requirements. They must also know how to establish the actual costs of the present system, how to project the costs for the future, and how to determine the costs of the proposed system. Because each project is so unique, systems analysis is often viewed more as an art than as a science. The way a project is handled or a system develops has no real regularity.

Perhaps the only consistent aspect is that, through the use of systems techniques, the analyst learns enough about an existing system to design and implement a better system, if necessary. Despite unique circumstances, every systems analyst must follow certain steps. Data has to be collected and documented. Processing operations are studied, and the data resulting from the study is organized, evaluated, and summarized. The outcome is a problem definition report, which defines the limitations of the present system and the contributions of the proposed system. In essence, the analyst is a methods person with the ability to start with a complex project, break it down to its key components, pinpoint the problem area, and then recommend practical solutions.

What qualities are descriptive of a systems analyst? The answer includes the thinking of the professionals as well as the expectations of users. The analyst must have:

1. an analytical mind to solve problems and recognize the problems not yet identified;

2. an ability to communicate with the user, write instructions, and develop procedures that are understandable to the operations staff; and

3. an adequate knowledge in the functioning of the organization. The analyst must be familiar with the organizational structure and understand the lines of authority, chain of command, and communication network of the system. Such background is extremely valuable for successful systems analysis.

Another important quality is the ability to deal with many different kinds of people, a characteristic necessitated by the systems analyst's dual role. In the role of a computer systems "expert," a knowledge of programming helps in communicating with the programming staff. In the role of an evaluator, an ability to interact with people makes it possible to work with the user and the staff to satisfy their requirements. This dual role becomes critical in systems work and requires a high level of competence in determining the future success (or failure) of all systems studies.

This "personal" qualification is especially important, because systems are designed around people. The tools used, the hardware employed, and the forms and reports generated are all designed by people who have an interest in the system. Since the information sought comes from people, the system analyst can overlook neither their role in the system nor their impact on its operation and success. Thus, regardless of the complexity of the system under study, humans—not machines—are the final judges of the effectiveness of the new system.

SUMMARY

1. Systems design provides information about a new system based on the objectives set in systems analysis. In conducting systems design, the analyst considers the user's objectives, the legal and financial constraints, the capabilities of the present computer system (if any), input-output and forms requirements, and the installation plan to operationalize the new system. In addition, the analyst provides the control to ensure proper auditing. All aspects of the new system design are checked for completeness, reasonableness, and integrity.

2. In systems design, the analyst must have knowledge about file organization and file processing. Data in a file is organized in a hierarchy ranging from the smallest unit (a bit) to the largest structure (a data base). Files are classified by content (master or transaction), method or processing (sequential or random), and storage (serial-access or direct-access). Files used for data processing applications are organized into sequential, random, or indexed-sequential order. A sequential file requires records to be stored in sequential order by record key. In random file organization, any record can be obtained directly if the address of that record is known. Finally, indexed-sequential organization combines the best features of sequential and direct-access organization via the index.

3. In input design, the analyst must consider input content and format, the method of input, and the sequence in which input is received for processing. In output design, the type and format of output is also important.

4. Forms design focuses on evaluating present documents and creating new or improved forms for the new system. Forms are classified as standard, snapout, fanfold, or NCR. A form is designed by a combination of captions, rules, and column headings. A well designed form with clearly stated captions should be self-instructing. Instructions should be placed in a location convenient to the user.

5. Before a system is implemented, it must be tested for program reliability and efficiency. Test plan activities include preparing test data for program testing, preparing the user training plan for job training, and compiling the program of the new system. The outcome should eliminate any syntactic and logic errors in the program.

6. The final stage of system implementation includes conversion, post implementation routines, and system maintenance. Conversion involves the creation of new files, training operating staff, and installation of new terminals. Post-implementation review ensures that the new system accomplishes its stated objectives. System maintenance takes on an increasingly important role in keeping systems up-to-date for the user.

TERMS TO LEARN

Audit trail
Bootleg form
Caption
Conversion
Data item
Direct-access storage
Fanfold form
Form

Forms design
Indexed-sequential file.
Logic error
Random processing
Sequential processing
Serial-access storage
System design

REVIEW QUESTIONS

1. What is systems design? In what way is it related to systems analysis?

2. Summarize the steps in systems design.

3. Distinguish between:
   (a) bit and byte
   (b) data item and record
   (c) file and data base
   (d) sequential and random processing

4. How are files classified? Explain briefly each classification.

5. Suppose that a 2,400-foot magnetic tape contains data stored at 1,600 characters per inch of tape. The size of the interrecord gap is 0.75 inch. Ten feet of tape are reserved for a header label and tape identification details. The last 12 feet are also reserved for end-of-file information.

   (a) What is the usable length of the tape?
   (b) What is the total storage capacity (in characters)?
   (c) If tape speed is 200 inches per second, how long would it take to read the entire tape?

6. How is indexed-sequential processing different from sequential processing? Illustrate.

7. Summarize the characteristics of action, memory, and report forms.

8. Explain the major requirements for good forms design.

9. Briefly describe each of the following forms:

   (a) snap-out forms
   (b) fanfold forms
   (c) NCR paper

10. If you were asked to organize a forms control program for your organization, show (a) how you would proceed in planning this activity and (b) how bootleg forms can be controlled.

11. What is system testing? Explain.

12. Describé the primary activities involved in developing a test plan.

13. How does system implementation differ from system testing?

14. Define conversion. List and briefly describe the procedures and documents unique to conversion.

15. Why is personnel training important in system conversion?

16. How does post-implementation review differ from system maintenance?

17. What are the primary forms of documentation? Explain each form briefly.

18. If you were in a position to recruit a number of analysts for a large computer installation, what qualifications would you look for? Explain in detail.

19. Assume that the daily transaction file of an inventory control application is written on tape and blocked 20 records to a block, with a tape density of 1,600 characters to an inch, an IRG of 0.75 inch, and a 2,400-foot tape reel. The first 15 feet are used for a leader. There are 1,500 transactions per day.

   (a) How many inches are used for IRG?
   (b) How many inches are occupied by records?
   (c) How many daily transaction files can be recorded on one reel of tape?
   (d) If the tape speed is 300 inches per second, how long would it take to read a daily transaction file?

Case Situation

A large retailer has a forms control which has been functioning for about 10 years. Recently, the function was turned over to a clerk. The official number of forms used by the store and its branches was 910.

Paper work was building up to unmanageable proportions. Recognizing the enormity of the problem, management called for a specialist on forms control. The first step the analyst took was to figure out the actual number of forms used. Instead of 910 forms, the store had 2,114 forms.

Most of the forms were produced on duplicating machines scattered in different offices. They were hard to fill in, write on, or even read. The disclosure shocked the general manager. She called a meeting of her department heads and discussed the problem. They weren't aware, themselves, since they produced their own forms independently.

Questions

a. What procedure would you use in solving the problem?

b. What measures should be taken to prevent the recurrence of the problem?

chapter 13

Computer Systems Software

Learning Objectives

A computer is expected to operate efficiently with a minimum of idle time. An operating system not only achieves such efficiency, but also provides processing services that reduce the user's programming requirements. By the end of this chapter, you should know:

1. what batch processing entails,

2. the basic programs in an operating system, and

3. the features of real-time, time-sharing, and virtual storage systems.

Basic Programs in an Operating System

Batch Processing

Supervisor Programs
Job Control Program
Sort/Merge Programs
Utility and Library-Maintenance Programs

Advanced Facilities of Operating Systems

Real-Time Systems

Primary Types of Real-Time Systems

Software for Time Sharing Systems

Space Allocation and Supervision
Computer Time Allocation
Polling Terminals
Input-Output Processing

Virtual Storage

Paging
Thrashing

Computer manufacturers of yesteryear used to design computers and then construct assemblers or compilers to operate the system. Since the late 1960s, however, the order of design has changed: The hardware and operating systems are now designed simultaneously. An **operating system (OS)** is a set of programs stored in library files on a disc pack, floppies, or on chips. It is designed to improve the efficiency of the computer in two ways:

1. by reducing the amount of computer idle time between jobs and

2. by providing processing services that reduce the programming effort required of the user.

Reducing idle time is achieved through batch processing programs, which improve operating and programming efficiency. Such programs include:

1. the supervisor,

2. job control,

3. sort/merge, and

4. utility and library-maintenance programs.

Basic Programs in an Operating System

Batch Processing

Traditionally, idle time occurs when the computer, completing one program, waits for the operator to load another program into memory through an input device. On the average, if the computer runs 60 programs a day and the operator takes 3 minutes to load each program, the computer system is idle 3 hours a day or 15 hours per 5-day work week. With computer time costing an average of $90 or more per hour, the total cost of idle time can be substantial.

Supervisor programs. The idle time problem is solved with a supervisory operating system. Programs are loaded automatically, one after another, without delay. Initially, all the company's jobs (programs) are stored in a library on a disc pack (or occasionally on tape). To initiate a day's computer operation, the operator loads a **supervisor program** into memory. The supervisor's primary function is to control the automatic loading of jobs into and out of the library (also called "system-residence"). The supervisor remains in memory during the execution of all programs.

The supervisor must be told which programs to execute. *Job control* cards, stacked in the card reader by the computer operator, control the activity of the supervisor. Job cards contain the names of the programs to be processed, the tape or disc drives, and supportive information to identify the desired sequence of programs. If a program requires data for processing, the data normally follows the job control card. As an example, Figure 13–1 shows five jobs to be

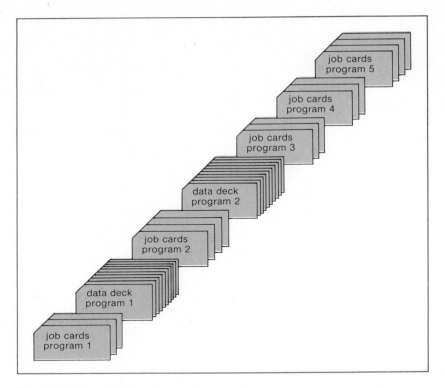

Figure 13–1. Batch processing – an example.

processed. Jobs 1 and 2 read data from the card decks following their respective job cards. Jobs 3, 4, and 5 require data input for processing.

When one program is executed, the next program is loaded and executed in four major steps. As shown in Figure 13–2, and the steps are:

Step 1. A. Program 1 is being executed and branches to the supervisor program.
B. Program 1 completes execution and branches to the supervisor program.

Step 2. A. The supervisor program loads the job control program into memory and branches to the first instruction in the job control program.
B. The job cards (in the card reader) are processed.

Step 3. A. When completed, the job control program branches to an instruction in the supervisor program.
B. The supervisor program loads the next program to be executed into memory.

Step 4. A. The supervisor program goes to the first instruction of program 2.
B. Execution of program 2 is initiated.

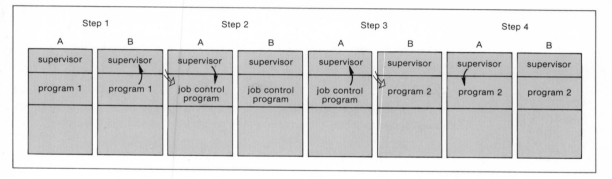

Figure 13—2.   Job-to-job transition in batch processing.

In this manner, the operating system performs the role of a resource manager, getting more "bang for your buck." The supervisor loads a program, which was identified by the job cards, into memory and then branches to it. A job control program not only eliminates some of the manager's work, but it also reduces the number of computer memory locations for the supervisor program. The program control requires main memory space only when it is loaded to read or to process job cards.

Although system residence may be a magnetic tape, it is more commonly a direct-access (disc) storage device. Direct-access (on-line) availability reduces the need to search sequentially for the programs (as on tape) and thereby improves transfer speed. Overall, it lessens the time required to load the program into memory and ultimately reduces computer idle time.

Job control programs.   A **job control program,** a supervisor that resides in memory, processes all the job control statements that specify the execution of a program. It also determines the availability of input-output devices. A program that is completed branches to the supervisor program, so the requested program can be loaded and executed.

Sort/merge programs.   A **sort/merge program** is a generalized program that can be employed in different jobs. In many computer applications, much of the processing involves sorting and merging records. For example, two or more tape files are often merged into one file with a given sequence. Although such an operation occupies a substantial amount of computer running time, the sort/merge programs are essentially the same. They differ primarily in the number of files to be sorted or merged, in the length of each record, and in the input-output devices to be used.

Utility and library-maintenance programs.   **Utility library** will include conversion programs, since they are designed to convert data from one input-output form to another. For example, utility programs supplied with operating systems can convert tape-to-tape, tape-to-disc, card-to-tape, or tape-to-printer. All the user has to do is specify (in coded form) the files or records involved.

A library-maintenance program simply provides up-to-date data availability of the programs needed for job processing. It can add new programs or delete old ones to update and maintain the library. The library is stored on a system-residence device.

Advanced Facilities of Operating Systems

Other than these programs that every operating system offers, some systems offer advanced facilities, particularly real-time and virtual storage systems.

Real-Time Systems

Real-time implies communication between the user and the computer while the program is executing. A *real-time system* may involve terminals, communication lines, one or more processors, direct-access devices, modems, and a supervisor program. It provides:

1. a direct connection between input-output devices and the central processor, and

2. fairly fast response time for two-way communication between the user and the system.

To carry out processing and to transmit the results fast enough to control an ongoing activity, a real-time system must meet severe time requirements. The measure of effectiveness in a real-time system is its **response time,** the time interval between the availability of input information and the computer's response to that information. Quicker results mean a more effective system. Adequate response time depends on the requirements of the application. For example, in a military defense application involving radar scanning, a response time measured in microseconds is mandatory. By contrast, a commercial airline reservation system requires response time of only 2 to 5 seconds, and a production control real-time system may find response time of 2 minutes quite adequate.

Programs in real-time operations must be detailed and stable enough to handle every conceivable probem that might arise during the operation. Users must be able to depend completely on the system, leaving only rare and exceptional matters for human manipulation. For example, overstocking a given item is checked manually because it does not justify a change in the overall program for proper handling.

Primary types of real-time systems.   There are two major types of real-time systems:

1. multiprogramming/multiprocessing and

2. time sharing systems.

1. In a **multiprogramming** real-time system, two or more programs are manipulated within the same time period by one central processor. Thus the utilization of the total computer system is increased. Whereas some programs require substantial input-output time but relatively limited computational time, others require little input-output time but considerable computational time. In multiprogramming, one type complements the other. When executed simultaneously, one utilizes the central processor, while the other takes advantage of the slower speed of the input-output devices.

In multiprogramming real-time systems, a supervisory program is used to control the central processor's switching from one program to another and to make sure that each processing phase is fully executed and handled in proper order (Figure 13–3). A multiprogramming system has three types of programs located in main memory:

a. The *supervisor* program, held in memory throughout processing, manipulates program switching. Main memory is divided into partitions for controlling the order of program execution and for protection against partial destruction of one program by another. Thus the supervisor program ensures the memory against loss of transactions during switchover. It also notifies the terminal operator how long the system may be unavailable as a result of the switchover phase.

Figure 13–3. Multiprogramming system, showing contents of main memory.

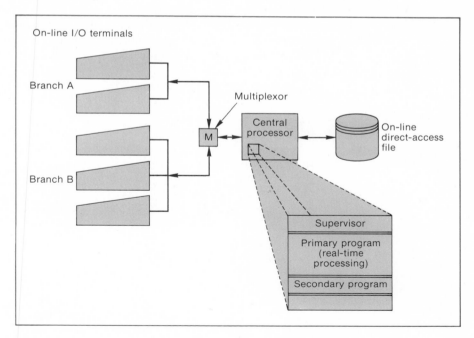

b. The primary program, often called the *foreground* program, has priority over all other programs in memory. It controls the computer system whenever data is received from an on-line input-output device.

c. The secondary, or *background,* program becomes operative when input-output devices are not in operation or while the system is not engaged in a real-time transaction. When input-output devices handle data, the processed results from the background program are stored, and the foreground program is reloaded for real-time operation. This switching back and forth between programs continues until the whole operation is completed.

Designed for maximum function, a **multiprocessing** real-time system uses two or more processors linked together for coordinated functioning and "computer-to-computer" communication. Smaller computers in such a system handle "housekeeping" routines, such as file maintenance and input-output processing. The larger computer is then free to perform computational tasks. Thus the larger computer becomes the master and the smaller computer the slave. Figure 13–4 illustrates a basic multiprocessing real-time system in which all existing terminals are interfaced with the smaller (peripheral) computer. This computer, in turn, is linked directly to the larger (master) computer. Storage devices, if needed, may be linked to the smaller computer for retrieving data. The real-time nature of this design depends on the linkage of an on-line direct-access file to the system's master computer or processor.

The reliability of a multiprocessing system can be further increased by two peripheral computers. Each computer interfaces with one half of the existing terminals. In this configuration, if either peripheral computer malfunctions, only one half of the system fails (Figure 13–5). The malfunction of the main com-

Figure 13–4. A basic multiprocessing real-time system.

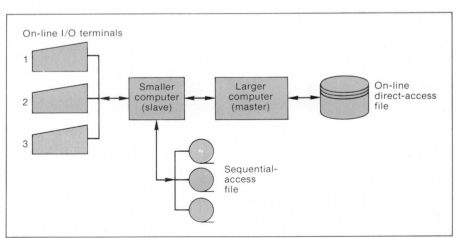

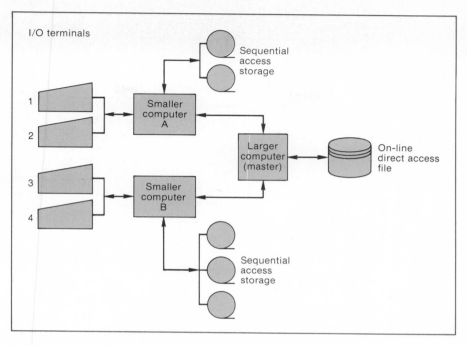

Figure 13–5. A multiprocessing system, using two peripheral computers.

puter, however, can still result in total system failure. In applications requiring "fool-proof" real-time system operation, this possibility is a special problem. To correct the loophole, a second master computer may be added, and both processors made directly accessible to either peripheral computer. During peak processing, either peripheral computer can alternate its tasks between master computers. In the event of a master computer failure, only one half the existing terminals will be inoperative (Figure 13–6).

Logically, an increase in the number of processors results in a positive increase in the system's reliability and throughput. The major constraint, however, is cost. In designing a real-time system, an organization should carefully plan the size and requirements of its proposed system at a realistic cost figure. A poorly implemented system-acquisition plan could easily multiply the figure agreed upon in the initial proposal.

2. *Time sharing* is defined in one of three ways:

a. A computer service bureau that offers a variety of application programs or specialized problem-solving languages to scientists to do on-line problem solving independent of other users.

b. An internal scheduling algorithm through which a "time slice" is offered by the central processor. Once the allotted time expires, control is switched to the next job.

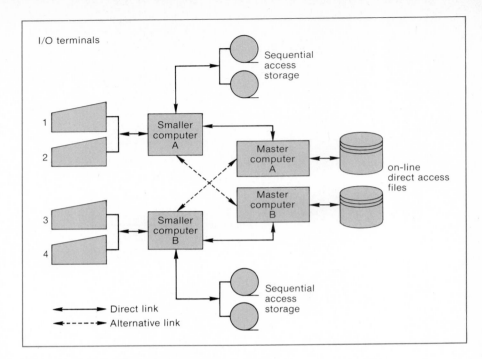

Figure 13—6. A multicomputer real-time system.

c. A computer system to which several on-line terminals are linked and through which many users communicate for solving various problems.

In this discussion, a time sharing system means an *organization of computers, communication equipment, and specialized programming that permit almost simultaneous utilization of the system by several users working at remote, on-line terminals.* A time shared computer can be used in a conversational mode or for remote batch processing. In the *conversational* approach, the user operates a terminal capable of sending and receiving information. *Remote batch processing* is basically the processing of accumulated data without requiring intervention of the user during program execution (Figure 13–7).

A typical time sharing system has the following characteristics:

1. *One-line operation.* The central computer receives data from and sends responses to remote input-output devices or terminals.

2. *Real-time processing.* The system handles all users' needs at a speed great enough for the applications.

3. *Almost-simultaneous access.* The system handles many users at the same time. One common method, called *queuing,* involves lining up all the waiting input instructions or messages from various terminals and processing them either on a first-come/first-served basis or according to a priority system controlled by a multiplexor routine.

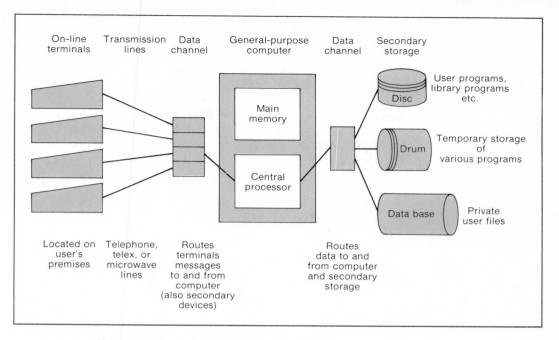

Figure 13—7. A typical time sharing system.

4. *Multiprogramming ability.* The system handles a variety of programs to meet various users' informational needs.

5. *Supervisory program control.* The program schedules and allocates working storage space and computer time for processing problems received through various terminals.

6. *Integrity.* The configuration provides privacy and protection against access to data and to programs by unauthorized individuals.

7. *Independence of operation.* Each on-line terminal functions independently of all other terminals, as though it were the only user. Each user can test and carry out programming details without any interference from other users.

8. *Flexibility.* The program handles a variety of applications such as simulation, forecasting, sales analysis, portfolio analysis, personnel scheduling, queuing studies, linear programming, inventory control, and production scheduling.

Functionally, time sharing systems are divided into three major categories, which differ by the degree of independence of the user:

1. *Unlimited systems* are general-purpose systems that accept a variety of programming languages and allow the users to create and write their own programs. Such systems are designed to run any program concurrently, in a batch or multiprocessing environment.

2. *Multiple-application systems* allow users to choose a program without making any alterations.

3. *Limited-application systems* offer users only one fixed application program, as is the case in airline reservation systems.

The first two categories, in effect, divide the computer system into a number of time slices and allot each programmer a time share for doing whatever work is needed.

Software for Time Sharing Systems

The time sharing software package generally consists of:

1. supervisor programs stored permanently in the system's memory, serving all operations, and

2. user programs available to the user for solving specific problems.

Each program carries out certain functions and has a variety of operating requirements. The supervisor program monitors the speed and capability of the computer, determining when and where the computer should be available. The program's complexity, ranging from a few to many thousands of words in length, depends on the type and size of the time sharing system. The supervisor program, separate from user programs, is mandatory in each operative system. Among the primary responsibilities assumed by the supervisor program are:

1. space allocation and supervision,

2. computer time allocation,

3. polling terminals, and

4. input-output processing.

Space allocation and supervision. The supervisor program allocates the exact physical memory location of certain data for processing and supervises the relocation of the user program during queuing and other operations. A set of constantly maintained tables is used for keeping track of data locations and for protecting transactions against accidental or intentional loss. The program also prevents unauthorized access. One common technique is to include a code within the user's number that specifies the memory areas containing his or her file. Other codes can also be used to allow the user to read but not change the data in the file, or vice versa.

Computer time allocation.   The supervisor program determines and assigns a specific slice of computer time (quanta) to each user. The length of computer time depends on the number of users and on the response time they require. The problem is compounded by the diversity of users and their computational needs. Conversational or interactive users, for example, require smaller quanta for their shorter computational problems than "production" users, whose programs are more lengthy. The supervisor program's role here is to swap programs into and out of the computer's main memory in order to serve all users with minimum delay.

One way of handling interactive and production users is to assign a high interrupt priority to interactive users, while assigning a low-priority status to production users. When a production job becomes available in main memory, it is processed without interruption, except when an interactive user requests computer time. In this case, the latter's job is promptly handled, with the former program "shelved" in the interim. Another method is to assign specific computing quanta to each user (30 milliseconds, for example). After the program uses its computer time, the interrupted program is allowed to continue processing.

Thus, the supervisor program not only allocates computer time for various jobs, but it also handles *priorities, program swapping,* and *response to interrupts* from system devices and programs. This overall scheduling function is a complex and involved task. The supervisor program is constantly determining which transactions should be processed next according to priority factors and monitoring the computer time allotted to each.

Polling terminals.   The time sharing system takes action on data transmitted from one terminal at a time. When several terminal users wish to transmit at the same time, only one user can do so, based on a predetermined priority or a first-come/first-serve basis. Other users have to wait their turn. However, since the waiting time is only a matter of seconds or sometimes a fraction of a second (depending on the number and usage of available terminals), each user feels as though he or she has a direct connection, independent of other users.

The supervisor program handles input from these terminals by **polling** (scanning) them. The time sharing computer has in memory a polling list that gives the sequence in which to poll the existing terminals. Certain terminals are high on the polling list and therefore have high priority. Others might be listed more than once on the same list so that they are polled twice as often as other terminals. Briefly, the supervisor program polls each terminal for input. Sensing input data, it gives control to the user program for processing. Otherwise, it moves on to poll the next terminal on the list, and so on until all terminals are polled and served. The supervisor program also keeps track of which terminal is related to which user program.

Input-output processing.   In time sharing systems with multiprogramming capability, the supervisor program controls the processing of two or more programs within quanta allotted in advance. To illustrate this key function, assume the availability of three user programs with each program allotted 25 milliseconds of computation time. Assume further that the supervisor program requires 5 milliseconds to do such routines as polling terminals and swapping user programs. Figure 13–8 shows the procedure as follows:

Phase 1: For the first 25 milliseconds, program A performs calculations while program B waits in the computer's main memory for processing. Program C is held in secondary storage. Once the 25-millisecond quanta is used by program A, the supervisory program uses 5 milliseconds to transfer program A to secondary storage, move program C to main memory, and release program B to perform calculations.

Phase 2: Program B is executed for the next 25 milliseconds, after which the supervisory program transfers it to secondary storage, moves program A to wait its turn in main memory, and releases program C to perform calculations.

Phase 3: Program C goes through 25 milliseconds of calculations, followed by the supervisory program's 5-millisecond routine of bringing program C to secondary storage, moving program B to main memory, and releasing program A for computation. Thus, the first 90 milliseconds constitutes a total cycle since each of the three user programs has gone through its slice of computing time, or quanta.

Phase 4: At 90 milliseconds the cycle starts all over, with program A computing while program B is waiting its turn, and program C is in secondary storage. At 115 milliseconds, the supervisory program interrupts program A, transfers it to secondary storage, and releases program B for computation.

Phase 5: In phase 5, program B runs for 10 milliseconds only, requesting more input data. The supervisory program moves it to secondary storage where it remains until input data are ready. Program A is brought into main memory, and program C (already in main memory) is allowed to run.

Phase 6: At the end of the 25-millisecond limit, program C is interrupted, giving control to program A.

Phase 7: The supervisory program bypasses program B and gives control to program C, since program B is still in storage waiting for input data.

Phase 8: Control again is transferred back to program A.

Phase 9: At 240 milliseconds, after only 15 milliseconds of processing, program A requests output. The supervisory program transfers it to secondary storage and, since program B is still without input, it allows program C to run. However, at 260 milliseconds, input for program B becomes available. The supervisory program waits until program C completes its quanta before it takes action.

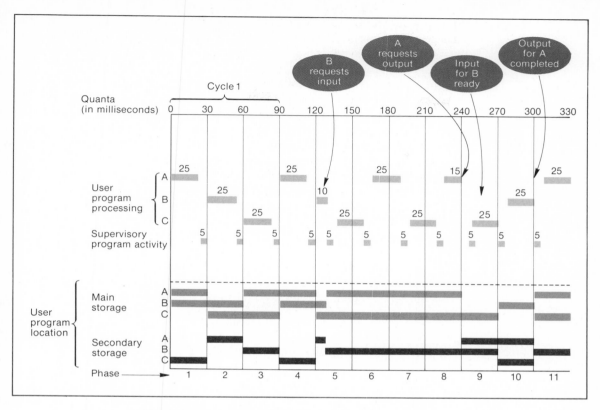

Figure 13–8. Program swapping—an example.

Phase 10: Program C is moved to secondary storage, and program B is allowed to run. Program A is still in the output phase.

Phase 11: At 300 milliseconds program A's output is completed. The supervisory program moves it to main memory and allows it to run.

The overall multiprocessing routine of processing input and output data continues until the whole operation is completed. The operation becomes more complex in time-sharing systems handling a large number of user programs with different priority levels.

Virtual Storage

In larger time sharing systems, an optional advanced technique employs a virtual control program. This program expands the functional capability of the computer by combining main memory and direct-access devices. In effect, the user treats secondary storage as an extension of main memory, giving the illusion of a very large main memory. The combination of secondary storage with main memory through direct-access devices is called **virtual memory.** Thus, virtual memory can be larger than the main computer memory.

Paging.   Virtual memory, real storage, and auxiliary storage are managed on a paging basis. A **paging** process involves moving uniform-size pages each back and forth between main and secondary storage. Managing the transfer is the function of the operating system. For example, when a user references a page in virtual memory, the control program checks on its availability in main memory. If available, processing proceeds. Otherwise, an interrupt occurs, allowing the supervisor program to "page in" the needed page into main memory.

While a page is being brought into main memory, the job needing a page is put into a "page wait" status, allowing the CPU to work on another job. When the page becomes available, the supervisor puts the waiting job in a ready state.

Virtual memory offers the following benefits:

1. Programmers need no longer be concerned with program size. They are free to concentrate on problem solutions and laying out a well designed efficient program.

2. The computer's main memory need not hold the entire program throughout its execution. Since the rest of the program may be kept on disc for immediate use, main memory may be used more efficiently.

3. The computer system's total storage is increased by as much as four times its real main memory. For example, in one of IBM's large systems, main memory is about 4 million bytes. With the virtual storage feature, the total available storage appears to be 16 million bytes.

4. Elaborate applications can be tested and debugged during prime time by giving each application to be tested a low priority so that it can be done during slack periods without interfering with the normal load.

Virtual memory storage hierarchy is sketched in Figure 13 – 9. Note:

1. The user views a large virtual memory for preparing and executing his or her programs.

2. Main memory contains only the pages needed for different programs being multiprogrammed.

3. Additional pages are "paged in" on demand (called *demand paging*). Unneeded pages are "paged out" to a primary paging device, usually a magnetic drum.

4. Since the primary paging device has limited storage capacity, infrequently used pages migrate to a backup (secondary) paging device for storage until needed.

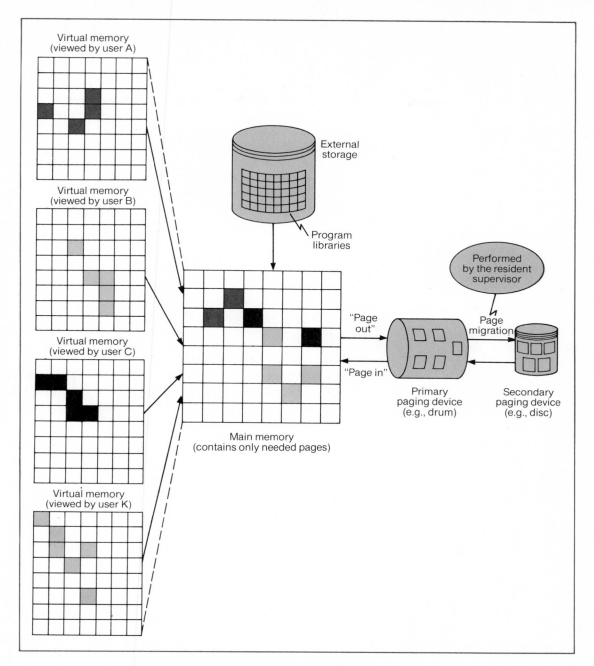

Figure 13−9. Virtual memory storage hierarchy.

Thrashing. One drawback of paged virtual memory is that individual programs may require more time for execution. The system may therefore **thrash** (or churn,) that is, make frequent page swaps between real and virtual storage, eventually compromising the efficiency of the system. One way to minimize thrashing is to use a priority scheduling algorithm that allows paging of only the highest priority jobs. Another remedy is to select a page size appropriate to the computer's operating system.

Virtual memory provides solutions to certain types of problems but not all. Only time and know-how can minimize inefficiency resulting from excessive thrashing. Furthermore, since additional equipment (and therefore more investment) is generally needed for an efficient virtual memory, perhaps better planning and review of the user's program to make more efficient use of real memory is a better alternative in some cases. Advance planning to determine the types and sizes of both programs and hardware components is also important.

SUMMARY

1. This chapter reviews the functions and types of operating systems. An operating system is a set of programs stored in library files on a disc pack. It improves computer efficiency by reducing computer idle time between jobs and by providing processing services that reduce the programming effort required of the user. The basic programs of an operating system are the supervisor, job control, sort/merge, utility, and library-maintenance programs. Each program serves a unique purpose.

2. Advanced facilities of operating systems include real-time and virtual storage systems. Real-time systems have three major types:
   a. Multiprogramming systems manipulate two or more programs within the same time period.
   b. Multiprocessing systems use two or more processors for simultaneous use.
   c. Time sharing systems are used in the conversational mode or for remote batch processing. The primary piece of software is the supervisor program, which handles space and computer time allocation and which polls terminals.

3. Another advanced facility of an operating system is virtual storage. It is an optional technique that expands the functional capability of the computer through a combination of main memory and direct-access devices. Virtual storage is managed on a paging basis through an operating system. The primary drawback is that individual programs may require more time for execution. The system may make frequent page swaps between real storage and virtual storage, eventually compromising the efficiency of the

system. Considering the likelihood of excessive thrashing, planning and reviewing the user's program to determine the proper utilization of real memory become all the more important.

TERMS TO LEARN

Job control program
Multiprocessing
Multiprogramming
Operating system (OS)
Paging
Polling

Response time
Sort/merge program
Thrashing
Utility program
Virtual storage

REVIEW QUESTIONS

1. What is a supervisor program? Explain briefly the responsibilities it assumes.

2. Illustrate the successive steps taken in loading and executing a program.

3. Define the function of a job control program. How does it differ from a sort/merge program?

4. What makes up a utility library?

5. Explain the makeup and provisions of a real-time system.

6. Briefly discuss the two major types of real-time systems.

7. What is the difference between a foreground and a background program?

8. Illustrate the unique features of a multi-computer real-time system. How does it differ from a multiprocessing system?

9. What is time-sharing? What are its major characteristics and categories?

10. Define virtual storage. Explain the storage hierarchy applied to virtual storage.

11. Distinguish between:
    (a) paging and polling
    (b) thrashing and program swapping

part four

Programming and Software Basics

chapter 14

Tools for Program Planning

Learning Objectives

Each application requires an application (as opposed to an operating) program. Before an actual program is written, however, the general instructions (telling the computer what to do with the data) are illustrated in flowcharts. Flowcharts describe graphically the operations and logic decisions performed on data. They become the logic diagrams for problem solutions. When you complete this chapter, you should know:

1. the varieties of flowcharts,

2. basic flowcharting symbols,

3. how looping is prepared, and

4. the structure and types of decision tables.

When a new system is designed, a program has to
system self-operational. If a program is simply a detailed s
tions, then the steps—or the program—must be mappe
actually written. The programmer therefore illustrates tl
form of a flowchart. From the flowchart, instructions
language suitable for computer processing. Flowcharts il
the programming languages called Basic and Cobol, whi
next two chapters. This chapter describes two special tool
in general: program flowcharting and decision tables. C
the next two chapters are best studied as a unit.

What Is a Flowchart?

A **program flowchart** is a *graphic* means of describing the operations and decision logic done on data. It details the flow of the computer's sequential steps necessary for the transformation of data. It is "graphic" because it uses a two-dimensional pictorial format, incorporating wording to identify the data and the operations. Flowcharts go by other names: block diagram, logic diagram, run diagram, flow diagram, and system chart. The diverse names simply reflect a lack of uniformity in nomenclature and the special interests of users in the field.

Varieties of Flowcharts

The two major varieties of flowcharts are the system and program flowcharts. A **system flowchart** depicts the entire data flow throughout a system. (Figure 14–1 shows a partial system flowchart.) It illustrates which data is used or produced at various points in a sequence of operations, along with input media, operations performed, output media, and the nature of output. It is a visual representative of the interaction among data, hardware, and personnel. Symbols representing input, processing, and output are frequently used in system flowcharting—as well as specialized symbols to emphasize a particular operation or device. (The symbols unique to system flowcharting are shown in Figure 14–3.) System flowcharting illustrates the components of the system.

Figure 14–1. General system flowchart for an accounts receivable file update.

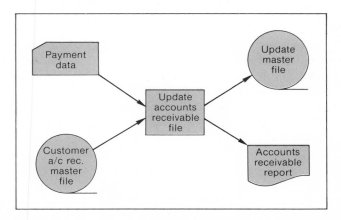

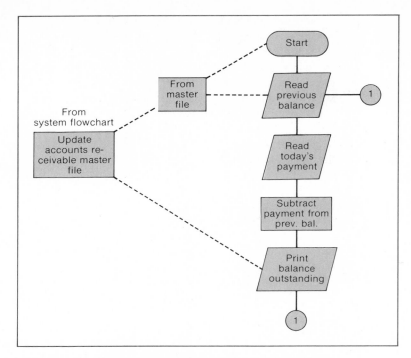

Figure 14–2. General program flowchart for updating an accounts receivable file.

By contrast, a **program flowchart** depicts the plan behind the system. The plan is known as an **algorithm,** which is a series of operations (steps) that the computer follows to generate the desired information. Since the program flowchart is usually an expansion of a simple process symbol in a system flowchart, it is usually more complex than the system flowchart. For example, Figure 14–2 evolves from the system flowchart in Figure 14–1. The second figure is an expanded representation of the "Update Accounts Receivable File" step in the system flowchart.

Major Uses

Program flowcharts are the most widely used graphic method for describing computer operations. Their major uses are in documentation and in programming. As a documentation tool, a flowchart helps a person communicate the nature of the operation, regardless of the programming language or the computer in use. Because of the considerable mobility of computer programmers, a company often finds itself modifying programs that were written by programmers who are no longer with the computer center. In such cases, a program flowchart is an invaluable aid to understanding the original programmer's logic flow.

Program flowcharts are more widely used than decision tables, due to their relative advantages:

1. They are *language-independent.* Flowcharts can be learned and applied without formal knowledge of a programming language.

2. By their very nature, flowcharts force the user to give attention to significant matters over the less significant ones.

3. As a visual representation, flowcharts provide an alternative to the usual narrative description of a system or a program. The graphic format enables the user to grasp a lot at a glance.

4. The wide range of detailed options available to the one who prepares the flowchart enhances the communication value of the flowchart.

Flowcharts also have limitations:

1. Some programmers complain that flowcharts are a waste of time. Since thinking in graphic terms is not normal, they cannot be viewed as a natural means of communication.

2. They are often unwieldy and costly to produce. Certain details that require only a few lines in descriptive form often take more than a page of space to present in flowchart form.

3. Sometimes, they do not highlight what is important. Each step receives as much attention in a flowchart as any other.

4. Flowcharts do not represent a programming language. They are actually more a person-to-person than a person-to-computer means of communication. A computer cannot accept a program described in flowcharting form.

5. Condensing details is subjective. Summarizing the wrong details can render the flowchart useless.

6. A flowchart generally tells *how* but rarely *why* a given set of operations is made.

Despite the limitations, a program flowchart can be translated into any one of a large number of programming languages. Since it graphically represents the logic of a computer program, it provides a convenient reference for locating logic errors. For complex problems, some installations use a special computer program designed to write program flowcharts. Once it is fed the data for each symbol and the squares into which the data goes, the program utilizes the printer to draw flowchart symbols on paper marked with numbered squares and to connect them to one another. This technique is quite efficient, convenient for the programmer to look over the results and make changes where necessary.

Symbol Standardization

Systematic use of graphic arts dates back to John von Neumann, the intellectual father of flowcharting. With the collaboration of associates at the Institute for Advanced Study at Princeton, he was the first to use and publish information on flowcharts. Although the symbols have changed over time, the concept and rationale of flowcharting remain the same.

National and international cooperation have resulted in the development of standards for computer processing. During the 1960s, the first formal U.S. attempt to develop a flowcharting standard was made. A committee worked with the Business Equipment Manufacturing Association (BEMA) and the American Standards Association (ASA). The latter association's members included representatives from computer manufacturers and a few computer users. The result was the drafting of a standard, which was approved in 1963 and published as the ASA X3.5. This American effort toward flowcharting standardization was matched by the International Standards Organization (ISO). The X3.5 standard was later revised in 1965, 1966, 1968, and 1970. In 1965 the name of the American Standards Association was changed to the United States of American Standards Institute (USASI), and the ASA X3.5 became USASI X3.5 Standard. When the name was again changed in 1969 to the American National Standards Institute (ANSI), the flowchart standard also changed to ANSI X3.5 Standard. The 1970 revision brought the X3.5 standard closer to the ISO standard.

Use of Templates

Proficiency in the art of flowcharting is developed with practice. No two persons draw flowcharts exactly alike. The only two persistent criteria are clarity of the presentation and validity of the symbols. Templates enhance the presentation of a flowchart. A good flowchart template should be flexible and transparent, with clearly visible registration lines to align the symbols as they are drawn. A sample flowcharting template is shown in Figure 14–3.

Figure 14–3. Flowcharting template

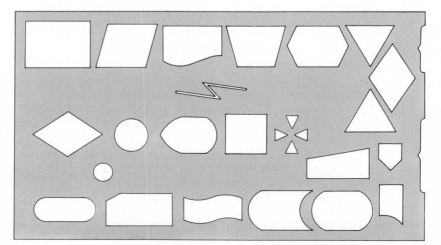

General Flowcharting Hints

Some helpful points in constructing a program flowchart are:

1. The flowchart should be legible, clean, and simple. Use a standardized template with clearly recognizable symbols. The flowchart will look neater and more presentable than a hand-drawn flowchart.

2. Each page should be numbered sequentially, and enough space should be allowed for the title of the application, the name of the programmer, and the data on which the flowchart was constructed. The title should be short and clear.

3. The language used in describing each step in the flowchart should be English or common notations, not coded language. The use of English contributes to a better understanding of the instructions by people other than the programmer who may not be familiar with the system used.

4. In each instruction, the wording should be clearly written within the symbol and consistent with the level of detail in the flowchart.

5. The flowchart should maintain a consistent, general flow direction—from top to bottom and from left to right. When this is done, arrowheads are not needed.

6. Where possible, only one entrance and exit flowline should be drawn for each symbol. Also, the flowline should be drawn so that it enters or exits at the visual midpoint of the symbol. Symbols that may require more than one exit flowline are decision and input-output symbols.

Basic Symbols

Some symbols are used primarily for system flowcharting, others for program flowcharting, while certain other symbols are used for both types. The flowcharting symbols approved by the American National Standard Institute (ANSI) are shown in Figure 14–4. They can be drawn directly from templates, obtainable everywhere.

1. The *input-output symbol* (a parallelogram) represents an instruction to an input or an output device. It is usually shown on both ends of a program flowchart. Occasionally, other symbols appear before the input symbol to initialize preparatory routines (such as to set a variable to zero) or to prepare the system for a new application (Figure 14–5).

2. The *processing symbol* (a rectangle) denotes an action to be taken by the CPU in the actual processing of data. Examples are "ADD A + B," "LET A = 40," "MULTIPLY A BY B GIVING C" (Figure 14–6).

3. The *annotation symbol* (assertion flag) is an open rectangle with a broken line connecting the symbol to another flowchart symbol. It does not signify any action in the program, but it is used to give descriptive comments or explanatory notes for clarification (Figure 14–7).

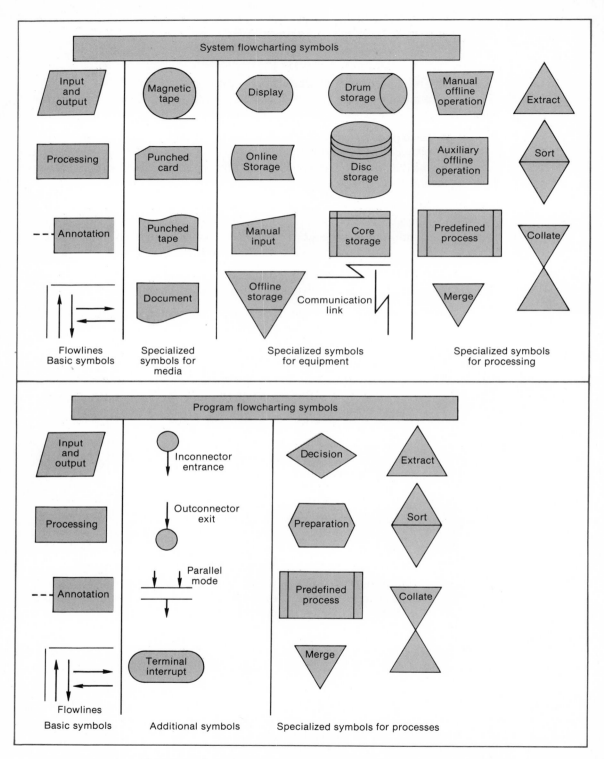

Figure 14–4. System and program flowcharting symbols.

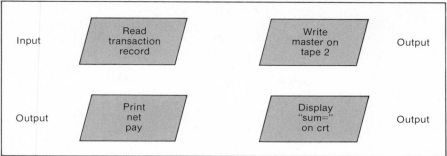

Figure 14–5. Input-output symbols—examples.

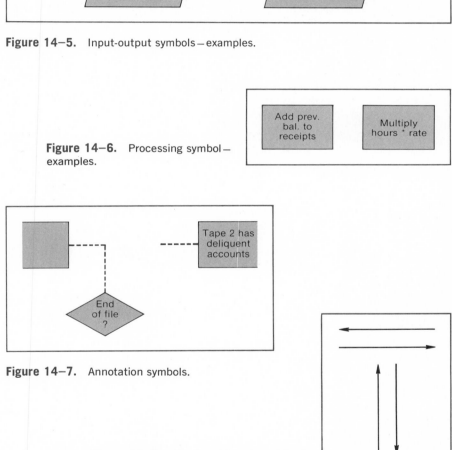

Figure 14–6. Processing symbol—examples.

Figure 14–7. Annotation symbols.

Figure 14–8. Flowline (direction-of-flow) symbols.

4. A *flowline symbol* (a straight line) is used to link symbols and to indicate the sequence of operations (Figure 14–8). Flowlines may cross, form junctions, or connect any two symbols so that the symbols follow a logical, meaningful flow. Occasionally broken arrows are used to specify a possible flow change in the computer during the program run, depending on the conditions dictated in the process.

Input-Output System Symbols for Media

Several specialized symbols (see Figure 14–4) have been developed for representing the input-output functions in system flowcharting. They are:

1. The *punched card symbol* represents an input-output function using a punched card, mark-sense card, stub card, deck of cards, and the like.

2. The *punched tape symbol* represents a punched tape routine.

3. The *magnetic tape symbol* represents a magnetic-tape routine.

4. The *document symbol* represents a printed document format.

System Symbols for Equipment and Processes

The primary system symbols under this category are:

1. The *display symbol* represents an input-output function in which the information is displayed for human use at the time of processing by means of video devices, console printers, plotters, or the like.

2. The *manual input symbol* represents entering input manually through a keyboard at the time of processing.

3. The *on-line storage symbol* represents an input-output function using any type of storage, such as magnetic tape, drum, or disc.

4. The *off-line storage symbol* refers to any storage not directly accessible by the computer system.

5. The *communication link symbol* represents data transmitted automatically from one source to another.

Program Symbols for Processing

Specialized program processing symbols (Figure 14–4) indicate specific processing functions and types of operations. The primary symbols are as follows:

1. The *decision symbol* represents the "thinking" part of a program. A branch is made based on a test or a condition.

2. The *predefined symbol* is a specialized process symbol that represents a named operation or programmed step not explicitly detailed in the program flowchart. As a subroutine symbol, it can be used when a procedure needs to be repeated several times. Rather than write the instructions for the procedure each time it is needed, the programmer may choose to make it a predefined process. It is written once, but can be available whenever it is needed in the program. Figure 14–9.

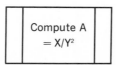

Compute A
$= X/Y^2$

Figure 14–9. Example of a predefined process symbol.

3. The *preparation symbol* is used to specify operations such as control, initiation, an index register, and anything that will alter the program's course of execution. In addition, some programmers use this symbol for various preparatory routines.

Other program flowcharting symbols include the following:

1. The *terminal symbol* (flat oval) is used to designate the beginning and the end of a program. It can also be used elsewhere in the flowchart for specifying error conditions, such as parity error checks or detection of invalid characters. In this case, manual intervention is required (Figure 14–10).

2. The *parallel mode symbol* consists of two parallel lines of any equal length. It represents the beginning or the end of two or more simultaneous operations (Figure 14–10).

3. The *fixed connector symbol* is a nonprocessing symbol used to connect one part of a flowchart to another without drawing flowlines. It denotes an entry to or an exit from another part of the flowchart. It conserves space by keeping related blocks near one another, reduces the number of flowlines in complex programs, and eliminates cross lines from taking place (Figure 14–11). Thus the fixed connector symbol aids in developing a clearer, better organized, and more simplified flowchart.

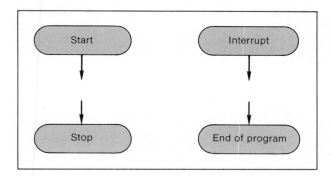

Figure 14–10. Terminal symbols.

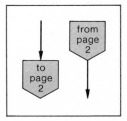

Figure 14–11. Interpage connector symbols.

Figure 14–12 illustrates the use of fixed connector symbols in blocks A to I. The cross line going from the output symbol "Print C" to the initialization routine has been eliminated, space is conserved, and the related blocks stand out in a clear and organized manner.

4. The *interpage* (off-page) connector, a nonprocessing symbol, is used to indicate an exit from one page to another. Complex problems often require a detailed flowchart extending over several pages. In Figure 14–13,

Figure 14–12. Program flowchart using connector symbols.

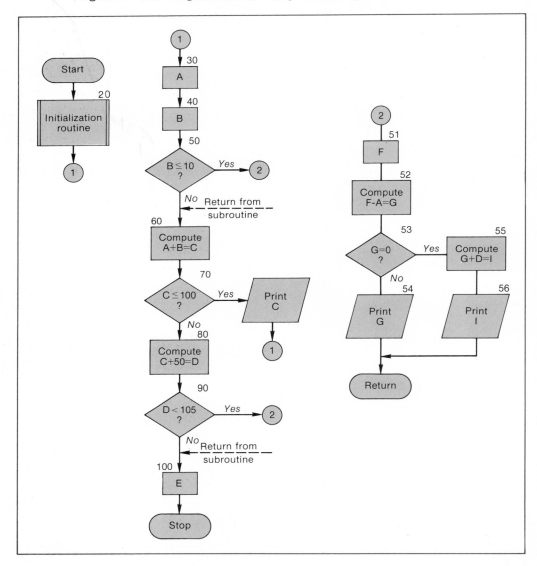

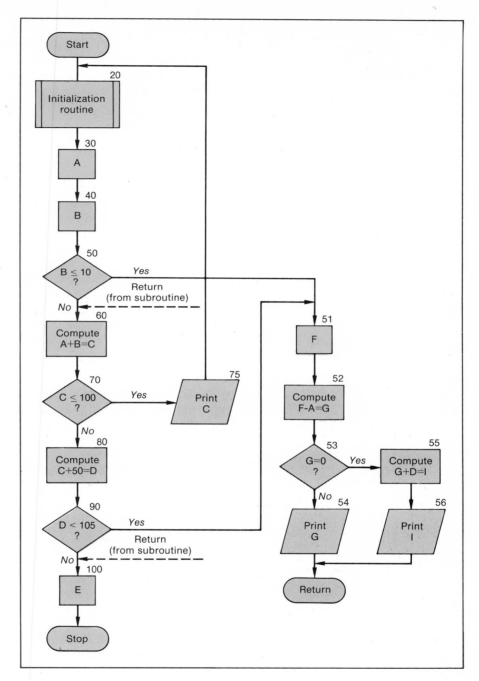

Figure 14–13. Hypothetical program flowchart.

the left symbol is the last symbol on the first page; it indicates continuation of the flowchart on the second page. The first symbol on the second page should be the same symbol, which refers to the continuation of the flow-charting from the first page.

Subroutines

To reduce programming and compiling costs, programmers often develop a set of instructions called *subroutines,* that are kept in a "library" and made available to the main program when needed. When in operation, the subroutine derives its information from the main program, performs the necessary routine, and relays the results back to the main program. Entrance to and exit from a subroutine are often called *entrance parameter* and *exit parameter,* respectively.

In Figure 14–12, a subroutine headed by connector symbol 2 is initiated from two separate decision points in the main flowchart. After execution, control returns to the instruction following the decision point that initiated the entry. For example, if an entry is made from the decision point "B < 10?," control returns to the instruction "Compute A + B = C." However, if entry is made from the decision point "D < 105?," control returns to the instruction "E." Since a subroutine can be initiated from several places in the main program, care must be taken to return control to the proper instruction.

Looping and "Decision Making"

A computer executes one instruction after another unless directed to alter the sequence. Changing the execution sequence is called **looping.**

A loop is illustrated in Figure 14–14. The computer reads the employee's ID, the hours worked, and the rate per hour. Next it checks whether the hours are equal to or under 40. If yes, it computes gross pay (hours × rate). All deductions are then subtracted from gross pay, resulting in net pay. Net pay is printed, followed by looping back to reading another employee record. On the other hand, in the case of overtime (over 40 hours), the computer loops to an overtime computation to arrive at gross pay. Then the program branches to the net pay calculation, prints net pay details, and loops back to read the next sequential record.

The loop that takes the program to overtime calculation is a *conditional* loop; that is, the program tests for a condition ("Hours ≤ 40?"). The loop following the overtime calculation, however, is an *unconditional* loop because no conditions are tested. Once overtime is calculated, the program branches automatically to the gross pay calculation.

A program may include one or more loops to test various conditions or to decide on a particular course of action based on the test. This "decision making" ability, symbolized by the logic symbol, represents the "thinking" part of a computer and relates to algebraic notations used to test a given relationship. These tests, called relational expressions, are in three forms: English expression, arithmetic form, and coded form (Table 14–1).

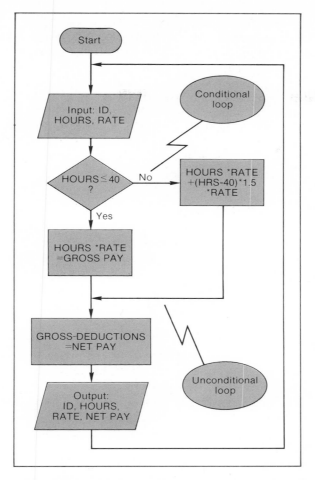

Figure 14–14. The use of loops in program flowcharts.

Table 14–1. The three forms of "decision making."

English expression	Arithmetic form	Coded form
A is equal to **B**	$A = B$	**A.EQ.B**
A is not equal to **B**	$A \neq B$	**A.NE.B**
A is greater than **B**	$A > B$	**A.GT.B**
A is greater than or equal to **B**	$A \geq B$	**A.GE.B**
A is less than **B**	$A < B$	**A.LT.B**
A is less than or equal to **B**	$A \leq B$	**A.LE.B**

Cross Referencing a Program Flowchart

Once a program flowchart has been completed, many programmers give each block a number based on its sequence in the flowchart. This optional step, called *cross referencing,* can be used later as a statement number in the coding phase of program preparation. In Figure 14–13, for example, the functional blocks constituting the main instruction flow are arbitrarily numbered from 20 to 100, in increments of 10. The numbers within an increment are used to label up to nine statements that might be derived from any given block. A case in point is the decision symbol, labeled 50: A "Yes" alternative leads to the execution of six instructions, which are given cross references 51 to 56. Thus the increment between any two blocks in the main program should be constant and sufficient for labeling secondary instructions.

Use of Notations

The use of ordinary English is often too verbose for specifying operations or naming data within flowcharting symbols. Although the American National Standards Institute (ANSI) does not specify any special language, several compact sets of notations are recommended. Figure 14–15 lists some of the more commonly used notations in flowcharting. Notations summarize within flowcharting symbols greater amounts of information than ordinary English, improving the flowchart's communication value.

Decision Tables

A **decision table** is an effective tabular approach used in planning programs, in showing cause-and-effect relationships, and in handling complex decision logic. It presents the original conditions and the courses of action to be taken if the conditions are met.

For many years tabular representation of data has been an effective means of communicating data clearly and concisely. A typical table is one that gives the status of various term test grades. Table 14–2 has a one-to-one relationship and reads as follows: *If* the test grade is between 90 and 100, *then* it is "excellent"; *if* the test grade is between 80 and 89, *then* it is "good"; and so on until *if* the test grade is below 60, *then* it is "fail." The table can also be turned around by stating that *if* the test is excellent, *then* the grade is between 90 and 100, and so on. Thus a decision table explains a situation involving more than one "if-then" relationship.

Table 14–2. Decision table – an example.

Score range	Rating Excellent	Good	Average	Poor	Fail
90 – 100	✔				
80 – 89		✔			
70 – 79			✔		
60 – 69				✔	
Below 60					✔

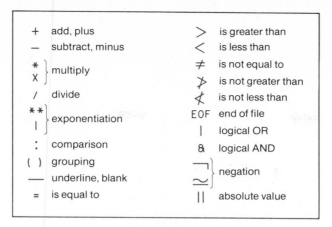

+ add, plus	> is greater than
− subtract, minus	< is less than
* X } multiply	≠ is not equal to
	≯ is not greater than
/ divide	≮ is not less than
** | } exponentiation	EOF end of file
	| logical OR
: comparison	& logical AND
( ) grouping	¬ ~ } negation
—— underline, blank	
= is equal to	|| absolute value

Figure 14–15. Primary notations used in flowcharting.

Decision tables are of use to everyone – programmers, analysts, supervisors, and managers:

1. As a documentation tool, they constitute a simpler and more concise form of data analysis than either the narrative or the flowchart form.

2. They can be effective tools for extracting details pertinent to a given problem and in formulating questions.

3. Unlike flowcharts, which are developed around the programmer's logical thinking and are arbitrarily made simple or complex, decision tables oblige the preparer to be concise and to consider all sets of conditions.

4. They serve as easy-to-follow communication devices between technical and nontechnical personnel. They are verbally oriented for managers and logically prepared for programmers and analysts.

5. They are easy to learn and to update, and they continue to function once the logic is developed.

Elements of a Decision Table

A decision table is divided into two parts: the stub and the entry. The left part is divided into an upper quadrant, called the **condition stub,** which sets forth in question form the conditions that may exist. The lower quadrant is called the **action stub,** which outlines in narrative form the action to be taken to meet each condition (Table 14–3).

Table 14–3. Elements of a decision table.

Condition Stub	Condition Entry
Action Stub	Action Entry

The right-hand part of a decision table is also divided into an upper section, called the condition entry, and a lower section called the action entry. The **condition entry** provides the answers to the questions asked in the condition stub quadrant. Answers are represented by a Y to signify "yes," an N to signify "no," or a blank to show that the condition involved has not been tested. In the **action entry,** a check mark or an X indicates the appropriate action resulting from the answers to the conditions entered in the condition entry quadrant. A number of columns are also available in the condition entry section, each representing a condition (an alternative plan). See Table 14–4. A number of rows are also available in the condition stub, each representing a logical question answerable by Y or N. The same logic applies to the columns and rows of the action entry and action stub; that is, the action entry shows completion of the action statement, and the action stub presents an indication of where to go next for each instruction or rule.

Table 14–4.   Detailed structure of a decision table.

			1	2	3	4	5	6	7
		Table Name							
IF (condition) · · · THEN (action)	Row 1								
	Row 2								
	Row 3								
	Row 4								
	Row 5								
	Row 6								
	Row 7								
		STUBS				ENTRIES			

Application of a Decision Table

The application of decision tables is easier illustrated than explained. Early in the morning you have to determine what to wear to school. Figure 14–16 is a flowchart that presents the basic decisions to consider and the actions to take. In the corresponding decision table (Table 14–5), the condition constitutes the input, while the action is the output. A look at either the flowchart or the decision table gives the answer immediately. The illustration of this simple decision shows the details that go into the construction of a simplified flowchart and a decision table.

The construction of a flowchart for an actual business application is likely to involve many more detailed logical and processing steps than those required for a personal procedure. In either case, decision tables are excellent communi-

Table 14–5. Decision table to determine what to wear to school.

What to wear table	Condition entry encountered			
	Alternative 1	Alternative 2	Alternative 3	Alternative 4
IF (condition) Raining and temperature over 70°	Y	N	N	N
Forecast clear and temperature under 70°		Y	N	N
Forecast rain and temperature under 70°			Y	N
THEN (action) Wear light clothes	X			
Wear regular clothes		X	X	
Wear summer clothes				X
Carry a sweater		X	X	
Wear a raincoat	X			
Carry a raincoat			X	
Carry an umbrella	X		X	
Wear overshoes	X		X	
Go to car	X	X	X	X
Drive to school	X	X	X	X

ACTION ENTRY

Legend:
Y = Yes
N = No
Blank = Irrelevant action (or condition)
X = Completion of action statement

cation aids to both programmers and users. In situations involving complex relationships between key variables, they can be very effective, while relatively simple to construct. The main rules to follow are:

1. Each table should be given a name, shown in the table header.

2. The development of a table begins at the top.

3. Although the logic of the decision table is independent of the sequence in which condition rules are written, the action takes place in the order in which the events occur.

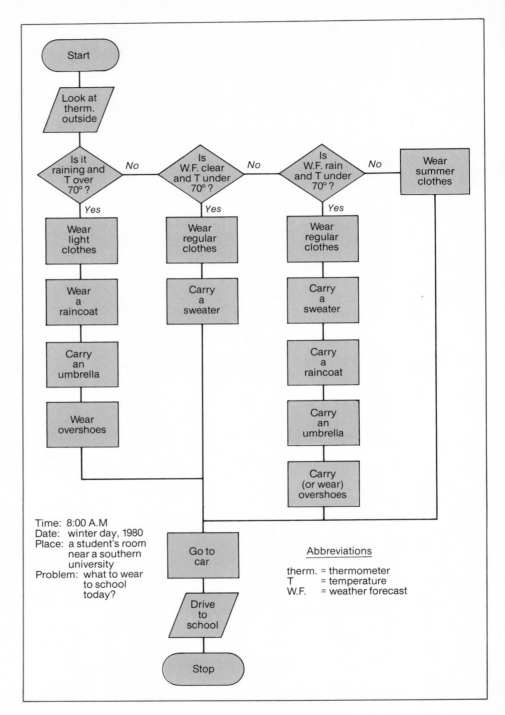

Figure 14–16. A flowchart to determine what to wear to school.

4. Use standardized language as much as possible.

5. Eliminate duplication, redundancy, and contraindication.

Types of Decision Tables

Decision tables are normally classified by the type of information they record:

1. limited entry,

2. extended entry, or

3. mixed entry.

Limited entry tables.   Probably the most widely used type, the **limited entry design** requires a fixed form of information in each quadrant and limits condition entries to Y, N, or a blank; action entries are also limited to X or a blank (Table 14–5). The condition stub must be written so that it is either true or false, and the action stub must completely describe the action to be taken.

Table 14–6 is a typical example of a limited-entry decision table. The problem here is to determine whether or not to extend a real estate mortgage loan against a table of key values. Note that the statements in the condition stub are written in question form, and they require either a yes or no response. The response to each statement is written in the condition entry accordingly. Likewise, the action is written in a narrative form in the action stub, with ×s in the action entry responding to each Y in the condition entry.

Table 14–6.   Limited entry decision table.

Mortgage loan table	1	2	3	4
Credit record excellent?	Y	N	N	N
Annual salary over $30,000?		Y	N	N
Net worth over $50,000?			Y	N
Approve loan for 20 yrs.	X			
Approve Collateral loan for 10 yrs.		X		
Approve Conditional loan for 8 yrs.			X	
Reject Application				X

Since they are limited to a yes or no alternative, as is the case in binary logic, limited-entry tables are suited for computer-oriented applications.

Extended entry tables.   In **extended entry decision tables,** the statements written in the stub section are extended into the entry section. The condition stub identifies the elements to be tested; the condition entry states those elements or defines the value in absolute or relative form. Similarly, the action stub states the action, and the action entry specifies the stated action. Table 14–7 presents an extended entry table of the information provided in Table 14–6. Extended entry tables offer the advantage of reducing the number of items listed in the condition and action stubs, while providing essentially the same information.

Extended entry decision tables resemble conventional data tables and are ideally suited to problems that have few variables, with each variable having many values.

Table 14–7. Extended entry decision table.

Mortgage loan table	1	2	3	4
Credit rating?	Excellent	Good	Fair	Poor
Salary (in thousands)		>30	<30	<30
Net worth (in thousands)			>50	<50
Decision	A	B	C	D
A. Approve loan for 20 yrs.				
B. Approve Collateral loan for 10 yrs.				
C. Approve Conditional loan for 8 yrs.				
D. Reject Application				

Mixed entry tables. As the name implies, a **mixed-entry table** is a combination of rows with extended entries and of rows with limited entries. One rule to remember is that, although the rows may be mixed, each row must be either entirely extended or entirely limited. In Table 14–8, rows 2 and 3 have an extended entry format, while the remaining rows have a limited entry format. Conversion from either extended entry or mixed entry is done by writing the value of each element as an independent condition or action and assigning Ys, Ns, or Xs where applicable.

Table 14–8. Mixed entry decision table.

Mortgage loan table	1	2	3	4
Credit record excellent?	Y	N	N	N
Salary (in 1000's)		>30	<30	<30
Net worth (in 1000's)			>50	<50
Approve loan for 20 yrs.	X			
Approve Collateral loan for 10 yrs.		X		
Approve Conditional loan for 8 yrs.			X	
Reject Application				X

In comparing limited and extended entry decision tables, we find that each type has certain advantages. In a limited entry table, for example, the status of each condition (true or false) and that of each action (applied or not applied) makes it more precise than either the extended entry or the mixed entry table. On the other hand, the extended entry table is best suited for problem solving. It offers the possibility of having two or more responses to a given condition.

The ELSE Rule

A catchall convention occasionally applied in decision tables is the **ELSE rule.** It represents any conditions (or rules) not mentioned in the decision table. In Table 14–9 the four rules mentioned are

1. If less than 400 units are sold, then the salesman's commission is 1 percent of total sales.

2. If between 400 and 499 units are sold, then the salesman's commission is 2 percent of total sales.

3. If between 500 and 599 units are sold and if the salesman has been with the company more than 1 year, then the salesman's commission is 3½ percent of total sales.

4. If between 500 and 599 units are sold, and the salesman has been employed by the firm for 1 year or less, then his commission is 3 percent of total sales.

Table 14–9. Decision table using the ELSE rule.

Salesman's commission table	1	2	3	4	5
units sold <400?	Y	N	N	N	E
units sold 400–499?		Y	N	N	L
units sold 500–599?			Y	Y	S
with firm more than 1 yr?			Y	N	E
1% commission of total sale	X				
2% commission of total sale		X			
3½% commission of total sale			X		
3% commission of total sale				X	
Investigate					X

The ELSE rule (written in the extreme right column of a decision table with an × in the action-entry section) simply calls for investigating the situation in the event that none of the first four rules or conditions applies. Its frequent use is discouraged, because it does not offer a clear-cut statement of the action to be taken and is likely to hide both logic and redundancy errors.

Logic Flow and Construction of Decision Tables

As indicated earlier, a primary objective of a decision table is to present the logic patterns of a basic problem in a clear, concise, and easy-to-follow sequence. However, major problems, especially those involving complex decision logic and relationships, often cannot be effectively written in one table. Thus, several tables encompassing the necessary details of logic groups must be constructed and linked together in a sequential order similar to the order applied in program flowchart construction.

In constructing a set of tables, the main logic flow is written in what is called **open end tables;** the set of actions and conditions common to these tables is written separately in **closed** tables. Linkage of these tables is accomplished by two control instructions:

1. A *GO TO instruction* (GO TO, followed by a table number or a table name) directs logic flow to another open end table, which then takes control. In a limited entry table, the name or number of the table to which control is transferred is written as a part of the GO TO instruction (Figure 14–17, the Begin Table and Table 2); in an extended entry table, the table name or number appears in the entry part of the table (Figure 14–17, Table 1). After the appropriate rule has been acted on, a GO TO instruction in the latter table directs the user to the next open end table for processing.

2. A *DO instruction* (DO, followed by a table number or a table name), on the other hand, directs logic flow from an open end table to a closed table.

After execution, the closed table transfers control back to the point of reference in the open end table.

Figure 14–17 depicts seven logic flow steps involving four open end tables and three closed tables. The steps are as follows:

1. The "GO TO Table 1" instruction in the Begin Table takes us to Table 1 and, following the execution of the appropriate rule, the last instruction in the action section leads to Table 2 — an open end table.

2. Table 2 takes control throughout the execution of the appropriate rule or rules. Then the next action is "DO Table 4" — a closed table. Table 4 takes temporary control and then returns to the next sequential instruction in Table 2 — "GO TO Table 3."

3. This instruction transfers control to Table 3 (open end table), which takes control throughout the execution of the appropriate rule or rules.

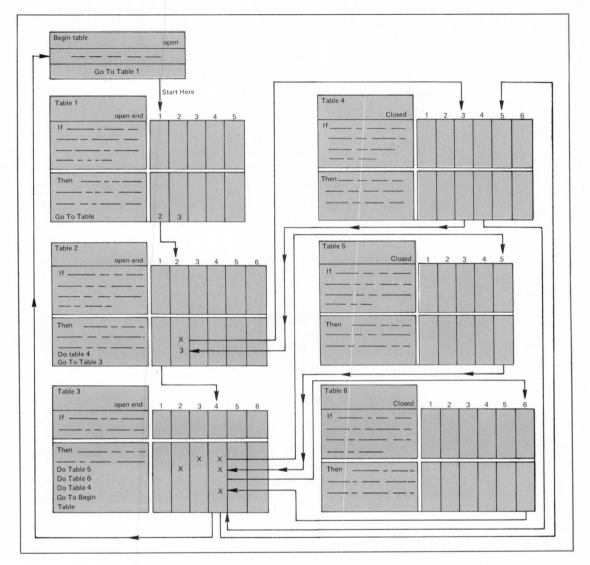

Figure 14–17. Flow of logic decision tables.

4. Next, the "DO Table 5" instruction in the action section of Table 3 is picked up, transferring temporary control to Table 5 (closed table); when the appropriate rule or rules have been executed, control is transferred back to the next sequential instruction in Table 3, which is "DO Table 6."

5. The "DO Table 6" instruction transfers control to Table 6, the appropriate rule is executed, and control is transferred back to the next instruction in Table 3, which is "DO Table 4."

6. This instruction uses Table 4 again and later returns to the next instruction in Table 3, which is "GO TO Begin Table."

7. The "GO TO Begin Table" instruction sends the user back to the Begin Table to continue this operation.

This illustration gives rise to several observations:

1. A closed table does not end with a special instruction on where to go next. Return of control to the table that originally caused the transfer is indicated by the word "Closed" in the table header; or sometimes a return or exit entry is made instead.

2. When both DO and GO TO control instructions are written in the action section of an open end table, the DO instruction is written first, followed by the GO TO instruction.

3. More than one open end table can reference a given closed table. In Figure 14–17, closed Table 4 was referenced by open end Tables 2 and 3.

Table 14–10

| | Combination (rule) | | | | | | | |
	1	2	3	4	5	6	7	8
1	Y	Y	Y	Y	N	N	N	N
2	Y	Y	N	N	Y	Y	N	N
3	Y	N	N	Y	N	Y	Y	N

In constructing a decision table, every possible useful combination or rule must be taken into consideration. The total number of combinations of Y and N in a given table is computed by raising 2 to a power equal to the number of rows involved. For example, in a three-row table, the total number of combinations of Y and N is 2^3 or 8. The combinations are shown in Table 14–10.

Thus each combination is covered by a separate rule in the table. Tables that do not have all required combinations but include an ELSE rule in the right column are considered complete tables, since the ELSE rule covers all missing combinations. However, its use, especially in computer-oriented projects, is not recommended, as it covers up inconsistencies and redundancies. In the absence of the ELSE rule, inconsistency occurs in a table when a number of its rules have comparable overall conditions but result in different actions or results. **Redundancy** also occurs when two or more rules in a table display or stress the same combination. Thus, to minimize redundancy, calculation of the required combinations should be made and no two rules should have the same combination.

Finally, regardless of the complexity of the problem at hand, the decision table should be of manageable size. Smaller tables are easier to read and comprehend and are relatively more complete and lacking in redundancy than the often unwieldy and data-loaded larger tables. Proper judgment as to size should be made as the details of the problems are gathered and the variables determined. Common sense, in this case, should lead to determining the size and number of tables that would best solve the problem.

SUMMARY

1. A program flowchart is a graphic means of describing the operation and decision logic done on data. It is a detailed flow of the sequential steps that must be performed by the computer. Flowcharts are either system or program flowcharts. System flowcharts present the broad data flow and operations of the system. Program flowcharts focus on the sequence of steps necessary for data transformation from input to output.

2. Basic and specialized symbols are used for developing both types of flowcharts. The symbols used are standardized through national and international efforts represented by the American National Standards Institute (ANSI) and the International Standards Organization (ISO).

3. The basic symbols used in describing or specifying computer program operations are input-output, processing, flowline, annotation, and terminal symbols. Looping and branching operations are represented by the decision (logic) symbol. Specialized input-output and process symbols for media or devices are often used for emphasizing a specific operation. A terminal symbol designates the beginning or end of a program. A connector symbol connects parts of a program together without drawing flowlines.

4. Flowcharting is an art and is time-consuming. In preparing flowcharts, the important factors to consider are neatness, consistency, and clarity of details.

5. Compared to the flowchart, decision tables offer a more concise documentation tool and a simpler form of data analysis. They are designed around the programmer's logical thinking and are verbally oriented for managers. They are easy to learn and continue to function once the logic is developed.

6. Decision tables are classified by the type of information recorded in their entries. They are limited entry, extended entry, or mixed entry. Limited entry tables are the most widely used and are ideally suited for computer-oriented applications. Extended entry tables resemble conventional data tables and are best suited for problem solving. A mixed entry table is a combination of rows with extended entries and rows with limited entries.

7. In constructing decision tables, every possible useful combination must be considered and covered by a separate rule in the table. The ELSE rule can be used to cover all missing combinations. In computer-oriented projects, however, its use is not recommended, since it may cover up inconsistencies and redundancies.

TERMS TO LEARN

Action entry	Extended entry table
Action stub	Limited entry table
Algorithm	Looping
Closed table	Mixed entry table
Condition entry	Open end table
Condition stub	Program flowchart
Decision table	Redundancy
ELSE rule	Systems flowchart

REVIEW QUESTIONS

1. What is a program flowchart? Summarize its advantages and limitations.

2. What guidelines must one consider in constructing a program flowchart?

3. Define and illustrate the major program symbols for processing.

4. Distinguish between:
    (a) fixed and interpage connector symbols
    (b) annotation and predefined symbols
    (c) conditional and unconditional loop
    (d) condition entry and condition stub

5. What is a decision table? Summarize its uses and elements.

6. What rules should be followed in constructing a decision table?

7. Explain the major types of decision tables. Which is the most widely used type?

8. How does an open-end table differ from a closed table?

Program Design and Structured Programming

Learning Objectives

Developing a program requires a number of of procedural steps. The problem must be defined, and flowcharts must be prepared and coded. The outcome is a program ready for testing. Recently, program design has taken a more structured approach than in times past. By the end of this chapter, you should know:

1. the steps making up the programming cycle,

2. how a program is converted into a machine-readable language,

3. the difference between symbolic and high-level lanugages,

4. the uses of computers and assemblers, and

5. the basics of structured programming.

The Programming Cycle

Problem Definition
Program Planning
Program Coding

Machine Languages
Machine-Oriented Assembler (Symbolic) Languages
High-Level Languages

Debugging and Testing
Documentation and Maintenance

Modular Programming

Top-Down Program Design
Structured Walkthrough
HIPO Diagrams
Structured Programming

The Structure Theorem

Modular Techniques in General

The Programming Cycle

Once provided with a valid program, the computer becomes self-operational; that is, it requires no human intervention during processing. The program instructions are executed one at a time in a single path. In the case of a special routine, the system takes an alternative path to execute the instructions. When the last instruction is executed, the program is terminated. This chapter explains the programming cycle from inception to implementation, providing an overview of structured methods of program design.

Developing a program requires the following well defined steps (Figure 15 – 1):

1. problem definition,
2. planning the solution (program planning),
3. program coding,
4. debugging and testing, and
5. documentation and maintenance.

Problem Definition

The programming cycle is initiated as soon as a decision is made to solve a problem with the computer. Problem definition, of course, presupposes the existence of a problem.

Figure 15–1. The programming cycle.

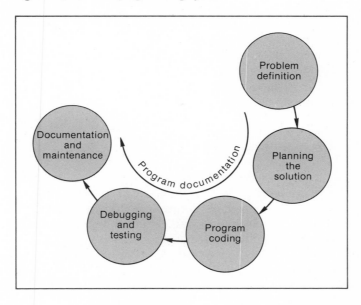

It also presupposes that the person in charge knows what the proposed program is supposed to do. That person may be an analyst, an analyst-programmer, or both. Depending on the specific computer installation, problem definition is usually under the jurisdiction of a systems analyst who designs the system and does the programming. It may be assigned to a programmer/analyst who has basic knowledge of systems design but who does the programming. Rather than have one person do both systems design and programming, many installations assign these functions separately to two people, on the basis of their qualifications and experience. Whoever the designer is must be familiar with the system requirements, with flowcharts, and with the steps in the passage of data from one stage to the next. The primary tasks are:

1. Plan to collect, organize, record, and process data. The data must reflect the actual application.

2. Design the input, output, and file formats. Input should be designed for ease of entry and processing. Output should also be designed to help the user make best use of the information. Special preprinted layout forms (such as the print chart, Figure 15–2) are used to format input and/or output data.

   In determining file layout, a number of factors are considered. For example, if the file is maintained on magnetic tape, items such as record length, the length of record blocks, the number of blocks to be maintained, and the capacity of the tape file should be specified. Figure 15–3 shows a tape storage format for organizing data on tape.

3. Create a procedure for program completion of each stage of development, to determine how to ensure progress toward program completion.

The main qualification of the person in charge of problem definition is this: He or she must know exactly what the program is supposed to do *before* it is written. Often, errors in program testing reflect the definers lack of understanding in some aspects of the problem. All aspects of the program that need clarification, therefore, are best thoroughly examined during this stage of program development.

Program Planning

The solution to a programming problem requires planning—deciding in advance what steps must be taken to solve the problem. Having defined the problem and recorded information on preprinted layouts, the programmer proceeds to describe the processing sequence of the operation. Working with program flowcharts of the planned solution, the programmer generally begins flowcharting at a broad (macro) level of general logic and proceeds to detailed (micro) charts as guides for coding.

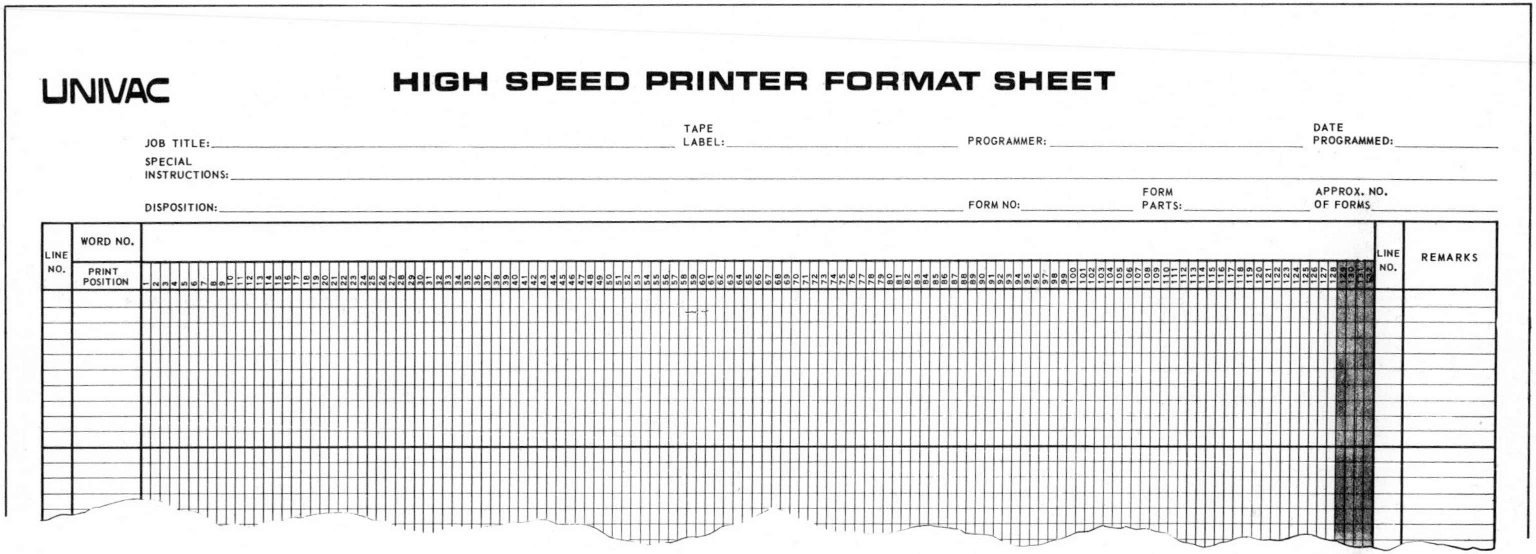

Figure 15–2. Print and file format.

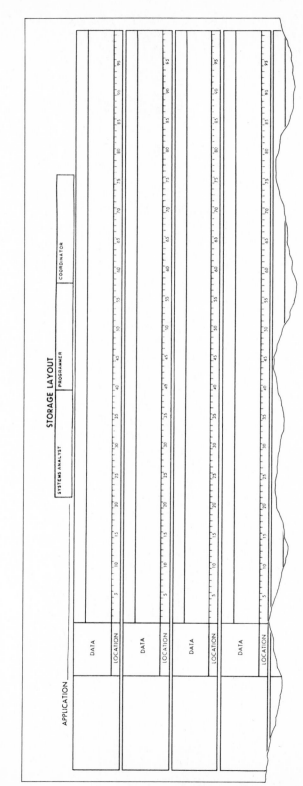

Figure 15–3. Tape storage format.

Program planning often divides the program into a number of modules (or subroutines) and tests them individually. A *subroutine* is a set of instructions, varying from a few to several hundred instructions, that derives its information from the main routine (program). After it executes its instructions, it sends the results back to the main program. Thus a subroutine may be viewed as a program within a program, with the following advantages:

1. It standardizes common functions that can then be used in any program when needed.

2. It reduces programming cost by eliminating the duplication of common logic in each program.

3. It cuts down on debugging cost and time, since it is easier to locate and correct errors by subroutine than by program.

4. It improves program maintenance, since only subroutines that are subject to modification need to be altered or updated.

During the seventies, new methods of designing and writing programs were introduced. The major methods (structured programming, top-down design, and HIPO) are explained later in the chapter.

Program Coding

After planning the solution, the programmer is ready for coding. Coding is the first of two steps: First, the steps on the flowchart must be transformed into written instructions, readable by humans; second, the human-readable instructions have to be converted into computer-readable form. Thus *coding* a program means simply writing coded instructions that are later translated into a machine language program understandable to the computer.

In the coding phase, the programmer converts the steps depicted in the program flowchart into readable instructions that make up the actual program, usually on special coding sheets (Figure 15–4). A coding form depicts the basic structure of the language used, helps the programmer minimize clerical errors in coding, and assists in the identification and organization of the program. After the program is coded, each line of code is punched into cards (or entered online), checked, and submitted to the computer for action. So ends the logical phase of devising a solution.

But how is the program converted into a language that the computer understands? To answer this question, we have to take a brief look at the programming languages used today. Historically, programming languages developed in the following order:

1. machine languages,

2. machine-oriented assembler (symbolic) languages, and then

3. high-level languages.

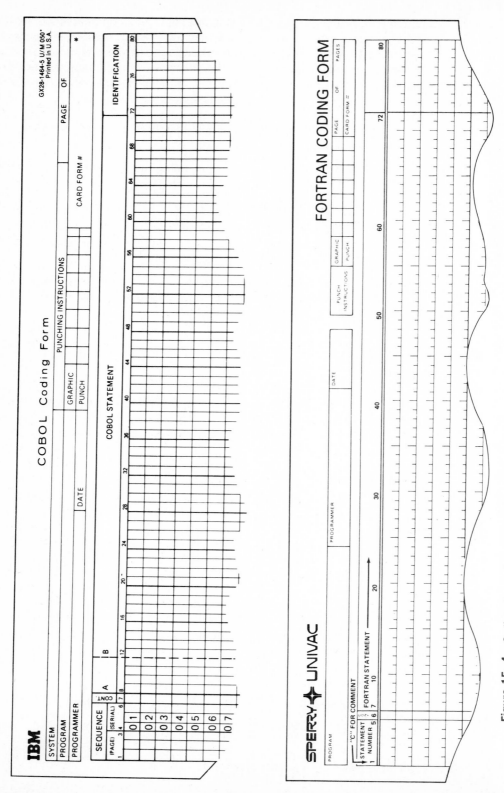

Figure 15–4. Coding forms for Cobol and Fortran programming.

Machine languages. The first generation of computer languages was represented by *machine languages,* which were tied to specific machines (computers). Writing a machine language program was complicated and often tedious. Programmers had to work with strings of numbers that represented each instruction's operation code and operand. They also had to remember a long list of code numbers of operation codes and keep track of the storage location of data and instructions. A *one-to-one* relationship existed between the instructions that the programmer coded and the operations that the computer performed.

The list of machine instructions, called an **object program,** required no translation the instructions were already written in computer language (Figure 15 – 5). The instructions were punched onto cards and read into memory for processing. Avoiding the conversion step was an efficient method of using main memory that made the program more immediately available for processing. However, the disadvantages outweighed the advantages. If the results showed errors in the program, the programmer had to check tediously each instruction to locate the error. If the correction meant adding or deleting one or more instructions, every instruction to the end of the program had to be changed. Furthermore, each program was written independently of other programs. Parts of an existing program could not be used as a part of a newly written program.

Machine-oriented assembler (symbolic) languages. Coding had to be made simpler. In the early 1950s, various software aids, called assembler or translating programs, were developed. An **assembler** allocated one line of coding for each machine instruction as it finally appeared in the output program. Whereas in assembly language there is only one line of coding for each instruction, a machine language instruction may require many lines of coding. Assemblers also allowed the use of easily remembered symbolic names or **mnemonics,** which are English-like words, instead of the numberical codes for machine operation. Symbolic languages eased the tedium of program coding and generally improved program preparation. Letter symbols were substituted for numeric machine language codes. Assigning and keeping track of instruction addresses was left up to the computer. Table 15 – 1 presents examples of symbolic and machine operation codes.

Figure 15–5. Processing run for a program in machine language.

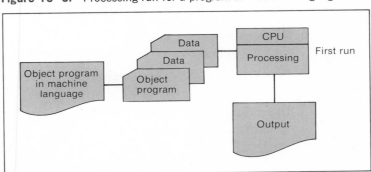

Table 15–1. Symbolic and machine language codes—example.

Command name	Symbolic code	Operation code
Input-output		
Halt input-output	HIO	9E
Start input-output	SIO	9C
Test input-output	TIO	9D
Data movement and manipulation		
Convert to binary	CVB	4F
Convert to decimal	CVD	4E
Execute	EX	44
Load address	LA	41
Move	MVI	92
Move characters	MVC	D2
Move numerics	MVN	D1
Store	ST	50
Translate	TR	DC
Arithmetic		
Add	A	5A
Divide	D	5D
Multiply	M	5C
Subtract	S	5B
Logic		
Compare	C	59
Transfer of control		
Branch on condition	BC	47
Supervisor call	SVC	0A

When the instructions of the assembler language program are organized, they comprised the **source program.** This program still had to be translated into an **object** (machine language) before its execution by the computer. As shown in Figure 15–6, the assembly routine includes the following steps:

1. The assembly program (provided by the computer manufacturer) is loaded into memory from a disc library.

2. During assembly, the source program is read one instruction at a time. Each source code is converted into object code.

3. If errors are detected during assembly, they are printed in a *diagnostic listing* along with the assembly listing.

4. After errors are corrected, the object program is produced and stored on disc for testing.

5. Data is read into memory under the control of the object program. When completed, the program is ready to be used for the actual application.

Initially, an assembler converted one symbolic instruction into one machine language instruction. As assembler languages developed, macroinstruc-

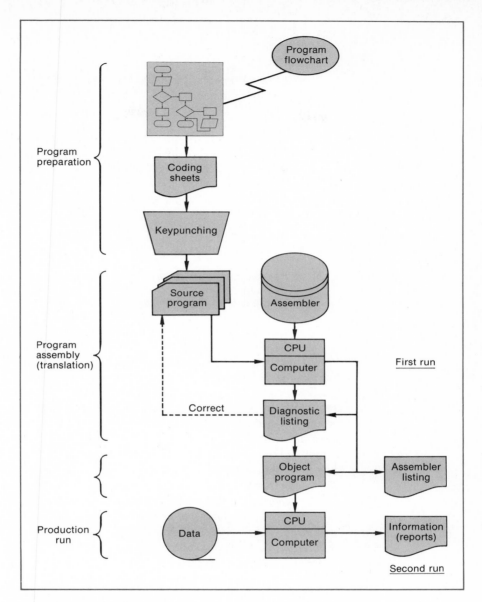

Figure 15-6. Assembly of a symbolic program.

tions were added. A **macroinstruction** assembles several lines of machine language instructions, reducing the coding requirements for the programmer. Despite these improvements, however, an assembler language had several limitations:

1. It was time-consuming and still tedious.

2. It was still a machine-oriented (low-level) language. The language was

translated on a one-for-one basis—one machine instruction for one symbolic instruction.

3. The programmer had to have detailed knowledge of the way a computer's instructions are handled.

High-level languages.   At the turn of the decade, the state of the art included complete macroinstructions in high-level programming languages. The latest languages are called "high level" because they are machine-independent. A programmer doesn't have to know much about the computer in order to write a program in a high-level language. The primary advantages of high-level languages are:

1. a reduced amount of coding,

2. compatibility with a wide range of computers with minor modification,

3. their ease of learning (easier than assembly languages), and

4. easy program documentation, updating, and maintenance.

Their major disadvantage, however, is that they take longer to execute than low-level languages, because the translation process within the machine is extensive and time-consuming. The conversion of a high-level source program into an object program is essentially the same as that of an assembly language program. The exception is that the assembler is called a **compiler,** which is a software aid written by the computer manufacturer and made available with the computer. The compiler is loaded into main memory from a disc library for execution. During execution, the source code is converted into an object code, which is then stored on disc ready for testing. Any error during conversion produces a diagnostic listing in addition to the compiler listing (Figure 15 – 6).

High-level languages are classified as procedure-oriented languages (such as Fortran, Cobol, Basic) or problem-oriented languages (such as RPG). A *procedure-oriented language* represents a system of computational procedures designed to solve a problem. For example, Fortran (FORmula TRANslator) is designed for mathematical computations, while COBOL (COmmon Business-Oriented Language) is designed for business problems. In contrast, a *problem-oriented language* is a descriptive language, used to describe problems. For example, RPG (Report Program Generator) does not require programmers to memorize a procedure for placing certain information in designated positions in the program. Instead, they work with coding sheets that indicate the exact location of the data to be coded. Because of the simplified procedures, programming in such language boils down to simply "fill in the blanks." Figure 15 – 7 shows sample Fortran and RPG programs.

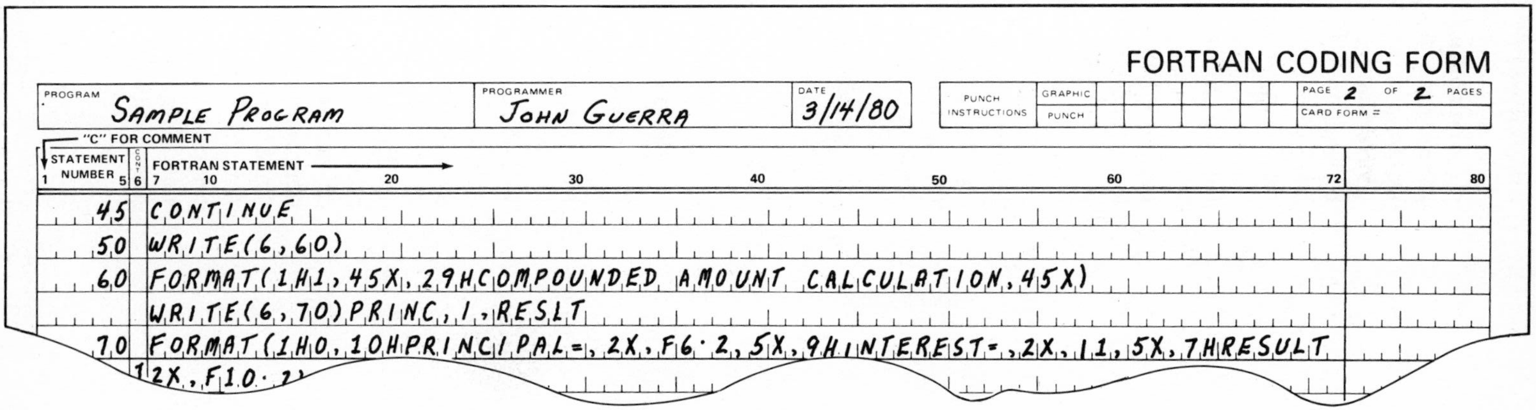

Figure 15–7. Fortran

Debugging and Testing

Human errors in programming are not rare. They tend to increase with the complexity of the program. Thus a program seldom runs perfectly the first time. **Debugging** entails locating and correcting programming errors, or "bugs," of which there are two types: clerical and logical. A *clerical* error often occurs in the coding phase. For instance, a programmer may inadvertently assign two unrelated values to a given instruction or the same statement number to two (or more) instructions. A *logical* error occurs due to the misinterpretation of a problem area or due to a lack of knowledge of a processing routine. For example, the failure to consider the overtime rate in computing gross pay creates a logical error. In this case, the computer calculates gross pay by multiplying an employee's total time (say 65 hours) by the regular rate. The result is obviously an error in logic, caused by the programmer's oversight.

Debugging can be facilitated by two methods. One is called *desk-checking*. After the program has been coded, it is reviewed manually by the programmer for obvious errors. In the second method, the program is loaded into memory for compilation. Most compiler programs are designed to detect and analyze errors through **diagnostics,** that is, an error message list that specifies the nature of the errors and their locations in the source program. Among the more common errors detected in compilation are:

1. invalid characters or statements in the source deck,

2. undefined symbols,

3. incorrect operation codes,

4. illegal names,

5. improperly sequenced statements,

6. spelling errors, and

7. omitted labels.

A *postcompilation* listing which reflects the status of the program in memory, can also be produced. The programmer uses this listing to modify the program so as to eliminate all errors.

Once the program has been debugged, it is tested for accuracy and reliability. Typically, a program is first tested with representative input data. Then another test with "exception" data normally checks the program's maximum limits or verifies out-of-the-ordinary details. For example, maximum gross pay for nonexempt employees should not exceed $400 per month. The final test runs "fake" and erroneous data that the program should detect as invalid.

In each case, the anticipated results must be worked out in advance for comparison with actual test results. If the results match, no diagnostics are generated. The program is considered "error-free." Actual data can then be processed with confidence. Otherwise, a series of **diagnostics** is generated by the language translator: This error message list helps the programmer eliminate most of the clerical and many of the logical errors. After corrections have been made, the program is read into memory and tested again. This procedure continues until an "error-free" run is achieved. At times, when desk-checking and diagnostics do not eliminate all errors, the programmer calls for a **memory dump**—a snapshot of the computer's memory—to search for logical errors. A memory dump is usually a last resort, since it is tedious and costly.

When a system is to be replaced by a new one, the important question is, "How should the substitution be implemented?" A common method, called **parallel run,** involves the simultaneous operation of both the old and the new systems to determine whether both systems produce identical output. Generally, a parallel run is carried out over a period of days, often weeks, before the new program can be allowed to handle the new operation on its own. The major limitation of this approach, however, is cost. The savings of going completely with the new routine has to be weighed against the security of retaining the old system as a backup.

Documentation and Maintenance

Program documentation, essentially a "carbon copy" of the work performed on the program, should be developed and maintained at every stage of the programming cycle. In the event that the programmer transfers out of the department or resigns from the company, good documentation enables someone else to modify or maintain the program. Documentation thereby simplifies program revision, not only by the originator but by 2 new comers as well. It provides key information about the status and operation of the program, guiding the console operator with operating instructions. Perhaps most important, documentation reduces the need for maintenance. The detail available in the documentation minimizes the need for a major program overhaul. Program maintenance, a continuing process that affects various phases of program development, usually gives programmers all they can do just to keep programs "up and running."

Some of the details included in a program documentation package are:

1. preflowcharting data,

2. a problem definition statement and the methodology used in program preparation,

3. a copy of the master program flowchart and other layouts,

4. a detailed description of input data preparation,

5. a master list of details in connection with the record layout and code forms used in writing the program,

6. a program run manual, listing the instructions the console operator must follow in running the program,

7. a sample of tested data and their output, and

8. storage dumps and diagnostic messages, if any.

Modular Programming

Never before has a programming development stirred as much interest and discussion as structured programming. Throughout the seventies, computer scientists and data processing personnel searched for ways to improve program design and to reduce the costs of program development and maintenance. The traditional view of programming is that a program is a personal creation, that no two programs are exactly the same. Although two programs may achieve the same results, programs generally are hard for anyone but the original programmers to understand and maintain.

The shortcomings of traditional program design led to the introduction of new techniques, especially:

1. top-down program design,

2. structured walkthroughs,

3. HIPO diagrams as design aids, and

4. structured programming.

Although in this book each technique is treated separately, in practice it is usually combined with other techniques. As a result, top-down program design is often viewed as one aspect of structured programming, and it will therefore be treated as such.

Top-Down Program Design

The idea for top-down design is attributed to Professor E. W. Dijkstra, who first began publishing papers on the overall subject of structured programming in 1965.[1] **Top-down design** is an orderly approach to designing a program. The first step is to identify major program functions (modules), along with their interfaces, and then to break each function into successively smaller functions. In other words, the highest-level segments of the program are written and tested first because they contain the highest-level control logic and are the most critical to the operation of the program. Then, the next lower-level modules are written and tested in the same manner. Thus, the details of the program are left until the lowest-level modules are designed. The outcome of this approach is a top-down program designed as a hierarchy of modules related to each other in a tree-like structure.

[1] E. W. Dijkstra, "Programming Considered as a Human Activity," *Proceedings of the IFIP Congress 1965* (Washington, D.C.: *Spartan Books,* 1965). See also Dijkstra, "GO-TO Statement Considered Harmful," Letter to the Editor, *Communications of the ACM* (March 1968).

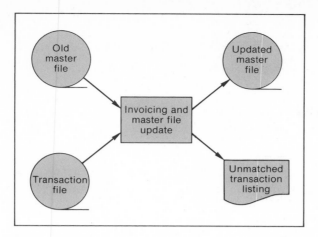

Figure 15–8. System flowchart for master file update.

To illustrate top-down design, consider the sequential master file update program shown in Figure 15–8. An old master file and a transaction file (input) are read into the computer, one record at a time. The outcome is an updated master file and a listing of any unmatched transaction records. Figure 15–9 is a flowchart detailing the steps laid out in the systems flowchart. When top-down design is used, the tree-like structure may be illustrated in a *structure chart* as shown in Figure 15–10. The chart shows the top (highest level) and its functional relationship to lower-level modules (top-down). The main module controls the processing of every other module directly below it in the hierarchy.

The complexity of the program determines the number of levels of processing modules. In our example, two more levels are added to the update master file program in Figure 15–11. Note that the "Update Master Records" block is now a processing and a control module. It controls three processing modules (4.1, 4.2, 4.3) directly below it. Likewise, modules 4.1 and 4.3 are processing and control modules. They control two processing modules, respectively.

Top-down design offers the following benefits:

1. It subjects the critical top modules of the program to the most testing. As each lower level is tested, the higher-level modules are tested again. This repeated testing assures that the most critical, main modules are tested the most.

2. If gives early indication of possible problems with the interfaces between modules.

3. It spreads testing and debugging over a greater part of the program development cycle.

With respecting to testing and debugging, note that each module has only one entrance and one exit point to facilitate the flow of control from one module to the next. Also, each module represents a single program function (such as,

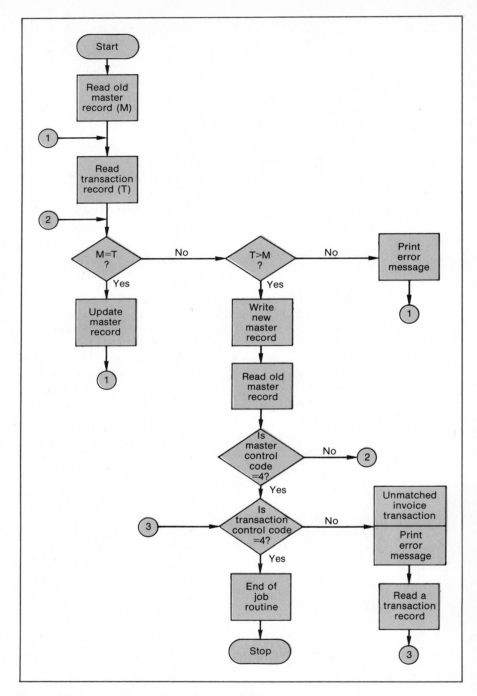

Figure 15–9. A master file update—an example.

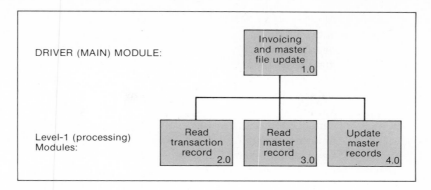

Figure 15–10. Structure chart for invoice tape update program showing one level of processing modules.

Figure 15–11. Structure chart for invoice tape update program showing three levels of processing modules.

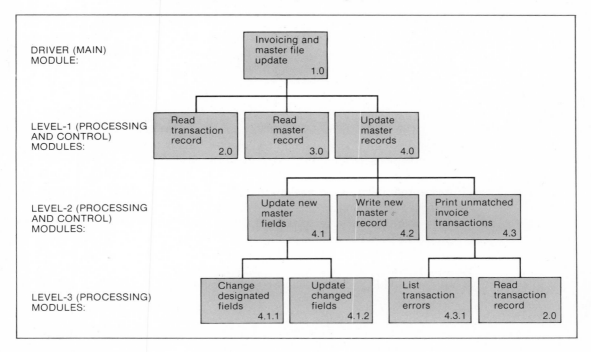

read a master record, read a transaction record) not to exceed one page (50 lines) of program code. Finding errors is thus simplified because the programmer need review only one page of code for each module in question. The outcome is that the program is fully debugged and tested by the time the lowest-level modules are completed. Traditional flowcharting methods emphasize procedures rather than functions. Testing a program in its entirety gives no indication to the location of a bug. If a program has several bugs, the entire program (rather than certain modules) has to be analyzed to determine the cause of each bug—a time-consuming and costly solution. Top-down programming eliminates the need for debugging a program in its entirety.

Structured Walkthrough

A **structured walkthrough** consists of a meeting at which the originator of the program design explains it to colleagues and users. This program technique is basically a reveiw of each other's work by a cross-section of planners, users, and anyone else involved in the system. The purpose is to detect and correct errors (after the walkthrough) as early in the process as possible when it is least costly.

HIPO Diagrams

Although the program flowchart has long been viewed as a primary piece of documentation, experience has shown that it is not an effective documentation tool. Except in complex programs, more and more programmmers maintain that they start writing a program before they have a complete flowchart. After they code, debug, and test the program, they backtrack to flowcharting for documenting their work. The result has been a mismatch between what the flowchart shows and what the program actually does.

The shortcomings of the traditional flowchart led to the development of other program documentation techniques. One is the **HIPO (Hierarchy plus Input-Processing-Output),** a combination of flowchart and cause-and-effect graph. It divides the task into work blocks that can be more easily managed and measured. Each task (function) is designed with listed inputs and outputs and specified processing.

A HIPO package consists of a set of diagrams that graphically describe functions from the general to the detailed levels. Each major function is initially identified and then subdivided into lower-level functions. Programs are developed starting with the functions described in the top-most level of the diagrams. A typical HIPO package, illustrated in Figure 15–12, consists of the following diagrams:

1. A *visual table of contents.* This diagram contains the names and identification numbers of all the overview and detailed HIPO diagrams in the package. It shows the structure of the diagram package and the relationships

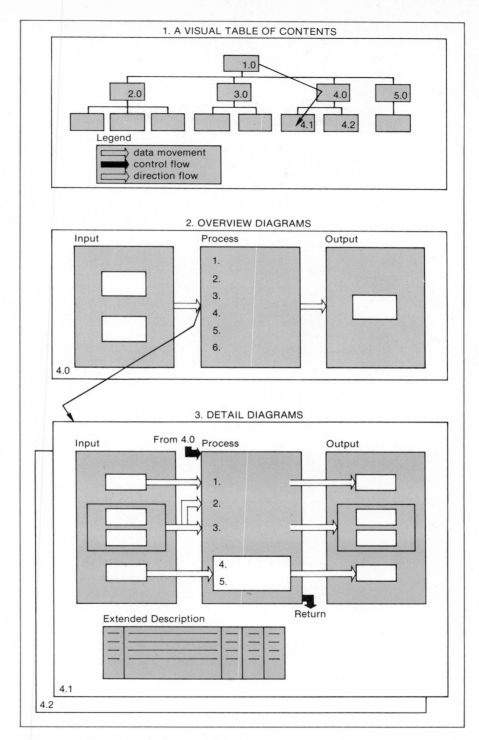

Figure 15—12. A typical HIPO package.

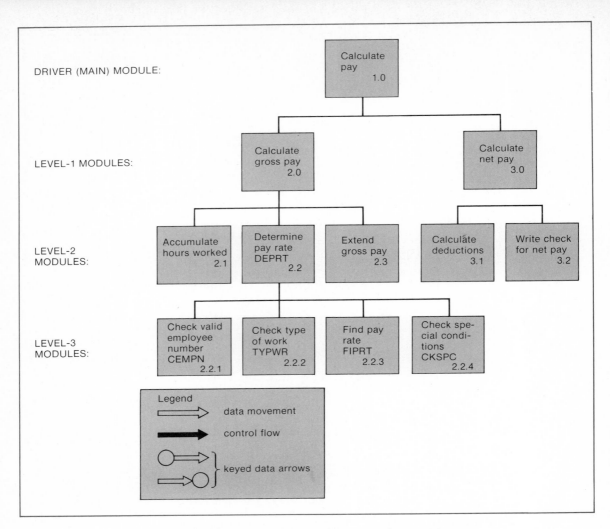

Figure 15–13. A visual table of contents — payroll example.

among the functions in a hierarchical fashion. It also contains a legend indicating how symbols in the package are to be used. With the visual table of contents, the reader can locate a particular level of information or a specific diagram without thumbing through the the entire package. Figure 15 – 13 is a visual table of contents for payroll calculation.

2. *Overview diagrams.* Overview diagrams are high-level HIPO diagrams. They describe the major functions and reference the detailed diagrams needed to expand the functions to sufficient detail. In general, they provide the input, process, and output. The process section contains a series of numbered steps that describe the function performed. The input section contains the data items used by the process steps. Arrows connect the input data items to the process steps. The output section contains the data

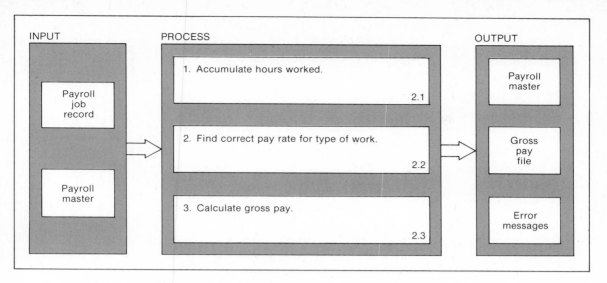

Figure 15-14. An overview diagram—payroll example.

items created by the process steps. Arrows connect the process steps to the output data items. An extended description area can amplify the process steps and input-output data items. Figure 15–14 is an overview diagram for a payroll calculation.

3. *Detail diagrams.* Lower-level HIPO diagrams contain the fundamental elements of the package. They describe the specific functions, show input and output items, and refer to other diagrams. The detail diagrams contain an extended description section that amplifies the process steps and references the code associated with the process steps. They also reference other HIPO diagrams as well as non-HIPO documentation, such as flowcharts or decision tables of particularly complicated logic, record layouts, and so forth. The number of levels of detail diagrams depends on the complexity of the material and the amount of information to be documented. Figure 15–15 illustrates a detail diagram for payroll calculation.

The details pertaining to all the alternative HIPO techniques are too numerous to itemize. Suffice it to say that HIPO is useful in program maintenance for educating new personnel on a particular system and in locating an area of program code that needs to be changed. It also serves the manager who needs an overview of a program. With all its advantages, HIPO represents a definite movement away from flowcharting.

Structured Programming

Structured programming (SP) is a rigorous form of modular programming that clarifies the structure of a program—interrelationships of its parts. The conventions of SP supply the discipline that makes a computer program a

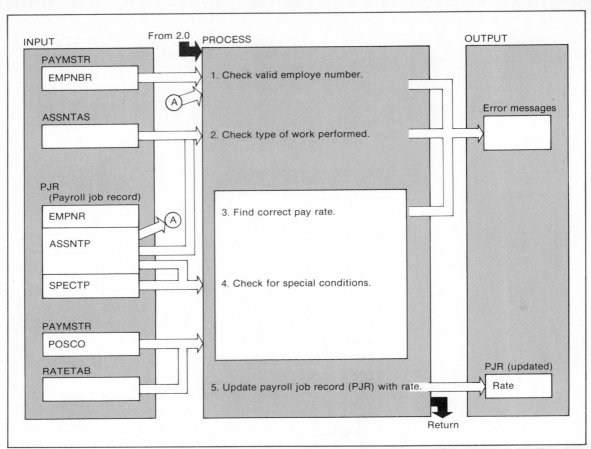

	Notes	Module	Segment	Reference
1.	If invalid, job records are bypassed and error message is printed.	DEPRT	CEMPN	2.2.1
2.	If type of work is incorrect, job records are bypassed and error message is printed.	DEPRT	TYPWR	2.2.2
3.	Use pay rate table (RATETAB) to find correct rate.	DEPRT	FIPRT	2.2.3
4.	Check for overtime, shift pay, or holiday pay and add to rate.	DEPRT	CKSPC	2.2.4

Figure 15–15. Detail diagram—a payroll example.

human-readable document. Properly executed, the listing reads clearly in an uninterrupted manner. Unlike reading a flowchart, the reader does not have to jump around from one page to another for a couple of instructions in the middle of subroutines. Structured programming has three major objectives:

1. To *vastly reduce testing time.* IBM claims to have developed a major project with only one bug per 10,000 lines of coding. The project has been run for two years with only a handful of minor bugs.

2. To *improve programmer productivity.* Programming productivity is related to testing. Several SP projects have shown five-fold improvement in the number of lines of code produced by programmers per day. Thus fewer programmers can work on a project, and communication problems with the user can be reduced.

3. To *clarify programming.* SP improves program clarity by:
   a. *standardizing* a style of programming
   b. organizing a program into modules no longer than one page of coding, and
   c. arranging program logic for top-to-bottom readability without "skipping around" through the program (typical of other program styles). A program that is easy to read, tends to be simpler, faster, and less expensive to maintain.

The structure theorem. The structure theorem states that any program can be written by following the control logic structures of:

1. sequence,

2. selection, and

3. iteration or loop control.

The program must have only one entry and one exit for program control, and paths from the entry to the exit lead through every part of the program.

The *sequence* structure means simply that program statements are executed in the order in which they appear in the program. For example, in Figure 15–16, Functions A and B may consist of a single statement or a complete module. The statements in Function A are executed before the statements in Function B. Control also flows from Function A to Function B.

The *selection* structure is the choice between two paths (actions) in the program based on a *predicate* or a true or false *condition.* As shown in Figure 15–17, if p (predicate) is true, Function A is completed, if false, Function B is completed. This structure is often referred to as IF THEN ELSE. Many programming languages have codes to handle this structure.

The **iteration** structure, also called *loop* structure, provides for the repeated execution of a function while a condition is true. The basic form of this structure is called the DOWHILE. In Figure 15–18, the DOWHILE is described as "*do* Function A *while* the condition represented by p is true." In this type of structure, Function A may never be executed if p is false when first tested. A closely related iteration structure is called the DOUNTIL pattern. Here, the pattern performs a function until a condition becomes true (Figure 15–19).

The difference between the DOWHILE and the DOUNTIL iteration structures is that with the DOWHILE, the condition is tested *before* executing the function. If the condition is false, the function is not executed at all. With the DOUNTIL pattern, the condition is tested *after* executing the function. The function is always executed at least once, regardless of whether the condition is true or false.

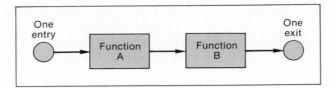

Figure 15–16. Sequence structure.

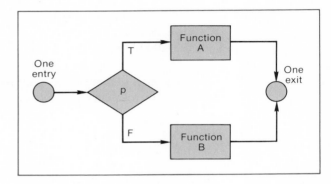

Figure 15–17. The selection(IF THEN ELSE) structure.

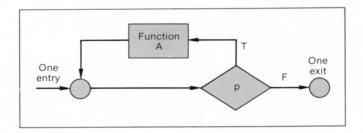

Figure 15–18. The iteration (DOWHILE) structure.

Figure 15–19. The DOUNTIL structure.

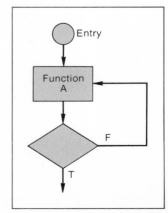

How widely used are the foregoing programming techniques? For all the fanfare, not enough structured programming has been adopted. A recent survey of some of the largest corporations on the West Coast showed that most firms were still experimenting with and evaluating the benefits and limitations of these techniques. Table 15–2 shows the following:

1. The most significant benefit of SP is its more efficient debugging and testing (2.5) and better quality programs (2.3), although it is not a method for lowering program processing costs (0.8).

2. SP is reasonably effective in activating clear and useful programming system documentation (1.9). If also increases productivity (1.8), but it is not very effective in improving programmer morale (1.4). The constraints posed by SP are not easy to adjust to.

3. Top-down design is moderately effective in the development and maintenance of application programs and in improving programmer/analyst performance. It is also somewhat responsive to user's needs.

4. Structured walkthrough was rated as very effective (2.3) for achieving better quality programs that are less costly to maintain (2.1). See Table 15–2. It is also effective in improving debugging and documentation. For program testing, on the other hand, this technique could be suspect for leading to poor staff morale (1.5). See Table 15–2.

Table 15–2. A summary of the rating of SP techniques.

Uses	Structured programming	Top-down design	Structured walkthrough
Impact on Software			
Lower development costs	1.5*	2.0	1.6
Faster implementation	1.5	1.9	1.6
Lower program processing costs	0.8	1.2	1.3
Better quality programs	2.3	1.9	2.3
Easier and less costly maintenance	2.1	1.7	2.1
Impact on Programming Staff			
Higher productivity	1.8	1.8	1.8
Better morale	1.4	1.5	1.7
More efficient debugging and testing	2.5	2.2	2.2
Clearer and more useful programming system documentation	1.9	2.1	1.9
Impact on Users			
More flexible and timely response to user needs	1.3	1.8	1.8
Less cost to users	1.4	1.7	1.3

*Effectiveness rating score (0–3)
Adapted from Holton, John B "Are the New Programming Techniques being Used?" *Datamation* (July 1977), pp. 97–100ff.

Overall, the concepts of structured programming are rather easy to describe, but the techniques are considerably more difficult. The ease with which programmers accept structured programming depends on the language they program in. The goal of all of these techniques is to make programs easier to read, write, debug, test, and maintain, resulting in more productive programs.

SUMMARY

1. Developing a program requires several steps. First, the problem must be defined. The programmer must know what the program is supposed to do before it is written. Having defined the problem, the programmer uses program flowcharts to plan the solution. The program is often divided into a number of modules as a way of deciding how it should be tested. After the planning of the problem solution, the program is ready for coding. Each line of coding is punched into cards or keyed in through a terminal to the computer for action.

2. The first generation of computer languages consisted of machine languages. Each language was tied to a specific machine. Writing a program was complicated and tedious. The next generation introduced symbolic language, which reduced program coding and improved program preparation. The assembler allowed the use of easily remembered symbolic names. Today's state of the art represents high-level, machine-independent languages. They are easier to learn than assembly languages and provide easier program documentation and maintenance.

3. Once a program is debugged, it is tested for accuracy. If the test data results show errors, a series of diagnostics is generated by the language translator. After the errors are corrected, the program is run through for another check. The process continues until an error-free run is achieved. In extreme cases, when neither desk checking nor diagnostics is enough to eliminate errors, a "memory dump" is used to search for and correct errors. It is a last resort, as it can be tedious and costly.

4. Program documentation is developed at every stage of the programming cycle. If includes preflowcharting data, a copy of the program flowchart, a master list of details regarding record layout and code forms, a program-run manual, and a sample of tested data and output. This information simplifies program maintenance and update.

5. The shortcomings of traditional program design led to the introduction of structured techniques. The major techniques are:
   a. *Top-down design* identifies major program functions (modules) and breaks each function into successively smaller ones in a tree-like struc-

ture. Each function, with one entry and one exit point, should not exceed one page of program code.

b. *Structured walkthrough* allows the originator of the program design to explain the material to colleagues and users in an effort to debug the program.

c. *HIPO diagrams* divide the task into manageable work blocks. Each function is designed with listed inputs and outputs and specified processing.

d. *Structured programming* is a form of modular programming in which the structure of the program is clarified by restricting control logic to three structures: sequence, selection, and iteration. The most efficient benefit of structured programming is providing efficient debugging and testing and better quality programs, although it is not a method for lowering program processing costs.

The goal of all these techniques is to make programs easier to read, write, debug, test, and maintain, resulting in more productive programs.

TERMS TO LEARN

Assembler
Compiler
Debugging
Diagnostics
HIPO
Iteration
Macroinstruction
Memory dump
Mnemonics
Object program
Parallel run
Source program
Structured programming
Structured walkthrough
Top-down design

REVIEW QUESTIONS

1. Describe in your own words the steps making up the programming cycle.

2. What is involved in program planning? Explain.

3. Distinguish between:

(a) subroutine and a program
(b) structured programming and top-down design
(c) source and object program

4. Summarize the major new methods of designing and writing programs.

5. Briefly describe the historical order of program language development

6. What advantages does assembler language offer over machine language? What are the limitations of an assembler language?

7. Summarize the basic steps in an assembly routine.

8. What is so unique about a high-level language? Explain.

9. Distinguish the difference between:

(a) problem-oriented and procedure-oriented language
(b) assembler and compiler
(c) desk checking and diagnostics
(d) iteration and selection structure

10. What is involved in program debugging and testing? Explain.

11. Explain the major features and procedure in top-down design. What benefits does it offer?

12. Explain carefully the HIPO package. How is it useful in program maintenance?

13. Explain and illustrate the structured theorem.

14. Compare and contrast the three structured techniques in terms of their respective impact on software, programming staff, and users.

chapter 16

Basic

Learning Objectives

Most of today's computers process programs written in Basic. For a beginning student or a first-time user, Basic is easy to learn, has few rules to remember, and uses ordinary English words and arithmetic symbols. It thus facilitates direct interaction with the computer for problem solving. By the end of this chapter, you should know:

1. how to sing on and enter program instructions into the system,

2. the fundamental system commands, elements, and structure of Basic,

3. Basic END, REM, PRINT, READ DATA, INPUT, and LET statements, and

4. Basic arrays and subscipts.

Sign-On and Program Entry

Basic (Beginner's All-Purpose Symbolic Instruction Code) is a higher-level programming language developed at Dartmouth College especially for time-sharing computer users. A mixture of plain English and algebra (arithmetic operations and exponentiation), it has a structure similar to that of Fortran. Competence in one language normally helps learning the other. In addition to being a powerful language, Basic is easy to use, has few rules to remember, and uses ordinary English words and arithmetic symbols. It provides a real-time environment in which the user interacts directly with the computer for problem solving.

Basic is designed for on-line processing in a time-sharing environment, which entails a conversational dialogue with the computer via a terminal. The terminal, whether a teletypewriter or cathode ray tube, is the communication link with the computer. The keyboard is used to enter commands and instructions to the system. Although the exact procedure depends largely on the type of terminal and on the requirements of the time-sharing computer system, entry protocol generally requires a sequence of steps as follows:

1. Turn power switch on.

2. Type LOGIN, followed by your password or account number. For example, LOGIN II 1521. The computer responds by displaying a line representing the job number, the name of the time-sharing facility, and the ID number of the terminal used. For example,

    ```
    JOB 10, FLORIDA INT'L UNIV., SIDIDI
    ```

3. Once displayed, the user enters his or her PASSWORD on the same line and depresses the *carriage return* key. The password is stored (not shown) by the system, because only the user knows it. The computer responds by displaying the time of the day, the date, and the day of the week. Then it types a period (.) at the beginning of the next line which means that the system is ready to accept commands. From here on, each command ends with a carriage return. No exception is made without this step.

4. After the system accepts the user's identification, the Basic computer is selected by typing @UBASIC. This signal accesses the Basic program. When ready, the computer types:

    ```
    READY, FOR HELP TYPE HELP
    ```

Typing HELP tells the computer to list the Basic commands and an explanation of each command. At this time, selected commands can be entered or a program can be typed in. (Basic commands are explained later in the chapter.)

5. If a new program is entered, the user types NEW. On the next line, the user types the file name for the program. In Table 16–1, the file name is (PROBCO).

6. The computer displays the word READY. The user types in the program. In Table 16–1, the program represents five instructions (statement numbers 10 through 50).

7. Once entered, the user types RUN. The system responds by typing identifying information such as the name of the program, time, date, and so on.

8. If the program is error-free, it is executed and the answer printed. The system then types READY, signaling a new operation.

9. When all operations have been completed, the user terminates by:
   a. typing BYE to indicate that there is no longer a need to use Basic;
   b. typing @FIN to specify that the user is done. At this time, the system prints or displays the user's statistics; or
   c. typing @TERM to turn off the terminal.

Table 16–1. Basic program entry and format.

Computer Messages	Typical response
	LOGIN
JOB 10 TTY 09	
#	II1521
PASSWORD:	
1801 24 – May – 80 SAT	
	UBASIC
READY	NEW
NEW FILE NAME	PROBCO
READY	
	10 READ A,B,C
	20 DATA 7,8,9
	30 LET S = (7*7) + (8*8)/5
	40 PRINT "VALUE IS" S
	50 END
	RUN
PROBCO 1802:04 24 – May – 80	
VALUE IS 22.60	
TIME: 0.002 SECS	
READY	BYE
JOB 10, USER II1521 LOGGED OFF TTY 09	1802:04 24 – May – 80
RUNTIME 1.02 SECS	

System Commands

A **system command** is a computer instruction that tells the system what specific action to take. Unlike Basic statements that begin with a statement number, system commands are written without a statement number. They are executed immediately after they're typed in. A response of READY verifies the execution.

Some of the more frequnetly used system commands are:

RUN Tells the computer to execute the current program. It is typed at the beginning of the next line, followed by returning the carriage.

SAVE Causes the existing program to be written onto a disc file for later use. The form of the command is SAVE (file name) or SAVE: for example, SAVE PROBCO.

OLD Retrieves a program (or a file) that has been stored on disc through the SAVE command: for example, OLD PROBCO. The program can be recalled by typing OLD and then the name of the program.

NEW Used when the user begins to establish a new file (or program) in the computer's memory. The general form is NEW (file name).

LIST Causes printing of a program statement or complete listing of the program.

SCRATCH Used when the user wishes to wipe out the working copy of the current program.

BYE
(or GOODBYE) Disconnects the terminal from the system.

Basic Elements and Structure

Constants and Variables

A **constant** is a number that remains fixed. It may be positive, negative, or zero; but it should be shown in decimal (not fractional) form. It is used with or without a decimal point as a part of a statement. If the constant is negative, it must be preceded by a minus sign. If positive, a plus sign is optional. Examples of data values are:

Correct	Incorrect	Explanation
4342	4,342	A comma between characters is not allowed.
42	$42	No dollar sign is permitted.
401	401–	A negative sign is not allowed at the end of a number.

Very large or very small numbers may be represented by using the letter E, which means "10 raised to a power." A number followed by E and an exponent represents the larger number. For example.

1. *17E4* means 17 times $(10)^4 = 17$ times $10,000 = 170,000$.

2. *.14E–2* means 0.14 times $(10)^{-2} = 0.14$ times $0.01 = 0.0014$.

Thus the negative exponent indicates the number of places to the left that the decimal point should be located. In the case of the second example, exponent −2 indicates that the decimal point should be moved two places to the left, causing two zeros to be written between digit 1 and the decimal point. The following Basic examples should clarify this point:

Before	After
1.4E3 is interpreted as	1400
1.4E−3 is interpreted as	0.0014
.8E−5 is interpreted as	0.000008

A **variable** represents a number or a value that is not fixed. A numeric variable must be either a single letter or a single letter followed by a single digit. In some Basic systems, it is a string variable that stands for a word (a combination of letters). A *string variable* consists of a letter followed by a dollar sign or a letter followed by a digit and then by a dollar sign. Examples of numeric variables are:

Correct Variable	Incorrect Variable	Explanation
A	10A	Alphabetic character must be the first character.
D4	ZIP	Only one alphabetic character is permitted.
D1	D11	Only one numeric digit is allowed.

Examples of string variables are:

C$ may stand for COSINE
S$ may stand for SQUARE
Z$ may stand for ZONE
A1$ may stand for first rating of a product

Arithmetic Operators

Arithmetic signs in Basic are called *operators*, and they are used in a manner similar to that of ordinary arithmetic. Arithmetic operators are as follows:

Arithmetic Notation	Operation	Basic Operator	Arithmetic Example	Basic Equivalent
a^n	Exponentiation	↑ or **	C^3, $X^{1/2}$	C ↑ 3, X ↑ .5
+	Addition	+	A + B + C, C + 10	A + B + C, C + 10
−	Subtraction	−	A − B, C − 4	A − B, C − 4
×	Multiplication	*	A × B, C × .41	A*B, C*.41
÷	Division	/	5 ÷ 2.5, C ÷ 14	5/2.5, C/14

Order of calculations. Basic arithmetic calculations follow normal mathematical rules. The order of priority is:

1. Calculations inside parentheses are performed first. If there are parentheses within the outer parentheses, calculations inside the inner parentheses are performed first. For example, $5 + (5 + 4*(7*2))$ is computed as follows:
   Step 1. $7*2 = 14$.
   Step 2. $4*14 = 56$.
   Step 3. $5 + (5 + 56) = 66$.

2. In the absence of parentheses, the order of calculation takes the following priority:
   a. exponentiation (represented by ↑ or **)
   b. division and multiplication, then
   c. addition and subtraction.

When a statement contains two or more computations on the same level of priority, they are handled from left to right. The following examples illustrate these rules.

	10 LET $A = 4 + 14/2 - 1*4$
Step 1: divide	$= 4 + 7 - 1*4$
Step 2: multiply	$= 4 + 7 - 4$
Step 3: add and subtract	$= 7$
	10 LET $A = 4 + 14/2*7 ↑ 3 - 9$
Step 1: find exponential value	$= 4 + 14/2*343 - 9$
Step 2: divide	$= 4 + 7*343 - 9$
Step 3: multiply	$= 4 + 2401 - 9$
Step 4: add and subtract	$= 2396$
	10 LET $Y = 4 + (10 ↑ 2/5)*(2 ↑ 3 - 4)$
Step 1	$= 4 + (100/5)*(8 - 4)$
Step 2	$= 4 + (20)*(4)$
Step 3	$= 4 + 80$
Step 4	$= 84$

Statement Numbers

Each statement in Basic is a separate computer instruction, standing alone on a separate line. Each line, starting with a number identifying the statement, thereby tells the computer the sequence of the instructions in the program. For example, statement numbers 100 – 150 represent the following instructions:

```
100   REM AN EXAMPLE OF INSTRUCTIONS IN BASIC
110   PRINT "BASIC IS A RELATIVELY EASY LANGUAGE"
120   READ A,B
130   DATA 54, 17.37
140   PRINT A,B
150   END
```

Notice that each line has a unique statement number. The statement numbers go from low (in this example, 100) to high. Beginning the numbering at 100 is arbitrary. Any other set of numbers will do as long as no two numbers are the same. Spacing between numbers is suggested to provide room for adding statements between existing lines, if necessary.

Statement Format

As explained earlier, a program consists of several related statements presented in a logical sequence for computer processing. A typical Basic statement is broken down as follows:

Statement (or Line) #	Special Basic Word	Variable Name		An Expression
120	LET[1]	E	=	A * B

The expression means multiply A times B and place the product in a memory location having variable name E. Thus a program designed to multiply two digits and print their product might require the following statements:

```
100   LET A = 5
110   LET B = 6
120   LET E = A*B
130   PRINT A,B,E
140   END
```

Basic Statements   You can begin writing a Basic program immediately after learning the major types of Basic statements, described in the order of their usage for generating output:

1. END, REM, and PRINT statements,

2. INPUT/OUTPUT statements,

3. assignment statements using LET and =, and

4. control statements.

END Statement

Every Basic program must conclude with a termination statement. An **END statement** defines the end of the program. It is assigned the highest line

[1]This statement is discussed later in the chapter.

number and placed at the end of the program. The general format of the END statement is, for example:

```
Line #      END
 999        END
```

REM Statement

Providing statements that descirbe what certain aspects of the program are supposed to do is often desirable. These REMark statements are a part of program documentation and are nonexecutable. The general format of the REM statement is:

```
Line #              REM (message or description)
 110        REM THIS PROGRAM COMPUTES SICK PAY
```

The number of REM statements that can be included in a program is not limited. They can be anywhere in the program, and they are not presented in a program flowchart.

PRINT Statement

The PRINT statement tells the computer to:

1. provide headings or print literals and

2. perform basic calculations that require no specific identification.

The general format of the PRINT statement is:

```
Line #    PRINT    { • headings or literals }
                   { • computations         }
                   { • numbers or values    }
```

Printing literals. A *literal* is a heading, an expression, or a label made up of alphabetic, numeric, or alphanumeric characters. As shown in the following examples, a literal is printed by placing it in quotes. A numeric literal, however, is printed without having to be placed in quotes, provided it does not contain special characters, such as commas.

1. Print alphabetic literals

```
140   PRINT "PROFIT STATEMENT"
199   END

RUN
```

Output: PROFIT STATEMENT

2. Print numeric literals

```
140   PRINT "1745" (or 140   PRINT 1745)
199   END

RUN
```

Output: 1745

3. Print alphanumeric literals

```
140   PRINT "GENERAL TIRE: 455"
199   END

RUN
```

Output: GENERAL TIRE: 455

Printing computations.   Another use of the PRINT statement is to perform limited computations. The following examples illustrate the single and multiple PRINT computations and headings:

1.
```
10   PRINT   (4*6)+42
20   END

RUN

66
```

2.
```
10   PRINT   "TOTAL", "TAX"
20   PRINT      14 , 14*.05
30   END

RUN

TOTAL      TAX
   14      .70
```

3.
```
10   PRINT   "TOTAL", "TAX"
20   PRINT   "AMOUNT", "DUE"
30   PRINT   (10+4), (10+4)*.05
40   END

RUN

 TOTAL      TAX
AMOUNT     DUE
   14      .70
```

4.
```
10   PRINT   "TOTAL", "TAX"
20   PRINT   "AMOUNT", "DUE"
30   PRINT
40   PRINT   "--------------------------"
50   PRINT
60   PRINT   (10+4),   (10+4)*.05
70   END
```

```
RUN

TOTAL       TAX
AMOUNT      DUE
-----------------------------------------
  14        .70
```

In this example, note the following:

1. A PRINT statement can be used to underline headings (Example 4).

2. Data or values placed in quotes are viewed as quoted expressions and are treated as literals. None of the computations used in our examples have quotes around them. Consequently, actual computations can be carried out via a print statement.

3. A blank line can be inserted between rows by adding a PRINT statement (Example 4, statement numbers 30 and 50).

Output spacing.   In some cases, two or more data items must be printed on one line. To do so, a comma is placed between the items in the PRINT statement. For example:

```
40   PRINT A,B,C,D
```

This PRINT statement prints the values of A, B, C, and D in 15 spaces each on one line. The comma sets the spacing at a field width of 15 spaces. (Some systems vary the field width slightly.) A semicolon allows two spaces between fields or variables.

Printing the output of two or more PRINT statements on one line is achieved by placing a comma after the last item of the first statement. For example, the statement:

```
40   PRINT A,B,
50   PRINT C,D
```

causes the four values to be printed on the same line. Again, to print the four values closer, semicolons are used instead of commas.

The PRINT USING Statement

To fully control the output format, the programmer uses the PRINT US-ING statement. It allows formatting outputs to have decimal point alignment and other forms of desirable spacing. Spacial formating specifications, listed in an IMAGE statement, format the output. The form of these statements is:

```
n PRINT USING nl, list
nl:(image specifications)
```

The common specification characters and their functions are as follows:

1. For numeric image specification:
   # shows how many digits to give for each number on the print lines. Zeroes fill in on both sides of the decimal number if the actual values are fewer than the actual number of signs given.
   indicates the decimal point.
   Example: #.##   #.#

2. For string image specifications:
   ' (an apostrophe) indicates the first character in the string. It is followed by as many of the characters C,L, or R as are necessary to output the string.
   C causes the string to be centered in the output field.
   L causes the string to be left justified in the output field.
   R causes the string to be right justified in the output field.

```
Example:
     100   DATA 3.912, 7.40, 8.1, .011, 900
     110   READ   A,B
     120   IF   A=900 THEN 190
     130   PRINT USING 140 , A,B
     140       #.##        #.#
     150   GO TO 110
      .
      .      statements missing
      .
     190   END
```

When executed, the program prints the data and gives the digits in statement number 100 based on the format specified in statement number 130.

The TAB Function

Output may be printed in any column on the page. The TAB statement positions output from left to right on the page for example, to print "WEEKLY PAYROLL REGISTER" beginning in column 33, write the statement:

```
110   PRINT TAB(32); "WEEKLY PAYROLL REGISTER"
```

The number in parentheses specifies the number of spaces from the left-hand margin to be skipped. In our example, the TAB statement (with the semicolon) causes the automatic skipping of the first 32 spaces; the printed phrase thus begins in column 33. If a comma had been used instead of a semicolon, it would have caused the phrase to be printed in column 46 or the beginning of the next available column after the thirty-third position. The following statement further illustrates the use of the TAB statement:

```
Required:  Print  "EMPLOYEE" in columns 1–8, "SALARY" in columns 15–20,
           "TOTAL DEDUCTIONS" in columns 25–40, and "NET PAY" in col-
           umns 45–51.

Statement:
           100  PRINT  "EMPLOYEE"; TAB(14); "SALARY"; TAB(24);
                "TOTAL DEDUCTIONS"; TAB(44); "NET PAY"
           110  END

           RUN

           EMPLOYEE      SALARY      TOTAL DEDUCTIONS      NET PAY
```

READ/DATA and INPUT Statements

The PRINT statement has limited capacity for placing data into a program. When a large amount of numeric data must be entered into a Basic program, the **READ/DATA statement** is used. The general formats are:

```
Statement #   READ    variable variable        variable
                      name , name , . . . , name

Statement #   DATA     data  , data  , . . . , data
```

Each of the variable names (except the last one) in the READ statement and each of the data items in the DATA statement is followed by a comma. No ending punctuation is required. The DATA statement specifies the data for use by the program to be accessed by the READ statement; thus the READ statement precedes a corresponding DATA statement. It lists variable names that take corresponding values from the DATA list. For example:

```
10   REM DATA AFTER READ
20   READ A,B,C
30   DATA 7,–8,9
40   PRINT A,B,C
50   END

RUN

7          –8          9
```

```
10   REM DATA VALUES MUST EQUAL READ VALUES
20   READ A,B,C
30   DATA 7
40   DATA −8
50   DATA 9
60   PRINT A,B,C
70   END

RUN

7              −8            9

10   READ A,B
20   DATA 7,−8
30   READ C
40   DATA 9
50   PRINT A,B,C
60   END

RUN

7              −8            9
```

The READ statement takes the data values 7, −8, 9 and assigns them to A, B, C, respectively. Note that the number of DATA statements does not have to equal the number of READ statements, but the number of constants in the DATA statements must be equal to the number of variables in the READ statement.

In a time-sharing environment, where the user "converses" with the computer through a terminal, a program can be fed through the terminal using an INPUT statement rather than the READ/DATA statements. The INPUT indicates to the computer that the data is to be entered from the user's terminal. The general format is:

```
Statement #   READ    variable variable        variable
                      name ,  name , . . . ,  name
```

For example,

```
10   REM   input statement is terminal-oriented
20   INPUT A,B,C
30   PRINT "SUM OF"; A ; "AND"; B ;
40   PRINT "AND"; C ; "IS"; A+B+C
50   END

RUN

?   5,6,7

SUM OF 5 AND 6 AND 7 IS 18
```

During execution, when input data is requrested by the computer, a question mark (?) appears on the terminal or teletype. At this time, the requisite values for input is entered. In the example above, the numbers 5,6,7 (separated by a comma without ending punctuation) are entered. Note that entering input data has the same effect as the placement of data in a DATA statement. Here is another example, using multiple input statements:

```
100  REM CASH FLOW
110  PRINT "WHAT IS INITIAL CASH AT HAND?"
120  INPUT I
130  PRINT "WHAT WAS CASH RECEIVED EACH WEEK DAY?"
140  INPUT M,T,W,T1,F
150  PRINT
160  PRINT "INIT. CASH "; I; "UNITS"
170  PRINT "                    DAILY RECEIPTS"
180  PRINT "               ---------------------------"
190  PRINT " MON.","TUES.","WED.","THURS."."FRI."
200  PRINT M,T,W,T1,F
210  PRINT
220  PRINT
230  PRINT "AMOUNT OF CASH RECEIVED THIS WEEK";M+T+W+T1+F
240  PRINT "FINAL CASH BALANCE"; I +(M+T+W+T1+F)
250  END

RUN

WHAT IS INITIAL CASH AT HAND?

?  60

WHAT WAS CASH RECEIVED EACH WEEK DAY?

?   142, 63, 49, 78, 692

INIT.  CASH 60 UNITS

                      DAILY RECEIPTS
                   ---------------------------
MON.           TUES.          WED.           THURS.          FRI.
 142            63             49             78             692


AMOUNT OF CASH RECEIVED THIS WEEK 1024
FINAL CASH BALANCE  1084
```

The Restore Statement

At times, a previously read data block must be read once more. The RESTORE statement causes the data previously read from storage to be replaced in storage. The data can therefore be reread as often as the RESTORE statement is encountered. The general format of the RESTORE statement is:

Statement #	RESTORE
100	RESTORE

The following program shows the use of the RESTORE statement:

```
100   REM COMPUTE AND PRINT A,B AND THEIR SUM
110   REM COMPUTE AND PRINT X,Y AND THEIR PRODUCT
120   PRINT "A", "B", "A+B"
130   READ A,B
140   DATA 4,2.0
150   PRINT A,B,A+B
160   RESTORE
170   PRINT "X", "Y", X*Y
180   READ X,Y
190   PRINT "X", "Y", X*Y
200   END

RUN

A             B             A+B
4             2             6
X             Y             X*Y
4             2             8
```

The initial data (4,2) corresponds to variables A and B. The RESTORE in statement 160 restores the data in statement 140 for use again. The next read instruction (statement 180) causes the data 4,2 to be assigned to the variables X and Y, respectively. Without the RESTORE statement, the second read statement could not be executed.

The LET Statement

The **LET statement,** an important assignment statement even though optional in most Basic systems, is a way of assigning values to variables or of evaluating expressions. The general format of the LET statement is:

$$\text{Statement \#} \quad \text{LET} \quad \text{(variable)} = \begin{cases} \text{constant} \\ \text{expression} \\ \text{variable} \end{cases}$$

The LET statement performs any of the following:

1. It assigns the values on the right side of the assignment operator "=" to the variables on the left side. For example,

$$100 \text{ LET } L=5$$

Value 5 is assigned to variable L, even if L had a prior value assigned earlier in the program.

2. It evaluates an expression, which is any constant or variable or constants, variables, and operators. For example,

$$100 \text{ LET } A=B*C \uparrow 3+D*E+F$$

The expression on the right side is evaluated and its value assigned to the variable A. The previous value of variable A (if any) is replaced by the value of the expression. Variables B, C, D, E, F must also have values assigned to them earlier in the program.

3. It updates a variable. For example, if an employee's current gross earnings (represented by Y) is $1,000 and this week's gross pay is $200, the gross earnings to date is done by the following LET statement:

100 LET Y=Y+200

Care should be taken to write valid LET statements.
Here are examples of invalid LET statements:

1. 100 LET B+C=A   The left side of the equals sign (=) can contain only a single variable. Variable A must therefore be on the left side, and the expression must be on the right side. The reason is that the equals sign is an assignment operator. It does not mean equality.

2. 100 LET B="BOY"   The string constant "BOY" must be assigned to a non-numeric variable. An alternative statement is:

100 LET B$="BOY"

Multiple LET Statements

In some cases, several variables must be assigned the same initial value or the same value of a computation. Rather than writing a LET statement for each assignment, one multiple LET statement does the job. For example:

1. Initializing three variables with the same value:

	Multiple LET Statement
100 LET A=0 110 LET B=0 120 LET C=0	100 LET A=B=C=0

2. Assigning a functional expression to a number of variables:

100 LET A=3.5 * 4 110 LET B=3.5 * 4 120 LET C=3.5 * 4	100 LET A=B=C=3.5*4

Control Statements

A computer's power lies with its ability to branch from one area in the program to another for a problem solution. The branching operation controls the sequence of statement execution. Thus a statement designed to allow branching, called a *control statement,* provides program flexibility by transferring control to a different program instruction to handle an exception or to satisfy a condition. There are two types of control statements:

1. Unconditional transfer of control, with the format:

Statement #	GO TO	Statement #
100	GO TO	140

A GO TO statement simply tells the computer to jump to the program instruction that carries the statement number indicated in the GO TO statement. In the example, the next instruction to be executed is statement 70.

2. Conditional transfer of control with the format:

Statement #	IF	Condition to be Tested	THEN (or GO TO) THEN (or GO TO)	Statement #
40	IF	A = B		80

A conditional statement transfers control to the statement number indicated only if the specified condition is met. In the example, if A (the subject) is equal to (the relation) B (the object), THEN the computer is told to transfer control to (or GO TO) statement 80. Otherwise, it automatically executes the next sequential instruction.

A conditional statement is further illustrated in the following program:

```
10  LET J = 1
20  PRINT J
30  LET J = J+1
40  IF J<101 THEN 20   or   40 IF J<101 GO TO 20
50  END
```

The program is designed to tell the computer to count from 1 to 100. Statement 10 sets the initial value of J to 1. Statement 20 prints the value of J. In this case, it is 1. Statement 30 increments the value in J by 1. Statement 40 is a conditional statement that tests the value of J for 101. *If* the value is less than 101, *then* the computer is told to jump to statement 20 (print the present value of J) and proceed with the rest of the program (in this case, statement 30 only). Otherwise, the computer will take statement 50, which ends the running of the program.

Relational Symbols

Conditional statements use six possible Basic relational symbols (Table 16–2). Two or more consecutive conditional statements may be used in the program if necessary. For example, to compare the values X, Y, and Z in order to find out which of the three is the largest value. A program similar to the following might be used:

```
10   READ X, Y, Z
15   DATA 14, 12, 17
20   IF X>Y THEN 90
30   IF Y>Z THEN 70
40   LET A = Z
50   PRINT A
60   GO TO 130
70   LET A =Y
80   GO TO 50
90   IF X>Z THEN 110
100  GO TO 40
110  LET A = X
120  GO TO 50
130  END
```

Table 16–2. Basic relational symbols.

Relational Symbol	Meaning	Basic Notation	Examples
$=$	Equal	$=$	$A4 = K7$
$\neq$	Not equal	$<>$	$K2 <> 6$
$<$	Less than	$<$	$B < 7$
$>$	Greater than	$>$	$Y4 > N9$
$\leq$	Less than or equal to	$<=$	$A4 <= 2$
$\geq$	Greater than or equal to	$>=$	$U4 >= U3$

Arrays and Subscripts

Loops are often connected with subscripted variables. Basic language offers instructions that make it possible to define these variables and, consequently, perform the necessary looping operation. Assume a single variable J is subscripted. The first 10 subscripts of J are:

Arithmetic Representation	BASIC Representation
J_1	$J(0)$
J_2	$J(1)$
J_3	$J(2)$
J_4	$J(3)$
.	.
.	.
.	.
J_{10}	$J(9)$

An *array* is a list of values or entries classed as a unit. Each entry is identified by the name of the list and by its position on the list. The name of an array must be a single letter, such as A, P, X. Any other arrangement is illegal. For example, assume a list of the following five entries with the name A:

```
A
1
2
3
4
5
```

The fourth entry is identified as A, or A(3) in Basic. Note that in Basic the subscript for the first entry is generally 0, for the second entry is 1, . . ., and for the fourth entry is 3. When we have a list of subscripted values in a single column, the list is called a *one-dimensional array*. Arithmetic notations use a lowered number (subscript). A subscript may be a whole, positive number such as 6, 8, or 40, or a variable name like *I, J, K, L, M,* or *N*. It must never be larger than the maximum number of entries in an array as specified in the DIM statement. In Basic, the subscript must be in parentheses. So the entries above are subscripted as follows:

Arithmetic Notation	BASIC Notation
A_1	A(0)
A_2	A(1)
A_3	A(2)
A_4	A(3)
A_5	A(4)

Basic provides 11 places in memory for any one-dimensioned array. If more than 11 places are desired, a Basic **dimension** (abbreviated **DIM**) **statement** can be used. The DIM statement format is

Statement #	DIM	$\left(\begin{array}{c}\textbf{Array}\\\textbf{Name (Size)}\end{array}\right),$	$\left(\begin{array}{c}\textbf{Array}\\\textbf{Name (Size)}\end{array}\right)$	$(, \cdot\cdot\cdot,$	$\left(\begin{array}{c}\textbf{Array}\\\textbf{Name (Size)}\end{array}\right)^n$
10	DIM	A (99),	B (55),	. . .	N (940)

Commas are used to separate the arrays listed in the dimension statement. Also, an array in Basic begins with a *zero subscript*. In the example, array A (99) reserves 100 cells [A(O), A(1), . . ., A (99)] in computer memory.

To illustrate the use of the DIM statement, suppose that we need a program to add five types of income and print out the sum. The five figures are 1,400, 670, 145, 716, and 801. Using a DIM statement, you have the following program.

Program	Comment
10 DIM A(5)	Reserves five computer locations (5 A's). Technically, there are six locations [A(0), . . ., A(5)].
20 READ A(1), A(2), A(3), A(4), A(5)	
30 LET X=A(1) +A(2) +A(3) +A(4) +A(5)	The five types of income are added together.
40 PRINT X	The sum is printed out.
50 DATA 1400, 670, 145, 716, 801	Each value corresponds to the sub-scripted values in the READ statement, respectively.
60 END	

The DIM statement is nonexecutable. It can be written anywhere in a Basic program, provided that it precedes the appearance of any entry of the array to be used in the program.

Looping

In a looping operation a segment of a program or a sequence of statements is repeated a specific number of times to solve a problem. The effect is to reduce the number of required instructions to run a program. In Basic programming, the special FOR-TO and NEXT statements are used for this purpose. The **FOR-TO format** is:

$$\text{Statement \#} \quad \text{FOR} \quad \begin{pmatrix} \text{Legal} \\ \text{Variable} \\ \text{Name} \end{pmatrix} = \begin{Bmatrix} \text{Constant} \\ \text{Variable} \\ \text{Expression} \end{Bmatrix} \text{TO} \begin{Bmatrix} \text{Constant} \\ \text{Variable} \\ \text{Expression} \end{Bmatrix}$$

The **NEXT format** is:

$$\text{Statement \#} \quad \text{NEXT} \quad \begin{pmatrix} \text{Legal} \\ \text{Variable} \\ \text{Name} \end{pmatrix}$$

Take the following partial program:

```
          30   FOR A = 1 TO 5
Partial   40   PRINT A
program   50   NEXT A
          60   END
          RUN
           1
           2
           3
           4
           5
          READY
```

Statement 30 initiates the sequence of statements that will be performed five times, with A successively incremented in value from 1 to 5. Thus every time the sequence is executed a printout is made of the value of A. The NEXT statement (number 50) merely tells the computer to continue executing the sequence. When A is equal to 5, the next statement (END) is executed, ending the program.

An important point to remember is that a FOR-TO statement is used when a set of statements is to be executed several times. Compare the following programs:

Looping with a GO TO Statement	Looping with FOR, NEXT Statements
10 READ B	10 FOR J=1 TO 5
20 LET A=B*5	20 READ B
30 PRINT A, B	30 LET A=B*5
40 GO TO 10	40 PRINT A, B
50 DATA 1.7, 6.9, 17.1, 8.4, 3.8	50 NEXT J
60 END	60 DATA 1.7, 6.9, 17.1, 8.4, 3.8
	70 END

The way the two programs are written produces the same result. However, the operation in each is different. In the program on the left, the computer reads from the DATA statement one value at a time, multiplies it by 5 (statement 20), prints the product along with the value of B, and returns to read another value when the GO TO statement is executed. This looping phase continues as long as there are values in the DATA statement.

In the program on the right, however, the special FOR-TO and NEXT statements are used as a pair to specify the number of times looping is to be made. The FOR-TO statement causes the computer to initiate a counter with the name J as it appears in the statement. It simply means: *Execute all subsequent statements up to and including the NEXT statement with variable name J, five times.* Here, the DATA statement must have five values. On the first round of execution, the computer sets the counter at 1. When it executes the NEXT J statement, the counter is incremented by 1, initiating the second round of execution (statements 20, 30, and 40). Looping continues until the counter exceeds 5, which means that the computer has executed the set of statements exactly five times. At that time, the computer jumps the loop and takes the statement following the NEXT statement in the program.

Two-Dimensional Arrays

When entries (variables) are to be subscripted in one-dimensional arrays, a DIM statement must be written if the number of entries to be dimensioned is larger than 11. A dimension statement is also used in a two-dimensional array. A *two-dimensional array*, also called a *matrix*, is one in which individual variables are identified by their row and column numbers. A matrix can be represented by a general double-subscript variable A (I, J), where I represents the number of rows and J the number of columns. Table 16–3 is a 3-by-4 matrix consisting of 12 variables. Elements in a two-dimensional matrix are represented by the subscripts I and J, where I represents values in rows 1, 2, 3, . . . , m of the matrix, and J represents values in columns 1, 2, 3, 4 . . . , n of the same matrix. A DIM statement 40 DIM A(3,4) reserves an area in computer memory for these variables. It tells the computer that the dimensions of the matrix are three rows and four columns, respectively. Items shown between parentheses are subscripts, are separated by a comma, and denote the location of a given constant in the matrix. For example, A(3,2) refers to 14—the intersection of the third row and the second column.

Table 16–3. Two-dimensional array A.

		Columns			
		1	2	3	4
	1	15	71	10	1
Rows	2	2	18	8	15
	3	9	14	4	3

Inner and Outer Loops

Basic programming allows one or more loops (called inner loops) to be inserted within a major (outer) loop. An example of the general format of loops within loops is shown in Table 16–4. In that table, one inner loop is controlled by counter B within an outer loop controlled by counter A. Execution is carried out by executing the inner loop three times for each execution of the outer loop. This means that the statements within the inner loop will be executed a total of 12 (3×4) times.

Another way of using the loop-within-a-loop concept is to set the elements of a two-dimensional array to a specific digit, depending on the problem. The following is a sample program:

Table 16–4.

```
                              20  FOR A=1 TO 4
                               .                    Statements
                               .                    missing
                               .
                              70  FOR B=1 TO 3
Outer      Inner              .                    Statements
loop       loop               .                    missing
                              .
                             110  NEXT B
                               .                    Statements
                               .                    missing
                             180  NEXT A
```

```
10   DIM A(4,3)
     .
     .
     .
40   FOR I=1 TO 4
45   FOR J=1 TO 3
50   LET A(I,J)=7
60   NEXT J
70   NEXT I
     .
     .
     .
     .
```

When execution is initiated, J cycles from 1 to 3 while I remains at 1. Then I advances to 2, followed by J cycling from 1 to 3 for the second time, and so on, until I advances to 4, followed by J cycling from 1 to 3 for the fourth time. At that stage, both loops (I being the outer loop and J the inner loop) will have been completed. The final values of I and J will be 4 and 3, respectively.

Sample Programs

Net Pay Calculation

To illustrate the use of the Basic statements explained in this chapter, suppose a company pays each of its 13 employees $4.25 per hour. No overtime is allowed. Also assume that total taxes withheld are based on the following schedule:

Gross Earnings ($)	Tax Withheld	
Under 100	0	
100 to 125	15%	of amount over $100
Over 125	20%	of amount over $125
	+	$3.75

So if gross earnings are $175, the tax withheld is 15 percent of $25 ($3.75) and 20 percent of $50 ($10) or $13.75. The program in Table 16–5 is designed to print the net pay and tax withheld for each employee.

Table 16–5. The program for payroll example.

```
10   REM THIS IS A SIMPLIFIED PROGRAM TO CALCULATE
20   REM NET PAY AND TAX DEDUCTIONS
30   DIM S(150), H(150), P(150), T(150)
40   READ N' NUMBER OF EMPLOYEES
50   DATA 13
60   FOR I = 1 TO N
```

```
70   READ H(I)' H(I) REFERS TO NUMBER OF HOURS WORKED
80   LET S(I) = H(I)*4.25' 4.25 IS WAGE RATE PER HOUR
90   NEXT I
100  DATA 36,40,15,28,40,34,26,38,20,40,31,40,34
110  PRINT "NET PAY AND TAX IN DOLLARS"
120  FOR I = 1 TO N
130  IF S(I) > 100 THEN 160
140  LET T(I) = 0' TAX DEDUCTIONS
150  GO TO 200
160  IF S(I) > 125 THEN 190
170  LET T(I) = .15*(S(I)—100)' TAX DEDUCTIONS
180  GO TO 200
190  LET T(I) = 3.75+.20*(S(I)—125)' TAX DEDUCTIONS
200  LET P(I) = S(I)—T(I)' NET PAY
210  PRINT P(I), T(I)
220  NEXT I
230  END

RUN

NET PAY AND TAX IN DOLLARS
143.65        9.35
157.25       12.75
 63.75        0
116.15        2.85
157.25       12.75
136.85        7.65
108.92        1.58
150.45       11.05
 85           0
157.25       12.75
126.65        5.10
157.25       12.75
136.85        7.65
```

Accounting Application Problem— Accelerated Depreciation

Depreciation charges are deductible when computing federal income taxes: the larger the depreciation charge, the lower the actual tax liability. Depreciation accounting aims to distribute the cost of the tangible capital assets over the estimated useful life of a unit in a systematic and rational manner. Of the four principal methods of depreciation, we shall illustrate the sum-of-years'-digits method.

Sum-of-years'-digits depreciation calculation. This method is applied by listing the life expectancy of the asset and each successive year through one. The cumulative years can be obtained with the following formula:

$$\text{Sum} = N\left(\frac{N+1}{2}\right)$$

where N is the life of the asset. Divide the number of remaining years by the sum-of-years'-digits, and multiply this fraction by the depreciable value of the asset as:

$$\text{Dep(I)} = \left(\frac{N-I+1}{\text{sum}}\right) \times (\text{Cost} - \text{Salvage Value})$$

Problem. Using this arithmetic formula, try to work out a Basic program for calculating a depreciation schedule by this method. As an example, use a $350 typewriter with a five-year life and a salvage value of $50 (see Tables 16–6 and 16–7, as well as Figure 16–1). The program is shown in Table 16–8.

Figure 16–1. Flowchart for sum-of-the-years digits method.

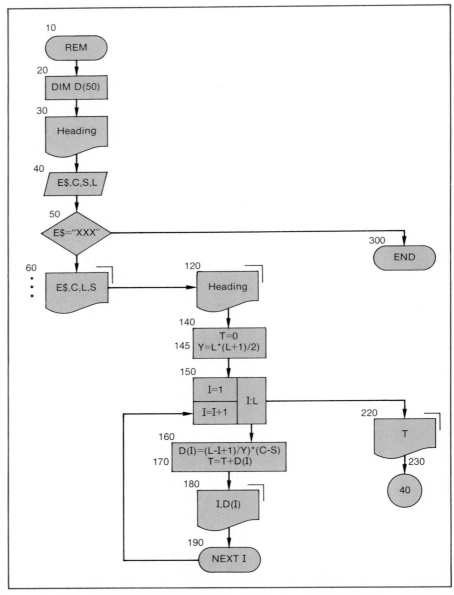

Table 16–8. Program and output for the accelerated depreciation problem.

```
10   REM DEPRECIATION SCHEDULE BY SUM-OF-YEARS-DIGITS METHOD
20   DIM D(50)
30   PRINT "DEPRECIATION SCHEDULE BY SUM-OF-YEARS-DIGITS METHOD"
40   READ E$,C,S,L
50   IF E$ = "XXX" THEN 300
55   PRINT
60   PRINT USING 65,E$
65   : ITEM 'LLLLLLLLLLLLLL
70   PRINT USING 75,C
75   : COST $#####.##
80   PRINT USING 85,L
85   : LIFE EXPECTANCY IN YEARS  ###
90   PRINT USING 95,S
95   : SALVAGE VALUE $####.##
100  PRINT
120  PRINT "YEAR    DEPRECIATION"
130  PRINT
140  LET T = 0
145  LET Y = L * ((L + 1)/2)
150  FOR I = 1TO L
160  LET D(I) = ((L – I + 1)/Y)*(C – S)
170  LET T = T + D(I)
180  PRINT USING 185,I,D(I)
185  : ##         #####.##
190  NEXT I
200  PRINT
220  PRINT USING 225,T
225  :     TOTAL  #####.##
226  PRINT
230  GO TO 40
240  DATA "TYPEWRITER E29",350,50,5
260  DATA "XXX",0,0,0
300  END
```

DEPRECIATION SCHEDULE BY SUM-OF-YEARS'-DIGITS METHOD

ITEM   TYPEWRITER E29
COST $ 350.00
LIFE EXPECTANCY IN YEARS 5
SALVAGE VALUE $ 50.00

```
YEAR      DEPRECIATION

  1          100.00
  2           80.00
  3           60.00
  4           40.00
  5           20.00
   TOTAL     300.00
```

Table 16–6. Table of variables

Program variable	Definition
E$	ITEM
C	COST
S	Salvage Value
L	Life expectancy in years
D(I)	Depreciation of the i th year
I	Year indication
T	Total depreciation
Y	Cumulative years

Table 16–7. Analysis of the problem.

1. Outputs: (i) E$, C, S, L (echo)
             (ii) I, D(I)
2. Inputs: (i) E$, C, S, L
3. Computations: $y = L\left(\dfrac{L+1}{2}\right)$

                    $D(I) = \left(\dfrac{L-I+1}{y}\right)(C - S)$

Marketing Application Problem— Calculation of Stock-Turnover Rate

Determining the level of annual sales is a significant aspect of merchandise control. The firm that increases its sales and resulting profits without having to carry larger inventories achieves a higher rate of return on its investment.

The relationship between sales and inventory investment is reflected in the ratio of sales achieved in a given time period to the average inventory carried to realize those sales. That ratio indicates the rate of stock turnover, which in turn represents the number of times during a given time period that the average inventory on hand was sold and replaced. The formula for calculating the rate of stock turnover is

$$\text{Rate} = \frac{\text{Net Retail Sales}}{\text{Average Retail Stock Value}}$$

The average retail stock value is derived from totaling the beginning stock on hand for each of the periods in the time span covered and the ending stock on hand for the last period. For example, if the data used is monthly, the twelve monthly beginning stocks on hand plus the ending stock on hand at the twelfth month are totaled. Then thirteen stocks on hand are totaled, and the average is computed from the total divided by 13. So if the span of time covered is 24 months and the data is monthly, the number of stocks on hand is 25. The formula for deriving the average stock on hand is

$$\text{Average Retail Stock Value} = \frac{\text{Sum of the Retail Values of the Inventory}}{\text{The Number of Inventory Values}}$$

Problem. Provide a program to calculate the stock turnover rate for one year with monthly data by utilizing the formulas for the rate of stock turnover. As an example, use a total sales figure of $236,542 for a twelve-month period and an average retail stock value of $1,525.04. Compute for the stock turnover rate. See Tables 16–9 and 16–10, as well as Figure 16–2. Table 16–11 contains the program.

Table 16–9. Table of variables.

Variable	Definition
N	Number of inventory values
V	Inventory value
S	Annual sales
T	Total inventory value
R	Rate of stock turnover
C$	Company name

Table 16–10. Analysis of the problem.

1. Outputs: N, S, A, R
2. Inputs: N, S, V
3. Computations:

$$A = \sum_{i=1}^{N} V_i/N$$
$$R = S/A$$

Table 16–11. Program and output for the stock turnover rate calculation problem.

```
10   REM STOCK-TURNOVER RATE CALCULATION
20   PRINT "STOCK-TURNOVER RATE CALCULATION"
30   LET T = 0
40   READ C$,N,S
50   FOR I = 1 TO N
60   READ V
70   LET T = T + V
80   NEXT I
90   LET A = T/N
95   LET R = S/A
100   PRINT USING 102,C$
101   PRINT
102   :COMPANY      'LLLLLLLLLLLLLL
105   PRINT USING 106,N,S
```

```
106   :TOTAL SALES FOR ### PERIODS = $######.##
108   PRINT USING 109,A
109   :AVERAGE RETAIL STOCK = $#####.##
110   PRINT USING 111,R
111   :RATE OF STOCK TURNOVER RATE = $###.##
120   DATA "XYZ",12,236542.00
121   DATA 1000.0,1200.0,1450.0,2010.5,1340.0,1400.0
122   DATA 1400.0,1350.0,1300.0,1800.0,2000.0,2050.0
200   END


READY
RUN


MARKT          12:00          22-JAN-80
STOCK-TURNOVER RATE CALCULATION
COMPANY  XYZ
TOTAL SALES FOR 12 PERIODS = $236542.00
AVERAGE RETAIL STOCK = $ 1525.04
RATE OF STOCK TURNOVER RATE = $155.11


TIME:  0.14 SECS.
READY
```

Figure 16–2. Flowchart for the stock turnover problem.

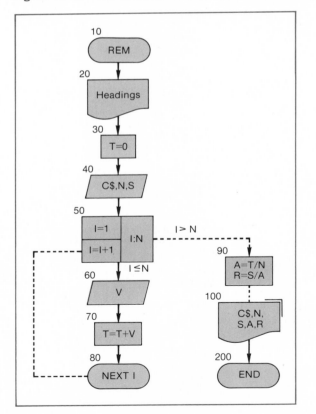

SUMMARY

1. Basic is a special, powerful language designed for on-line processing in a time-sharing environment. Using plain English and familiar arithmetic symbols, a user can feed a program via a terminal. Several system commands are used to tell the computer what action to take. The computer can be instructed to SAVE an existing program, LIST a program, retrieve an OLD program, signal the END of program instructions to be executed, RUN a program that has just been entered, and disconnect the terminal by printing a BYE message.

2. Like Cobol, Basic uses constants, variables, and arithmetic operators to form statements. In the absence of parentheses, the order of calculation is exponentiation, division or multiplication, and addition or subtraction. The Basic statements include the following:
   a. END defines the end of the program.
   b. REM is nonexecutable, for program documentation.
   c. PRINT provides headings and labels, prints literals, or performs basic calculations.
   d. TAB specifies the location of labels to be printed on a line.
   e. READ reads the variable names that take corresponding values for the DATA list.
   f. DATA specifies the data for use by the program to be assessed by the READ statement. It follows the READ statement.
   g. INPUT indicates to the computer that the data is to be entered from the user's terminal.
   h. RESTORE causes the data previously read from storage to be replaced in storage.
   i. LET is a way of either assigning values to variables or defining an expression.
   j. Control statements are designed to allow conditional (IF-THEN) or unconditional (GO TO) transfer of control within the program.

3. Basic also offers instructions that make it possible to define subscripted variables and, consequently, perform looping routines. When more than eleven memory places are needed, a DIMension statement is used to define the necessary computer memory area for processing. It is also used to define a two-dimensional array. A looping routine utilizes the FOR-TO and the NEXT formats to allow repetitive execution of the statements placed between the two formats.

TERMS TO LEARN

Basic   NEXT
Constant   READ
DIM   RUN
END   SAVE
FOR-TO   SCRATCH
LET   System command
LIST   Variable

REVIEW QUESTIONS

1. Explain briefly the characteristics of Basic. What similarities and differences are there between Basic and Cobol?

2. Distinguish between:

   a. a constant and a variable.
   b. END and RUN.
   c. FOR, NEXT, and GO TO.
   d. END and STOP.
   e. One- and two-dimensional arrays.
   f. SAVE and HELP.

3. For what purpose are the following input-output statements used?

   a. DATA
   b. INPUT
   c. READ
   d. PRINT

4. Explain the difference between a conditional and an unconditional statement. Give an example.

5. Explain the Basic procedure involved in inner and outer loops.

6. Which of the following variables are invalid? Why?

   a. 3P
   b. P3
   c. P3A
   d. 7

7. Write a Basic program to multiply 17 by 8. Enter the appropriate messages to the computer.

8. Find the value of X in each of the following statements:

```
LET X = 19+20/4*3 ↑ 3−8
LET X = 4+(10*6 ↑ 2)*3 ↑ 3 − 4
LET X = (3+12)/3*2 ↑ 4 − 1)
```

9. Write the basic set of instructions to find the square root of $4x^2 + 5$, where $x = 10$.

10. Write a partial basic program to cause the computer to print out digits 1 to 50.

11. Write a partial BASIC statement to print the heading "DAILY VALUE IS"

12. Write a partial program to input five values into A and print them out.

13. What does the following program accomplish?

```
10   READ A
20   LET B = 2*3.1416*A
30   PRINT B,A
40   GO TO 10
50   DATA 1.7,2.8,3.9,4.5,7.5
60   END
```

chapter 17

Cobol

Learning Objectives

Cobol is the language of business applications programming. Since it is the most commonly used language in industry, business students should be especially familiar with the makeup and structure of this important language. Learning Cobol also makes it easier to learn other programming languages. By the end of this chapter, you should know:

1. the nature of Cobol

2. the main divisions of a Cobol program, and

3. the main instructions that make up a program in COBOL.

Introduction

Cobol is the most extensive programming language used in business applications today. No language rates as high in programming business applications as Cobol. For over a decade Cobol has maintained its rank as the most commonly used commercial programming language, if not always the most well liked. In a recent survey[1] of 138 sites, it was used for some 70 percent of all programming. By industry, the average use of Cobol is 75 percent in banking, 80 percent in health care, 76 percent in insurance, 81 percent in manufacturing, and 64 percent in retailing and distribution. With this background, Cobol occupies a major role in business data processing.

Cobol is an acronym for COmmon Business-Oriented Language — a high-level procedure-oriented language. The title explains the general purpose of this unique language. Cobol is "business" and "English-language" oriented in the following ways:

1. It allows program instructions to be constructed in paragraph- and sentence-like form, using words encountered in business situations.

2. Programs are written in English to communicate data processing procedures to businesspersons as well as to serve as source programs for computers. For example, the Cobol sentence MULTIPLY QUANTITY BY PRICE GIVING TOTAL PRICE is self-explanatory and easy to understand.

3. It is particularly applicable to business (rather than to scientific) data processing problems.

No single company can claim full credit for the creation of the Cobol language. Several users and computer manufacturers (including IBM) contributed to its development. The Conference on Data Systems Languages (CODASYL) regularly revises and updates Cobol specifications. In addition, the American National Standard Institute (ANSI) has issued a standard for Cobol language and regularly reviews suggested changes in the language. Cobol implementations based on the ANSI standard are referred to as ANSI Cobol.

Finally, Cobol provides its own documentation. The documentation needed in Cobol involves occasionally only remarks or notes added to the overall program.

Reserved Words

One of Cobol's unique aspects is its English-like words or phrases referred to as **reserved words.** A reserved word represents a particular meaning and is used for a specified purpose. The programmers can choose the appropriate words for his or her program from a list of over 250 words. No change in either their meaning, spelling, or definition is allowed. Also, any word that is defined by the programmer — a **programmer-defined** word — must not duplicate any reserved

[1]Phillippakis, Andreas S. "A Popularity Contest for Languages," *Datamation* (December 1977), p. 81ff.

word. Examples of some reserved words and their special purposes are:

Reserved Words	Purpose
ADD	Specifies addition to be taken
COMPUTATIONAL	Denotes a specific function
ENVIRONMENT	Specifies a program unit
PICTURE	Identifies a part or parts of an entry
ZERO	Represents a data value (zero)

Program Organization

Coding Sheet

A Cobol program must be arranged in a standard format, normally on standard coding forms. The Cobol coding sheet is designed for entering source program entries, which are later keypunched onto Cobol program cards. Each sheet provides room for 80 columns of data to correspond to the standard 80-column card (Figure 17-1).

- Columns 1 to 3 are reserved for a three-digit page number. Page 1 is numbered 010; page 2, 020; and so on.

Figure 17–1. COBOL coding sheet

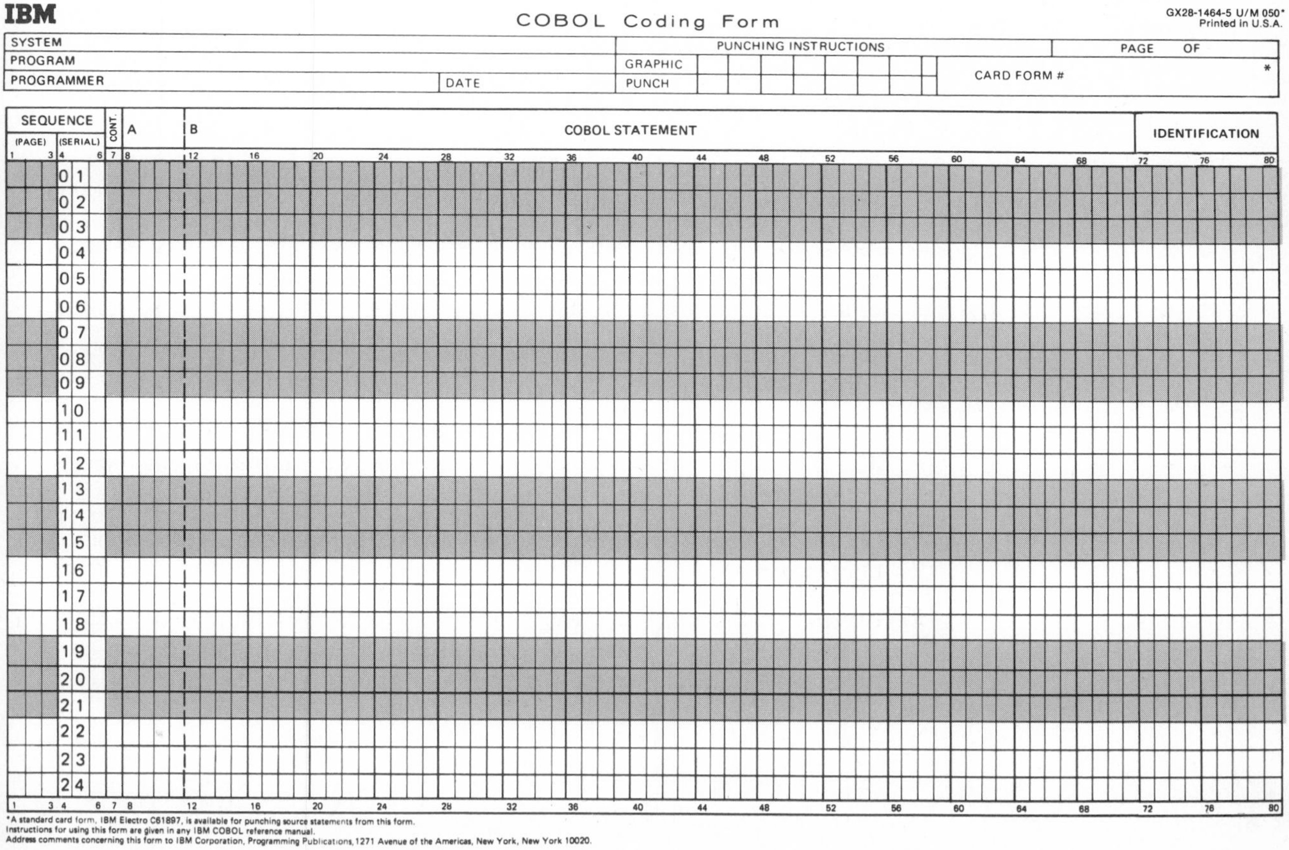

- Columns 4 to 6 indicate the line or statement number. The first line is numbered 010; the second, 020; and so on. Thus, when using columns 1 to 6, 010080 would mean page 1 and line 8.

- Column 7 is reserved for indicating the continuation of literals (non-numerics). For example, if a non-numeric literal requires three lines, enter a hyphen in column 7 of the second and third lines.

- Columns 8 to 72[2] are reserved for program entries. They are divided into margin A (columns 8 to 11) and margin B (columns 12 to 72). The entries that must begin in column 8 are:
  — division headers,
  — section headers,
  — paragraph headers,
  — declaratives and end declaratives in the procedure division, and
  — file-description entries in the data division. A file-description entry begins with the reserved word FD (file description). It is written in columns 8 and 9. The remaining part of the entry is entered beginning in column 12.

Entry-Recording Specifications

Level numbers *may* be written in margin A. All other entries *must* be written in margin B, beginning in column 12 or indented to a column number that is a multiple of 4: The indent must be to column 16, 20, 24, and so on. Other entry-specifications include:

1. An entry that must begin in margin A is written on a new line. The next entry, consequently, is also written on a new line.

2. Although each entry commonly begins on a new line, an entry not required to start on a new line may be written on the same line as the preceding entry, separated by one or more spaces.

3. An entry that can be written on one line may be arbitrarily written on two or more lines.

4. In addition to a hyphen in column 7 for every continuation line, a quotation mark is also written in margin B, followed by the remaining characters of the literal.

5. No space is allowed immediately after a left parenthesis or a beginning quotation mark.

6. No space is allowed immediately preceding a right parenthesis, an ending quotation mark, a comma, a semicolon used to punctuate a program entry, or a period written at the end of an entry.

[2]Columns 73 to 80 are reserved for program identification. The use of this field, however, is optional.

A Cobol program consists of four divisions presented in the following sequence:

1. identification division,

2. environment division,

3. data division, and

4. procedure division.

To understand the unique structure of Cobol, you must examine a complete Cobol program and be able to identify the four divisions (Figure 17–2).

Identification Division

The **identification division** provides key information for identifying the program. It states primarily the name of the program, the name of the programmer, the date it was written, and remarks related to the job for which the program was written.

The identification division requires three entries: IDENTIFICATION DIVISION (division header), PROGRAM-ID (paragraph header), and a program name enclosed in single quotation marks.[3] Up to six optional paragraphs may also be added. Represented by reserved words, these paragraphs are entered in the sequence shown in Table 17–1. Any number of entries can be added to each paragraph at the discretion of the programmer. An example of the identification division is presented in Figure 17–3.

Table 17–1. Identification division format.

IDENTIFICATION DIVISION.

PROGRAM-ID.
  'program name'
(AUTHOR.
  entry. . . .)
(INSTALLATION.
  entry. . . .)
(DATE-WRITTEN.
  entry. . . .)
(DATE-COMPILED.
  entry. . . .)
(SECURITY.
  entry. . . .)
(REMARKS.
   entry. . . .)

LEGEND: A line under a word is used to refer to a required reserve word. Brackets are used to refer to optional paragraphs or portions of the format.

[3]A program name must not exceed eight characters. The first character must be a letter. The remaining characters may be letters or digits, but not special characters. The program name may be written on a separate line or on the same line as the paragraph header.

```
//JTESTING JOB (10137,1),'CYNTHIA MA',MSGLEVEL=1,CLASS=A        ] CONTROL STATEMENTS
//  EXEC    COBUCLG                                            ]
//COB.SYSIN DD *
        IDENTIFICATION DIVISION.
        PROGRAM-ID.
            'PAYROLL'.
        AUTHOR.
            SANDY TREMAINE.
        INSTALLATION.
            ACCOUNTING DEPARTMENT.
        DATE-WRITTEN.
            DECEMBER 11, 1980.
        DATE-COMPILED.
            DECEMBER 18, 1980.
        REMARKS.
            THIS PROGRAM PROCESSES THE PAYROLL OF THE
            STAFF OF THE ACCOUNTING DEPARTMENT. IT IS
            DUE BY THE LAST DAY OF EACH WEEK.
    *********************************************
        ENVIRONMENT DIVISION.
        CONFIGURATION SECTION.
        SOURCE-COMPUTER.
            IBM-370.
        OBJECT-COMPUTER.
            IBM-370.
        INPUT-OUTPUT SECTION.
        FILE-CONTROL.
            SELECT FILE-1
                ASSIGN TO UT-S-SYSIN.
            SELECT FILE-2
                ASSIGN TO UT-S-SYSPRINT.
    *********************************************
        DATA DIVISION.
        FILE SECTION.
        FD  FILE-1
            LABEL RECORDS ARE OMITTED
            DATA RECORD IS EMPLOYEE-CARD-REC.
        01  EMPLOYEE-CARD-REC.
            02 SOC-SEC-NO       PIC X(9).
            02 EMPLOYEE-NAME     PIC A(20).
            02 HOURLY-RATE       PIC 99V99.
            02 FILLER            PIC XX.
            02 HOURS-WORKED      PIC 999V99.
            02 FILLER            PIC X(40).
        FD  FILE-2
            LABEL RECORDS ARE OMITTED
            DATA RECORD IS PRINT-AREA.
        01  PRINT-AREA          PIC X(133).
        WORKING-STORAGE SECTION.
        77  WEEKLY-WAGE         PIC S9(4)V99 VALUE ZEROS.
        77  KOUNTER-W           PIC S9(5)V99 VALUE ZEROS.
        01  HEADING-1.
            02 FILLER           PIC X(30) VALUE SPACES.
            02 FILLER           PIC X(21) VALUE 'WEEKLY PAYROLL REPORT'.
        01  HEADING-A.
            02 FILLER           PIC X(45) VALUE SPACES.
            02 TOTAL-A          PIC X(22).
            02 TOTAL-B          PIC $ZZZZZ.99.
        01  SUB-HEADING.
            02 FILLER           PIC X(4) VALUE SPACES.
            02 FILLER           PIC X(23) VALUE 'SOC-SEC-NO'.
            02 FILLER           PIC X(15) VALUE 'NAME'.
            02 FILLER           PIC X(12) VALUE 'HOURLY-RATE'.
```

Figure 17–2. Illustrative program, simplified payroll application.

```
            02 FILLER              PIC X(16) VALUE 'HOURS-WORKED'.
            02 FILLER              PIC X(13) VALUE 'WAGE'.
        01  PRINT-LINE.
            02  FILLER             PIC X(5) VALUE SPACES.
            02 SOC-SEC-NO-P         PIC 9(9).
            02 FILLER              PIC X(5) VALUE SPACES.
            02 EMPLOYEE-NAME-P     PIC X(20).
            02 FILLER              PIC X(5) VALUE SPACES.
            02 HOURLY-RATE-P        PIC $ZZ.99.
            02 FILLER              PIC X(7) VALUE SPACES.
            02 HOURS-WORKED-P       PIC ZZZ.99.
            02 FILLER              PIC X(4) VALUE SPACES.
            02 WEEKLY-WAGE-P        PIC $ZZZZZ.99.
        ************************************************
        PROCEDURE DIVISION.
        PARA-1.
            OPEN INPUT FILE-1, OUTPUT FILE-2.
            MOVE HEADING-1 TO PRINT-AREA.
            WRITE PRINT-AREA BEFORE ADVANCING 1 LINES.
            WRITE PRINT-AREA FROM SUB-HEADING AFTER ADVANCING 4 LINES.
        PARA-2.
            READ FILE-1 AT END GO TO PARA-4.
            MOVE SOC-SEC-NO TO SOC-SEC-NO-P.
            MOVE EMPLOYEE-NAME TO EMPLOYEE-NAME-P.
            MOVE HOURLY-RATE TO HOURLY-RATE-P.
            MOVE HOURS-WORKED TO HOURS-WORKED-P.
        PARA-3.
            COMPUTE WEEKLY-WAGE ROUNDED = HOURLY-RATE * HOURS-WORKED.
            MOVE WEEKLY-WAGE TO WEEKLY-WAGE-P.
            MOVE PRINT-LINE TO PRINT-AREA.
            WRITE PRINT-AREA AFTER ADVANCING 2 LINES.
            ADD WEEKLY-WAGE TO KOUNTER-W.
            GO TO PARA-2.
        PARA-4.
            MOVE 'TOTAL WEEKLY-WAGE' TO TOTAL-A.
            MOVE KOUNTER-W TO TOTAL-B.
            WRITE PRINT-AREA FROM HEADING-A AFTER ADVANCING 4 LINES.
        END-JCB.
            CLOSE FILE-1, FILE-2.
            STOP RUN.
/*
//GO.SYSPRINT  DD  SYSOUT=A
//GO.SYSIN DD *
234455678ROBERT ALLAN          0320   04500
345566789MARY JOHNS            0650   04000
346677890JOHN JOHNSON          0575   03600
456678901JOAN KELLY            0850   05000
467789542PETER SMITH           1050   02000
346678234JAMES WELLS           0650   04000
/*
```

CONTROL STATEMENTS

DATA

CONTROL STATEMENT

Fig 17-2 (cont.)

9

WEEKLY PAYROLL REPORT

SOC-SEC-NO	NAME	HOURLY-RATE	HOURS WORKED	WAGE
234455678	ROHERT ALLAN	$ 3.20	45.00	$ 144.00
345566789	MARY JOHNS	$ 6.50	40.00	$ 260.00
346677890	JOHN JOHNSON	$ 5.75	36.00	$ 207.00
456678901	JOAN KELLY	$ 8.50	50.00	$ 425.00
467789542	PETER SMITH	$10.50	20.00	$ 210.00
346678234	JAMES WELLS	$ 6.50	40.00	$ 260.00
		TOTAL WEEKLY-WAGE		$ 1506.00

Fig 17–2 (cont.)

Figure 17–3. Identification division.

IBM COBOL Coding Form

SYSTEM		PUNCHING INSTRUCTIONS		PAGE OF
PROGRAM		GRAPHIC	CARD FORM # *	IDENTIFICATION 73 80
PROGRAMMER	DATE	PUNCH		

```
SEQUENCE   A   B                                    COBOL STATEMENT
(PAGE)(SERIAL)
Ø1Ø 01     IDENTIFICATION DIVISION.
    02     PROGRAM-ID.
    03         'PAYROLL'.
    04     AUTHOR.
    05         SANDY TREMAINE.
    06     INSTALLATION
    07         ACCOUNTING DEPARTMENT.
    08     DATE-WRITTEN.
    09         DECEMBER 11, 198Ø.
    10     DATE-COMPILED.
    11         DECEMBER 11, 198Ø.
    12     REMARKS.
    13         THIS PROGRAM PROCESSES THE PAYROLL OF THE
    14         STAFF OF THE ACCOUNTING DEPARTMENT. IT IS
    15         DUE BY THE LAST DAY OF EACH WEEK.
    16
    17
    18
    19
    20
    21
    22
    23
    24
    25
    26
```

*A standard card form, IBM Electro C61897, is available for punching source statements from this form.
Instructions for using this form are given in any IBM COBOL reference manual.
Address comments concerning this form to IBM Corporation, Programming Publications, 1271 Avenue of the Americas, New York, New York 10020.

Form No. X28-1464-4 U/M 025
Printed in U.S.A.

Environment Division

The second division of a Cobol program, the **environment division,** provides information about the computers to be used in compiling and executing the object program; also, using problem-oriented names, it assigns data files to input-output devices. Thus, this division is primarily computer-dependent, since it is directly involved with the specifications of the computers to be used. The general format is shown in Table 17–2.

Table 17–2. Environment division format.

```
ENVIRONMENT DIVISION.
CONFIGURATION-SECTION.
(SOURCE-COMPUTER.
   computer's name (model – number).)
(OBJECT-COMPUTER
   computer's name (model – number).)
INPUT-OUTPUT SECTION.
(FILE-CONTROL
   SELECT-entry. . . .)
(I-O-CONTROL
   APPLY-entry. . . .)
```

The primary entries and sections of the environment division are illustrated · in Figure 17–4. Line 01 indicates the first required entry, ENVIRONMENT DIVISION, followed by the division's two main sections: the configuration section and the input-output section. The *configuration section* identifies the source computer (the computer in which the program is compiled) and the object computer (the computer in which the computed program will be executed). Normally, the source and object computers are the same machine. Thus the two required paragraph headers in the configuration section are SOURCE-COMPUTER and OBJECT-COMPUTER. Each header is followed by the computer's name and model number (Figure 17–4).

The *input-output* section assigns data files to input-output devices and specifies certain input-output conditions. File assignment is carried out by a file-control paragraph, FILE-CONTROL; following this paragraph is an entry that selects the file by a programmer-defined name and assigns it to an "external" file name[4] and an input-output device. The key words SELECT and ASSIGN are reserved words and must be written exactly as they appear (Figure 17–4, lines 09 to 12).

Three device types are used with an ASSIGN entry. They can be UNIT-RECORD, UTILITY, or DIRECT-ACCESS. The UNIT-RECORD class refers to card read-punch and printer machines; the UTILITY class refers to input-output devices capable of reading and writing data sequentially. Examples are magnetic tape, magnetic disc, and magnetic drum devices. The DIRECT-ACCESS class

---

[4]An external file name must begin with an alphabetic character, followed by no more than seven alphabetic and/or numeric characters. Special characters are not allowed. The file name is enclosed by single quotation marks.

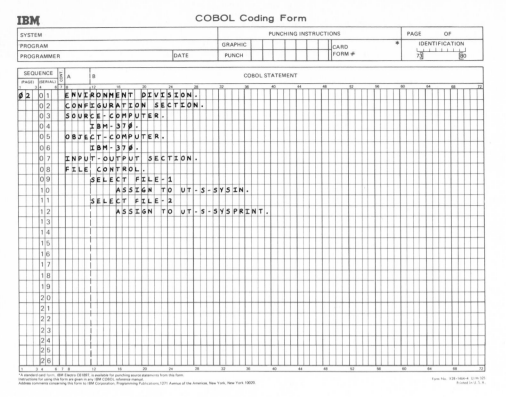

Figure 17–4. Environment division.

includes devices that can read and write data in a random manner. Examples are magnetic disk and magnetic drum devices. When one of these device classes is used, it should be entered with its model number. For example, lines 10 and 12 assign FILE-1 to SYSIN for the card reader and FILE-2 to SYSPRINT for the printer, respectively. Both of these units are IBM UNIT-RECORD devices.

Data Division

The primary functions of the **data division** are to describe:

1. the data files and the records they contain, and

2. the items in working storage.

The two most frequently used sections are the *file section,* which describes the data files (stored externally)and their records, and the *working-storage section,* which describes internal storage used for processing records and elementary data items. The general format of the data division is shown in Table 17–3.

File Section. The file section is mandatory in every program that processes input or output data files. It consists of a file-description entry for every file named in a SELECT entry in the environment division. Each file description must be followed by two or more record descriptions or one record description for each record in the file.

The *FD (file-description) entry* specifies the number of data records, the number of characters per record, label records (if any), and the name of each data record. These details must be entered in the sequence shown in Table 17–4. A detailed example is shown in Figure 17–5.

Table 17–3.   Data division format.

```
DATA DIVISION.
[FILE SECTION.
   (file-description. . . .
   record-description. . . .)]
[WORKING-STORAGE SECTION.
   (independent-item-description . . .)
   (record-description. . . .)]
```

Table 17–4.   File-description format.

```
FD file-name
      RECORDING MODE IS (mode)
      BLOCK CONTAINS (integer) RECORDS
(or) BLOCK CONTAINS (integer) CHARACTERS
      RECORD CONTAINS (integer) TO (integer) CHARACTERS
      LABEL RECORD IS      ⎡STANDARD⎤
                           ⎢  (or)  ⎥
(or) LABEL RECORDS ARE ⎨ OMITTED ⎬
                           ⎢  (or)  ⎥
                           ⎣data-name⎦
      DATA RECORD IS (record-name)
(or) DATA RECORDS ARE (record-name)
```

Record-description entries are almost self-explanatory. After a given data file has been described, each record it contains must also be described. In the example given in Figure 17–5, the data record clause gives the name of the record, EMPLOYEE-CARD-REC, which must appear as level 01 as follows:

01 EMPLOYEE-CARD-RECORD.

This initial entry is then followed by item-description entries that describe the items in that record. Each item-description entry also takes an appropriate level number, depending on its *level* in the record structure.

To illustrate, suppose that we wish to describe the items of an employee record, as shown in Table 7–5. Obviously, the record is divided into four smaller items, with the social security number, name, hourly rate, and hours worked. In subdividing a record, the record name (in this example, EMPLOYEE-

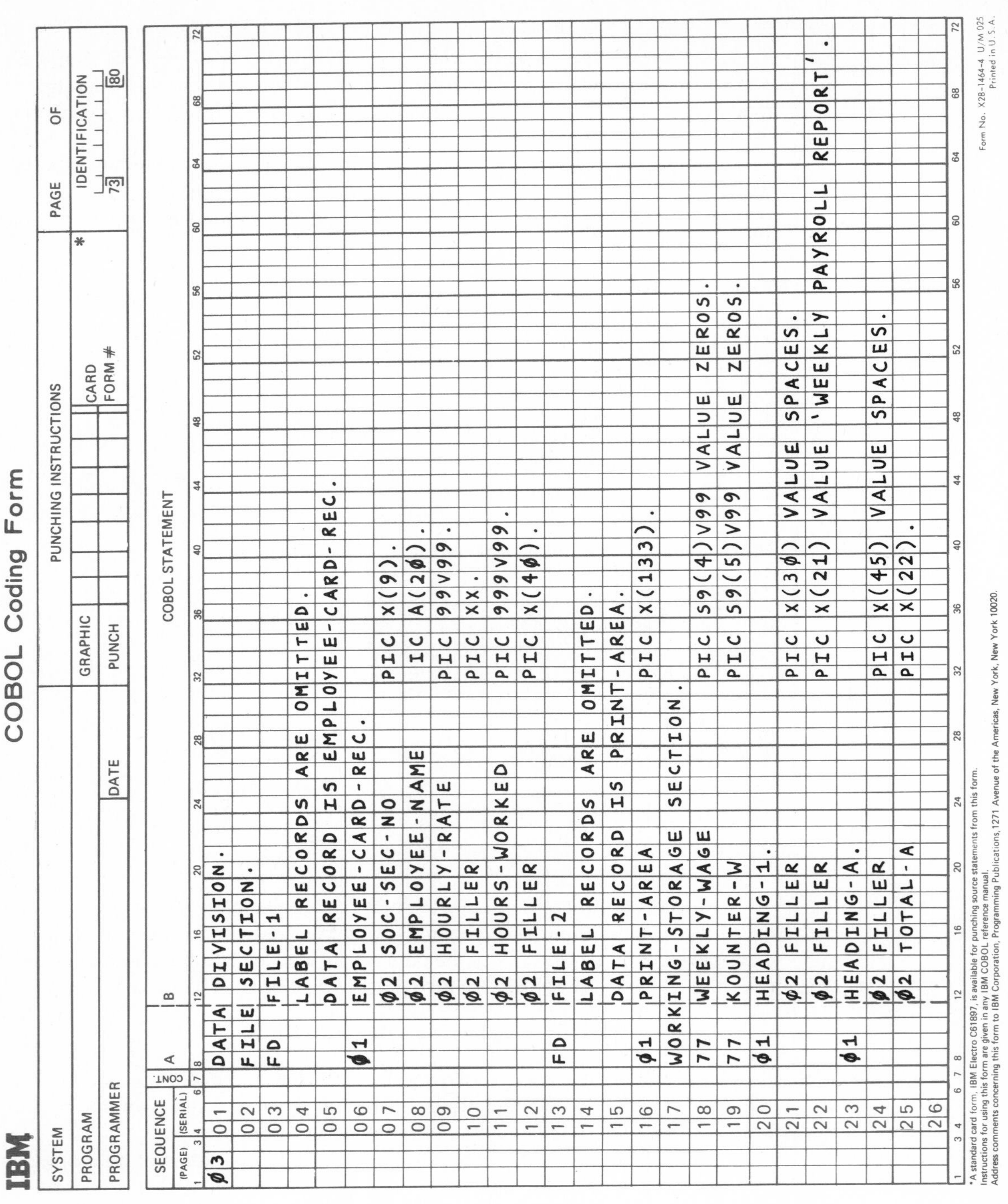

COBOL Coding Form

SYSTEM		PAGE	OF
PROGRAM	PUNCHING INSTRUCTIONS	IDENTIFICATION	
PROGRAMMER	DATE	GRAPHIC	PUNCH	CARD FORM #

```
Ø3 01   DATA DIVISION.
   02   FILE SECTION.
   03   FD  FILE-1
   04       LABEL RECORDS ARE OMITTED.
   05       DATA RECORD IS EMPLOYEE-CARD-REC.
   06   Ø1  EMPLOYEE-CARD-REC.
   07       Ø2  SOC-SEC-NO        PIC  X(9).
   08       Ø2  EMPLOYEE-NAME     PIC  A(2Ø).
   09       Ø2  HOURLY-RATE       PIC  99V99.
   10       Ø2  FILLER            PIC  XX.
   11       Ø2  HOURS-WORKED      PIC  999V99.
   12       Ø2  FILLER            PIC  X(4Ø).
   13   FD  FILE-2
   14       LABEL RECORDS ARE OMITTED.
   15       DATA RECORD IS PRINT-AREA.
   16   Ø1  PRINT-AREA            PIC  X(133).
   17   WORKING-STORAGE SECTION.
   18   77  WEEKLY-WAGE           PIC  S9(4)V99 VALUE ZEROS.
   19   77  KOUNTER-W             PIC  S9(5)V99 VALUE ZEROS.
   20   Ø1  HEADING-1.
   21       Ø2  FILLER            PIC  X(3Ø) VALUE SPACES.
   22       Ø2  FILLER            PIC  X(21) VALUE 'WEEKLY PAYROLL REPORT'.
   23   Ø1  HEADING-A.
   24       Ø2  FILLER            PIC  X(45) VALUE SPACES.
   25       Ø2  TOTAL-A           PIC  X(22).
   26
```

Figure 17–5. Data Division.

* A standard card form. IBM Electro C61897, is available for punching source statements from this form. Instructions for using this form are given in any IBM COBOL reference manual. Address comments concerning this form to IBM Corporation, Programming Publications, 1271 Avenue of the Americas, New York, New York 10020.

Form No. X28-1464-4 U/M 025
Printed in U. S. A.

IBM

COBOL Coding Form

SYSTEM		PUNCHING INSTRUCTIONS		PAGE OF
PROGRAM		GRAPHIC	CARD FORM # *	IDENTIFICATION 73–80
PROGRAMMER	DATE	PUNCH		

```
SEQUENCE  A   B                                     COBOL STATEMENT
ø4 01             ø2  TOTAL-B                  PIC $ZZZZZ.99.
   02         ø1  SUB-HEADING.
   03             ø2  FILLER                   PIC X(4)  VALUE SPACES.
   04             ø2  FILLER                   PIC X(23)  VALUE 'SOC-SEC-NO'.
   05             ø2  FILLER                   PIC X(15)  VALUE 'NAME'.
   06             ø2  FILLER                   PIC X(12)  VALUE 'HOURLY-RATE'.
   07             ø2  FILLER                   PIC X(16)  VALUE 'HOURS-WORKED'.
   08             ø2  FILLER                   PIC X(13)  VALUE 'WAGE'.
   09         ø1  PRINT-LINE.
   10             ø2  FILLER                   PIC X(5)  VALUE SPACES.
   11             ø2  SOC-SEC-NO-P             PIC 9(9).
   12             ø2  FILLER                   PIC X(5)  VALUE SPACES.
   13             ø2  EMPLOYEE-NAME-P          PIC X(20).
   14             ø2  FILLER                   PIC X(5)  VALUE SPACES.
   15             ø2  HOURLY-RATE-P            PIC $ZZ.99.
   16             ø2  FILLER                   PIC X(7)  VALUE SPACES.
   17             ø2  HOURS-WORKED-P           PIC ZZZ.99.
   18             ø2  FILLER                   PIC X(4)  VALUE SPACES.
   19             ø2  WEEKLY-WAGE-P            PIC $ZZZZZ.99.
   20
   21
   22
   23
   24
   25
   26
```

*A standard card form, IBM Electro C61897, is available for punching source statements from this form.
Instructions for using this form are given in any IBM COBOL reference manual.
Address comments concerning this form to IBM Corporation, Programming Publications, 1271 Avenue of the Americas, New York, New York 10020.

Form No. X28-1464-4 U/M 025
Printed in U.S.A.

Fig 17–5 (cont.)

CARD-REC) or the most inclusive record is assigned the highest level number, 01, with each succeeding level given a larger number.

Table 17–5. Example of the employee record.

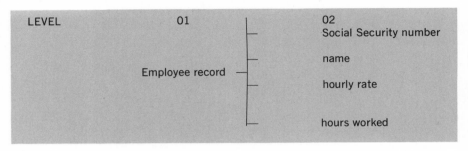

In this example there is a hierarchy of two levels:[5] 01 to 02. An item that is further subdivided is called a *group item;* an item that is not further subdivided is called an *elementary item.* Thus the date item is a group item, whereas the month, day, and year items are elementary. The record-description entries are shown in Figure 17–5.

Item-description entries are also nearly self-evident. A separate entry is made for each item included in the record involved. The entry specifies the characteristics of the data it contains, using a format that begins with a *level number,* followed by a *data name* or the word FILLER, and normally a descriptive clause, which begins with a word such as PICTURE, USAGE, or VALUE.

A *level number* must be the first element of an item description entry. As we see in Figure 17–5, the level number 01 indicates that the item is the most inclusive record. The level number 02 is assigned to group items that compose the record defined in the previous entry 01. The level number 03 would be given to smaller items if the 02-level items were subdivided.

Though not a name, "FILLER" is used to specify the unused part of a logical record or to indicate that the information will not be processed. For example, suppose the first 30 columns are unused and the next 21 columns (used for the information 'WEEKLY PAYROLL REPORT') are not to be processed. The word FILLER can be used as in Figure 17–5;

```
02 FILLER      PIC X(30) VALUE SPACES.
02 FILLER      PIC X(21) VALUE 'WEEKLY PAYROLL REPORT'.
```

A PICTURE clause is used only in describing an elementary item. It specifies item size, class, sign, assumed decimal point, and certain other editing requirements. Three classes of data items can be described: alphabetic, numeric,

[5]Level numbers need not be in consecutive order. For example, the form levels may be numbered 01, 03, 05, and 07, or 01, 05, 10, and 15. The important point is that the level numbers should be assigned in consecutive order in line with the order in which the hierarchy is subdivided.

and alphanumeric. These types of data fields are designated by such characters as:

A	alphabetic
9	numeric
X	alphanumeric

A PICTURE clause defines an *alphabetic item* by the letter A for each alphabetic character or space (Table 17–6). A PICTURE clause defines a *numeric item* if its character strings consist of the digit 9 or the letters V, S, or P (Table 17–7). The functions of these characters are as follows:

9	Indicates a numeric character 0 through 9.
V	Indicates the position of the assumed decimal point.
S	Indicates the presence of an arithmetic sign.
P	Indicates an assumed decimal point scaling position. That is, it positions the decimal point away from the actual number. It intends to show assumed zeros in the data item, one P for one zero.

Table 17–6. Alphabetic PICTURE clauses.

Item Value	Picture Clause	
ABC	PICTURE IS AAA (or) PICTURE IS A(3).	
CREDIT FILE	PICTURE IS AAAAAAAAAAA. (or) PICTURE IS A(11).	

Table 17–7. Numeric PICTURE clauses.

Item Value	PICTURE is	Item Value treated as
1294	9999	1294
1294	9(4)	1294
1294	99V99	12.94
129	S99V9	+12.9
25	99PP	2500
25	PP99	0.0025
25	P(3)99	0.00025
3795	9(4)PPV	379500
3795	V9(4)	0.3795

A PICTURE clause describes an *alphanumeric item* if its character strings contain a combination of the characters X, A, or 9. However, the data item is treated as though it contained all X's. Characters A and 9 have already been described. The letter X stands for a character of any kind—that is, a letter, a digit, a special character, or a space (Table 17–8).

Table 17–8. Alphanumeric PICTURE clauses.

Item Value	PICTURE
BD20	XXXX or X(4)
CD10–9	XXXXXX or X(6)

A PICTURE clause can also be used in *editing* a data item. Editing involves preparing certain data for printing. For example, the dollar amount might be stored in computer memory as 12345, with an assumed decimal point between the digits 3 and 4. Although the dollar sign and the decimal point are not required for processing, they are necessary for the printout to appear as $123.45. In this case, an editing picture of $999.99 will accomplish the result. The period represents the decimal point for alignment purposes.

Some of the common symbols used in the character strings of an edited picture are 9, Z, $, +, and −. Character 9 has already been discussed. The functions of the remaining characters are as follows:

Z Represents the leftmost positions that are to be zero-suppressed; that is, a leading zero is replaced by a space for each Z included in the character string. For example, if the actual value of the item is 004, it will be treated as 4 if its editing picture is ZZ9.

$,-,+$ Each of these symbols occupies the same character position in the actual result as the editing picture character string and is counted in the size of the item (Table 17-9).

Table 17-9. Editing PICTURE clauses.

Actual Value of Item in Storage*	PICTURE is	Edited Result
123	$999	$123
123	+$999	+$123
123	−ZZ999	− 123
0014	$ZZZZZ	$ 14
0001	$ZZ99	$ 01

*A dash above the unit's position indicates a negative sign.

A USAGE clause, used in data division entries at all levels, specifies the form in which an item is represented in computer storage. For a more efficient program, it is necessary to determine how a given item will be used most frequently and to specify the appropriate usage. This clause has the following general format:

```
USAGE          COMPUTATIONAL
                    (or)
                 DISPLAY
```

USAGE DISPLAY tells the computer to store a particular data item in character form, one character per byte. The word DISPLAY is optional, as in:

```
03 SHIPPING-CODE PICTURE XXXX.
```

The USAGE COMPUTATIONAL clause is used if the item represents a value to be used in computations and if it must be numeric. For example, the following entry is a computational entry:

```
02 GROSS, USAGE IS COMPUTATIONAL PICTURE $9(4).
                            or
02 GROSS USAGE COMPUTATIONAL PICTURE $9(4).
```

Working-storage section. The working-storage section describes independent data items and/or logical records. An independent item is defined in a separate data-description entry with level number 77. Level 77 begins in column 8, and the following data name begins in column 12.

In the working-storage section, a value clause is used when the initial value of an item must be specified, when a constant must be set up, or when a working area must contain a certain value prior to program execution. The VALUE clauses shown in the sample program are:

```
77 WEEKLY-WAGE PIC S9(4)V99 VALUE ZEROS.
77 KOUNTER-W PIC S9(5)V99 VALUE ZEROS.
```

Several rules apply to the use of the VALUE clause:

1. The value of the literal must be the same class as the item: That is, for a numeric item, the value of the literal must be numeric. Likewise, for an alphabetic item, the value of the literal must be alphabetic.

2. The size of the literal used in the VALUE clause must not exceed the size of the item.

3. The value of a numeric literal must be within the range of values defined by the picture clause. For example, if the picture clause is PICTURE 999, the literal must be within the range 000 to 999.

Procedure Division

The programmer-defined **procedure division** consists of one or more paragraphs that determine the required processing steps for solving a given problem. Each paragraph consists of a heading entry and one or more sentences. The PROCEDURE division starts with the entry 'PROCEDURE DIVISION'. Then procedural statements begin with a *reserved verb*, which specifies actions to be taken, such as data movement, input-output, and arithmetic. The general format of a procedure division is as follows:

```
PROCEDURE DIVISION.

paragraph-name-1.
              processing steps
paragraph-name-2.
              processing steps
paragraph-name-n.
              processing steps
```

The most commonly used procedural statements (Figure 17 – 6) are explained under five headings:

IBM

COBOL Coding Form

SYSTEM	PUNCHING INSTRUCTIONS	PAGE OF
PROGRAM	GRAPHIC / CARD FORM # *	IDENTIFICATION 73–80
PROGRAMMER / DATE	PUNCH	

```
SEQUENCE    CONT. A   B                              COBOL STATEMENT
(PAGE)(SERIAL)
Ø5 01             PROCEDURE DIVISION.
   02             PARA-1.
   03                 OPEN INPUT FILE-1, OUTPUT FILE-2.
   04                 MOVE HEADING-1 TO PRINT-AREA.
   05                 WRITE PRINT-AREA BEFORE ADVANCING 1 LINES.
   06                 WRITE PRINT-AREA FROM SUB-HEADING AFTER ADVANCING 4 LINES.
   07             PARA-2.
   08                 READ FILE-1 AT END GO TO PARA 4.
   09                 MOVE SOC-SEC-NO TO SOC-SEC-NO-P.
   10                 MOVE EMPLOYEE-NAME TO EMPLOYEE-NAME-P.
   11                 MOVE HOURLY-RATE TO HOURLY-RATE-P.
   12                 MOVE HOURS-WORKED TO HOURS-WORKED-P.
   13             PARA-3.
   14                 COMPUTE WEEKLY-WAGE ROUNDED = HOURLY-RATE * HOURS-WORKED.
   15                 MOVE WEEKLY-WAGE TO WEEKLY-WAGE-P.
   16                 MOVE PRINT-LINE TO PRINT-AREA.
   17                 WRITE PRINT-AREA AFTER ADVANCING 2 LINES.
   18                 ADD WEEKLY-WAGE TO KOUNTER-W.
   19                 GO TO PARA-2.
   20             PARA-4.
   21                 MOVE 'TOTAL WEEKLY-WAGE' TO TOTAL-A.
   22                 MOVE KOUNTER-W TO TOTAL-B.
   23                 WRITE PRINT-AREA FROM HEADING-A AFTER ADVANCING 4 LINES.
   24             END-JOB.
   25                 CLOSE FILE-1, FILE-2.
   26                 STOP RUN.
```

*A standard card form, IBM Electro C61897, is available for punching source statements from this form.
Instructions for using this form are given in any IBM COBOL reference manual.
Address comments concerning this form to IBM Corporation, Programming Publications, 1271 Avenue of the Americas, New York, New York 10020.

Form No. X28-1464-4 U/M 025
Printed in U.S.A.

Figure 17–6. Procedure division.

1. *program comments,*

2. *input-output,*

3. *data movement,*

4. *arithmetic,* and

5. *sequence control.*

Program comments — remarks.   A remarks sentence allows the programmer to write explanatory remarks that will be produced on the compiler listing, but that will not be included in the object program. The remarks can be of any length and may include any words or characters. If a paragraph's first word is RE-MARKS, the entire paragraph is treated as remarks.

Input-output.   The input-output procedural statements allow the efficient processing of data into and out of the computer. Included in this group of statements are OPEN, CLOSE, READ, and WRITE.

Open. The OPEN statement conditions one or more data files for reading or writing. Although it does not retrieve or release the first data record for processing, it opens a file before any records can be read or written. For example:

```
OPEN INPUT FILE-1, OUTPUT FILE-2.
```

Close. The CLOSE statement is used to terminate the processing of input and output files that were opened; only a single file may appear in each CLOSE statement. For example:

```
CLOSE FILE-1, FILE-2.
```

Read. The READ statement makes the next logical file record available for processing and, in sequential files, causes specified action to be taken after the last file record has been processed. When the last record has been processed, control switches to the close file for further processing. For example:

```
READ FILE-1 AT END GO TO PARA-4.
```

Write. The WRITE statement releases a logical record to an opened output file. The *record name* must be the same as the one described in the file section of the data division. The use of the ADVANCING clause is optional. It allows manipulation of the vertical positioning of each printed line on the page. The *integer* part represents the number of lines the page is to be advanced. For example:

```
WRITE PRINT-AREA BEFORE ADVANCING 1 LINES.
WRITE PRINT-AREA FROM SUB-HEADING AFTER ADVANCING 4 LINES.
```

Data movement — move. A key operation in programming is transferring selected data from one area in computer storage to another. The MOVE statement executes such a transfer based on the data description established in the data division. The general format is:

```
MOVE    {Area-name-1}    TO Area-name-2
        {   (or)    }
        {  Literal  }
```

For example:

```
MOVE HEADING-1 TO PRINT-AREA
MOVE SOC-SEC-NO TO SOC-SEC-NO-P.
```

In using a MOVE statement, several points should be noted.

1. An alphabetic item must not be moved to a numeric item (as described in the PICTURE clause), or vice versa.

2. A numeric item whose decimal is not directly to the right of its low-order position cannot be moved to an alphanumeric item.

3. Data transferred from a sending area to a numeric receiving area are positioned according to the decimal point in the latter area, with excess characters truncated. If no decimal point is specified, the data received will be right-justified.

4. Data transferred from a sending area to a non-numeric receiving area will be left-justified and any excess characters truncated. If the data received is smaller than the size of the receiving area, any unused character positions are left as spaces instead of zeros.

Arithmetic. The five arithmetic statements presented in this section are ADD, COMPUTE, DIVIDE, MULTIPLY, and SUBTRACT. Although each statement has its own unique format and rules, the following rules are applicable to all of them:

1. Literals used in an arithmetic statement must be numeric.

453   *COBOL*

2. A data name used in an arithmetic statement must be numeric and defined in data division as an elementary data item.

3. A data item or a numeric literal must not exceed 18 digits in length.

Add. An ADD statement adds two or more numbers and stores the sum according to the following format:

| ADD | { Literal-1 (or) Data-name-1 } | { Literal-2 (or) Data-name-2 } . . . | TO (or) Data-name-n GIVING {rounded} |

Compute. A COMPUTE statement assigns to a data item the value of a numeric data item, literal, or arithmetic expression. For example,

ADD WEEKLY-WAGE to KOUNTER-W ROUNDED.

This is the same as the following statement, in which you should note the location of the word ROUNDED:

COMPUTE KOUNTER-W ROUNDED = KOUNTER-W + WEEKLY-WAGE

The SUBTRACT, MULTIPLY, and DIVIDE verbs function very similarly to ADD. The ROUNDED option is identical. The characters for subtraction, multiplication, and division are —, *, and / respectively.

Program instruction execution control. Control flows automatically from one statement to the next in the order in which they are written except when:

1. a GO TO statement causes the program to branch to a procedure in the program,

2. an IF statement causes the program control to skip over certain statements,

3. a PERFORM statement passes temporary control to another procedure, or

4. a STOP statement stops or terminates program execution.

These statements are explained next.

Go To. The GO TO statement causes the transfer of program control from one part of the procedure to another, either unconditionally or conditionally. The general format of the unconditional GO TO statement is

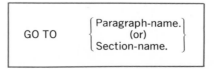

| GO TO | { Paragraph-name. (or) Section-name. } |

454

For example,

GO TO PARA-2.

directs the computer to branch unconditionally to the part of the procedure division, PARA-2. The general format of the conditional GO TO statement is:

GO TO procedure-name-1 Procedure-name-2 . . . Procedure-name-n DEPENDING on data-name.

For example:

GO TO ROUTINE-A, ROUTINE-B, ROUTINE-C, DEPENDING ON ROUTINE-CODE.

In executing this statement, the computer branches to ROUTINE-A, ROUTINE-B, or ROUTINE-C, depending on the current value of the ROUTINE-CODE (defined in the data division). If the ROUTINE-CODE contains integer value 1, the computer will branch to ROUTINE-A; if integer value 2, the computer will branch to ROUTINE-B; and if integer value 3, the computer will branch to ROUTINE-C. However, if the ROUTINE-CODE contains either a zero, a negative value, a value that is not an integer, or a value greater than the number of ROUTINES listed (that is, greater than 3), then the GO TO DEPENDING statement is ignored and the next sequential instruction is handled instead.

If. The IF statement evaluates the data and causes one or more statements to be executed if a certain condition exists. The reserved word IF is followed by a description of the data condition and the action to be taken if the data condition is true. Then the reserved word ELSE is written, followed by the action to be taken if the data condition is false. These groupings of words make up what is called a conditional statement. The general format is:

IF	Test-Condition	Statement-1	{ELSE}	Statement-2.
IF	TEST	TRUE ACTION		FALSE ACTION

In this general format, *statement-1* and *statement-2* represent one or more imperative statements. Any number of statements may follow the test condition. If the test condition is true, the statements following it (represented by statement-1 in the general format) are executed. However, if the test condition is false, the next sequential statement in the program is executed; or, if an ELSE clause is included, the statement following ELSE is executed. For example:

IF SOC-SEC-NO = 0 ADD 0 TO KOUNTER-W ELSE ADD 1 TO KOUNTER-W.

A *test-condition* may specify a relation condition, class condition, sign condition, or overflow condition. Only the first two conditions need be explained now; the last two explained later.

The test condition can be a relational or a class test. In a *relational test,* one data item is compared with another data item (each of which may be a data name or a literal) and some action is indicated based on the relation that exists. One data item is called the *subject operand* and the other the *object operand.* The general format is:

$$
\left\{ \begin{array}{c} \text{Data-name-1} \\ \text{(or)} \\ \text{Literal} \end{array} \right\} \quad \text{Relational operator} \quad \left\{ \begin{array}{c} \text{Data-name-2} \\ \text{(or)} \\ \text{Literal} \end{array} \right\}
$$

The *relational operator* (preceded and followed by a space) specifies the type of comparison to be made. It may be one of the following:

> IS EQUAL TO (or =)
> IS GREATER THAN (or >)
> IS LESS THAN (or <)
> IS NOT EQUAL TO
> IS NOT GREATER THAN
> IS NOT LESS THAN

A *class test* determines whether the contents of one operand are *all* numeric (characters 0 to 9) or *all* alphabetic (A to Z, space). The use of this test can be helpful in verifying incoming data. The general format is:

$$
\text{IF data-name} \quad \left\{ \begin{array}{c} \text{IS} \\ \text{(or)} \\ \text{IS NOT} \end{array} \right\} \quad \left\{ \begin{array}{c} \text{NUMERIC} \\ \text{(or)} \\ \text{ALPHABETIC} \end{array} \right\}
$$

Perform. The PERFORM statement is similar to a subroutine in that it causes a branch to one or more procedures in the program and, following their execution, returns control to the statement after the PERFORM statement. The general format is:

> PERFORM   Procedure-name-1 [THRU procedure-name-2]

For example:

> PERFORM PARA-3

Stop. The STOP statement causes either a temporary or a permanent halt in the execution of the object program. The general format is:

```
            ⎧ Literal ⎫
STOP        ⎨   or    ⎬
            ⎩  RUN    ⎭
```

If the RUN option is used, execution of the program is permanently halted. If the literal option is used, the literal is communicated to the operator and a temporary halt occurs. Continuation begins with the execution of the next sequential statement. Examples are:

```
STOP RUN.
STOP 'ERROR'.
```

SUMMARY

1. Cobol is a business-oriented language that allows instructions to be constructed in paragraph- and sentence-like form, using English words encountered in business situations. Cobol language makes use of symbols, reserved words, level numbers, programmer-defined words, literals, and pictures. *Symbols* represent a special meaning to the compiler. There are condition (e.g., $=$, $<$, $>$), arithmetic (e.g., $+$, $-$, $/$), and punctuation (e.g., ., ;) symbols.

2. A *reserved word* has a particular meaning and is used by the programmer for a specific purpose. *Level numbers* are used to indicate the level of various data items in relation to others in the program. *Programmer-defined* words or data names are supplied by the programmer to represent data items or procedures involved in the problem. They may contain alphabetic or numeric characters as well as hyphens. Hyphens may be anywhere in the name but not at the beginning or end of it.

3. A *literal* is a value defined by the programmer. It may be numeric or non-numeric. A numeric literal is a string of characters (0 to 9); a decimal point is allowed anywhere except in the right-most position. A non-numeric literal is a string of up to 120 characters enclosed by single quotation marks.

4. A *picture* is a string of special alphabetic, numeric, or alphanumeric characters that gives certain characteristics of data items. Each picture entry must be preceded by the word PICTURE.

5. A Cobol program is a structured hierarchy arranged in division, sections, paragraphs, and entries. A division is made up of paragraphs, and a para-

graph is made of up of entries. The four main divisions are identification, environment, data, and procedure. Each division is entered on a separate line in the coding sheet and is identified by a division header, which consists of the name of the division and the word DIVISION, followed by a period.

6. The *identification division* provides information for identifying the program (such as the program name, date, and name of the programmer). The *environment division* provides information about the computer to be used in computing and executing the object program and, using problem-oriented names, assigns data files to input-output devices. The *data division* describes the data files and records the items in working storage. The *procedure division,* consisting of one or more paragraphs, is programmer-defined; each paragraph consists of a heading entry and one or more sentences. Each sentence, in turn, may be one or more statements constructed within the constraints of a pre-established format.

7. Input-output procedural statements allow the processing of data into and out of the computer. Among the more commonly used are the OPEN, CLOSE, READ, and WRITE statements. Arithmetic, compute, and move statements are also used in handling the details of a program. Program control flows automatically from one statement to another, except in situations requiring special attention, which involve the use of GO TO, IF, PERFORM, or STOP statements. These and other statements perform a vital role in effective processing of business problems in Cobol.

TERMS TO LEARN

COBOL
Data division
Environment division
Identification division
Literal

Picture
Procedure division
Program-defined word
Relational test
Reserved word

QUESTIONS

1. Explain the general purpose of Cobol.

2. List and describe Cobol's primary language elements.

3. What types of symbols are used in Cobol programming? Illustrate.

4. Define and give an example of each of the following terms, a. reserved word; b. level number; c. data name; d. literal; and e. picture.

5. Describe briefly the primary structure of a Cobol program.

6. List and explain Cobol's required divisions.

7. Briefly explain the primary entries and sections of the environment division.

8. What is the primary function(s) of the data division? Distinguish between its file section and working-storage section.

9. Describe and illustrate the use(s) of each of the following:
   a. FILLER;
   b. picture clause;
   c. usage clause;
   d. note sentence;
   e. OPEN;
   f. WRITE;
   g. MOVE;
   h. COMPUTE;
   i. GO TO;
   j. IF;
   k. PERFORM.

10. Flowchart and code a program to compare A to B. If A is greater than B, the program is to go to ALPHA-1. Otherwise, it should go to ALPHA-2.

11. Flowchart and code a program based on the following information:
    IF A is greater than B and A is greater than C, THEN add B to C and go to ALPHA-1.
    IF B is greater than A and B is greater than C, THEN add A to C and go to Alpha-2.
    IF B is greater than A but less than C, THEN subtract A from B and go to ALPHA-1.

12. Simplify the following statement:
    IF A > 10 and if A < 14, subtract A − X. If A < 10 and if A > 14, go to WORK-ROUTINE.

part five

Management Considerations of the Computer

chapter 18

Acquisition of Computer Resources

Learning Objectives

To operate an effective computer operation, a business must acquire computer resources from a reliable source in the computer industry. A basic understanding of the makeup of the industry and of the evaluation process in computer acquisitions is essential background for successful computer installations. By the end of this chapter, you should know:

1. the makeup of the computer industry,
2. the criteria for evaluating computer acquisitions,
3. financial considerations in computer acquisitions, and
4. the cost of computer resources.

The Computer-Based Environment

The Computer Industry

Hardware Suppliers
Software Suppliers
Computer Service Suppliers

Evaluating Computer Acquisitions

Current System Performance Evaluation

Hardware/Software Monitors
Job Accounting
System Tuning
Revisions in System Software

Hardware/Software Evaluation

Benchmark Programs
Experience of Other Users
Product Reference Manuals

Proposal Evaluation

The "Ad Hoc" Approach
The Scoring Approach
The Cost-Value Approach

New System Performance Evaluation

The Role of the Outside Consultant

Financial Considerations in Computer Acquisition

The Rental Contract
The Lease Contract

Categories of Lease Contracts

The Purchase Contract
The Present Value Method

The Cost of Computer Resources

System Design and Implementation Costs
Operating Costs
Administrative Costs

The Implementation Phase of Computer Selection

To operate a computer system effectively, a business must acquire computer resources from a reliable source in the computer industry. Furthermore, a formal commitment to computerization often requires a study of the company's present needs and future requirements. This chapter therefore provides a basic understanding of how computer users should evaluate the acquisition of computer resources by looking into:

1. the makeup of the computer industry,

2. the evaluation of computer acquisitions,

3. the costs of computer resources, and

4. the steps of a feasibility study.

The Computer-Based Environment

The role of the computer industry in the American economy is highly significant. In 1980, the United States had a computer population well over 300,000 and total computer expenditure close to $100 billion. The industry represented approximately 6 percent of the gross national product and employed over 3 million people in computer-related jobs.

The ever increasing dependence by business (and, in fact, society) on computers means an ever increasing risk when computers break down. In 1965, for example, computer failure of one or more weeks meant reverting to the manual replacement system until the computer was "up" again. In 1980, an equivalent failure would cause chaos in an organization, not to mention potentially significant delays in the delivery of essential operational services. Quite likely, a computer failure in 1990 could force a cessation of business until the computer is restarted. This heavy reliance by businesses on computerization serves to point out the increasing importance of a viable relationship between the user of computer goods or services and the vendor.

The Computer Industry

Computer operations of a business takes place in a computer-based environment. An established computer services department participates in an industry that today consists of over 2,000 vendors who provide a wide range of computer goods and services to business and government. Table 18 – 1 lists some of the major firms in the computer industry. They are classified into three major groups:

1. hardware suppliers,

2. software suppliers, and

3. computer service suppliers.

Table 18–1. Major computer firms.

Computer systems

AMDAHL CORP
BURROUGHS CORP
COMPUTER AUTOMATION
CONTROL DATA CORP
CRAY RESEARCH INC
DATA GENERAL CORP
DATAPOINT CORP
DIGITAL EQUIPMENT
ELECTRONIC ASSOC.
ELECTRONIC ENGINEER.
FOUR-PHASE SYSTEMS
FOXBORO
GENERAL AUTOMATION
GRI COMPUTER CORP
HEWLETT-PACKARD CO
HONEYWELL INC
IBM
MANAGEMENT ASSIST
MANUFACTURING DATA S
MICRODATA CORP
MINI-COMPUTER SYST
MODULAR COMPUTER SYS
NCR
PRIME COMPUTER INC
PERKIN-ELMER
SPERRY RAND
SYSTEMS ENG. LABS
TANDEM COMPUTERS INC
WANG LABS.

Leasing companies

BOOTHE COURIER CORP
COMDISCO INC
COMMERCE GROUP CORP
COMPUTER INVSTRS GRP
CONTINENTAL INFO SYS
DATRONIC RENTAL
DCL INC
DPF INC
ITEL
LEASCO CORP
LEASPAC CORP
PIONEER TEX CORP
U.S. LEASING

Software and EDP services

ADVANCED COMP TECH
ANACOMP INC
APPLIED DATA RES.
AUTOMATIC DATA PROC

COLEMAN AMERICAN COS
COMPU-SERV NETWORK
COMPUTER HORIZONS
COMPUTER NETWORK
COMPUTER SCIENCES
COMPUTER TASK GROUP
COMPUTER USAGE
COMPUT AUTO REP SVC
COMSHARE
CULLINANE CORP
DATA DIMENSIONS INC
DATATAB
ELECTRONIC DATA SYS.
INSYTE CORP
IPS COMPUTER MARKET.
KEANE ASSOCIATES
KEYDATA CORP
LOGICON
NATIONAL CSS INC
NATIONAL DATA CORP
ON LINE SYSTEMS INC
PLANNING RESEARCH
PROGRAMMING & SYS
RAPIDATA INC
REYNOLDS & REYNOLD
SCIENTIFIC COMPUTERS
TYMSHARE INC
URS SYSTEMS
WYLY CORP

Peripherals and subsystems

ADDRESSOGRAPH-MULT
ADVANCED MEMORY SYS
AMPEX CORP
ANDERSON JACOBSON
APPLIED DIG DATA SYS
BEEHIVE INT'L
BOLT, BERANEK & NEW
BUNKER-RAMO
CALCOMP
CAMBRIDGE MEMORIES
CENTRONICS DATA COMP
COGNITRONICS
COMPUTER COMMUN.
COMPUTER CONSOLES
COMPUTER EQUIPMENT
COMPUTER TRANSCEIVER
COMPUTERVISION CORP
COMTEN
CONRAC CORP
DATA ACCESS SYSTEMS
DATA 100

DATA PRODUCTS CORP
DATUM INC
DECISION DATA COMPUT
DELTA DATA SYSTEMS
DOCUMATION INC
DATARAM CORP
ELECTRONIC M & M
FABRI-TEK
GENERAL COMPUTER SYS
GENERAL DATACOMM IND
HAZELTINE CORP
HARRIS CORP
INFOREX INC
INFORMATION INTL INC
INFOTON
INTEL CORP
LUNDY ELECTRONICS
MSI DATA CORP
MEMOREX
MOHAWK DATA SCI
OMEX
PARADYNE CORP
PENRIL CORP
PERTEC CORP
POTTER INSTRUMENT
QUANTOR CORP
RECOGNITION EQUIP
SCAN DATA
STORAGE TECHNOLOGY
T BAR INC
TALLY CORP.
TEC INC
TEKTRONIX INC
TELEX
TESDATA SYSTEMS CP
WILTEK INC

Supplies and accessories

AMERICAN BUS PRODS
BALTIMORE BUS FORMS
BARRY WRIGHT
CYBERMATICS INC
DUPLEX PRODUCTS INC
ENNIS BUS. FORMS
3M COMPANY
MOORE CORP LTD
NASHUA CORP
STANDARD REGISTER
TAB PRODUCTS CO
UARCO
WABASH MAGNETICS
WALLACE BUS FORMS

Hardware suppliers. The primary manufacturers of computer hardware are the computer manufacturers, peripheral manufacturers, supplies vendors, computer leasing companies, and used equipment vendors. According to sales volume, seven manufacturers of hardware lead the others with over $100 million of annual computer sales. Dominating sales is IBM, which approximates 70 percent of the total hardware market. The leading vendors are:

1. IBM,

2. Burroughs,

3. NCR,

4. Sperry Rand,

5. Honeywell,

6. Digital Equipment, and

7. Control Data Corporation.

Secondary computer manufacturers, with under $100 million, include companies such as Computer Automation, Data General, Interdata, Varian Data Machines, and Amdahl Corporation.

Peripheral manufacturers supply components used in conjunction with computers. Examples of peripherals are tape drives, disc drives, printers, card readers, and specialized equipment from companies such as Ampex and Memorex.

Supplies vendors provide both consumable and nonconsumable supplies. *Nonconsumable supplies* include such items as disc packs, tape reels, printer ribbons, tape library shelves, and fireproof vaults. *Consumable supplies* refer to items such as cards, paper tape, and printer forms. Hundreds of independent vendors are available in this field.

User companies do not always have to purchase a computer or computer components from the original manufacturer. Used computer companies purchase second-hand equipment from computer users and sell them at a substantial discount. Also, computer **leasing** companies generally finance the acquisition of equipment and of software; and they may also be used to underwrite or to insure the development of a computer system. Typically, they purchase specific computers desired by a user and then lease it to the user for a long period, usually five years. Leasing arrangements usually include maintenance, a purchase option, and a reduction in lease charges after a minimum time period.

Software suppliers. During the past decade, computer users have a choice of buying their programs from the computer manufacturer or from independent software suppliers for virtually every application imaginable. Although the manufacturers themselves are the largest source of software operating systems and service programs, most "bread and butter" applications—such as payroll, accounts receivables, and the like—are available through software houses at a fraction of the cost of developing them from scratch. In most cases, only minor modifications are required for the program to run properly. Other computer users occasionally develop unique application programs that can be utilized by other computer users. Although very few packages are suitable to different users, they may be purchased or leased for a reasonable fee.

Computer service suppliers.   External services are widely used by small firms or users with first-hand exposure to computer processing. Of the several sources of computer *service suppliers* (also called **servicers**), the major ones are:

1. *Computer manufacturers* supply a variety of services such as systems design, contract programming, specialized consulting, computer-based education and training, and hardware maintenance.

2. *Service bureaus* process jobs of users whose firms are too small to have their own computer systems. Larger firms often contract service bureaus for specialized applications or during peak volume periods. The primary services supplied include contract programming, data conversion service, remote batch processing, system conversion, system design, and training.

3. *Time-sharing servicers* provide on-line, real-time service to subscribers using remote terminals linked to a central processing system. The service makes it possible for firms to use the large computer system of the servicer without the commitment of acquiring one of this size.

4. *Facilities management (FM)* provides for the establishment of a data processing staff to operate, develop, and maintain computer systems, on the customer's premises, using the customer's equipment. In some cases, the service may consist of the development of application programs for customers on a computer. The customer operates his or her own system but calls on the service organization for development and maintenance only.

External services, such as facilities management and "canned" applications firms, have two major benefits. First, the customer generally pays only for the services needed. Second, they eliminate the personnel problems for the user organization caused by the employment of analysts and programmers in a rapidly changing and competitive field. Among the drawbacks, however, are:

1. loss of control over the EDP operation,

2. vulnerability and unauthorized access to company information, and

3. higher costs of service compared to a company-run operation.

Evaluating Computer Acquisitions

Gone are the days when a user could call IBM to order a gray 360 system. Today, selecting the proper system from the variety of alternatives and features is a serious and time-consuming task. Evaluating and acquiring a computer system therefore deserve serious consideration, in the light of such considerations as its impact on the organization, the complexity of the technology, and the variety of available alternatives. A mistake could cost millions of dollars in rental fees or in wasted system development time. Two major alternatives in selecting a computer are:

1. a computer maker, other than IBM, who has established a good reputation in terms of product quality and service reliability, or

2. the used computer market where computers of all sizes and brands are sold at heavily discounted prices. Because of the high dollar value of these systems, savings can run from $200,000 to $600,000 when compared with the vendor's retail price.

Computer evaluation and selection begins with a set of systems specifications defined during systems design. Minimum acceptable standards of performance for hardware and software must also be established as a basis for evaluating the bids to be received from the vendors. In deciding on a vendor, several selection criteria are considered. The influence of each of the following factors becomes evident as the buyer approaches the final phase of the selection decision. The most important criteria (ranked in their order of importance) are:

1. quality of service,

2. price/performance advantage (estimates of total run time versus costs),

3. overall reputation of the supplier,

4. software availability,

5. existing relationship to vendor,

6. delivery availability,

7. ease of installation, and

8. terms and conditions.

Current System Performance Evaluation

Before a new system is even considered, however, the performance of the current computer system should be thoroughly evaluated. Until all the facts are available to justify the need for an alternative system, top management cannot be assured that the new computer system is really necessary.

Several techniques are available for evaluating the performance of an existing computer system. These techniques are fostered by the increasing complexity of today's computer with its multiprogramming/multiprocessing, real-time, time-sharing, and other complex functions. Their key purpose is to enable the analyst to take a close look at the performance level and potential of the present system before deciding on acquisition. Trained analysts can often improve performance simply by identifying overloaded or underloaded components or by locating bottlenecks in the system. They use such techniques as:

1. hardware/software monitors,

2. job accounting,

3. system tuning, and

4. revisions in system software.

Hardware/software monitors.   A **hardware monitor** is a signal recording device attached to specific points in the computer circuitry to determine when the CPU is in a wait state, a problem state, or a supervisor state. It also counts instructions executed in computer systems such as IBM's system 370. The monitor has proved useful in many installations in determining overall system performance. Its most attractive feature is the ability to obtain accurate, detailed data without affecting the performance of the host computer.

In contrast to hardware monitors, **software monitors** are designed to check other programs as they are executed. They interrupt the system's software at periodic intervals and determine hardware usage, supervisory routines, and other programs. The primary drawback is the additional load they place on the system—sometimes as much as 20 percent on CPU activity.

Job accounting.   A unique form of self-monitoring software, called **job accounting software,** is designed to gather data on the start and finish times of each program, as well as on the amount of memory and CPU time used. Its objective is to reduce bottlenecks by making changes in the scheduling of programs that are run concurrently in a multiprogramming environment.

System tuning.   A typical problem in multiprogramming is *input-output contention* (thrashing), where several programs make concurrent requests to the same I/O device (disc, drum, and the like). The device then ties down the system by responding to all requests. The function of system tuning is to balance the use of the computer resources (CPU time, channel time, and file usage), so that the overall concurrent requirements do not cause system bottlenecks. System tuning can also be achieved by reducing the number of programs loaded or by trying a more responsive storage device (such as a drum rather than a disc).

Revisions in system software.   Revisions or changes in system software often result in major savings. The software market abounds in up-to-date supervisory control programs, utility routines, and other special-purpose packages, many of which reduce the execution time required by most application programs. Many standard software programs are offered free of charge by the hardware vendor. Exercise care, however, in weighing the efficiency of the vendor software against that of software specialists. The net benefit could easily justify the rental cost of the software specialist.

Hardware/Software Evaluation

Several sources of information are used in evaluating computer hardware and software. The basic sources include:

1. benchmark programs,
2. experience of other users, and
3. product reference manuals.

Benchmark programs.   A **benchmark program** is a representative application program run on the vendor's computer system. The program should be typical of the processing done on the system and also capable of testing the capabilities of the hardware/software to be used most frequently. Benchmark testing times the computer run of the application. The outcomes of comparative testing and resultant costs help in determining the proper vendor for the order.

Experience of other users.   Since benchmarks only help validate the claims in a vendor's marketing literature, other sources of information are necessary. Another source is the experience of other users with the same system, software, and service. Vendors are generally happy to provide a list of "reference accounts" and people to check with. Experience shows that the people on such a list happen to be the most satisfied customers who do not necessarily represent other users. Yet seeking objective users on your own can be a most frustrating effort. Even if the "ideal" user is found, the information is useful only if the user's system resembles your own in terms of hardware configuration, applications, and the size of the EDP staff. Major deviations in these elements distort the usefulness of the information received.

Product reference manuals.   Another source of information is the vendor's product reference manuals. A good policy is to read the product reference manuals that evaluate the features and capabilities of all computer systems. Since studying such manuals is often laborious and tedious work, one alternative is to seek the services of organizations that specialize in computers and their applications. They also publish unbiased information based on ongoing research and system testing in various sites. For example, Auerbach, Inc. (Philadelphia, Pennsylvania) publishes loose-leaf references in information processing, telecommunications, and computer graphics. The reports elaborate on computer products and often include price information. Considering the benefits of such information, the costs are relatively low.

Proposal Evaluation

Upon receipt of bids from all vendors, each bid should be reviewed to ensure not only that all information is valid and reliable, but also that it meets the requirements submitted initially by the user. The technical content of the bid should be summarized for comparative evaluation. Proposals that don't meet the mandatory requirements should be rejected. Although the proposals received are considered final, the vendor may be allowed to provide missing information or major omissions to meet the requirements of the user.

After all proposals have been validated, the selection of the final vendor is determined by one of three methods:

1. the "ad hoc" approach,

2. the scoring approach, and

3. the cost-value approach.

The "ad hoc" approach. This method refers to the user's inclination to favor one vendor over others. A change of mind is made only if overwhelming evidence supports another vendor. This "halo" effect often makes bidding on a project difficult for other vendors, if the user is known to favor a particular vendor at the outset.

The scoring approach. In a *scoring system,* the characteristics of each computer system are itemized and given a score in relation to a maximum point rating, such as 25. Then each proposal is rated according to the characteristics specified. Table 18–2 rates three proposals according to uniform computer and vendor evaluating factors. Proposal B has the most points for the total performance score. All other factors being equal, it should be the user's first choice.

Table 18–2. A sample scoring approach to computer acquisition.

	Proposals		
	A	B	C
C P U:			
Addressing	6	12	7
Arithmetic	3	4	1
Communication capability	23	19	14
Environmental requirements	1	5	4
Input/output capability	4	9	2
Main memory capacity	11	13	9
Multiprogramming capability	3	9	2
Physical size	6	7	4
Secondary storage capacity	16	21	11
Word size	19	20	14
Subtotal	92	119	68

Table 18–2. (cont.)

	Proposals		
	A	B	C
Vendor:			
Delivery time	9	5	12
Maintenance charges	18	19	21
Number installed	2	11	9
Past performance	6	9	8
Quality of service	6	9	5
Training	5	8	7
Subtotal	46	61	62
Total (performance score)	138	180	130

The cost-value approach. With this technique, often used as the main criterion for vendor selection, a dollar credit amount is applied to the proposal that best meets the user's desirable characteristics. This credit is subtracted from the vendor's quoted price. The proposal with the lowest price is the one selected.

To illustrate the cost-value approach, assume that, in a given application, the manufacturer's response for repair is a key criterion. The cost value of a quick response for repair is determined by estimating the cost of hiring additional help to do the required work manually while the system is waiting for service. This amount depends on how quickly the vendor responds to the request for service: Let's say one day of downtime means an expenditure of $1,000. A day and a half of downtime would be $1,500, and three breakdowns in a year would total $4,500. Any savings through quick response and repair time is thus a credit for the vendor. After evaluating all desirable factors and assigning the appropriate credits (or penalties), the total cost of each system is computed. The system with the lowest cost is the one selected.

New System Performance Evaluation

A system is only as good as its weakest link. Evaluating a proposed computer system entails consideration not only of the individual hardware and software components but also of the system as a whole. Hardware acquisitions require an analysis of several categories of performance, of which the major ones are:

1. *System availability.* When will the new system be available?

2. *Compatibility.* To what extent is the system compatible with existing hardware and programs?

3. *Cost.* What is the cost (lease or purchase) of the system? What about maintenance and operation costs?

4. *Performance.* What is the capacity and throughput of the system?

5. *Availability.* What is the "uptime" record of the system? How frequently is maintenance required?

6. *Support.* How competent and adequate is the vendor's technical staff for supporting the system?

7. *Usability.* How easy is it to operate, program, and modify the system?

Software evaluation factors are similar to those used for evaluating hardware and include the following:

1. the nature of the programming language and its suitability to the applications,

2. the ease with which the system software can be applied,

3. the availability of control programs in the new system, since they can save a lot of time in writing an additional program, and

4. the extent to which the system software can handle its data processing assignment without major modifications or "patching."

Given adequate hardware and software, the quality of the vendor's services should next be evaluated. While some services are offered free of charge, others have to be contracted. The major vendor support services are:

1. *Backup.* What emergency computer backup is available from the vendor?

2. *Conversion.* What programming and installation service does the vendor provide during conversion?

3. *Hardware/software.* How adequate is the selection list of compatible hardware and software?

4. *Maintenance.* How good and reasonable is equipment maintenance? How quickly does the vendor respond to a request for service?

5. *System Development.* Are analysts and programmers available for system development? How competent are they? What fees are charged?

The role of the outside consultant. A user may seek the services of an independent computer consultant for a final decision on computer selection. The user must understand, however, that the consultant's services are not synonymous with a sound computer acquisition. Satisfaction occurs only through proper participation by both the consultant and the user. A competent consultant can perform the following tasks:

1. evaluate current operations,

2. design and plan the implementation of the computer site,

3. select new equipment and convert the system to the new equipment and software,

4. train user personnel in the operation of the new system, and

5. manage the entire installation.

A vendor's representative also offers current and useful technical information on computer systems and peripherals. The "rep" is usually versed in the capabilities of each system and in the applications it can process. However, the representative is sales-oriented. Consequently, heavy reliance on his or her recommendations can obviously bias the buyer in favor of the rep's computer system. For the serious user, established vendors provide support staff, including systems analysts, to help the user make a final choice.

In addition to vendor representatives and computer consultants, the user may seek the advice CPA (certified public accountant) firms. Many CPA firms, including the larger ones, specialize in computer feasibility studies and computer acquisitions. Their combined experience in accounting and computer systems can prove invaluable to the user, especially in cost analysis. If the company conducting the computer acquisition study is already a client of the CPA firm, the firm's computer specialist could very well be the consultant to hire. Smaller firms usually acquire independent consultants for the same purpose.

Financial Considerations in Computer Acquisition

Deciding to acquire a computer system may be relatively easier than deciding on *how* to acquire it. In other words, should the system be rented, leased, or purchased? Computer manufacturers offer all three methods of financing, although the peripheral vendors usually offer only purchase or lease arrangements.

The Rental Contract

Under a rental arrangement, the user agrees to a minimum payment. The contract can be terminated without penalty by a minimum 90-day advance notice. Rental charges are based on a 176 usage hours (8 hours per day $\times$ 22 working days) per month. Added usage means higher total charges per month. Computer users favor renting a system for several reasons:

1. Expenses such as insurance and maintenance are included in the rental price.

2. The company maintains *financial leverage* due to the relatively short time commitment under the rental contract. The renting firm makes no investment in the equipment, so the user's money can be invested in other projects. Furthermore, rental charges can be deducted as an expense against the user's gross income.

3. Renting a computer provides *flexibility* in changing to better systems, thus reducing the risk of technological obsolescence, since the user has no commitment to purchase the rented equipment.

The primary drawback of a rental contract is the higher total cost incurred if the user rents the system for more than four years and for more than 176 hours per month. In such a case, purchasing the system would be more cost-effective than renting it.

The Lease Contract

In the computer industry, a **lease** contract is available indirectly through a "third party" or directly from the computer vendor. The third party purchases the equipment from the manufacturer and leases it to the user. Lease terms range from 6 months with month-to-month renewals to seven years. The lease terms can be flexible, depending on the risk to the lessor (the third party). Longer-running leases carry more favorable terms, but they also entail a higher risk of being "strapped" with a system for the duration of the contract. With a short-term lease, the user's risk is low, because the system can be replaced, removed, or upgraded. The cost for this low risk, however, is higher short-term lease payments.

In general, leasing offers several advantages:

1. Leasing does not require financing, and it is less expensive than renting the system for the same time period.

2. Lease charges are fully deductible.

3. The risk of equipment obsolescence is shifted to the lessor under the lease contract.

4. Lease charges decline after a minimum period and include maintenance and overtime usage.

The primary drawbacks of leasing are:

1. In the absence of a purchase option, the lessee (user) loses residual rights to the system upon the termination of the lease.

2. Lease charges are generally higher than the purchase price of the system. Since the lessor borrows funds for purchasing the equipment to be leased, the rent is based on the debt factor and a profit margin.

3. The long period of the lease cannot be terminated without payment of a heavy penalty.

4. In the absence of an upgrade clause, the user may not be able to sell or exchange the leased system for a newer or better model. Furthermore, if

interest rates decrease, the user continues to pay lease charges at the former rate. If the system is purchased, he could refinance the debt at a lower rate.

5. Unlike a purchased system, a leased system does not provide for the user tax benefits from accelerated depreciation and interest deductions in the early years of usage. Thus there are no cash savings in a lease arrangement.

Categories of lease contracts. Lease contracts may be financial or operating leases. In the *financial lease,* the lessee (user) has the right to purchase and assumes the risks normally assumed by the purchaser. The legal title, however, remains with the lessor. At the termination of the lease contract, the lessor still owns the equipment, although the lessee has the option to purchase. The *operating lease,* on the other hand, has the characteristics of rental contract, differing only in the length of the commitment (2 – 10 years). Monthly payments average around 25 percent less than the manufacturer's rental price.

The Purchase Contract

Purchasing a computer system outright has both benefits and drawbacks. Under a purchase contract, the users assume all the risks of ownership including taxes, insurance, and technological obsolescence. However, they obtain all the services and support that are available under the lease or rental agreement. Comparing purchase with renting or leasing, the primary benefits of purchasing are:

1. flexibility of modifying the system at will,

2. usually much lower continuing cash outlays than those for a leased system, due to the cash savings from depreciation and investment tax credit, and

3. usually a lower total cash outflow if the user kept the system for over 5 years.

Among the drawbacks of purchasing are as follows:

1. The initial cost of purchasing a system is high in relation to the initial cost of leasing. The user has to pay for the system in full upon delivery.

2. Insurance coverage and various taxes are assumed by the user. A service contract must also be taken on the system at the expiration of the vendor's warranty.

3. The overall risk is high. If the system turns out to be ill-suited for the user's needs or obsolete, the user is stuck with it. Selling a used computer can be a real headache.

The Present Value Method

One way to decide whether to rent, lease, or purchase a computer is by the **present value method,** which converts future cash flows into present values depending on the interest rates. In general, the present dollar value of a system is not accurately reflected in its absolute purchase price. The money laid out for a purchase may be better utilized to earn interest in other investments. So the *actual* present value of the system's cost is rarely what the bottom line states. For example, Figure 18–1 presents a hypothetical present value cost for varying discount rates under different contractual conditions. Assuming an 8-year commitment at a 10-percent discount rate, trace the 10-percent discount rate line vertically. A financial lease has a present value of $600,000; an operating lease, $630,000; and purchase, $730,000. At higher rates of interest, lease arrangements seem to be more economical, while at lower rates, purchasing the system is preferred.

Figure 18–1. Comparison of types of contracts.

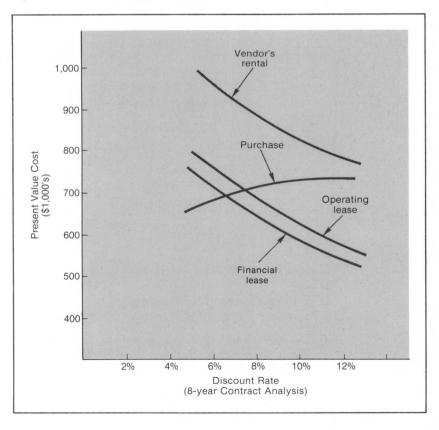

Computer acquisition involves a substantial expenditure in different ways. A recent study of budget allocations to electronic data processing in 1980 is summarized in Table 18–3. Hardware costs are only a part of total EDP costs. Today's trend shows that the costs of personnel are steadily increasing and that the costs of equipment are decreasing. The classic way to assess the cost of computer resources is to break it down into three general areas of importance:

1. systems design and implementation,
2. operating, and
3. administrative costs.

Systems Design and Implementation Costs

Systems design and implementation costs include the salaries of the systems analysts, of the programmers, and of the staff in charge of designing, testing, and implementing the computer system. Other costs incurred in preparing the computer facility for the new operation are:

1. testing the system,
2. training the user's staff in the operation of the new system,
3. the cost of file and form conversion,
4. the cost of new furnishings for the center,
5. the cost of air conditioning, false flooring, and emergency equipment, and
6. the cost of money borrowed for system implementation and initial supplies.

Operating Costs

Rental or lease charges, the salaries of operations personnel and of maintenance programmers, the cost of software and supplies are all *operating* costs. Other costs include maintenance of the computer center and the salaries of the security staff.

Administrative Costs

All costs incurred in the supervision, management, or clerical services of the center are included under administrative costs. The major costs are the salaries of the manager of the computer center, managers of various EDP departments, and secretarial staff.

In summary, the true benefit of a computer system is based on the user's ability to use it in a way that produces optimum information for decision making. The benefits are commensurate with the organization's commitment to computer processing, with the attitude of top management to the use of computer-based information, and with the availability of talented personnel to operate and manage the computer facility. The proper selection of a computer system from the right vendor is certainly an important step toward effective computerized operation.

The Implementation Phase of Computer Selection

When top management approves the acquisition of the recommended computer system, some time elapses before it is actually installed — between 3 months and 2 years, depending on the complexity of the system. Once the choice has been made, an order is placed with the computer vendor. The order lists in detail the hardware and supportive software the firm needs. Upon receipt of the order, the vendor sets tentative delivery and installation dates. Meanwhile, the user takes several preparatory preinstallation steps. As outlined in Figure 18–2, the primary steps are as follows:

1. *Planning the computer facility.* A management committee plans the makeup of the new facility and the hiring of a manager and staff.

2. *Hiring a data processing manager.* A manager is hired to coordinate the procedural plans for the facility with the committee. Given experience and authority, he or she begins to recruit new talent or to train qualified company employees for console operation, programming, and other required jobs. Meanwhile, he or she supervises the preparation of the new quarters for the installation. This involves extending utility lines, installing air-conditioning, and purchasing furniture and other necessary items.

3. *System design.* This phase can be quite critical. System analysts and other specialists lay out the system's requirements, implement the preparation of software, and write, test, and document the necessary programs. The vendor also arranges for the company's programmers to have access to a compatible system for test runs.

Execution of the foregoing steps requires careful planning and timing. During this phase, outside consultants become extremely helpful. Not only can they implement the conversion phase, but they can also employ temporary help in programming, systems design, and file conversion. Often, outside short-term help remains with the facility on a fulltime basis. Several aspects of implementation must be considered:

1. *Standards* relate to developing a scale by which the performance of the new system can be evaluated for efficiency and economical operation.

2. *Systems analysis and design* involve gathering and recording data related to required reports and developing procedures for the operation of the

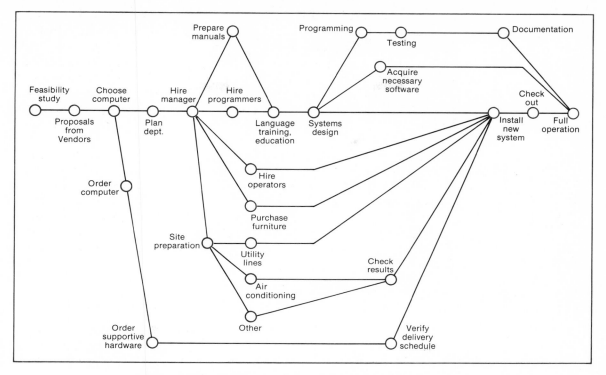

Figure 18–2. Critical path schematic of installation of a computer system.

new system. Once completed, the design phase establishes input-output and general operating routines for each user department.

3. *Programming* converts systems design into machine-readable instructions for computer processing.

4. *Testing* each component is necessary before it is integrated into the overall system. Programs are also checked out for errors before they are released for future processing.

5. *Documentation* relates to a detailed description of each program so that it can be modified in the future, if necessary. The documentation is presented in a special manual that also includes copies of flowcharts and related information. Examples of manuals are operators' manuals, which explain the operation of the computer system, and systems manuals, which lay out the functions, procedures, and input-output details of the system.

6. *Training of operators* in the procedures required for proper handling of various devices of the system includes handling input data, loading the program, and setting up and controlling the system in general.

Table 18-3. A typical allocation for EDP, broken down by category.

	Percent	
EDP Personnel:		
Programmer/analyst	28	
Others	16	
Subtotal		44
Hardware:		
CPUs	15	
Peripherals	12	
Minicomputer	3	
Terminals	5	
Subtotal		35
Outside Services:		
Processing	1	
Software	3	
Education	2	
Maintenance	3	
Communications	4	
Other	8	
Subtotal		21
Total		100%

Once the new system is installed, it should be ready for operation. Now that the company has a viable tool for processing applications, management should encourage the departments to look into new applications and better ways of processing existing files. How well the system performs in the future depends on the users' support and on the utilization of the facility as a whole.

SUMMARY

1. This chapter summarizes how users evaluate computers systems for acquisition. Computer operations take place in a computer-based environment. The computer industry is made up of hardware suppliers, software suppliers, and computer service suppliers. The hardware suppliers include the computer manufacturers, peripheral manufacturers, supplies vendors, and computer leasing companies. Computer manufacturers are also the largest source of software operating systems and service programs. The primary sources of computer service suppliers are computer manufacturers, service bureaus, time sharing servicers, and facilities management. They provide the benefits of charging only for the services provided. Among the drawbacks are relatively high service charges, loss of control over the EDP operation, and vulnerability of company information to unauthorized access.

2. The task of acquiring a computer is a serious business. In deciding on a vendor, the most important criterion includes quality of service, price/performance advantage, reputation of the supplier, software and delivery availability, and ease of installation. An evaluation of the *current* computer system's performance should be made prior to an acquisition decision. Once such a decision is available, the user follows a procedural routine in evaluating system performance, the vendors' proposals, and a choice of whether to rent, lease, or purchase the system.

3. Evaluating the current computer system's performance is carried out through techniques such as hardware/software monitors, job accounting, system tuning, and revisions in system software. Hardware and software are evaluated through benchmark programs, the experience of other users, and product reference manuals. After the tests are conducted, the vendors' bids are evaluated to ensure that all informais valid, reliable, and meets the requirements set by the user. The selection of the final vendor is normally determined by "ad hoc," scoring, or cost-value approach. The cost-value approach gives credit to the proposal that best meets the user's desirable characteristics. After subtracting the credits from the vendor's quoted prices, the proposal with the lowest price is the one selected by the user.

4. Evaluating hardware acquisition entails analysis of the system's availability, compatibility, cost, performance, reliability, and the vendor's technical support. Software evaluation factors also include a look at the suitability of the programming languages, ease of the application of the software, and the availability of control programs in the new system. Once hardware and software are evaluated, vendor support services should be checked. They include backup, conversion capability, and the quality of the maintenance service.

5. The final decision to acquire a computer boils down to a rent, lease, or purchase choice. Under a rental arrangement, charges are based on usage hours. Although higher costs are normally incurred than in a lease or purchase, the benefits of financial leverage and flexibility in changing systems to better ones favor renting a system.

    Either a financial or operating lease contract is less expensive than renting for the same time period. Equipment obsolescence is shifted to the lessor. Lease charges, however, are higher than the purchase price of the equipment. The long period of the lease cannot be terminated without a heavy penalty.

    A purchase choice provides flexibility in modifying the system, lower total cash outflow, and cash savings due to depreciation and the investment tax credit. The primary drawbacks, however, include the initial high cost of purchase relevant to the initial cost of leasing and the risk resulting from being "strapped" with one's own system should it turn out to be a "lemon."

6. Hardware costs are only a part of the total cost of computer acquisition. Other costs include the costs of systems design and implementation, operating costs, and administrative costs. In the end result, the total costs should be justified in the light of the true benefits of the system and its ability to produce optimum information for decision making.

7. After all costs are computed and the vendor is chosen, the system is implemented by planning the computer facility and hiring a manager and qualified staff. Other aspects of implementation include developing performance standards, programming, testing, documentation, and training of operators.

TERMS TO LEARN

Benchmark Program
Facilities Management
Job accounting
Lease
Monitor
Present value method
Service bureau
Servicer

REVIEW QUESTIONS

1. How are computer vendors classified? Explain each classification?

2. List and briefly describe the major computer service suppliers available to the user.

3. What is facility management? In your opinion, how does it rate compared to a company's own EDP staff?

4. What selection criteria are considered in deciding on a vendor? Explain.

5. Distinguish between:
   a. service bureau and facility management
   b. hardware monitor and job accounting
   c. financial and operating lease
   d. scoring and cost value approach

6. Explain in your own words the information one needs to evaluate hardware/software. Which source would you consider the most reliable? Why?

7. Describe and evaluate the approaches used in selecting a vendor?

8. Elaborate on the major performance criteria for hardware acquisition.

9. In what respect is an outside consultant helpful in deciding on the final selection of a computer system? Explain.

10. Discuss carefully the financial considerations in computer acquisition. Which method of financing would you choose? Why?

11. Differentiate between leasing and renting a computer. What categories of lease contracts should one be familiar with?

12. What costs are incurred in preparing the facility for a new computer operation.

13. Outline the major steps taken by the user prior to the arrival of the computer. What other aspects of implementation must be considered?

chapter 19

Managing Computer Resources

Learning Objectives

Computer acquisition requires detailed planning and staffing with qualified personnel under the direction of a competent manager. Thus management serves as the springboard for the successful operation of a computer facility, by providing leadership in information handling and control of the facility against unauthorized access. By the end of this chapter, you should know:

1. the major functions of the computer center,

2. what personnel positions make up a computer center,

3. the different approaches to locating a computer center, and

4. the control measures designed to safeguard data against fraud or embezzlement.

The Major Functions of the Computer Center
System Development
Computer Operations
General Administration

The Organizational Structure
Structural Variations of a Computer Center
  Size of Staff
  Age of System
  Managerial Control
Primary Job Areas of a Computer Center
  Administration
  Systems Analysis and Design
  Programming
  Operations/Clerical

Key Personnel Positions
Manager of the Computer Center
  General Qualifications
  Training

Manager of the Systems Department
  Project Management
  General Qualifications
  The Staffing Function

The Programming Manager
Manager of Computer Operations
Support EDP Staff
  The Systems Analyst
  The Programmer
  The Operations Group

Location of the Computer Center
Centralized Location Under One User
Centralized Location Independent of All Users
Centralized Location Above User Level
Decentralized Location

Controlling Computer Operations
System Security and Control Measures
  Identification
  Access Control
  System Integrity

Installing a computer is not an easy task. Just selecting a computer system requires detailed planning and cost justification. Once installed, the next step is to staff up with qualified personnel under the leadership of a competent manager. The failure of high-cost computer center to provide useful and timely information due to the lack of competent personnel is a well-known story. In this chapter, therefore, we shall discuss:

1. the basic functions performed by the computer center,

2. the makeup and organization of the center, and

3. the management of systems development and computer operations.

The Major Functions of the Computer Center

A computer center (also called "computer facility," "information system," "computer service department," among many other names) performs three major functions:

1. system development,

2. computer operation, and

3. general administration.

System Development

The *system development* function includes analysis, design, implementation, and maintenance of computers and applications in a computer-using organization. Additional activities include:

1. *Data base management.* The design and update of data bases and data base software.

2. *System programming.* The design and development of operating systems and other control programs.

3. *System standards.* The design, development, distribution, and update of standards that guide the actual operation of the computer system.

4. *Technical consultations.* Consultation with users and EDP staff on matters related to training, operations, documentation, and manuals.

Computer Operations

Computer operation activities relate to the actual handling of the equipment and software to convert data into useful information. They include vital functions such as:

1. *Data preparation and entry* involve converting source documents into a

form understandable to the computer and entering the data via a card reader, key-to-tape, key-to-disc, or similar device for processing.

2. *Machine operation* includes the operation of such devices as the computer console, data communication terminals (Touch-Tone™ phones, CRTs, and so on), magnetic tape drives, disc drives, line printers, CRTs, and the like.

3. *System scheduling and control* includes the scheduling of equipment use, data files, and supplies and supervision of the overall facilities of the computer center. Other activities, such as maintenance of operations documentation and safeguarding the physical security of the computer center, are also included.

General Administration

General administration of the computer center requires demonstration of specific managerial skills:

1. The *planning* function specifies in advance *what* is to be performed on system projects, hardware and software acquisition, and various aspects of the operations of the computer center.

2. The *organizing* function focuses on specifying the jobs and procedures to be performed and deciding how they will be carried out.

3. The *controlling* function deals with evaluating computer operations, system procedures, and programs against standards or plans for measuring performance. It also includes the preparation and implementation of a plan to protect the computer center and equipment from physical danger, theft, or sabotage.

4. The *staffing* function essentially determines the job requirements for various EDP jobs, screening and selection of personnel, staff training, employee evaluation, and administration of the salary schedule.

5. Other general administration functions include meeting and dealing with computer vendors and suppliers, analyzing and controlling the costs of running the computer center, and providing cost estimates of the needed equipment for planning purposes.

The Organizational Structure

Insofar as a successful computer center employs qualified staff operating under the direction of experienced supervisors, the organizing function is an important part of the overall management effort. By grouping work elements and assigning them to appropriate departments and individuals within the computer center, a manager organizes and defines the relationships among the staff.

The **organization structure** of a computer center consists of the organizing efforts on a number of managerial levels, of authority relationships, and of the general pattern of functions performed by employees at all levels. In Figure 19–1, a typical organizational structure of a computer center, the chain of command—or line of authority—flows from the director of computer services (top, center) to the supervisors of different areas, and ultimately to the subordi-

Figure 19–1. A general organization chart of a computer center.

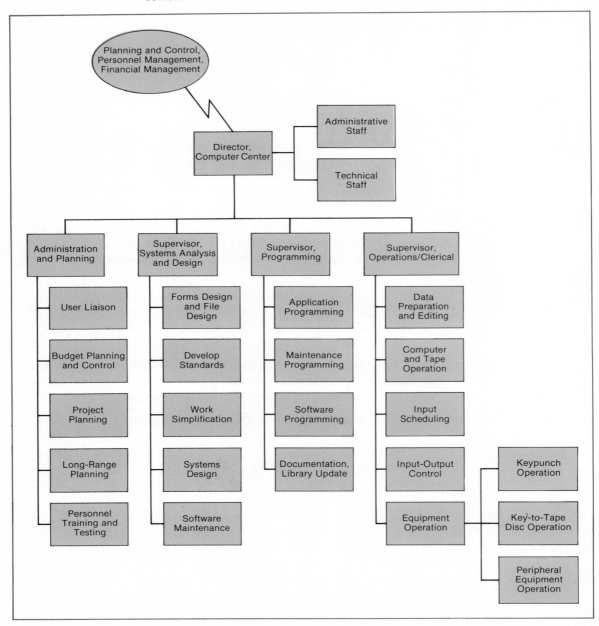

nates. The delegation of authority—to issue instructions, to direct the work of others, and to implement plans and goals—serves plainly and simply to make the department work by evoking action from subordinates.

Structural Variations of a Computer Center

The organization structure of a computer center depends on factors such as:

1. the *size* of the staff
2. the *age* of the computer system in operation, and
3. the extent of managerial *control* required.

Size of staff. In small computer centers (fewer than ten employees),systems analysis and programming are merged into one position. For example, the title "analyst/programmer" or "programmer/analyst" indicates that the persons holding the title perform both functions to one degree or another. Likewise, machine operation and clerical tasks are combined into a single job for the same purpose. Medium-sized computer centers (10–45 employees) usually isolate clerical functions as a separate unit.

Age of system. The relative age of the system already in operation is reflected in the importance placed on system planning versus system operations. In a new installation, more time is devoted to planning and development work than to operations. In an established system, greater attention is given to system operations, since much of the development work has already been completed.

Managerial control. Management has to adjust to its **span of control,** or the number of subordinates who directly report to a supervisor. The optimal span of control varies considerably, depending on the competence of the superior and subordinates, on the similarity of functions performed, and on the level of standardization of existing procedures. When emphasis is on stability and control, weight is given to a *narrow* span of management (Figure 19–2).Although a narrow span implies a limited number of specialists reporting to the manager, such a design provides control over the quantity and quality of work. In this respect, the manager is expected to be a specialist in his or her field. Overall, an effective span of control requires some form of skill grouping in a hierarchy, starting with the manager of the computer center and running down to the technical specialists. Figure 19–3 shows the managerial levels and key supervisory positions in a typical computer center.

Primary Job Areas of a Computer Center

Although the size of a computer center determines the number of supervisory levels necessary for control, most centers perform similar functions. In large centers, each job area is large enough to constitute a separate managerial

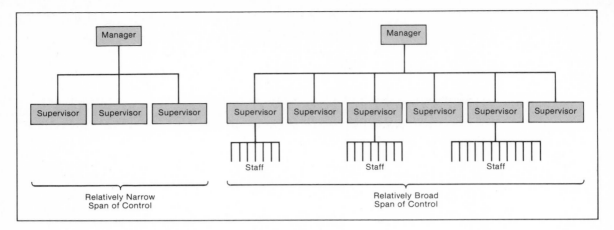

Figure 19–2. Variations of the span of control.

unit. Smaller centers merge a number of jobs into one unit. The makeup of a any computer center is designed around four major job areas (Figure 19–3):

1. administration,
2. systems analysis and design,
3. programming, and
4. operations/clerical.

1. Administration. This area includes the following activities:

a. the *user-systems relationship,* which promotes a sound interface between the user and staff,

b. *personnel* selection, recruitment, and training, as well as upgrading employee skills,

c. *application development and planning* for changes in the systems hardware or software, and

d. *budget administration and control* of the computer center's operating expenses.

2. Systems analysis and design. The organization of this area may be *project-based, pool-based,* or *functional.* A *project-based* structure is organized around a team of analysts with a specific project in mind. Each team is led by a project leader who reports directly to the manager of the systems department. This type of structure is typical of small computer centers that handle a limited number of projects (Figure 19–4).

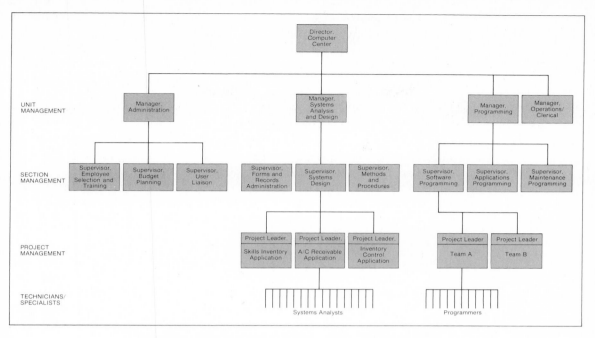

Figure 19–3. A partial organization structure illustrating key managerial levels.

Figure 19–4. A project-based structure.

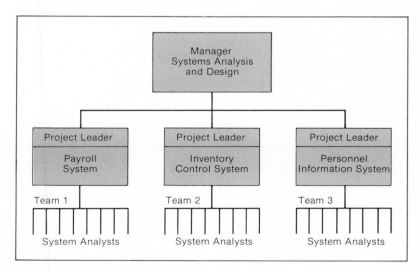

A *pool-based* structure calls for the "pooling" of all available systems analysts to work on any project within the company on a first-come/first-served basis. The analysts return to the pool after the completion of the project for another assignment. As shown in Figure 19–5, several system teams are on loan to the production, personnel, and accounting departments. This unique arrangement not only gives each operating department better control over its own applications than under the project-based arrangement, but it also means greater user participation and support throughout the duration of the project.

In the *functional* structure, descriptive of a large computer center, systems analysts are assigned specific projects within designated departments in the organization. For example, in Figure 19–6, a group of analysts is assigned to Project A in the personnel system. Each project is the responsibility of a project leader who is normally a senior systems analyst. The project leader reports to the manager of the system. The manager, in turn, reports directly to the director of systems development.

3. Programming. The programming function is organized around three major areas: applications, software, and maintenance (Figure 19–3). *Applications* programmers work directly on the applications designed by the analyst. *Software* programmers modify and maintain compilers and other software items used in existing applications. *Maintenance* programmers handle all changes and modifications necessary for keeping the existing programs up-to-date.

The reporting relationships of programmers are similar to those of systems analysts. Small computer centers use the pool-based structure: Programmers, clustered into a pool, report to a common supervisor and prepare a program through all stages. Larger centers use the team-based structure: Programmers are assigned to a team, in charge of a complete project, and report directly to a team or project leader (Figure 19–3).

4. Operations/clerical. The *operations function* includes computer operation, data preparation and entry, job scheduling, and support services. Support services entail activities such as program storage, decollating and bursting, and messenger service (Figure 19–3). They are handled in coordination with the programming and systems design functions as a part of a master plan in systems implementation and maintenance.

Key Personnel Positions

The organization chart of a typical computer center emphasizes four key positions (Figure 19–3):

1. manager of the computer center (sometimes aided by an administrative manager),

2. manager of the systems department,

3. programming manager, and

4. manager of computer operations.

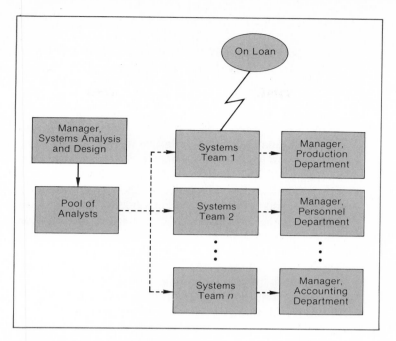

Figure 19-5. A pool-based structure.

Figure 19-6. A functional structure of systems analysis.

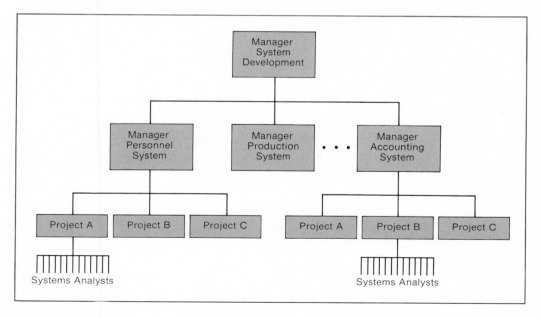

Manager of the Computer Center

Management means dealing with people for achieving preplanned objectives. In an in-house facility, the manager is in charge of the entire operation—responsible to the user for all work performed in the computer center. He or she plans, organizes, coordinates, and directs the activities of personnel and procedures on a regular basis.

General qualifications.   Effective management of a computer center requires *educational, technical,* and *managerial* experience. Persons beginning a career in this area are expected to have a college degree. In many cases, a master's degree is desirable. Although the college major required varies with each installation, a degree in business administration—with major emphasis on information systems or systems analysis—has, over the years, proved to be the ideal educational background.

EDP managers prove their worth by the actions they take and the applications they implement. The outcome of their operations reflects on their ability to provide the information required by users. Technical knowledge of the system's makeup, the design details undertaken by the systems group, and other hardware or software problems enhance their visibility in the eyes of subordinates. Therefore, a technical background is highly desirable.

A technical background for managers is useful in two ways. First, by keeping abreast of current developments in the field, they make sure that computer systems are upgraded so that they do not suffer from technological obsolescence. Second, technical knowledge in applications programming and systems work is necessary for handling staff problems. Managers who diagnose and help solve design and programming errors command a lot of "expert power" in the department.

In addition to having educational and technical background, managers of computer centers must be capable of handling people. Coping with people requires understanding and perception of their vocational needs, since needs are highly individualized. Managers who can fulfill these needs are generally able to keep employees satisfied while achieving company goals. Task-oriented needs can be satisfied by:

1. showing appreciation for honest effort,

2. praising the employee for good work done,

3. promoting an attitude of job security and opportunities for advancement,

4. paying competitive wages and developing standards for regular salary increases,

5. offering work that sustains interest and motivation, and

6. providing good working conditions.

The role of the computer has changed. Once, businesspersons viewed it as a "super" adding machine, spewing out financial data. Now the computer is seen as an information tool for the entire organization. This new view has awarded managers greater responsibility than before. In addition to normal managerial duties, they now have to work with executives at all levels. In essence, managers have to become executives — agents of change — making decisions that can affect the functioning of the entire organization. Because of this new role, managers require certain qualities for effectiveness in a computer-based environment:

1. skill in planning, organizing, and controlling the work of the center,

2. a current technical knowledge base in computer systems and software,

3. the capacity to logically deal with complex problems and to cope with "out-of-the-ordinary" situations,

4. an ability to relate to users and subordinates alike, and

5. a broad knowledge of the company business and its environment.

Training.   Since a person with all these qualifications is not easy to find, many installations settle for less and thus compromise the overall effectiveness of the computer center. Others spend a lot of time looking for qualified managers or enrolling senior supervisors in management training programs. Most such programs are designed to develop communication and human-relation skills, as well as leadership in management. The practicality of this training depends on the size of the computer center, on the caliber of the staff, and on the requirements set by management for the top position in EDP.

Manager of the Systems Department

A second-level managerial position in the computer department is the systems manager, whose primary functions are:

1. long-range planning of future organizational systems projects,

2. identifying and authorizing systems projects,

3. organizing and staffing project teams to implement each project,

4. controlling all forms,

5. coordinating and advising department managers on the development of interdepartmental systems and procedures, and

6. preparing and maintaining procedures as required.

Although the systems superivsor technically performs all these functions, senior systems analysts often perform similar functions. In larger systems departments and in more complex projects, the duties of the supervisor are more likely distributed among analysts for optimum performance.

Additionally, the systems department supervisor assumes the following responsibilities:

1. conducts systems surveys, recommends systems changes, and shares in installing approved new systems;

2. establishes standards and specifications on office machines and other supportive equipment when needed;

3. cooperates with the organization's education and training department in conducting special training programs on administrative projects;

4. assists departments with form layout, and also prepares form layouts for reproductions;

5. maintains control over record storage; and

6. develops basic operating procedures.

Project management. In large computer centers, systems management includes the formation of project teams to handle complex projects. A project team usually consists of systems analysts, programmers, user representatives, and an outside consultant. A project leader reports to the supervisor of the systems department.

Leading a project means managing resources and costs in detail. The responsibilities involved with **project management,** which includes the entire system development cycle, are:

1. feasibility analysis,

2. systems design,

3. system specifications,

4. programming,

5. system testing,

6. conversion, and

7. implementation.

The most important activities in project management are (1) establishing goals, (2) developing plans, and (3) comparing project progress with the plan. A project is based first on definable objectives, which include priority planning, problem definition, and anticipated benefits. Once goals are set, then a typical plan is made up of:

1. the description of various tasks,

2. the estimated project startup and termination dates, and

3. the time, cost, and manpower required for each activity.

The third phase, comparing actual progress with the plan, is perhaps most critical. Project control is therefore an important aspect of project management, because it ensures that all project objectives are accomplished on schedule. To implement a project control plan:

1. define tasks and their interrelationships;

2. assign a man-day estimate to each task and adjust the estimates as needed for experience and training;

3. develop and use tools such as Gantt or PERT charts to monitor progress on the project and update the tools regularly to reflect changes or adjustments on the project;

4. collect project status information on activities and resource consumption at review points predefined in the plan; and

5. review each job phase (set of tasks) and keep the user informed at all times.

General qualifications. These project activities and functions make the systems manager's job obviously unique. Working through the analysts and with officers of the organization, systems managers are expected to have a *technical* as well as an *administrative* background. A technical background gives systems managers "expert" power, gains them respect from the staff, and enables them to become an active participant in operations. An administrative background is also necessary if they are to solve human problems, to evaluate the work of the staff, and to assess their performance in ways that match the standards of the organization. Systems work that produces the most effective results is invariably a shared team effort. To get the job done, systems analysts have to work with people — with department personnel and users throughout the organization. Specifically, the systems manager must therefore have:

1. the ability to design systems and to write procedures,

2. the ability to sell ideas pertaining to revised systems or new equipment to department heads and other line officers,

3. the ability to discuss procedures with the user in an objective, mature manner,

4. the forcefulness and tact in handling members of other departments, as well as outsiders,

5. imagination in exploring new and better ways of converting existing operations,

6. integrity in dealing with hardware representatives and safeguarding company records and supplies, and

7. perceptiveness in understanding subordinates and how they react to him or her and to the work situation.

The staffing function.   In developing a systems department, a major function of the systems supervisor is staffing the department with competent analysts and support personnel. An applicant's past experience in systems work and letters of recommendation provide excellent input for a final decision. Unfortunately, however, no established standard, no valid test, no foolproof acid test for competence in new applicants is available. Research in this area, however, suggests the following attributes are desirable characteristics in a systems analyst:

1. the ability to express opinions and sell ideas to others;

2. an open mind that does not reject other people's ideas or shut off outside sources of information;

3. analytical ability;

4. experience with computer hardware;

5. honesty and fairness in dealing with others;

6. imagination and curiosity — wanting to know the "why" of every interesting episode —

7. initiative, drive to achieve useful goals, and a tendency to be impatient with perfunctory work;

8. maturity, balance, humility, and the ability to exchange ideas without giving the impression of being a "wise guy",

9. knowledge of the theory and tools of systems work; and

10. two or more years of college — generally a college graduate in business administration, accounting, or management science.

Of all the requirements, a college background seems to be the foremost. Current hiring practices favor college graduates and offer them the best prospects for advancement in this area. Again, the college major desired depends on the kind of installation and on the particular projects. Generally, a balanced background in mathematics, computer science, and business management is desirable.

Larger computer centers often have a program review group, consisting of systems analysts and selected senior programmers, that evaluates and revises proposed data processing procedures. In smaller installations, the group may be required to develop mechanized procedures in addition to the regular assignments. The combined background of the group ensures that all procedures and programs evaluated are workable and efficient.

The Programming Manager

On the second managerial level in the organization structure is the programming supervisor. This person has the total responsibility for the development of programs and for the activities carried out by his or her systems, applications, and maintenance programmers. Interacting with systems analysts in charge of the application under development, programming supervisors make certain that the right approach and the right programs are developed for testing and implementation. Additional responsibilities are:

1. consulting with colleagues in order to acquire special programming guidance or system knowledge,

2. consulting with programmers to determine detailed design and program flow,

3. evaluating the impact of proposed changes on existing programs,

4. ensuring systems analysts and the user that all performance requirements and program specifications are met and that programs work properly, and

5. interacting with user personnel to ascertain program requirements and data flow.

Manager of Computer Operations

The manager of computer operations, on the second managerial level, must direct the computer installation, plan the scheduling of computer time, allocate personnel, maintain the program library, and control operations within the center. Specifically, operations management entails:

1. developing and administering a viable budget for the computer center and evaluating the performance of the department against the expenditures;

2. evaluating the performance of the personnel and the computer system in terms of labor turnover, systems "downtime," and the capacity at which the system is operated;

3. monitoring the quality of input data preparation, processing, and output and controlling the facility's data files against unauthorized access;

4. scheduling specific systems and other applications for computer processing; and

5. supervising the testing and implementation of a new system.

Educational requirements for operations management vary considerably, depending on the size and functions of the computer center. Although many computer operations managers currently do not have college degrees, the trend is toward hiring and promoting those who do — particularly, degrees in computer science or business administration. College studies should include business management, programming languages, basic systems analysis and design, and statistics. In today's competitive market, the usefulness of the high school diploma is all but gone.

Support EDP Staff

The systems analyst.   In charge of directing the "task force" for systems work, systems analysts comprise the focal point in the overall systems concept. They ensure that the company's systems operate efficiently by using the latest managerial techniques, systems, and peripherals. Management techniques, such as PERT, give information for making better decisions and allow executives to offer better services at low cost. Systems analysts regularly examine new techniques in an effort to design better systems for the firm.

Although detailed knowledge of *all* available hardware is unnecessary, analysts should be able to distinguish among the various requirements and know the capabilities of the equipment involved. They must also be prepared to evaluate cost differentials and assume responsibility for incorporating the system as an integral unit into the business. Their business is to make sure that the record-keeping and paperwork of a business meet the desired specifications smoothly and efficiently.

In the past, systems analysts dealt with machine operators and key-driven devices. They thought mechanistically of reports and procedures passing from person to person and from department to department. This pattern of thinking has gradually yielded to an evaluation of increasingly larger segments of the total business. In an attempt to integrate a human's superior reasoning ability with the machine's superior speed and accuracy, the analyst must make reports ever more current, integrate many intermediate steps into fewer ones, and free people of routine duties so they can devote more time to creative work.

Since systems analysis and design carry such considerable responsibility, the job's status and salary are the highest in the department. No other EDP personnel can function without the design details provided by the analyst. The vertical job mobility of computer operators and programmers within the computer facility continues as long as they remain within their divisions. To become systems analysts, they must cross division lines.

While systems analysts have the highest status, the operations group has a relatively low status. Within each group, the jobs closer to the manager's level bear higher status'. For example, senior systems analysts enjoy a higher status (with greater responsibility and higher pay) than junior systems analysts. The same relationship exists in the programming and operations groups.

The programmer.   The programmer's job is a creation of the computer. Before 1950, this job did not exist. Not until early 1951 was the first commercial computer installed; by the end of that year, there were 10 computers. By 1960, there were 5,400. Today, over 300,000 computers are in operation. With the steadily increasing demand for computers comes an equivalent demand for programmers at all levels to put the computers to work. It is estimated that as many as 500,000 computers and 600,000 programmers will be needed by 1985.

Programming requires a logical mind and attention to detail. Except for sophisticated or scientific applications, programming does not require a college degree. Nevertheless, a college education in business or in related areas is still helpful. Some of the top talent in programming have college educations in music, philosophy, or the arts.

How do you know if you have an aptitude for programming? A number of computer users, manufacturers, and employment services offer various *programming aptitude tests*. Most tests measure:

1. attention to detail and facility with numbers,
2. the ability to grasp abstract representations,
3. logical or reasoning ability, and
4. problem solving ability.

Some extensive tests also measure general intelligence and verbal ability. Anyone interested may inquire about these tests through the school guidance counselor, the state or federal employment service, or the educational center of a computer manufacturer.

The operations group. A key person in the operations area is the computer operator, in direct command of the computer during a program run. Operators load and unload programs, prepare input data for entry, and stay on hand to monitor error messages and to keep the machines operating smoothly. They should be intelligent, alert, and mindful of the costly hardware in operation. At present, most computer operators are high school graduates who have previously run less sophisticated systems. However, the more sophisticated computer systems on the market today demand additional educational operators.

Training for computer operators is provided through private business and technical schools, junior colleges, and some high schools. Most operators have learned on the job and through schools conducted by the computer manufacturers for their customers' personnel. Most of those who train for computer operating jobs either have high school diplomas or are undergoing preliminary training in data processing at a junior college.

Location of the Computer Center

The location of a computer center differs in different firms. One alternative is to locate the center under the "department of most use." Another alternative is to organize it as an independent department not tied directly to any other. Either way, an ideal choice depends on the type of organization, the capabilities of the staff, the type of management involved in the final decision, and the historical development of data processing in the organization.

Centralized Location Under One User

Although a "one-user" structure is designed to serve all departments, it is directly under the primary user or the "department of most use" — usually the finance or accounting department (Figure 19–7). Even though is appropriate when most of the applications relate to the sponsoring department, its primary drawback is that other departments have to cross organizational lines to get service. Hence the EDP staff often view them as "secondary" users. Some organizations either limit computer use by other departments or authorize the computer center manager to integrate their work into an already tight schedule.

Centralized Location Independent of All Users

An independent, centralized location provides equal service to all users, with no allegiance to any particular department. The manager of the computer facility, at the same level as other department heads, reports directly to a top executive (Figure 19–8). The cost of operating the center is absorbed by the company, and each department is "billed" for a portion of the total cost based on usage.

Placing the computer center on the same level as other departments allows the manager of the center to negotiate projects with users on an equal footing. Furthermore, if all users have access to the same facility, the facility itself can work toward standardizing data-processing activities common to all departments and make such data available when needed.

Centralized Location Above User Level

Placing a centralized computer center above the level of other departments reflects top management's view of the center as a major source for accommodating and controlling the informational needs of the organization. The center's manager has tremendous power to determine how user applications are to be implemented. This arrangement is practical in organizations that rely heavily on the operations of the computer center (Figure 19–9).

Decentralized Location

The development of microcomputers, minicomputers, intelligent terminals, and distributed processing makes it practical to decentralize computer services within the organization. A decentralized arrangement is usually more responsive to the user's needs, encourages more efficient integration of the computer system, and improves the accuracy of data preparation and entry (Figure 19–10). On the other hand, a centralized computer center is ideal for companies with a high volume of repetitive applications. It often makes more efficient and therefore more economical use of the hardware, software, and technical

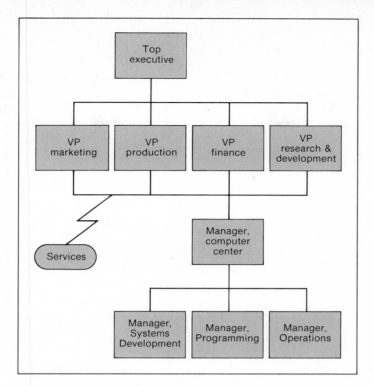

Figure 19–7. Organization chart showing a centralized EDP structure, reporting to the vice-president of finance.

Figure 19–8. Organization chart showing a centralized autonomous EDP line structure.

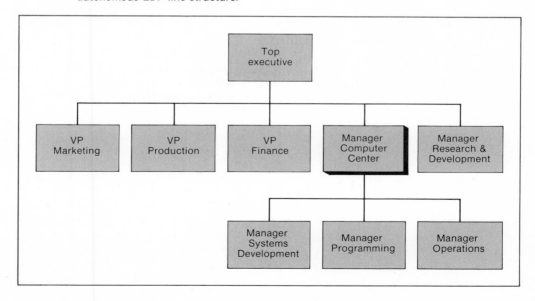

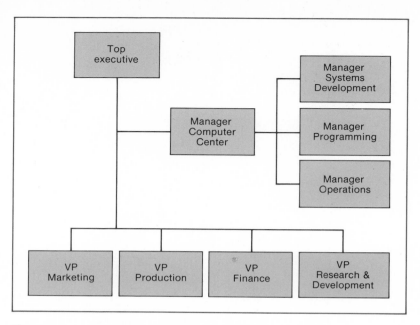

Figure 19–9. Organization chart showing a centralized EDP line structure above the departmental level.

Figure 19–10 Organization chart showing a decentralized data processing line structure.

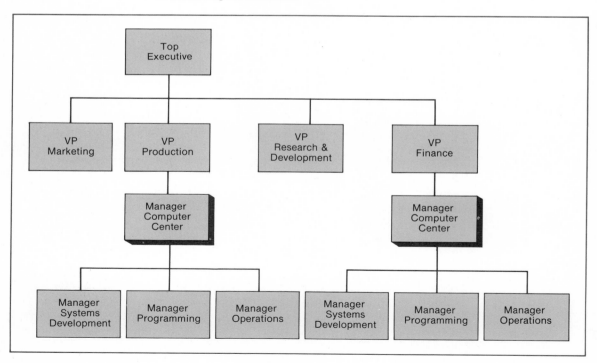

staff. It also promotes integration and standardization of EDP procedures and routines within the organization.

Controlling Computer Operations

Since the possibilities for major theft via computer are staggering, the manager of the computer center must institute and implement procedures for system integrity and security. **System security** is comprised of computer operations designed to:

1. ensure the accuracy of information,
2. safeguard data against fraud, and
3. secure data against unauthorized access.

System Security and Control Measures

Tight security is expensive, but appropriate security is cheap when compared with the catastrophe associated with no protection at all. There are three major motives for system security of a computer center:

1. The nearly total dependence of most organizations on the continued operation of a computer center. Rarely can a firm resort to a manual mode of processing.
2. Data is regarded as a major asset. If lost, it can be replaced only at substantial cost.
3. Private information must be protected from unauthorized access.

In order of decreasing probability the major threats to systems and data are primarily programmer and operator errors, secondarily dishonest and disgruntled employees, and finally fire and natural disaster. Bringing risk within tolerable limits at the lowest costs should be the aim of every manager. Each security measure should therefore be quantified for comparison with its respective cost. Basic, common sense measures can be taken at little cost. For example, management can screen analysts, programmers, and operators carefully. In some centers, an employee is subjected to a polygraph test before being assigned to a sensitive project.

After assessing the risks and costs of a computer center's security, the next step is the selection of internal and external control measures. Fundamentally, these measures are identification, access control, and system integrity.

Identification. The purpose of identification is to uniquely identify people and associate them with the actions they perform. Schemes for identifying people to the computer center fall into three classes: *something you know* (such as a password), *something you are* (your fingerprints, for example) or *something you have* (like a credit card).

Access control.   The threat from fraud or mischief necessitates effective access controls. One of the most prominent means of access control is the card access system. A sophisticated system utilizes plastic, uniquely encoded cards, which serve as keys to unlock doors including tape storage areas and file cabinets containing classified information. The card, which has a photograph of the bearer, also doubles as employee identification badge.

Against possible fraud and embezzlement by EDP personnel, the following measures may be taken:

1. Programs and program changes are restricted to programmers.

2. Duties are rotated to prevent an operator or programmer from dominating a file.

3. At least two persons are always in the computer room.

4. Final program assemblies are controled so that only the approved program is installed.

Because fraud or embezzlement is often difficult to detect, auditing must be done frequently. Internal auditors should have some control over programs to discourage unauthorized program changes. They must have a copy of all necessary programs and receive information on program changes.

System integrity.   **System integrity** entails the proper functioning of hardware and programs, effective physical security, and correct operating procedures. The most costly type of software error is a program error. Elimination of such errors depends on proper test program procedures: Parallel runs, for instance, are used whenever a new system is being implemented.

Finally, a system security "chain" is only as strong as its weakest link — and the weakest link is people. The manager of the computer center can implement effective security measures by fostering an awareness of their importance among the EDP staff and by enforcing the security standards equally on everyone.

Obviously, the organization and society in general suffer many adverse effects by the computer, because individuals or computer center staffs violate the profession's code of ethics and proper control measures set up to ensure the privacy and integrity of data. Like other powerful tools, the computer possesses the potential for good or evil. Company users, managers of computer centers, and their staffs must accept the responsibility for its functioning and proper use.

SUMMARY

1. A computer center has three major functions: system development, computer operations, and administration. It employs qualified staff operating under the direction of experienced supervisors. The chain of command flows from the director of the center to the supervisors of different areas, to

the subordinates. The organization structure depends on factors such as the staff size, the age of the system, and the extent of managerial control. The need for stability and control favors a narrow span of management.

2. The makeup of a computer center is designed around four job areas: administration, systems analysis and design, programming, and operations. Each area is headed by a manager or a supervisor. Managers of the computer center plan, organize, and coordinate the activities of personnel and procedures on a regular basis. In addition to an educational and technical background, they must be capable of handling people. They also have to deal with executives at all levels.

    Managers of system departments are in charge of long-range planning—authorizing systems projects, staffing project teams, and controlling forms and procedures. They conduct systems surveys, assist departments in form layout, and maintain control over record storage. A technical as well as an administrative background is necessary for solving systems problems and human relations, respectively. Other attributes include the ability to design systems and to discuss procedures, tact in handling users, integrity in dealing with vendors, and perception in understanding and recognizing subordinates at work.

    Programming managers are responsible for the development of programs, applications, and maintenance programmers. They consult with programmers on detailed design and program flow, follow through on program testing and implementation, and interact with user personnel to establish program requirements and data flow.

    Supervisors of computer operations direct the computer installation, plan the scheduling of computer time, allocate personnel, and control the operations of the center. Although educational requirements for this position vary with each center, college education is becoming increasingly essential for a senior position in this area.

3. The support staff in a computer center include systems analysts, programmers, and the operations group. Systems analysts are in charge of directing the "task force" for systems work. No other EDP personnel can function without the design details provided by the analysts. They have the highest status and salary. In contrast, programming is a more tedious task than analysis: It requires a logical mind and attention to detail. Following the programmer is the computer operator whose job is loading and unloading programs, preparing input data for entry and monitoring error messages during computer runs. Most of those who train for this position either have high school diplomas, or they are currently undergoing training in data processing at junior college.

4. The location of the computer center differs in different firms. One approach is to locate it under the department of "most use" or organize it independently or other departments. The final choice depends on the

type of organization, on the capabilities of the staff, on the type of management, and the historical development of data processing in the organization.

5. Computer operations should be designed to control the accuracy of information, safeguard data against fraud, and secure data from unauthorized access. The manager of the computer center is responsible for handling the control function and for implementing procedures for system integrity and security.

6. The primary control measures taken by a typical computer center are identification, access control, and system integrity. These measures center around physical security, file control, and documentation control. The center's manager can implement effective security measures by fostering an awareness of their importance among the EDP staff and by enforcing the security standards equally on everyone.

TERMS TO LEARN

Controlling
Management
Organization structure
Organizing

Planning
Project management
Span of control
System integrity
System security

REVIEW QUESTIONS

1. What are the primary functions of a computer center?

2. Distinguish the difference between:
   (a) data base management and systems management
   (b) systems standards and system scheduling
   (c) planning and organizing
   (d) organization structure and chain of command
   (e) project-based organization and functional organization

3. Explain carefully the factors that determine the organization structure of a computer center.

4. What makes up the administration area of the computer center?

5. In what respect is the position of manager of computer center different from that of the systems department? Explain.

6. Is there any relationship between system management and project management? In what way?

7. What characteristics or attributes must a systems manager have? Why are they important?

8. Write a 300-word essay on the attributes and role of the systems analyst in a computer-based environment.

9. What makes up a support EDP staff? Explain.

10. What factors determine the location of a computer center?

11. How is a centralized computer center different from a decentralized center?

12. Comment on the primary control measures taken by a typical computer center.

Word Processing

Word Processing as a System
The Bases for the Installation of Word Processing Systems

    Productivity
    Ballooning Paperwork
    Increasing Cost of Clerical Labor
    Business Letter Costs
    The Private Secretary and the Boss

Identification of Problems for Word Processing
Word Processing — A Summary

The term "word processing" was originally coined by Ulrich Steinhilper of IBM to describe the overall information processing function of the office that deals with words as distinguished from data or numbers. His premise was that numbers or data are processed by means of calculators, while words are processed by means of typewriters. Word processing deals with *words*. It transforms ideas or useful information into a communication format acceptable to the user. The whole process is carried out through the combined efforts of people, hardware (equipment), and specialized procedures. Words originate through machines, shorthand dictation, oral or written instructions, or a rough draft copy. They are then processed by transcription, keyboarding, formatting, editing, revising, or proofreading. Additional activities, such as duplicating and microfilming, may be used as auxiliary processing steps.

Overall, word processing is a practice that affects all managerial levels in the organization. It entails the office function as well as the processing or production of word output. In fact, the area of word processing (WP) has expanded to include the concept of administrative support (AS). The combined concepts are often expressed as the **WP/AS concept,** meaning a new form of office organization and a method of support for providing written communications. The more recent systems incorporate computer-like technology, which makes it possible for organizations to multiply the speed and efficiency of their word processing routines.

Word processing has the potential for improving the effectiveness of information processing. It is the key to the total integration of the office and to the creation of a comprehensive management information system. Here are some supportive reasons for its importance:

1. After an idea is originated, it is captured and stored for later use. The *availability* of such *information* makes it possible to revise or process it with minimum effort or loss of time. No additional keyboarding is necessary.[1]

2. Words are used for *communication* throughout all organizations. They represent the ideas (messages, reports, and the like) that are communicated from the originator (source) to the users (destination) in the system.

3. Of the total volume of information processed, approximately two-thirds deals with words while the remaining third consists of numbers. This suggests the importance of word processing in providing information for decision making. In most cases, total understanding of information cannot be communicated by numbers alone but must be interpreted by means of accompanying words.

4. The increasing flood of paperwork and high handling costs have created a need for better ways of processing information and providing the support

[1]It should be noted that in the conventional mode, ideas are initially captured on paper. In contrast, word processing eliminates rekeyboarding because the ideas are stored directly on media where they are available for later use.

that management needs. Words communicated in written form, to interpret or to *convey ideas* efficiently processed and distributed.

5. The *speed* factor is also critical. For example, after the televising of the 1976 Presidential Debates, transcript copies were printed, bound, and distributed to the candidates and Associated Press within two hours. In contrast, for the 1960 Kennedy-Nixon Debates, it took 1.5 days to produce the same kind of information.

Word Processing as a System

The systems concept has been subject to a great deal of misunderstanding and indiscriminate use. To date, most of the work on developmental systems has been related to computers and to data processing functions. The WP/AS concept represents a system designed to provide various supportive subsystems for management. Today's word processing systems are composed of subsystems such as machine dictation for input and sophisticated keyboarding equipment for output.

A unique feature of a word processing system is its capability of supporting special-purpose subsystems for carrying out specialized functions. For example, a word processing typewriter may have an optional device designed to provide two-way communication with remote users. Such a device makes it possible to transmit or receive information from other terminals,[2] establishing the basis for electronic mail or a telecommunications system.

In addition to telecommunication, word processing systems may be used for in-house printing and production. For example, automatic typewriters using magnetic media may be programmed with both the text material and the directions for layout of the text by phototypeset equipment. Such applications are time-saving and cost effective.

In addition to the use of magnetic media as a form of storage, information stored on magnetic tape cassettes or floppy discs may be converted to computer-compatible tape and later stored or used for preparing computer output microfilm (COM) file. The transformation to microfilm through the integration of special-purpose subsystems contributes to the *effective* implementation of an overall total system of information processing.

The foregoing illustration points out the importance and interactive role of the computer in a word processing system. This electronic, high-speed capability means that applications, such as a manuscript incorporating the most up-to-date inventory figures, are easily and quickly accomplished. Also, by means of special packages programmed for text processing, computers may be used to perform the entire information processing function quickly, economically, and on time. Thus, the obvious benefits of word processing behooves management to design a total systems approach to information processing to handle its overall word processing needs.

[2]Examples are communicating typewriters, Telex, TWX, and a variety of computer terminals.

In today's business, office-related work is a primary service. However, the cost of service is continually spiraling upward. The inflationary trend is increasing office costs which, in turn, affects profitability. Word processing is a concept designed to reduce paperwork, improve productivity, and cut clerical and secretarial labor costs.

Productivity

Office productivity has not increased as quickly as office costs have risen. In a conventional office, productivity per typist has shown no gain in the last fifty years. Even with the introduction of the electric typewriter, typing speed has not increased (50–60 words per minute). With the explosion of administrative work and an avalanche of paperwork, the same old typewriter and telephone (with the addition of some dictation and copying equipment) are still the basic tools. Although data processing systems have impacted roughly one-fifth of the activities of the office, the greatest part have remained unstructured, unsystematized, and unimproved.

With the implementation of a word processing system, productivity increases greatly for a number of reasons. Job specialization results in much better use of employee time. The same number of employees can carry a greatly increased workload. Less duplication of effort occurs and the dull repetitive typing may be eliminated. When revisions are made, retyping is avoided and only the material that has been changed needs proofing. Experience shows that efficient word processing systems often increase typing productivity (as measured by output of lines) from 200 to 300 percent. Management's effectiveness may be improved significantly through (1) the use of machine dictation, (2) the time saved in proofing revised material, and (3) the improved assistance with the implementation of an administrative support program.

Ballooning Paperwork

Literally a deluge of paperwork inundates today's business. Over 15 trillion pieces of paper in business offices and a million new pages are added every minute of each working day. Government-required paperwork accounts for much of the paper. In recent years, Congress has established a Commission on Federal Paperwork. Former President Ford initiated a personal paper-cutting crusade, intended to reduce the number of forms under the President's administrative control. Here are two representative examples of the volume of cost of paperwork:

General Motors estimates that it spent $190 million on government paperwork and related administrative costs in 1975; a hefty chunk of it to satisfy the Environmental Protection Agency that G.M's cars met federal emissions standards.

Eli Lilly & Co., reports that the cost of its government paperwork is about $15 million a year, and that more man-hours are devoted to paperwork than to research on drugs for cancer and heart disease. A lot of Lilly's paperwork is accounted for by the Food and Drug Administration's requirements for information about studies conducted to ascertain the effects of new drugs. When Lilly asked the FDA to approve a new drug for arthritis in 1976, its application ran to 120,000 pages.

Several reasons can be cited for so much paperwork:

1. *Increased need for information.* Management mandates that more information be processed to provide adequate, accurate, and timely information to enable them to reach the best decisions.

2. *Increased need for data and records.* Each new governmental policy or piece of legislation, requires new procedures, forms, and reports. For example, the Equal Employment Opportunity (EEO), the Occupational Safety and Health Act (OSHA), and the Employee Retirement Income Security Act (ERISA) have all generated considerably more paperwork than before.

3. *Growth and complexity of our economy.* As companies expand, merge, or diversify, relationships become more complex and often exist at great distances. The growth in the number of executives also creates more paperwork. The trend is toward more management members over specialized areas which necessitates the distribution of information to a wide range of executives within relatively short periods of time.

Given the foregoing factors, the higher levels of productivity achieved through word processing systems make it possible to handle the ever increasing volume of paperwork. Word processing further facilitates the measuring of productivity for a given task. Accurate measurement enables better control through evaluation of the performance of the activity and effecting changes when necessary.

Increasing Cost of Clerical Labor

Office labor costs are increasing at a higher rate than total office costs. A recent estimate of the costs for office expenditures for one year showed that 84 percent of office costs were spent on office labor. The average salary for a clerical job was around 12 percent higher in 1978 than in 1977 and 9 percent higher in 1979 than in 1977. Related to increase in labor costs is the dramatic increase in clerical and secretarial jobs. Employment in clerical jobs is expected to rise from present estimates of 16 million to 20 million in 1985. Likewise, secretarial positions are expected to increase from 4.5 million in 1979 to over 6 million in 1985.

The literature abounds with case histories of the cost savings resulting from installation of modern word processing equipment, which adds greater efficiency to the typewriting function. Although dollar savings vary in different situations, cost comparisons between old and new systems generally result in 15–30 percent reduction in clerical costs. Full implementation of a WP/AS system provides not only cost savings but also cost prevention.

Business Letter Costs

All too often, the cost of a business letter is viewed only as the cost of the stationery and envelope. In reality, the time of the dictator (writer) and secretary (plus the costs for fixed overhead, filing, and nonproductive labor time (sick leave and vacation) must be considered as well as mailing and material costs. The Dartnell Corporation has studied letter costs since 1930 when a team of researchers first put the cost of a business letter at 29.6¢. By 1953, the cost was $1.17; in 1975, $3.79. In 1976, the cost was $4.17, and in 1980 it is estimated to be around $5.25 — an increase of 362 percent over 1953 (Figure 1).

Figure 1. The increasing cost of letter writing.

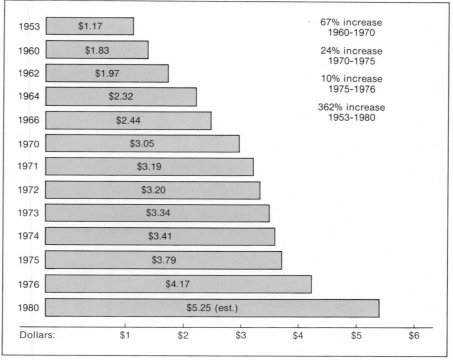

1953	$1.17
1960	$1.83
1962	$1.97
1964	$2.32
1966	$2.44
1970	$3.05
1971	$3.19
1972	$3.20
1973	$3.34
1974	$3.41
1975	$3.79
1976	$4.17
1980	$5.25 (est.)

67% increase 1960-1970
24% increase 1970-1975
10% increase 1975-1976
362% increase 1953-1980

Dollars: $1 $2 $3 $4 $5 $6

Table 1. Determining the Cost of One Letter (1976).

Cost Factor	Average Cost	Your Cost	Determining Cost
Dictator's Time . . . For this cost, it is assumed that the executive receives a weekly salary of $326, and he takes approximately 7 minutes to dictate a single business letter.	$0.95		Based on a 40-hour week, this cost is determined by dividing an executive's salary by 7 minutes. For example, at a salary of $326 a week, the executive earns $8.15 an hour or 13.5¢ a minute. Thus, 7 minutes of his time costs 95¢. ($326 ÷ 40 hrs. = $8.15 per hour) ($8.15 ÷ 60 min. = 13.5¢ per min.) (13.5¢ × 7 min. = 95¢ per letter)
Secretarial Time . . . Based on a salary of $159 a week this figure includes all time but filing. It is estimated that the total figure is 18 minutes.	1.19		The cost is determined by dividing the secretary's salary (40-hour week) by 18 minutes to learn the total cost of taking dictation, doing "extra" work, and transcribing the letter as well as addressing envelope, etc.
Nonproductive Labor . . . This is the time consumed by both dictator and secretary in waiting, illness, vacations, etc. This has been set at 15% of labor costs for both.	0.32		This cost is a basic percentage arrived at from previous studies. It includes absenteeism factors but does not include all fringes. It **does** include interruptions due to phone calls.
Fixed Charges . . . A catchall charge that wraps up overhead, depreciation, cost-per-square-foot, taxes, interest, and such things as maintenance and light and heat. Fringe benefits are included. This is now 50% of **total** labor costs.	1.07		This particular cost is the most difficult to determine, but studies have indicated that the 50% of labor factor is about as close as you can come. It is a combination of time charge and fixed charges.
Materials Cost . . . Stationery, envelopes, carbon paper, copy machine sheets, typewriter ribbons, and other types of necessary supplies.	0.15		This cost is fairly easy to arrive at if you maintain records covering your supplies. It reflects the fact that many firms make machine copies as well as carbons.
Mailing Cost . . . First class postage (13 cents). Includes the work of gathering, sealing, stamping, sorting done by personnel other than the secretary.	0.28		The number of letters sent Special Delivery can change this given figure. It includes wages of mail room help and office boy or mail pickup, also delivery to post office in majority of cases.
Filing Cost . . . Clerk's time (% of salary) and reflecting fact that secretary does filing in 77% of offices. Also includes prorate on equipment and cost of supplies.	0.21		This cost can be determined if you have facts on who files, where letter is filed, cost of office space, etc.
Total Cost	$4.17		YOUR COST

It should be pointed out that the costs figured here are strictly for the traditional boss-secretary type of business letter. The use of Word Processing is gaining momentum, but it is still generally accepted that most businesses use the secretary with steno pad and typewriter as their mode of business correspondence.

Most of this increase is due to rising salaries. Dictators' salaries rose 8 percent and represent a direct cost of 95¢ of the total; secretaries' salaries rose 11 percent and represent a direct cost of $1.17 of the total cost (Table 1). Studies by other researchers indicate that the Dartnell figures are conservative, because the salary computations are below average. Actually, many business letters cost as high as $10 each.

The Private Secretary and the Boss

For a number of years, the position of the private secretary has remained sacrosanct. Although executives considered it an important and necessary function, they did not consider that secretarial problems were significant or had much impact on administrative costs. Each executive expected to have a private secretary as a matter of course. Research has shown, however, that secretarial problems are extremely costly to a business organization, both in terms of labor charges and low productivity levels. The traditional private secretary position is wasteful and inefficient.

Most private secretaries spend each work day performing many unrelated tasks, often being interrupted in the middle of any one task. The average private secretary has been known to be interrupted up to 44 times a day. While attempting to type a letter, a typist may be interrupted by the telephone, by people arriving at the office, or by the executive calling for other work. In fact, three interruptions per typed page were noted. Each interruption results in a break in the secretary's train of thought; thus many start-up times occur each time that work on the task is resumed.

Another factor that affects employee productivity is waiting-for-work time (idle time) as a percentage of the total available work time. Figures on waiting-for-work time vary from secretary to secretary, with the same secretary, and with different circumstances. The fact remains, however, that most secretaries spend considerable time waiting for work. Figure 2 illustrates the average secretarial waiting-for-work time in 13 companies.

The high cost of labor, together with the erratic workload of secretaries, has led to a somewhat different trend lately. According to a survey conducted by the Darnell Corporation, the exclusive one-secretary-per-boss relationship in the business office appears to be passing into legend. Two-thirds of those holding the title of executive secretary serve more than one person on a regular basis. This also holds true for those at all career levels — with the titles of secretary to (56 percent), administrative assistant (52 percent), secretary/stenographer (72 percent), senior secretary (73 percent), and junior secretary (82 percent).

Word processing systems alone do not solve the problem of secretarial utilization. Besides word processing, administrative support tasks can be sharpened. Organizing and systematizing dictation and typing also require careful attention, as do many other office tasks — mail handling, telephone, supplies, fast copies, filing, information retrieval, and clerical activities. Two related systems should therefore, evolve — word processing and administrative support. A well-organized administrative support system can provide dollar savings, secretarial job enrichment, and better utilization of human resources.

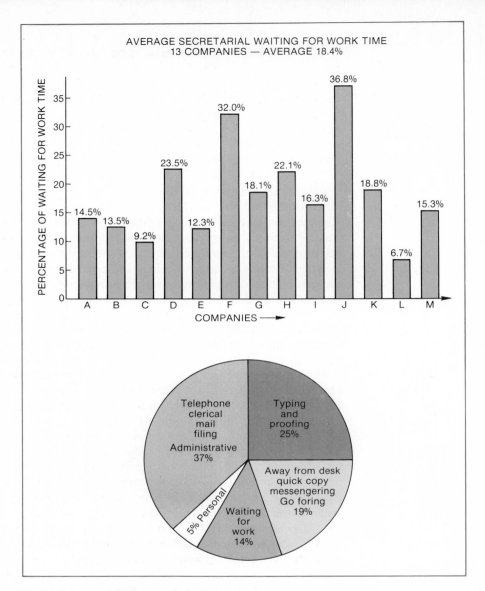

Figure 2. Secretarial waiting time.

Identification of Problems for Word Processing

Every organization should survey its operation systematically to determine its need for word processing. Among the steps to be considered is identification of the problems that exist in the present system. A list of problems might include:

1. low productivity,

2. poor quality,

3. inadequate turnaround time and workflow,

4. high percentage of overtime and turnover,

5. user dissatisfaction,

6. lack of supervision and evaluation of secretarial activities,

7. irrational assignment of secretaries to users,

8. lack of personnel training,

9. morale problems, and

10. excessive costs.

The presence of many such problems provides the basis for implementation of the full word processing/administrative support concept. The adoption of a systems approach to word processing leads to a modification or restructuring of work and workflow; and it is expected to have four important contributions: elimination of unnecessary functions, combination of related functions, realignment of work and/or its distribution, and simplification of the present system.

A properly implemented word processing system can eliminate a number of unnecessary functions. The tedious time-consuming input of longhand can be eliminated through the use of dictation equipment. The dictator can be freed for more higher-level administrative duties. The use of editing typewriters can eliminate the high-volume rekeying of input by putting the keystrokes into an inventory to be recalled as needed for repetitive and revision typing. Much duplication of effort in retyping is eliminated. Only proofreading of revised material is necessary. Properly implemented procedures and job specialization permit the secretarial activities to be controlled and carried out in the most economical and efficient manner.

Through a properly implemented word processing system, all of the related functions in the processing of words (from origination to final distribution or storage) may be combined into one smoothly operating system. By combining dictation equipment with an editing typewriter, information can be typed at the same time it is listened to. The originator may dictate anytime without pulling the secretary away from other activities. A system that combines editing typewriters, communication, and typesetting input capabilities can virtually eliminate the need to rekeyboard data for Telex or TWX transmission, for entry into a computer, or for typesetting purposes.

Work specialization and centralization contributes to increased efficiency throughout the entire operation. Those who typewrite or keyboard have the advantage of a controlled environment (without interruptions), together with the equipment that enables them to perform much more productively. Proofreading of all typewritten documents can be assigned to one individual with proven proofreading skills. Certain other functions that all secretaries repeat daily can be assigned to a specialist. For example, copy requests can be routed to a department specialist who is responsible for handling an entire department's copying needs. This eliminates the need for all secretaries to leave their desks, wait in line, and make copies for their boss only. Thus, job specialization and the combination of activities reduce the time that must be expended upon these activities.

Finally, a well implemented and well managed word processing system simplifies the clerical organization for many reasons:

1. Input methods are standardized, and input channels are established in order to input work to centralized word processing centers.

2. The most up-to-date tools are utilized to process the work in the fastest time and in the most efficient manner.

3. Duplicate and unnecessary tasks are eliminated.

4. Similar jobs are combined and centralized.

5. Organized management, measurement, and control of clerical personnel and clerical functions are possible because secretarial personnel are supervised by a manager of the word processing function — not by managers of unrelated functions.

6. Career paths are possible for secretarial personnel, because word processing can create a distinct, separate organizational entity within which several clearly defined job levels can be created.

Word Processing — A Summary

Word processing is an emerging field with roots in past technology and management practice. It is a viable way of dealing with the world of today's business. Although it has not yet come of age, the concept is quickly maturing. Only a relatively short time has intervened between its inception and its present state of development.

Word processing as a subset of the larger field of information systems has undergone various stages of growth. These stages are based on technological development in hardware, patterns of growing applications, increased personnel specialization, and most importantly a shift in management focus. The processing of words by the "typewriters" of the 1880s has developed through stages ranging from the use of private secretaries and typing pools to today's word processing by means of electronic hardware and technology. An ever increasing breadth of applications is apparent including integration with such other systems as phototypesetting and telecommunications. As the field has become more complex, the specialization of personnel has followed and many more job opportunities have been created.

Word processing has hurtled through its earliest stages of growth. The technology is here: Except in isolated progressive organizations, it yet remains for management to view and recognize word processing as an integral part of information processing. Such a critical step is bound to be taken. The input of today's word processing is the key to much of the integrated office of the future. Word processing has an unquestionable role to play in the total information processing systems of tomorrow.

Terms to Learn

Abacus: A manual calculating device that uses beads to represent decimal values.

Access Time: (1) The time interval between the instant at which data is called for from a memory device and the instant delivery is completed (i.e., the read time) is (2) The time interval between the instant at which data is requested to be stored and the instant at which storage is completed (i.e., the write time).

Action Entry: Lower right quadrant of a decision table, specifying the action to be taken.

Action Stub: Lower left quadrant of a decision table, listing every possible action that can be taken.

Address: (1) An identification, as represented by a name, label, or number, for a register, location in storage, or any other data source or destination, such as the location of a station in a communications network. (2) Loosely, any part of an instruction that specifies the location of an operand for the instruction.

Algorithm: A mechanical or recursive computational procedure

Analog Computer: A computer that represents variables by physical analogies. Thus, any computer that solves problems by translating physical conditions such as flow temperature, pressure, angular position, or voltage into related mechanical or electrical quantities and that uses mechanical or electrical equivalent circuits, such as an analog for the physical phenomenon being investigated. In general, a computer that uses an analog for each variable and produces analogs as output. Thus, an analog computer measures continuously, whereas a digital computer counts discretely.

Aperture Card: A standard 80-column card with a precut rectangular hole for holding 35-mm. microfilm.

Arithmetic Logic Unit (ALU): The unit of a computing system that contains the circuits that perform arithmetic and logical operations.

ASCII: An acronym for American Standard Code for Information Interchange, used when transmitting data between computers.

Assemble: To prepare a machine-language program from a symbolic-language program by substituting absolute operation codes for symbolic operation codes and absolute relocatable addresses for symbolic addresses

Asynchronous: Operating independently.

Audit Trail: A routine designed to allow the analyst, the user, or the auditor to verify a process in the new system.

Bar Code: A special machine and human-readable code adopted by the grocery and retail industries to automate data gathering and processing.

Base Address: A given address from which an absolute address is derived by combination with a relative address.

Basic: An acronym of Beginners All-purpose Symbolic Instruction Code. A widely used time-sharing language developed by Professors Kemeny and Kurtz with a structure similar to that of Fortran.

Batch Processing: A technique by which items to be processed must be coded and collected into groups prior to processing.

Baud: A unit of signaling speed that amounts to 1 bit per second.

Benchmark Program: Running a representative application program on the vendor's computer system.

Binary: (1) Pertaining to a characteristic or property involving a selection, choice, or condition in which there are two possibilities. (2) Pertaining to the number representation system with a radix of 2.

Binary-Coded Decimal: Pertaining to a decimal notation in which the individual decimal digits are each represented by a group of binary digits; e.g., in the 8-4-2-1 binary-coded decimal notation, the number 23 is represented as 0010 0011, whereas in binary notation, 23 is represented as 10111.

Bit: (1) An abbreviation of binary digit. (2) A single character in a binary number. (3) A single pulse in a group of pulses. (4) A unit of information capacity of a storage device.

Block: A set of things, such as words, characters, or digits, handled as a unit.

Bootleg Form: A form used by the company's staff without prior authorization or approval.

Bubble Memory: See magnetic bubble

Business Organization: A framework by means of which the activities of a business are tied together to provide for integrated performance. Also, a human relationship in group activity.

Byte: A set of consecutive binary digits (usually, 8-bit set) operating as a unit.

Calculator: (1) A device capable of performing arithmetic. (2) Generally and historically, a device for carrying out logic and arithmetic digital operations of any kind.

Caption: A word on a form that specified what information to write in the space provided.

Central Processing Unit (CPU): A major device containing the arithmetic logic unit, main memory, and control unit.

Chain Printer: A device that uses a chain of several links, each of which contains alphabetic and numeric characters. The chain rotates horizontally at constant speed. Hammers from the back of the paper are timed to fire against selected characters on the chain, causing the printing of a line.

Channel: A parallel track on a magnetic tape, a band on a magnetic drum, or a path along which information flows.

Character: An elementary mark or event that is used to represent data. A character is often in the form of a graphic spatial arrangement of connected or adjacent strokes.

Chip: A memory device made from wafers of silicon which is externally wired, sealed in plastic for building the main memory of a computer.

Classifying: Arranging data in a specific form, usually by sorting, grouping, or extracting.

Closed Table: A decision table that consists of a set of rules which are accessed to by other decision tables for processing.

COBOL: Common Business-Oriented Language: A procedural language developed for business data processing. The language is intended as a means for direct presentation of a business program to a computer with a suitable compiler.

Compile: To prepare a machine-language program from a computer program written in another programming language by making use of the overall logic structure of the program, generating more than one machine instruction for each symbolic statement, as well as performing the function of an assembler.

Computer: A calculating device that processes data represented by a combination of discrete (in digital computers) or continuous (in analog computers) data.

Computer-Assisted Instruction: A concept that applies computers and specialized input/output display terminals directly to individualized student instruction.

Computer-Output Microfilm: An output system in which computer output is automatically photographed onto microfilm.

Computer Word: A sequence of bits or characters treated as a unit and capable of being stored in one computer location. Synonymous with machine word.

Condition Entry: Upper right quadrant of a decision table, indicating all the possible combinations of conditions listed in the condition stub.

Condition Stub: Upper left quadrant of a decision table, listing the conditions related to a particular problem.

Constant: Any specific value (number) that does not change during program execution.

Control: (1) The part of a digital computer or processor that determines the execution and interpretation of instructions in proper sequence, including the decoding of each instruction and the application of the proper signals to the arithmetic unit and other registers in accordance with the decoded information. (2) Frequently, in any mechanism, one or more of the components responsible for interpreting and carrying out manually initiated directions. Sometimes it is called *manual control*. (3) In some business applications, a mathematical check. (4) In programming, instructions that determine conditional jumps are often referred to as *control instructions,* and the time sequence of execution of instructions is called the *flow of control.*

Control Unit: The part of a computer used to specify the sequence of operations to be performed in an electronic system according to a program of instructions.

Data Processing: Any operation or combination of operations on data.

Data-Processing Cycle: The sequence of steps involved in manipulating business information.

Data Word: A word that may be primarily regarded as part of the information manipulated by a given program. A data word may be used to modify a program instruction, or to be arithmetically combined with other data words.

Debug: To detect, locate, and remove mistakes from a routine or malfunctions from a computer. Synonymous with *troubleshoot.*

Decision Table: A documentation format; a table of the contingencies to be dealt with in defining a problem and the actions to be taken.

Demodulator: See MODEM

Density: The number of characters that can be stored in a given unit of length such as an inch of magnetic tape.

Diagnostics: Messages transmitted by a computer during language translation or program execution which pertain to the diagnosis or identification of errors in a program or malfunctions in equipment.

Digital: The representation of data using a discrete medium, such as fingers, rocks, bits, or anything that is counted to determine its value.

Digital Computer: A computer that operates on discrete data by performing arithmetic and logic processes on these data. Contrast this with *analog computer.*

Dim: Commonly used in array programming, a statement that establishes a dimensioned computer-memory area of a specific size for processing.

Direct-Access Storage: (1) The process of obtaining information from or placing information into storage where the time required for such access is independent of the location of the information most recently obtained or placed in storage. (2) A device in which random access, as defined in (1), can be achieved without effective penalty in time.

Direct Costs: Costs that are normally applied directly to the operation in question.

Disc Pack: A device containing a set of magnetic discs for storing secondary information.

Distributed Processing: Also called Distributed Data Processing (DDP); A decentralization of electronic data processing made possible by a network of computers "dispersed" throughout an organization.

Documentation: As a means of communication, a written record of a phase of a specific project; it establishes design and performance criteria for various phases of the project.

Data: Unprocessed or "raw" facts, concepts, characters, or quantities available for processing into information by a manual, mechanical, or electronic data processing system.

Data Base: A single file containing information in a format applicable to any user's needs and available when needed.

Data Communication: Transmitting or receiving processed data, sound, or other bits of information over telephone wire, radio, or other electromagnetic means.

Data Division: The part of a COBOL program describing the data to be processed by the object program. It contains primarily a file section that describes the file(s) used and a working-storage section that reserves memory space for storage of results.

Data Item: One or more bytes combined for describing some attribute of an object.

Data Manipulation: The performance of all necessary routines on input data.

Data Origination: Determination of the nature (origin) of source data.

Data-Phone: A device which facilitates data communication over telephone channels.

Dual-Gap Read-Write Head: A device used in magnetic tape data processing to insure the accuracy of recorded data on tape. A character written on tape is read immediately by a read head to verify its validity.

Dump: A snapshot of the computer's internal storage.

Duplex: A data channel that allows simultaneous transmission in both directions.

EBCDIC (Extended Binary-Coded Decimal Interchange Code): An 8-bit code first used with the IBM 360 system.

Electronic Data Processing: The processing of data by an electronic device such as a computer.

Electronic Funds Transfer (EFT): An automated version of our current national check clearing system. Each retail store user would have their cash (less) register *on-line* to a regional transaction clearing house. Funds are transferred immediately from a customer's bank account to the retail store's bank account, even when the two banks are thousands of miles from each other.

End User: The final (authorized) user of the output or report produced by a computer system.

ENIAC: Electronic numerical integrator and calculator (the first all-electronic general-purpose computer), built in the early 1940s by Prosper Eckert and John W. Mauchly while at the University of Pennsylvania.

Environment Division: The part of the Cobol program describing the physical characteristics of the equipment being used and the aspects of the problems that are dependent on the program. Its two main sections are the configuration and the input/output section.

Equalization: A process by which a modem maintains the quality of a transmission line.

Extended Entry Table: A decision table in which the statements written in the stub section are extended into the entry section.

Facilities Management: The use of an external service organization to operate and manage the electronic data processing facilities of an organization.

Fanfold Form: A multiple unit form joined in a continuous strip with perforations between each pair of forms.

Feedback: The part of a closed loop system that automatically brings back information about the condition under control.

Field: A specified area of a record used for a particular category of data; e.g., a group of card columns used to represent a wage rate, or a set of bit locations in a computer word that are used to express the address of the operand.

File: A collection of records relating to a class of objects.

Fixed Costs: One-time or sunk costs

Floppy disc: A small, single magnetic disc made of material so thin it is not rigid, used for recording input data and in intelligent terminals.

Flowchart: A graphical representation for the definition, analysis, or solution of a problem, in which symbols are used to represent operations, data flow, and equipment.

For: A statement that initiates a program loop.

For-To: A special Basic statement word used when a set of statements is to be executed several times.

Form: A data (or information) carrier.

Forms Design: Focuses on evaluating present documents and creating new or improved forms that offer useful information for action.

Fortran (From formula translations): Any of several specific procedure-oriented programming languages.

Fortran IV: A problem-oriented language, initially designed for scientific application, which allows the programmer to think in terms of the problem rather than the computer used in solving it. The language is quite convenient for many business applications.

Frequency: The number of times a signal is repeated over a given period.

Full-Duplex Channel: A channel that facilitates simultaneous transmission in both directions.

Gantt Chart: A static systems model used for scheduling. Portrays output performance against a time requirement.

General-Purpose Computer: A computer that is designed to solve a wide class of problems.

Hardware: Physical equipment; e.g., mechanical, magnetic, electrical, or electronic devices. Contrast with *software.*

Reader Label: An identification record at the beginning of a reel of tape (see also trailer label).

Help: A Basic system command that asks for system assistance in resolving errors and references information about the system.

Hexadecimal: Relating to a number-representation system using base sixteen.

Hollerith: A widely used system of encoding alphanumeric information onto cards, hence *Hollerith cards,* as synonymous with *punched cards.*

HIPO: (Hierarchy + Input/Processing/Output). A design and documentation tool or structured programming utilized to record input/processing/output details of the hierarchical program modules.

Identification Division: The part of the program that identifies the name of the programmer, the title of the Cobol program, and the compiler listing associated with it.

Imperative Statement: A statement that commands the computer's immediate execution of specific sequential statements following it. Imperative statements include the DO statement, CONTINUE statement, and the STOP and END statements.

Indexed-Sequential File: Storing records in a file such that most of the records are in sequential organization and the file is equipped with an index to the locations of records.

Information: The results of processing data, in a form that will be useful to people (see also data).

Information Retrieval: A technique of classifying and indexing useful information in mass-storage devices, in a format that is amenable to interaction with the user.

Input: (1) The data to be processed. (2) The state or sequence of states occurring on a specified input channel. (3) The device or collective set of devices used for bringing data into another device. (4) A channel for impressing a state on a device or logic element. (5) The processes of transferring data from an external storage to an internal storage.

Input Device: The mechanical unit designed to bring data to be processed into a computer; e.g., a card reader, a tape reader, or a keyboard.

Instruction: A set of characters that defines the details of an operation.

Instruction Word: A computer word that contains an instruction.

Integer Variable: A series of alphanumeric characters with the first letter being I, J, K, L, M, or N.

Intelligent Terminal: A key terminal that performs such functions as editing and verifying keyed data, inserting standard information into keyed data, requesting particular pieces of data to be keyed, or requesting corrections to previously keyed data.

Interblock gap: The space between blocks on a magnetic secondary storage medium. Such spacing is used to prevent errors through loss of data or overwriting and permits tape stop/start operations.

Interrecord Gap: An interval of space or time deliberately left between recording portions of data or records.

Interrupt: A break in the normal flow of a program, usually caused by an external source. The interrupt causes the computer to handle a particular set of events before resuming the ordinary operation.

Iteration: Pertaining to the repeated execution of a series of steps.

Job Accounting: Self-monitoring software designed to gather data on the start/finish times of each program that was run and the amount of money and CPU time used.

Job Control Program: A program containing instructions necessary for the operating system to properly set up hardware and execute a program.

Key Punch: A keyboard-operated device that punches holes in a card to represent data.

Keyboard: A group of marked levers operated manually for recording characters

Label: One or more characters used to identify an item of data. Synonymous with *key*.

Lease: A way of acquiring the use of a computer system. A lease contract requires no financing and is less expensive than renting the system, although lease charges are generally higher than the purchase price of the system.

LET: A special BASIC word or assignment statement. It is a way of assigning values to variables or for evaluating expressions.

Library Subroutine: A set of tested subroutines available on file for use when needed.

Limited-Entry Table: A widely used type of decision table requiring fixed information in each quadrant. Condition entries are limited to "Y," "N," or a blank, while condition stubs are answered with either "Y" or "N," with "X"s in the action entry, responding to each "Y" in the condition entry.

Line-At-A-Time Printer: A device capable of printing one line of characters across a page — i.e., 100 or more characters simultaneously — as continuous paper advances line by line in one direction past type bars or a type cylinder that contains all characters in all positions.

Literal: A true value defined by a programmer.

Load Point: A tape marker, indicating the beginning of the usable portion of the tape when writing or reading is to begin.

Logic: (1) The science dealing with the criteria or formal principles of reasoning and thought. (2) The systematic scheme that defines the interactions of signals in the design of an automatic data-processing system. (3) The basic principles and application of truth tables and interconnection between logical elements required for arithmetic computation in an automatic data-processing system.

Logic Error: Deals with problems such as incorrect data fields, division by zero, and invalid combinations.

Longitudinal Check Character: An extra character placed at the end of every block of data to permit accuracy of the data recorded in that block to be checked through either an even or odd parity check.

Loop: A sequence of instructions that is repeated until a terminal condition prevails.

Looping: Executing repeatedly a set of computer instructions until a terminating condition is met.

Macro Instruction: (1) An instruction consisting of a sequence of micro instructions that are inserted into the object routine for performing a specific operation. (2) A more powerful instruction that combines several operations in one instruction.

Magnetic Bubble: A negatively magnetized cylindrical island in a positively magnetized film made of amorphous material.

Magnetic Core: A configuration of magnetic material that is, or is intended to be, placed in a spatial relationship to current-carrying conductors, and whose magnetic properties are essential to its use. It may be used to concentrate an induced magnetic field as in a transformer, induction coil, or armature, to retain a magnetic polarization for the purpose of storing data, or for its nonlinear properties as in a logic element. It may be made of such material as iron, iron oxide, or ferrite, and in such shapes as wires and tapes.

Magnetic Disc: A rotating metal disc having two magnetized surfaces for storing data.

Magnetic Drum: A right circular cylinder with a magnetic surface on which data can be stored by selective magnetization of portions of the curved surface.

Magnetic Ink Character Recognition (MICR): See MICR

Magnetic Tape: A tape coated with magnetizable material, on which information may be recorded in the form of magnetically polarized spots.

Management: A procedure, art, or science of getting things done through others.

Management Games: A small-scale simulation of the decisions made in a real-life business situation.

Management Information System: An all-inclusive system designed to provide instant information to management for effective and efficient business operation.

Manipulation: The actual work performed on source-data processing.

Mass-Storage File: A type of temporary secondary storage that supplies the computer with the necessary data for an immediate, up-to-date report on a given account.

Master File: A collection of records of semi permanent data, usually containing at least one record for each and every entity in a class of objects.

Memory Dump: (See Dump)

Memory: (1) A device into which data can be entered, in which it can be held, and from which it can be retrieved at a later time. (2) Loosely, any device that can store data.

MICR: Magnetic-Ink Character Recognition, a technique involving the use of a device that senses characters printed with an ink containing magnetized particles and encodes them into a machine language.

Microcomputer: A computer smaller than a minicomputer; also referred to as personal computer.

Microfiche: A sheet of microfilm several inches long and several inches wide.

Micrographics: A medium that provides pictorial data using on-line display console with manual input capability.

Microprocessor (MPU): A microcomputer central processing unit (CPU) on a chip and without input/output or primary storage capabilities in most types.

Microsecond: One millionth of a second.

Millisecond: One thousandth of a second.

Minicomputer: A low-cost, small, general-purpose, digital computer with a 4,000-basic-word memory and a price tag of less than $25,000, stripped down.

Mixed-Entry Table: A decision table which consists of a combination of rows with extended entries and rows with limited entries.

Mneumonics: A word or abbreviation to aid memory.

Modeling: A (often abstract) representation of a system in some form different from the system.

MODEM: (Modulator/Demodulator) A device designed to interface between the computer and the communication system.

Modularity: Operating system programs which permit the user to expand the existing system to meet increased processing demands or to handle new applications.

Monitor: Software or hardware that observes, supervises, controls, or verifies the opertions of a system.

Multiplex: Making simultaneous use of a communication channel for transmitting a number of messages.

Multiplexing: See multiplex.

Multiprocessing: Relating to a system involving more than one arithmetic and logic unit for simultaneous use.

Multiprogramming: Running two or more programs simultaneously by interleaving their operations.

Nanosecond: One billionth of a second.

NEXT: In a Basic language, it tells the computer to continue executing the sequence in a For-To statement.

Object Program: The program that is the output of an automatic coding system. Often the object program is a machine-language program ready for execution, but is may well be in an intermediate language.

Object Time: The time span during which a stored program is in active control of a specific application.

Off-Line: Pertaining to equipment or devices not under direct control of the central processing unit.

On-Line: Pertaining to peripheral equipment or devices in direct communication with the central processing unit.

On-line Processing: Data processing by means of a system, and of the peripheral equipment or devices in a system, in which the operation of such equipment is under control of the central processing unit, and in which information reflecting current activity is introduced into the data-processing system as soon as it occurs; thus, directly in line with the main flow of transaction processing.

On-Line, Real-Time: Pertains to a system which receives input data, processes them, and returns results (output) fast enough to affect an ongoing process.

Open-End Table: A decision table where the last action instruction transfers logic flow to another open-end table.

Operand: That which is operated upon. An operand is usually identified by an addressed part of an instruction.

Operating System: A set of routines for monitoring the operations of a computer system.

Operation Code: A code that represents specific operations. Synonymous with *instruction code*

Optical Character Recognition (OCR): A technique which relies on electronic devices and light to detect, and convert into machine language, characters which have been printed or written on documents in human-understandable form.

Optical Scanning: Translation of printed or handwritten characters into machine language.

Organization Structure: The mapping of the number of managerial levels, authority relationships, and the general pattern of functions performed by employees at all levels.

Organizing: Developing a procedure or a plan to carry out predetermined plans for action.

Origination: Determination of the nature, type, and origin of some documents.

Output: (1) Data that has been processed. (2) The state or sequence of states occurring on a specified output channel. (3) The device or collective set of devices used for taking data out of a device. (4) A channel for expressing a state of a device or logic element. (5) The process of transferring data from an internal storage to an external storage.

Output Device: The part of a machine that translates the electrical impulses representing data processed by the machine into permanent results, such as printed forms, punched cards, and magnetic writing on tape.

Overhead: Allocated costs; costs that are neither fixed nor variable.

Overlapped Processing: Pertaining to the ability of a computer system to increase the utilization of its central processing unit by overlapping input/output and processing operations.

Packed Decimal: A method of coding numbers in 8-bit bytes where each byte except one contains two digits, coded in binary, and one byte contains one digit, coded in binary, and a sign.

Packing Density: The number of useful storage elements per unit of dimension; e.g., the number of bits per inch stored on a magnetic tape or drum track.

Paging: A process which automatically and continually transfers pages of programs and data between main memory and direct access storage devices. It provides computers with advanced mutliprogramming and virtual memory capabilities.

Parallel Processing (run): Concurrent processing of two or more programs stored in memory.

Parameter: A variable that is given a constant value for a specific purpose or process.

Parity Check: A check that tests whether the number of 1's (or 0's) in an array of binary digits is odd or even. Synonymous with *odd-even check.*

Participant Observation: The process of collecting data through direct observation.

Peripheral Equipment: Components which work in conjunction with, but which are not a part of, the central processing system—for example, a card reader, a printer.

Phase: The duration of signal in time.

Picosecond: One thousandth or 10^{-12} seconds.

Picture: A string of specified alphabetic, numeric, or alphanumeric characters which gives certain characteristics of data items.

Planning: Determining in advance *what* is to be done. It is the first step in management.

Point-of-Sale (POS) Input System: A technique geared to automating a collection of source data through on-line computer systems.

Polling: A request to each available computer console for a message or for readiness to accept a reply.

Present Value Method: A method of deciding on computer acquisition by converting future cost flows into present values.

Problem-Oriented Language: A machine-independent language requiring only statement of the problem (not the procedure) for proper solution.

Procedure Division: In Cobol, the part of the program that is programmer-defined and determines the operations that will perform the necessary processing of data. Its structure includes sections and paragraphs, as well as conditional, imperative, and compiler-directing classes of sentences/statements.

Procedure-Oriented Language: A machine-independent language designed to simplify stating the necessary procedures for solving the problem; e.g., Fortran and Cobol.

Process: A general term covering such terms as *assemble, compile, generate, interpret,* and *compute.*

Processor: The CPU; an assembler or a compiler translator routine.

Processor Program: A programming aid that prepares an object program, first by reading symbolic instructions and then comparing and converting them into a suitable computer language.

Program: (Noun) (1) A plan for solving a problem. (2) Loosely, a routine (Verb) (3) To devise a plan for solving a problem. (4) Loosely, to write a routine.

Program Flowchart: A graphic representation of a computer problem, using symbols to represent machine instructions or groups of instructions.

Programming: Preparing a logical sequence of events which the computer must follow and execute to solve a problem.

Program Specification: A list of the information requirements of the system with emphasis upon the input and output specifications, existing files, and the processing details. Related to *systems specifications.*

Programmer-defined Word: Also called data name—In Cobol, it is a word supplied by the programmer to represent data items or data procedures involved in the problem.

Project Management: A detailed procedure for managing system resources and costs.

Protocol: A specific set of rules defining the exchange of special signals and characters when a connection is made between two data communications terminals, and before and after each transmission of a data communications message.

Queuing: A computer technique which involves lining up input instructions or messages from various terminals and processing them on a first-come, first-served basis or according to a priority system controlled by a multiplexor- programmed routine.

Random-Access Memory (RAM): One of the basic types of semiconductor memory used for temporary storage of data or programs during processing. Each memory position can be directly sensed (read) or changed (write) in the same length of time, irrespective of its location on the storage medium.

Random Processing: Retrieving and updating any records without examining intervening records.

Read: To acquire or interpret data from a storage device, a data medium, or any other service.

Read-Only Memory (ROM): A basic type of semiconductor memory used for permanent storage, can only be read, not "written," i.e., changed. Variations are "programmable Read-Only Memory" (PROM) and "Eraseable Programmable Read-Only Memory" (EPROM).

Real-Time: Pertains to the processing of information or transactions as they actually occur. It is actually a concurrent operation for computing and physical processing.

Real-Time Processing: The processing of data as received and in time for the result to affect a decision.

Real Variable: A series of alphanumeric characters with the first letter being any letter other than I, J, K, L, M, or N.

Record: A collection of related items of data, treated as a unit.

Recording: The process by which an input device facilitates the presentation of source data for processing.

Redundancy: A situation where two or more rules in a decision table depict the same combination.

Register: A device capable of storing a specified amount of data, such as one word.

Relational Test: A test shown in a conditional statement, in which the subject operand is compared with the object operand and some action is taken based on the relation that exists.

Reserved Word: A Cobol word which represents a particular meaning to be used in prescribed context.

Response time: The time required by the system to react to an input stimulus.

Run: A single continuous performance of a computer program or routine.

Save: In *Basic,* it is a system command that causes the existing program to be written onto a disc file for later use.

Scientific Computer: A computer designed to handle a large amount of mathematical computations of a scientific problem.

Sequential Data Processing: A technique by which items to be processed must be coded and collected into groups prior to processing.

Scratch: In *Basic,* it is a system command used when one wishes to wipe out the working copy of the current program.

Sequential Processing: Processing logical data elements or records according to a prescribed sequence.

Selector Channel: A channel that is active with only one input/output device at a time.

Self-directing: Automation; performing a given job independently of human intervention.

Serial-access Storage: Pertaining to the process of obtaining data from or placing data into storage, where the access time is dependent upon the location of the data most recently obtained or placed in storage. Contrast with direct access.

Serial Processing: An early computer operation, whereby a read-computer-print cycle is performed in series or one operation after another.

Service Bureau: Business firms renting computer time to users.

Servicer: An organization that provides data processing services to other organizations for a fee.

Shared Processor: Descriptive of a key-to-disc system which offers editing and data control, reduced error rates, and improved data entry input format flexibility.

Simplex: Transmission of information in one direction only.

Simulation: Symbolic representation (in terms of a model) of the essence of a system for testing an idea or a product before operationalizing its full-scale production.

Software: (1) The collection of programs and routines associated with a computer; e.g., compilers, library routines. (2) All the documents associated with a computer; e.g., manuals, circuit diagrams. Contrasts with *hardware.*

Sort/Merge Program: A program that places the records of a file in a specified order or merges them based upon the values in each record's key field.

Sorting: Arranging numeric or alphabetic data in a given sequence.

Source Data Automation (SDA): (1) Data capture at the source. (2) In intelligent data entry, the data is entered, validated, and edited using an intelligent terminal under stored program format.

Source Document: A document from which basic data is extracted.

Source Program: A program written in a source language, a language that is an input to a given translation process.

Span of Control: Pertains to the number of employees a supervisor can effectively handle.

Special-purpose Computer: A computer that is designed to solve a restricted class of problems.

Stored Program: A series of instructions in storage to direct the step-by-step operation of the machine.

Structured Interview: An interview in which the question and the alternative responses are fixed.

Structured Programming: A programming methodology which involves the use of a "top-down" program design and use a limited number of control structures in a program to create highly structured "modules" of program code.

Structured Walkthroughs: A structured programming methodology which requires a peer review by other programmers of the program design and coding to minimize and reveal errors in the early stages of programming.

Stub Card: A card containing a detachable stub to serve as a receipt for future reference.

Subsystem: A component of a system (for example, in a punched-card data processing system, the keypunch is a primary subsystem).

Summarizing: Condensing a mass of data into a concise and meaningful form.

Supervisor Program: (Synonymous with *monitor routine*), a program which handles the loading and relocation of various program segments or runs.

Synchronous System: A computer whose operations are handled in set time intervals fixed by pulses emitted by a clock.

Syntax Error: Error in the grammatical correctness of instruction structure or rules of instruction design.

System: (1) An organized collection of parts united by regulated interaction. (2) An organized collection of men, machines, and methods required to accomplish a specific objective.

System Command: A keyword that causes prompt system action.

System Flowchart: A graphic representation of a system in which data provided by a source document are converted into final documents.

System Integrity: Refers to the proper functioning of hardware and programs, appropriate physical security and operating procedures, and the required degree of safety against eavesdropping and wiretapping.

System Security: Refers to the technical innovations and managerial procedures applied to the hardware, programs, and data to protect the privacy of the records of the organization and its customers.

System Study: The detailed process of determining a system or set of procedures for using a computer for definite functions or operations, and establishing specifications to be used as a basis for the selection of equipment suitable to the specific needs.

Systems Analysis: (1) Analyzing in detail the components and requirements of an existing system. (2) Analyzing in detail the information needs of an organization, the characteristics and components of presently utilized information systems and the requirements of proposed information systems.

Systems Analyst: A person skilled in the definition and development of techniques for the solving of a problem, especially those techniques for solution on a computer.

Systems Design: The step in the system life cycle when a business system or application is designed to meet the needs set in systems analysis.

Systems Proposal: Also called a problem-definition report — a detailed summary of the investigation that has been carried out on the present system.

Thrashing: (also called churning) — a page swap between real storage and virtual storage.

Throughput: The total output during a given time period.

Time-Sharing: A data processing technique where two or more terminals can concurrently utilize a central computer system for various routines.

Top-Down Design: A methodology of structured programming in which a program is organized into "functional modules," with the programmer designing the "main module" first, and then the lower-level modules.

Transaction File: A data file containing relatively transient data to be processed in combination with a master file. Synonymous with detail file.

Turnaround Document: The elapsed time between submission of a job to a computing center and the return of the results.

Turnaround Time: The amount of time required for a given routine to reach the computer for processing and get back to the programmer in the form of desired output.

Unit Record: (1) A separate record that is similar in form and content to other records; e.g., a summary of a particular employee's earnings to date. (2) Sometimes, a piece of nontape auxiliary equipment; e.g., card reader, printer, or console typewriter.

Ultrafiche: Microfilm images reduced more than 90 times.

Unstructured Interview: An interview in which neither the questions nor their responses are specified prior to the interview.

User's Request: A statement of what a proposed system is expected to produce and whom it will accommodate, source of data input, desired output information, and anticipated deadline. A phase of project initiation.

Utility Program: A standard set of routines which assists in the operation of a computer system by performing some frequently required process such as sorting, merging, etc.

Validity Check: A control measure to verify the reasonableness of the value of a given computation.

Variable: A name that is arbitrarily chosen to represent numbers and computer locations where the numbers are located.

Variable Costs: Costs that are incurred in proportion to the volume of work processed.

Variable-Word-Length: Having the property that a machine word may have a variable number of characters. It may be applied either to a single entry whose information content may be changed from time to time, or to a group of functionally similar entries whose corresponding components are of different lengths.

Virtual Storage: Managing the location of program and data by a combination of storage devices, paging, and software, such that a programmer is unaware of constraints on amount of available storage.

Word: An ordered set of characters that occupies one storage location and is treated by the computer circuits as a unit and transferred as such. Ordinarily, a word is treated by the control unit as an instruction, and by the arithmetic unit as a quantity. Word lengths may be fixed or variable depending on the particular computer.

Word Length: The number of bits (or bytes) or characters in a word.

Word Processing: Pertains to the use of automated and centralized typing, dictation, copying, and filing systems that are utilized in modern offices.

Zoned Decimal: A method of coding digits in 8 bits in which each digit has a 4-bit zone and a 4-bit numeric portion, coded in binary.

Index xxx